CAMBRIDGE LAT. ~~~~~~ ~ ~ ~DIES

EDITORS

DAVID JOSLIN JOHN STREET
TIMOTHY KING CLIFFORD T. SMITH

15

SILVER MINING AND SOCIETY
IN COLONIAL MEXICO

ZACATECAS 1546–1700

THE SERIES

SILVER MINING AND SOCIETY IN COLONIAL MEXICO

ZACATECAS
1546-1700

BY

P. J. BAKEWELL

Fellow of Trinity College, Cambridge

CAMBRIDGE

AT THE UNIVERSITY PRESS

1971

PUBLISHED BY THE PRESS SYNDICATE OF THE UNIVERSITY OF CAMBRIDGE
The Pitt Building, Trumpington Street, Cambridge, United Kingdom

CAMBRIDGE UNIVERSITY PRESS
The Edinburgh Building, Cambridge CB2 2RU, UK
40 West 20th Street, New York NY 10011–4211, USA
477 Williamstown Road, Port Melbourne, VIC 3207, Australia
Ruiz de Alarcón 13, 28014 Madrid, Spain
Dock House, The Waterfront, Cape Town 8001, South Africa

http://www.cambridge.org

First published 1971
First paperback edition 2002

Library of Congress Catalogue Card Number: 78-158553

ISBN 0 521 08227 7 hardback
ISBN 0 521 52312 5 paperback

CONTENTS

TABLES

ILLUSTRATIONS

ACKNOWLEDGEMENTS

The debts of gratitude I have incurred in preparing this book are very numerous, and far larger than I can properly repay in a few words of thanks. My first acknowledgement must be to Professor J. H. Elliott, who guided my research from its beginnings to the stage of a Ph.D. thesis, and for whose advice, enthusiasm and encouragement at all times I am deeply grateful. Hardly any less do I owe to Dr John Street, who first introduced me to the study of Latin American history. Both for that introduction and for his friendship and support in many different ways I wish to thank him. This is the last work in the series of Cambridge Latin American Studies that Professor D. M. Joslin edited before his sudden and untimely death. That it has reached the form of a book at all is the result, in considerable part, of his kind offices on my behalf over the last three years. He was always generous in his advice and in giving me the benefit of his wide knowledge of economic history. He pointed out to me many pitfalls, around which, I hope, I have warily trod.

The community of Latin American colonial historians is, of course, international, and yet is still small enough for the beginner, with luck, to make the acquaintance of many of its leading members. All are drawn at some time or another to the Archivo General de Indias in Seville, the great focus of *americanista* studies. On my first arrival there, I was fortunate enough to find 'in residence' Dr F. V. Scholes and Dr Enrique Otte, from both of whom I received much-needed guidance in that sea of papers. Indeed, it was on Dr Otte's advice that I first turned my attention to Zacatecas. Dr Scholes, with his long acquaintance with the Mexican sources in the Archive, directed me along several useful channels of research and pointed out valuable individual manuscripts.

Various other historians of New Spain in North American universities have made my way much easier. I should like to acknowledge the help given to me by Professor Woodrow Borah of the University of California at Berkeley, who has been a valuable correspondent, consented to read and criticise my Ph.D. dissertation, and supplied me with essential microfilm. During my short visit to Berkeley he received me with much kindness. On the same occasion I benefited from discussions with Dr D. A. Brading, with whose work on eighteenth-century mining in New Spain my own on an earlier period has much in common. Another Californian Mexicanist, Professor Philip Powell, whom I met, aptly

Acknowledgements

enough, in Zacatecas, gave me great encouragement then, and has followed my research since with much interest.

Academic debts of a less immediate kind I owe to the staffs of the libraries and archives in which I have worked: in Seville, the Archivo General de Indias and the Escuela de Estudios Hispanoamericanos; in Mexico City, the Archivo General de la Nación and the Museo Nacional de Antropología; in Zacatecas, the Presidencia Municipal and the Biblioteca Pública del Estado; in Ann Arbor, Michigan, the William L. Clements Library; in London, the British Museum. Everywhere I received freely-given help and made friendships. I cannot mention Seville without expressing my gratitude to two distinctive residents of that pleasant city: Don Miguel Maticorena Estrada, a prodigious walking bibliography; and the late Don Santiago Montero, who was always ready to put his matchless palaeographic skill at the service of stumbling beginners. His death in the autumn of 1969 deprived the Archivo de Indias of one of its most faithful devotees – he had been working there for more than fifty years – and researchers of one of their most useful allies.

In a way, I am more conscious of my non-academic debts than of those that are directly related to research and writing. Having arrived as a total stranger in Zacatecas, I was soon fortunate enough to make the acquaintance of Don Federico M. Sescosse and his family, without whose unfailing hospitality and interest my months in that city would have been far less enjoyable and less profitable than they were. Don Federico, an enthusiastic local historian, put his extensive collection of 'Zacatecana' at my disposal. And in the United States, it was only the great and undeserved generosity of Dr and Mrs Richard Garner, then of Ann Arbor, that enabled me to visit and work in the Clements Library of the University of Michigan, with its valuable collection of Zacatecas Treasury papers.

Part of the research for this study was carried out with the aid of a generous grant from the William Waldorf Astor Foundation, which altogether resolved financial difficulties.

Lastly, I am deeply indebted to the Master and Fellows of Trinity College, Cambridge, for having admitted me to their distinguished company as a Research Fellow. Without the time that my Fellowship has given me for research and writing, this book would not have appeared.

ABBREVIATIONS AND CONVENTIONS

Archives, Collections and Printed Material

AA.Z (LC)	Archivo del Ayuntamiento de Zacatecas (Libro de Cabildo)
AGI	Archivo General de Indias, Seville
AGN	Archivo General de la Nación, Mexico City
AHH	Archivo Histórico de Hacienda, Mexico City
AN.Z	Archivo de Notarías, Zacatecas
AT.Z (/VO)	Archivo de la Tesorería de Zacatecas (Viceregal orders)
BM	British Museum
BNM	Biblioteca Nacional, Mexico City
CDHG	*Colección de documentos históricos inéditos o muy raros referentes al Arzobispado de Guadalajara (publicados en forma de revista trimestral ilustrada por el Ilmo. y Rvmo. Sr Dr y Mtro. Don Francisco Orozco y Jiménez)*, 6 vols., Guadalajara 1922–7
DII	*Colección de documentos inéditos relativos al descubrimiento, conquista y organización de las antiguas posesiones españolas de América y Oceanía, sacados de los archivos del Reino y muy especialmente del de Indias*, 42 vols., Madrid 1864–84
HAHR	*Hispanic American Historical Review*
MA Mexico	Museo Nacional de Antropología, Mexico City
Recopilación 1680	*Recopilación de leyes de los reinos de las Indias, mandadas imprimir y publicar por la majestad católica del rey Don Carlos II, nuestro señor* . . ., Madrid 1680

Abbreviations and conventions

Notaries of Zacatecas

BN	Blas Núñez Hurtado
DV	Diego Vázquez Borrego
FE	Felipe de Espinosa
IG	Ignacio González de Vergara
JL	José de Laguna
JM	Josephe de Santa María Maraver
LF	Lucas Fernández Pardo
MH	Mateo de Herrera
MR	Manuel Rodríguez
PC	Pedro de Covarrubias

Other abbreviations

n.f.	no foliation
n.e.d.	no exact date

Conventions

The word 'miner' is used throughout with the same sense as 'minero' in colonial Mexico; that is, a mining entrepreneur, the owner of workings and ore refining plant – and usually, of both. As used here, it never means a mine labourer.

Spelling in Spanish titles, and in quotations given in Spanish, is modernised. Spanish Christian names, surnames and place names are also spelt in the modern fashion, wherever possible. Thus Bicente de Saldivar Mendoça becomes Vicente de Zaldívar Mendoza; but Joseph de Villarreal is not modified to José de Villarreal. Punctuation in titles and quotations is added where necessary.

'México', with accent, is widely used in references with the meaning of Mexico City.

References to the *Recopilación* of 1680 are given in the order: book, title, law. Thus *Recopilación* 1680, X x 10 signifies Libro 10, Título 10, Ley 10.

References to sums of money in cash are given in *pesos de oro común*, valued at 272 *maravedís*. Where, in the original source, a sum was given in another unit, it has generally been reduced to pesos of 272 maravedís, and the original figure indicated in parentheses.

The letter R. in references to manuscripts in the Archivo General de Indias signifies *Ramo*: a subdivision of a bundle (*legajo*) of documents. Occasionally there is still further subdivision into *Números*. Thus Patronato 80, R. 5, No. 1 is Patronato, Legajo 80, Ramo 5, Número 1.

Spanish words recurring in the text are italicised only at their first appearance. Some technical terms and some unusual words of which there is no good translation are commonly left in the Spanish original. Their meanings are explained. There is a Glossary of common mining terms. Some familiarity has been assumed with certain characteristic terms and institutions of colonial Spanish America; for example, encomienda, repartimiento, mita, asiento, consulado.

Si la de San Bernabé
No diera tan buena ley,
No casara Diego de Ibarra
Con la hija del virrey.

Zacatecan rhyme

THE SETTING

'... And that men should be made aware of the great Treasure hidden in these hills, God was pleased to create them in such a form that their very appearance, being so strange, made it clear that they held something precious within them, for in the wide plains that lie all around, God created this rugged chain, in length some six or eight leagues, which, considering its height in the midst of these plains, we could compare to a protruding navel on a smooth belly.'[1] So runs the description of the Serranía de Zacatecas made by Alonso de la Mota y Escobar, bishop of New Galicia, who undertook an extensive tour of his diocese between 1602 and 1605. His account is never lacking in stylistic panache, nor in graphic description. But the modern visitor to Zacatecas, with la Mota's image in mind, will be disappointed. For in truth the Serranía is an unremarkable range of low hills, one of many such ranges running northeast and south-west across the plateau of northern Mexico. The city of Zacatecas lies in a small basin in these hills at a height of some 8,000 feet; while the hills themselves rise only a few hundred feet above the *altiplanicie*, the great elevated plain stretched east-west between the Sierras Madre Occidental and Oriental, and north-south between the volcanic tumult of central Mexico and the plains of the United States.[2] The altiplanicie slopes gradually downwards towards the north, to heights of about 3,000 feet at the border;[3] but Zacatecas is sufficiently near its southern end to be one of the highest cities of Mexico.

As the crow flies, Zacatecas is some 350 miles to the north-west of Mexico City. The modern road from the capital runs over the plains of the southern part of the altiplanicie – plains which are more properly described as flat-floored and interconnected basins, the beds of former lakes.[4] It passes through Querétaro and the fertile lands of the Bajío, then to strike more directly northwards to Aguascalientes, renowned in modern times for its vineyards. The journey facing the traveller from Aguascali-

[1] Alonso de la Mota y Escobar, *Descripción geográfica de los reinos de Nueva Galicia, Nueva Vizcaya y Nuevo León*, written probably 1602–5, ed. used here, Guadalajara 1966, p. 63.

[2] Bataillon states that the plateau of northern Mexico corresponds, north of the border, not to the Great Plains of the United States, as might be supposed at first sight, but to the plateaux lying between the Rockies and the Sierra Nevada. See Claude Bataillon, *Les régions géographiques au Mexique*, Paris 1968, p. 15.

[3] Robert C. West, 'Surface Configuration and Associated Geology of Middle America', in *Handbook of Middle American Indians*, vol. 1, ed. Robert Wauchope, Austin, Texas 1964; pp. 33–83, here p. 40.   [4] West, 'Surface Configuration', p. 45.

The Setting

entes to Zacatecas is short, but presents him with an abrupt change of scene. For from irrigated and heavily cultivated land he passes into a region of semi-desert, and approaches Zacatecas from the town of Ojocaliente across a drab plain which only the rainy season brings to life. Such plains are the characteristic geographical feature of the Zacatecas district, spreading, beyond the Serranía, north and west to Mazapil and Sombrerete. Distant horizons are limited here and there by low hills. The plains, with rare local exceptions, are infertile. Their soils are thin, capable of supporting a natural vegetation of only xerophytic scrub, consisting of various sorts of shrubs and cacti, together with rough grass. Of larger plants, the most common are the nopal cactus (*Opuntia vulgaris*), the palmilla cactus (*Yucca rigida*), the maguey (*Agave mexicana*), the mezquite (*Prosopis juliflora*) and the huizache (*Acacia* of several varieties). Cultivation of all but a few crops is difficult. Maize and beans (the inevitable *frijoles* of Mexico) are the only true successes. Livestock, though, finds adequate grazing in the scrub, and the region has long produced cattle and sheep in quantity. In the last resort, goats are put out to pasture on the barest of the land.

While this infertility is true of the majority of the modern state of Zacatecas, there are exceptions in the west and the south of the region. The west forms part of a long and narrow basin–range area running along the eastern edge of the Sierra Madre Occidental and extending far to the north. The basins are filled with detritus and are often well watered.[1] Such, for example, is the valley of Valparaíso, recognised from earliest colonial days as a rich agricultural area. And the south of the present state of Zacatecas, extending tongue-like into Jalisco in the direction of Guadalajara, is a region of broken relief, crossed by what may be regarded as the foothills of the Sierra Madre Occidental. Streams flowing into the River Santiago have cut these hills to form an area known as *los cañones*. This is a geographical zone quite distinct from the rest of the Zacatecas district, being in general lower, warmer, better watered and more fertile.

The streams that have cut these deep southern valleys drain the land to the south of the Serranía, and their water is ultimately carried by the River Santiago to the Pacific. Water also reaches the sea from a small basin in the extreme west of the region between Sombrerete and Chalchihuites. But the majority of the present state, and of the historical district of Zacatecas, drains northward into the region of La Laguna at the southern tip of the state of Coahuila. The pattern of inland drainage is characteristic of semi-deserts and deserts, and typical of large areas of the northern altiplanicie. The principal stream in this northern basin is the Aguanaval,

[1] West, 'Surface Configuration', p. 48.

2

The Setting

known in the sixteenth and seventeenth centuries as the Río Grande.[1] It provides irrigation over a small area of its narrow valley, but does not flow the year round; nor, indeed, do most of the streams of the plains and the hills of Zacatecas. The city itself receives no more than 20 inches of rain a year, three-quarters of it between June and October.[2] Except for the south and the west the whole area of the modern state is deficient in rainfall, and is classified as arid or semi-arid. But its great height means that temperatures are moderate, and for most of the year animals can be adequately watered from springs and wells. It is none the less true, though, that growth of pasture is inhibited by lack of rain, and that grazing normally begins to be exhausted by January, some five months before the summer rains begin. Livestock in some areas is then obliged to have recourse to the fleshy, juicy leaves of perhaps the most typical of Zacatecan plants, the nopal cactus.[3]

To this dry, lofty and unpromising land the Spaniards came in 1546.

[1] Calling the Aguanaval the 'Río Grande' is perhaps a sign of the enthusiasm of Spanish settlers of the region in the sixteenth century, for the river is anything but large. An inhabitant of the town of Fresnillo gave the lie to the name in 1585 when he said that the river was not in the least 'grande', but only so called because there was no other river at all in the vicinity. 'Relación de Fresnillo', 17 January 1585, by Alonso Tabuya, in F. del Paso y Troncoso, *Papeles de Nueva España*, 2a. serie, México 1905–48, 9 vols., vol. 8, p. 298.

[2] Preston E. James, *Latin America*, New York 1950, p. 797.

[3] Except where otherwise stated, geographical information is taken from Moisés T. de la Peña (ed.), *Zacatecas económico*, México 1948, ch. 1, 'El medio físico'; and from personal observation.

CHAPTER I

DISCOVERY AND SETTLEMENT

On 8 September 1546 Juan de Tolosa, leading a small force of Spaniards and Indian auxiliaries, made camp under a hill crowned by a peculiar semi-circular crest of bare rock. The place lay 150 miles north-north-east of Guadalajara. From the summit of the Cerro de la Bufa, as the Spaniards later called the hill, a group of Zacatecos Indians watched the strangers' activities.[1] Tolosa in due course made friendly approaches to them, and the Indians, in appreciation of his good intentions, showed him stones which, on subsequent examination, were found to be rich in silver. And in this way, according to the traditional account, was the wealth of Zacatecas uncovered to the civilised world.[2] How did Tolosa come to be there?

His arrival on the future site of Zacatecas proved to be the culmination of a movement of exploration and expansion in search of wealth that had started immediately after the conquest of Tenochtitlan. The search for a route to the East, and then the quest for the fabled Seven Cities of Cíbola, had led Spaniards westward and northward from central Mexico in the very early years of the settlement of New Spain. By 1528, Cortés' lieutenants and followers had explored large areas of land to the south of the Lerma–Santiago river system, in what is today the state of Michoacán. And in 1529 began the conquests to the north of the Santiago of Beltrán Nuño de Guzmán, traditionally the blackest of figures among Spanish conquerors of Mexico. Over six years he ranged through regions of northern Michoacán, southern Zacatecas, Jalisco and Culaicán, laying the foundations of the province of New Galicia, which is the geographical setting of this book. He and his lieutenants founded towns, of which the most important at this early date was Compostela, in the west of the region. But far more central to this study, and of far greater subsequent fame, was Guadalajara, first established in 1531 by one of Guzmán's subordinates, Cristóbal de Oñate, and after various hesitations finally

---

[1] 'Bufa' was the name often given to the rounded crests of hilltops in northern Mexico. Perhaps this was an analogy with the meaning of the word (from Italian 'buffa') in armoury – the grand guard, or curved piece of accessory armour for the left shoulder used in jousting.

[2] Elías Amador, *Bosquejo histórico de Zacatecas*, vol. I, Zacatecas 1892, p. 186–7.

4

Discovery and Settlement

sited in 1542 in its present position to the south of the Santiago river (see plan 3).[1] Guzmán did not, of course, achieve settlement of New Galicia without meeting Indian resistance, and while this was temporarily overcome without great difficulty on early exploratory marches, it nevertheless remained a threat to permanent Spanish occupation of the land, and indeed grew as Spaniards sought to make use of Indian labour in the encomiendas granted to them by Guzmán. Resistance stiffened too as Spanish occupation advanced northward beyond the Santiago and Lerma rivers, leaving behind the sedentary Indian cultures of the centre of Mexico and encountering progressively more nomadic peoples. After various lesser revolts, a decisive confrontation came in 1540 with the outbreak of the Mixton war, in which the northernmost of the sedentary, agricultural peoples, the Caxcanes, attempted to halt and reverse the Spanish advance. This people occupied land to the north of the Santiago, extending into the canyon zone of present-day Zacatecas, and shared borders with the Zacatecos nation to the north. It appears to have formed something of a frontier between civilisation and barbarity in this region of Mexico, for beyond it lay the lands of the true nomads. Of these, the Zacatecos occupied much of the north of the modern state named after them and the north-east portion of Durango. Their lands bordered westwards with those of the Tepehuanes, and eastwards with those of the Guachichiles (see plan 4). These three tribes shared a primitive hunting–collecting culture, based on the gathering of mezquite on the fringes of Durango and *tunas* (the fruit of the nopal) in the region of nopal vegetation in eastern Zacatecas and western San Luis Potosí. They were in continuous conflict, and evidently communicated their aggressiveness to their Caxcan neighbours to the south. For despite the Caxcanes' more advanced sedentary way of life, they had waged constant war on the peoples beyond the Santiago, and now turned their efforts against the Spaniards.[2]

It took two years, the participation in the field of the viceroy himself, Antonio de Mendoza, and the efforts of 30,000 Aztec and Tlaxcalan auxiliaries, to subdue the Caxcanes in the Mixton revolt.[3] But subjugation, once achieved, was an important advance towards stability and permanence

[1] For the history of exploration by Cortés' agents and Guzmán, see J. H. Parry, *The Audiencia of New Galicia in the Sixteenth Century. A Study in Spanish Colonial Government*, 1948, pp. 19–25; H. H. Bancroft, *History of the Pacific States of North America*, vol. 5 (*Mexico*, vol. 2, 1521–1660), San Francisco 1883, pp. 344–71; J. Lloyd Mecham, *Francisco de Ibarra and Nueva Vizcaya*, Durham, North Carolina 1927, pp. 22–5.
[2] For a fuller account of the culture of the peoples mentioned here, see M. Othón de Mendizábal, 'Carácter de la conquista y colonización de Zacatecas', in *Obras completas*, vol. 5, México 1946, pp. 75–82.
[3] Parry, *The Audiencia*, p. 28.

5

Discovery and Settlement

of the Spanish occupation of New Galicia. Its most useful result, as far as the story of Zacatecas goes, was to open the way for exploration to the north-east further than any had gone before, by establishing at long last solid Spanish domination over the lands of the Caxcanes.[1]

It was nevertheless some years before explorations in that direction were to bear fruit. In the meanwhile Spanish settlers in New Galicia still faced considerable difficulties. The value of encomiendas fell as the Indian population was reduced by pestilence, and agriculture afforded a poor livelihood to colonists. Some relief came in 1543 with the first mining strikes in the region. Gold was found at Xaltepec and silver at Espíritu Santo, both near Compostela on the western margin of New Galicia. Further east, in the same year, came silver strikes at Guachinango, Xocotlán and Etzatlán. The prosperity of these mines was short-lived; their rich ores were quickly exhausted. But the strikes encouraged permanent settlement in New Galicia, not only through the possibility of wealth they offered, but also through the demand they created for food, and a consequent development of agriculture.[2] The mining discoveries were a result of the efforts of Cristóbal de Oñate, now lieutenant-governor of New Galicia, to find economic resources rich enough to support and stabilise the population of the province. Oñate did not fail to extract personal benefit from these mines, and some five years later used the wealth he had derived from them in the establishment of a settlement at Zacatecas.

The years after the Mixton war were in general, then, ones of consolidation of settlement. Typical devices of Spanish colonisation in the New World come into play at this time. A vanguard of priests moved slowly northwards, attempting to root the nomads in townships; while Mendoza himself appears to have supervised the founding of a number of Indian settlements in the north of the Caxcan region, as a bulwark against the nomads of the plateau.[3] At the same time, administration of the province

[1] One of Guzmán's lieutenants, Peralmíndez Chirinos, is said to have reached the site of Zacatecas, without realising its mineral potential, in 1530. The itinerary of Chirinos' journey is not clear. See José López Portillo y Weber, *La conquista de la Nueva Galicia*, México 1933, pp. 224–8; Fray Antonio Tello, *Crónica miscelánea y conquista espiritual y temporal de la Santa Provincia de Jalisco en el Nuevo Reino de la Galicia y Nueva Vizcaya y descubrimiento del Nuevo México*, 1635; in ed. of Guadalajara 1891, pp. 107–10.

[2] Matías de la Mota Padilla, *Historia de la conquista de la Provincia de la Nueva Galicia, escrita por ... en 1742*, Guadalajara 1920, p. 270; Parry, *The Audiencia*, p. 28.

[3] There is no record of these foundations in the chronicles of New Galicia or in modern secondary sources, but that they took place is indicated by a document belonging to the pueblo of Susticacán, about 35 miles south-west of Zacatecas, showing that Mendoza established the town in 1542. I am grateful to Don Federico Sescosse for a copy of this document. It is a royal order of 1602 addressed to Viceroy Velasco the younger, referring to complaints by the Indians of Susticacán about a land dispute with the neighbouring town of Tepetongo.

Discovery and Settlement

began to be regularised, though until 1545 the only constant thread in government was Cristóbal de Oñate, for many years lieutenant-governor of New Galicia, and in practice the chief executive official in the frequent absences of the governors themselves.[1] Oñate appears always to have acted with great credit to himself, but there was a need for more permanently institutionalised administration, and when Lorenzo de Tejada, oidor of the Audiencia of Mexico, arrived in Guadalajara in 1544 to enact the New Laws, he recommended the establishment of an Audiencia for New Galicia. Tejada drew the province more closely under the control of Mexico City by annulling all grants of encomienda made by Guzmán and Coronado, and placing the Indians so released under Crown administration. The Consejo de Indias subsequently issued orders for the creation of the Audiencia of New Galicia at Compostela in January 1548. In the interim, government was in the hands of an alcalde mayor, Baltasar de Gallegos, appointed from Mexico City.[2]

In the stable and slowly expanding New Galicia of 1545, the most respected and possibly the richest man in the province, Cristóbal de Oñate, who was now relieved of his lieutenant-governorship, continued to encourage the search for wealth. The expedition led by Juan de Tolosa that by chance located the silver ore deposits of Zacatecas seems to have been part of Oñate's exploratory enterprise, though it is not clear to what extent he participated in financing it. According to Amador's account, Oñate had heard of silver deposits in the direction of Zacatecas and commissioned Tolosa to locate them. The party of Indians and Spaniards left Guadalajara in August 1546 and arrived on the site of Zacatecas on 8 September.[3] Mota Padilla elaborates this, saying that part of Tolosa's force of Indians came from the recently subjugated town of Tlajomulco in Michoacán, and part from Juchipila, where Tolosa stopped to augment his force on his march northwards.[4] The surviving documentary evidence, however, does not support the eighteenth- and nineteenth-century statements of Mota Padilla and Amador. According to an account

[1] After Guzmán's departure from New Galicia in 1536, the Crown having finally removed him for his excesses against the Indians and for insubordination, the governorship was held by Diego Pérez de la Torre. But he was killed in 1538 in an Indian uprising. His successor, Francisco Vázquez Coronado, spent most of his term of office at the head of his celebrated expedition to Cíbola and Quivira, far from New Galicia; though he was actively in office from 1542 to 1545, in which year he resigned, under censure for negligence and corruption injustice. Mendoza administered New Galicia directly during part of the Mixton campaign, and apparently for a short time afterwards. Parry, *The Audiencia*, pp. 26–30.

[2] Parry, *The Audiencia*, pp. 30–1.

[3] Amador, *Bosquejo histórico*, p. 186.

[4] Mota Padilla, *Historia*, ed. México 1870, p. 194; as quoted in P. W. Powell, *Soldiers, Indians and Silver. The Northward Advance of New Spain, 1550–1600*, University of California Press, Berkeley and Los Angeles 1952, p. 229, note 25.

Discovery and Settlement

(*información*) of Juan de Tolosa's services, dating from 1550 (less than four years after the event), he made several expeditions in search of mines from the town of Nochistlán.[1] On one occasion, being in Tlaltenango with a group of Spaniards, he was shown a piece of ore of some promise, and asked the local Indians where it came from. On being told, he led out an expedition consisting of Indian slaves, and Spaniards of his own force and that of one Miguel de Ibarra, on a search which resulted in the Zacatecas strike. At first the discovery was disappointing, for the earliest deposit to be found was 'the poor mine of Miguel de Ibarra'. The date of the find is not given. Witnesses merely say that it was more than three years before – that is, some time before the middle of 1547.[2] Tolosa then took three or four mule-loads (*cargas*) of ore to Nochistlán, where he found Miguel de Ibarra with his nephew Diego. The ores were assayed, with a result promising enough to cause the Ibarras to agree to co-operate with Tolosa in further exploration and development of the mines.[3] So about three days later, Tolosa and Diego de Ibarra returned northwards to the site of Zacatecas and within a short time brought in more settlers.

This account of the discovery is borne out by witnesses to the Tolosa *información*. Juan Michel, one of the earliest miners to arrive in Zacatecas, relates that when news of the strike spread he hurried to the site and there found Tolosa and Diego de Ibarra with slaves and horses.[4] Michel claims he was the second person to arrive after the initial group gathered by Tolosa and Ibarra. So it seems quite clear that Tolosa must be given credit for the discovery of ores itself. He was obviously engaged with the Ibarras in the search for mineral wealth, since his expedition included some of Miguel de Ibarra's men; and their convenient presence at Nochistlán only confirms that they were exploring the resources of the north. The name of Cristóbal de Oñate is not to be found in the Tolosa *información*, and while it is possible that Tolosa and the Ibarras were

---

[1] AGI Patronato 80, R. 1, No. 5, 'Información de los méritos de Juanes de Tolosa, fundador de la ciudad de Zacatecas; y otras informaciones de los descendientes del dicho Juanes de Tolosa y del Marqués Hernando Cortés y del emperador Moctezuma para la pretensión de ... Don Juan de Zaldívar Cortés Moctezuma.' This document has two distinct parts. The first is dated Nochistlán, June 1550, and is the *información de méritos* drawn up by Tolosa himself before Hernán Martínez de la Marcha, oidor of Guadalajara. The second part (beginning at f. 21v.) is dated Guadalajara, May 1594, and was drawn up by Tolosa's son, D. Juan Cortés Tolosa Moctezuma. The first account and petition of 1550 had brought Tolosa no reward from the Crown.

[2] AGI Patronato 80, R. 1, No. 5, 'Información ... de Juanes de Tolosa', ff. 8v.–11.

[3] AGI Patronato 80, R. 1, No. 5, 'Información ... de Juanes de Tolosa', f. 3v.

[4] AGI Patronato 80, R. 1, No. 5, 'Información ... de Juanes de Tolosa', ff. 11–13, testimony of Juan Michel.

Discovery and Settlement

acting under the general directive of Oñate, it seems that he had no direct part to play in the discovery. His contribution to the history of Zacatecas, in the form of capital for the establishment of a permanent settlement in a situation made hostile both by the barrenness of its surroundings and the ferocity of its Indian inhabitants, came soon afterwards. With justification he may occupy his position, with Tolosa and Diego de Ibarra, as one of the traditionally honoured founders of Zacatecas. The founders, as today commemorated in a decorative fountain in the city, are generally accounted as four. The last, not yet mentioned here, is Baltasar de Temiño de Bañuelos, who, like Oñate, goes unacclaimed in the Tolosa información of 1550. In the later account of 1594 he appears as a witness, stating merely that he was 'one of the first settlers to come to the said mines after the said Juanes de Tolosa had discovered them'.[1]

In the origins and careers of the four founders of Zacatecas there are interesting similarities, and their biographies are illustrative of certain common themes in the history of Zacatecas as a mining settlement. It is clear that the most distinguished of them at the time was Cristóbal de Oñate, who had many years of experience as a senior administrator and mining entrepreneur in New Galicia. Born in Vitoria, in the Basque province of Alava, in 1504 or 1505, the son of *hijosdalgo*, he crossed the Atlantic to New Spain in 1524 as the assistant (*ayudante*) of Rodrigo de Albornoz, accountant (*contador*) of the Treasury office of New Spain. He was one of Guzmán's lieutenants in the conquest of New Galicia from the beginning of that enterprise in 1529, and seems always to have been a moderating influence in that ruthless group. In the course of his career he was awarded two encomiendas, one at Culuacán, close by Mexico City, and the other at Tacámbaro in Michoacán. He also gained useful connections by his marriage to Doña Catalina de Salazar y de la Cadena, daughter of the Treasury officer Gonzalo de Salazar, an accomplice of Guzmán's. His wealth of later years derived from mining enterprises in various parts of New Galicia after the Mixton war and was reinvested in further mining activities at Zacatecas. But although he encouraged prospective miners to go to Zacatecas and supported them while they were there, he seems to have been resident very little himself. In the period immediately after the discovery of the mines, Oñate was in Mexico City, as is evident from his testimony in the información of Diego de Ibarra, dated at Zacatecas, 22 March 1550. Oñate there states that his agents (*criados*) in Zacatecas had written to him in Mexico City saying that they wished to

---

[1] AGI Patronato 80, R. 1, No. 5, 'Información ... de Juanes de Tolosa', f. 54 v., testimony of Baltasar de Temiño de Bañuelos, Zacatecas 14 May 1594.

9

Discovery and Settlement

leave the mines because of shortage of food and the poor quality of ores.[1] And one of the informaciones relating to Oñate himself definitely describes him as a householder (vecino) of Mexico City.[2] If Oñate was not normally resident in Zacatecas up to the time of his death, about 1570, his children became active members of the mining community and proceeded to greater fame. The most illustrious of them was Don Juan de Oñate y Salazar, conqueror, adelantado and governor of New Mexico. His brother, Don Alonso de Oñate y Salazar, was first a miner in Zacatecas and later solicitor general (procurador general) for the collectivity of miners of New Spain, New Galicia and New Biscay. The eldest son, Don Fernando Pérez de Narriahondo y Oñate, succeeded to the family encomienda at Tacámbaro and later became alcalde mayor of Puebla. Like the other founders of Zacatecas, Cristóbal himself is said to have died in poverty. In another información relating to him, presented by his grandson Cristóbal de Oñate Rivadeneira in México on 23 January 1584, there is a statement that he had extracted more than a million and a half pesos from the mines in which he held interests; but this enormous sum had been completely consumed in financing campaigns against Indians and in pacification. So great had been his services to the Crown that his children were left indigent: the constant aggrieved complaint of a conquistador's descendants.[3]

About the early activities of Juan de Tolosa, information is slighter and less certain. Neither the place nor the date of his birth is known, though it has been suggested that he was from Guipúzcoa – a plausible idea in view of the existence of the town of Tolosa.[4] Mecham states that he took part in the Mixton campaign, but neither in the información of 1550 nor in that of 1594 is such service claimed by him or by his descendants, and it would not have been a point to be passed over lightly. His first definite appearance on the scene is in 1546, with his arrival at Zacatecas at the head

---

[1] AGI Guadalajara 28, 'Información de oficio recibida en esta real audiencia de México de la Nueva España, sobre la que dió Diego de Ibarra, caballero de la orden de Santiago, vecino de México', México 9 August 1582. Most of the actual probanza is dated Zacatecas 22 March–20 April 1550.

[2] AGI Patronato 75, R. 5, No. 1, 'Información de los servicios de Cristóbal de Oñate en la conquista del Nuevo Reino de Galicia'; presented by Fernando de Oñate, his son, in Mexico City, 31 October 1577. N.f.; reference is to Q. 6 of the interrogatorio.

[3] AGI Patronato 78, R. 1, No. 1, 'Probanza de los méritos y servicios de Cristóbal de Oñate, conquistador de la Nueva Galicia ...', México 23 January 1584; here, interrogatorio, Q. 10. Other information on Oñate from: J. I. P. Dávila Garibi, La sociedad de Zacatecas en los albores del régimen colonial, actuación de los principales fundadores y primeros funcionarios públicos de la ciudad, México 1939, 13; López Portillo y Weber, La conquista, p. 137; AGI Mexico 1064, No. 1, f. 224.

[4] Dávila Garibi, La sociedad, 29; AGI Patronato 80, R. 1, No. 5, 'Información ... de Juanes de Tolosa', f. 4v.

Discovery and Settlement

of his troop. Then, some time in the early 1550s he married the daughter of Hernán Cortés and Doña Isabel Moctezuma, Doña Leonor Cortés Moctezuma, who in due course gave birth to three children: Don Juan Cortés Tolosa Moctezuma, a miner and active cabildo member until his death in 1624; Doña Isabel Cortés Moctezuma, later to marry Don Juan de Oñate, the adelantado of New Mexico; and Doña Leonor Cortés Moctezuma, wife of Cristóbal de Zaldívar Mendoza, a distinguished participant in the campaigns against the Chichimec Indians in the 1570s and 1580s, and a Basque in descent.[1] The date of Juan de Tolosa's death is unknown, though he was certainly no longer alive in 1594 when his children presented their información. In it they claimed, like Oñate's descendants, that he had died in poverty, leaving only a few abandoned ore-processing mills (haciendas de minas). His early mining fortune from Zacatecas had been wholly dissipated in further explorations he undertook during the 1550s in search of other mines.

Of the third of the recognised founders of Zacatecas, Diego de Ibarra, a good deal is known. Born in the town of Eibar in Guipúzcoa about 1510, he arrived in New Spain in 1540, in time to take part in the Mixton campaign. He appears to have fought that war in the company of his uncle, Miguel de Ibarra, and after the defeat of the Indians they began explorations together into the north of New Galicia, combining efforts with Juan de Tolosa, as has already been noted. Diego de Ibarra drew his share of Zacatecas' prosperity in the early 1550s, and, a wealthy man, married in 1556 Doña Ana de Velasco y Castilla, daughter of the second viceroy of New Spain, Luis de Velasco. He became important later as the principal source of credit for the expeditions of his nephew, Francisco de Ibarra, who, in a short period before his early death in 1575, explored vast areas to the north-west of Zacatecas, creating the province of New Biscay and becoming its first governor. After Francisco's death, Diego de Ibarra assumed the governorship in his place in 1576. He lived thereafter to an advanced age. In 1600 he was still claiming recompense for his great expenditure in the conquest of New Biscay, which had amounted, so he claimed, to over 200,000 pesos. Thus had his personal fortune drained away. But in fact he was not quite so destitute, for he failed to mention that in the last quarter of the century he had assembled an enormous estate to the west of Zacatecas, centred on the hacienda of Trujillo. This estate, together with other lands in New Biscay and extensive mining interests in Zacatecas and other mining towns of the north, was incorporated into a mayorazgo in 1578, which was inherited by his daughter, Doña Mariana de Velasco. His only son, Luis, had died in 1576. This

[1] Dávila Garibi, La sociedad, genealogical table No. 11.

mayorazgo was one of a very few ever created in the sixteenth and seventeenth centuries by miners and citizens of Zacatecas.[1]

Baltasar de Temiño de Bañuelos is usually taken to be the fourth founder of Zacatecas, but is worthy of the title only in the limited sense that he may have been present at the formal foundation of the settlement in 1548. For that was the year in which he appears to have arrived, and there were indisputably many others on the site before him. He was doubtless the youngest of the four, having been born about 1530, a son of the Temiño family from Burebe in Old Castile. In later life he was a leading miner and citizen of Zacatecas, and was appointed lieutenant captain-general of New Galicia in 1572 by Viceroy Enríquez in the war against the Chichimec Indians. He later protested that the cost of equipping forces for this struggle was his ruin, and in his last years, like his companions, claimed to be poor. He died in 1600, after playing a part in the local administration of Zacatecas for many years. The family name persists in the town throughout the seventeenth century, but his descendants never attained his position in the society of the city, nor riches approaching his.[2]

These were the four men whom Zacatecas recognises today as its founders. Their careers are characteristic of those of many of their fellow citizens in later years – a rapid rise from obscurity to an esteemed social position through the accumulation of wealth; high marriages; ascent to important military and civil office; descent from silver-lined middle years to indigent old age. The fact that three of them were Basques, and one from the northern limits of Old Castile, is also of interest. The history of the exploration and settlement of northern New Spain is dominated by Basque names in this period, and indeed into the seventeenth century: Francisco de Ibarra and Francisco de Urdiñola in New Biscay, Juan de Oñate in New Mexico, Martín de Zavala in New León. There was a tendency among emigrant Basques, above all other Spaniards in America, to congregate with others of the same tongue and regional origin.[3] But Zacatecas was not a city numerically dominated by Basques at any time, as can be seen from many name lists of miners and inhabitants in the sixteenth and seventeenth centuries. Basque families were influential but

---

[1] On Ibarra, see: Dávila Garibi, *La sociedad*, pp. 37–41, and genealogical table No. 15; Mecham, *Francisco de Ibarra*, pp. 42, 223, 239; AGI Mexico 1064, No. 1, f. 221; AGI Guadalajara 28, 'Información de oficio recibida ... sobre la que dió Diego de Ibarra', México 9 August 1582.

[2] Mecham, *Francisco de Ibarra*, pp. 42, 48.

[3] This effect is noted by P. Boyd-Bowman in 'La emigración peninsular a América: 1520–1539', *Historia Mexicana*, vol. 13, No. 2, October–December 1963, pp. 165–92; here p. 168.

few. Above all, Basques were great explorers; and Zacatecas the source of finance for their expeditions and the base from which they set out. How did that base develop from the small beginnings made by Juan de Tolosa and Diego de Ibarra in the autumn of 1546? The beginnings were not indeed very auspicious. The news of the discovery at Zacatecas spread quickly, but it did not seem that the deposits were more remarkable than those already found further south in New Galicia. The Treasury officials of the province, in December of 1547, were less enthusiastic about Zacatecas than about Culiacán, where silver strikes had just been made.[1] At Zacatecas there was difficulty in attracting and holding settlers. At one point Diego de Ibarra and his servants constituted the whole population.[2] While mines were few and poor, and attack by Indians an ever-present threat, there was little to recommend Zacatecas. One of the witnesses to the Tolosa información of 1550 relates that Tolosa, after making the initial discoveries of ore, quickly extended his explorations (in characteristically energetic fashion) to Tepezala. Returning thence to Nochistlán, he heard that the pioneers of Zacatecas were leaving for fear of the Indians; and at Mecatabasco, eighteen leagues south from Zacatecas, he found a group of fugitives from the mines, including Diego de Ibarra himself. In an attempt to preserve the settlement he and one Tomás de Arrayaiza returned to Zacatecas, and with Ibarra began to build solid houses, strong enough to withstand Indian attack. These were flat-roofed dwellings (*casas de terrado*), probably of *adobe* construction.[3] All this appears to have taken place early in 1547, and it was the only occasion on which there was a serious possibility of Zacatecas being abandoned. The Indian danger, which still remained a mere threat, was to become far more urgent in later years; but by then the town had grown to such a size that there was little chance of dislodging it. Now, in 1547, Diego de Ibarra, providing a nucleus of his own men, gave shelter, food and protection to newcomers, and indeed positively sought to encourage settlement by writing to those who he thought would be interested in the venture. At times he was maintaining seventy or eighty Spaniards in his house (variously referred to as a *casafuerte* or *posada*), although such large numbers were probably not reached until 1548, when the rich silver discoveries made in that year finally removed all danger of abandonment of the camp and attracted

---

[1] AGI Guadalajara 31, Treasury officials of New Galicia to Charles V, Compostela 15 December 1547. Of the Zacatecas mines they merely said 'they are held to be rich'.

[2] AGI Guadalajara 28, 'Información de oficio recibida ... sobre la que dió Diego de Ibarra', 1582, f. 11v.; testimony of Bartolomé de Mendoza.

[3] AGI Patronato 80, R. 1, No. 5, 'Información ... de Juanes de Tolosa', 23 May 1550, ff. 4, 7v.–8, testimony of Juan de Amuseo.

Discovery and Settlement

a flood of fortune seekers.[1] It is hardly an original observation to point out that Ibarra's mode of procedure in establishing Zacatecas is typical of the contemporary Spanish method of conquest and settlement, which delegated exploration to private enterprise and capital in return for promised future reward in the form of cash, concessions or honours of one sort or another. The founders of Zacatecas were later to be disappointed in their petitions for rewards for their efforts.[2]

The date of the founding of the town of Zacatecas is usually given as 20 January 1548. It was the day, according to various chronicles, on which the four founders met on the site for the first time. There is no documentary evidence for this, but the date of foundation is of no more than local patriotic interest in any case. The year 1548, though, was possibly the most important in the history of Zacatecas, for it was then that the major ore discoveries were made. The three principal groups of silver-bearing veins (*vetas*) in the Serranía were located in the months from spring to autumn: the vein christened La Albarrada (or in particular the mine of San Benito on it), forming part of the all-important Veta Grande, was found on 1 March; the veta of San Bernabé, two and a half miles north-east of Zacatecas, was located on 4 June; and the first of the veins of the Pánuco group, some eight miles north of Zacatecas, were discovered on 1 November.[3] These veins, with others occurring in association with them, yielded a large part of the wealth of Zacatecas until the beginning of the twentieth century. And although other deposits were later found in the immediate vicinity of the town, and other mining centres grew and flourished in what became the Zacatecas silver district, it was principally the veins in the hills of the Serranía, as far north as Pánuco, that yielded the mass of silver. The most important of the veins discovered in 1548 was the Veta Grande, in which were sunk many of the mines responsible for the great and later boom of 1615 to 1635. Today, around the centre of the Veta Grande, there is a small, decayed village, which seems to be of eighteenth-century origin. But in the sixteenth and seventeenth centuries there was no permanent settlement there, since the road to Zacatecas was short – no more than four miles – and access easy. There were, however, huts and shelters at the mine-heads for temporary

[1] AGI Guadalajara 28, 'Información de oficio recibida ... sobre la que dió Diego de Ibarra', 1582, *passim*.

[2] There is a traditional story, often repeated in local histories of Zacatecas and its region, demonstrating that Cristóbal de Oñate followed Ibarra's example in supporting settlement in Zacatecas. It is said that a bell was rung at mid-day in his house, inviting passers-by to a free lunch. See J. Arlegui, *Crónica de la Provincia de N.S.P. S. Francisco de Zacatecas*, México 1737, ed. used México 1851, p. 123.

[3] Amador, *Bosquejo histórico*, pp. 188–90; Mota Padilla, *Historia*, ed. Guadalajara 1920, p. 270. The precision of dates in these sources must be regarded with suspicion.

housing of workers and storage of ores and equipment. Pánuco was further off; and partly for that reason, partly because it yielded very rich ores right at the beginning, a separate camp grew up there. The discovery of Pánuco was claimed for Diego de Ibarra by his descendants.[1]

The strikes of 1548 led to a rush to Zacatecas, beginning in that year, and continuing for some years to come. The massive influx of population led to problems of public order and control, and there arose a need for regular civil government. In late December 1548 the citizens of Zacatecas applied to the Audiencia of New Galicia for the appointment of an alcalde mayor. The first recorded holder of the office was one Pedro Mejía, in 1549. There was evidently serious conflict among prospectors for claims, leading to violence and deaths. Abuses in the employment of Indians were also common. Indians were flooding into Zacatecas, while others were being seized for use as carriers (*tamemes*) and having their crops illegally confiscated as the demand for food at the mines soared.[2] In October 1549 it was reported that there were in Zacatecas 300 Spaniards skilled in mine work.[3] Many of these had come from Mexico City and had begun to remit silver there directly from Zacatecas, thus robbing New Galicia of taxes, which disturbed the Treasury officials of the province. But possibly a more important effect of the early silver remittances was the establishing of regular communication between the northern part of the plateau and the central region of Mexico.[4]

In the autumn of 1549 the *Licenciado* Hernán Martínez de la Marcha, one of the first four *oidores* of the Audiencia of New Galicia, arrived at Compostela, the seat of the Audiencia, to take up his post.[5] In the following year he undertook a *visita general* of the whole of the province, in the course of which he spent some time in Zacatecas. By now the Audiencia had appointed an alcalde mayor, but his effect in the preservation of order seems to have been small. For la Marcha found, in March 1550, a turbulent mining camp, full of prospectors from all parts of New Spain, who abandoned mines as quickly as they opened them up, jumped claims and neglected to register their workings. They likewise failed to pay any tax on the silver they produced. La Marcha made an inspection of the claims then being worked, and forwarded a report drawn up by the *alguacil mayor* of the town. Fifty mine owners were currently working stamp-mills and ore-refining plants. Cristóbal de Oñate, and others in company

[1] AGI Guadalajara 7, 16 September 1614, Doña Ana de Ibarra Velasco to king.
[2] *CDHG*, vol. I, p. 102, Guadalajara 29 December 1548, 'Petición para que la Audiencia no se asiente en Compostela sino en Guadalajara'.
[3] AGI Guadalajara 31, 22 October 1549, Juan de Ojeda to Charles V.
[4] AGI Guadalajara 31, Compostela, 20 December 1548, Treasury officials to Charles V.
[5] Parry, *The Audiencia*, p. 44.

with him, owned a number of mines, thirteen *ingenios* (stamp-mills), buildings to house slaves, a house and a church (probably a chapel attached to his hacienda de minas). Oñate also owned 101 slaves. Besides the owners of mines there were about a dozen vecinos engaged in other trades. Many of these were merchants. There were also some whites who owned neither houses nor mines. All the more prosperous miners employed slaves or *naborías* (voluntary Indian workers).[1]

While he was in Zacatecas, la Marcha issued two series of Ordinances. The first, given on 20 April 1550, regulated mining. It aimed principally at regularising claims. All mines should be registered before ores were taken from them. Claims, once registered, should be worked to a depth of three *estados* (about eighteen feet) within one year. They should be 80 varas along the vein and 40 varas across it, if they were the first on it; but subsequent claims should measure only 60 by 30 varas (a vara being slightly less than a yard). The Ordinances are of no great interest, and deal mainly with technical and purely legal matters. A week later, though, la Marcha issued a second series of orders, this time on the treatment of Indian labourers and other points relating to labour and mining. This series, in contrast with that on mining, is of great interest, and various parts of it will be discussed in due course. At this very early stage patterns in labour systems are discernible that last through the whole period under consideration.[2] Before leaving Zacatecas, la Marcha also made provisional arrangements for the taxing and stamping of silver at the mines. Up to then, it had gone either to Compostela or to Mexico City, and the absence of an authority on the spot to collect tax meant that there was much opportunity for fraud. La Marcha therefore appointed an inspector (*veedor*) at Zacatecas, to be assisted by representatives of the treasurer and auditor of New Galicia. The royal tax was thenceforth to be sent to the Treasury branch at Compostela every six months under armed escort.[3]

Thus Zacatecas survived its first visita, which had brought a crop of Ordinances and no doubt some inquietude to the vecinos and miners of

---

[1] Parry, *The Audiencia*, pp. 50–1; A. S. Aiton, *Antonio de Mendoza, First Viceroy of New Spain*, Duke University Press, Durham, North Carolina 1927, pp. 184–5. The original of la Marcha's letter, dated 18 February 1551, and quoted by Parry as being in AGI Guadalajara 5, is no longer in that legajo.

[2] AGI Guadalajara 5. The second part of this legajo is a vellum-bound volume entitled 'Averiguaciones hechas por el ilustre señor Licenciado Contreras y Guevara, oidor y alcalde mayor de la audiencia mayor del nuevo reino de Galicia y el más antiguo; sobre lo tocante a la visita del Real Consejo de Indias'; dated 10 March 1570. (Hereafter it is referred to as 'Averiguaciones ... Contreras y Guevara ... 1570'.) Ff. 105–14 contain la Marcha's mining Ordinances; ff. 115–21, his Ordinances for the treatment of Indians.

[3] Parry, *The Audiencia*, p. 52, quoting la Marcha's letter of 18 February 1551.

the town, as later visitas were always to do. But the town had not yet had time to develop the resistance to outside interference that was later to characterise its reaction to attempts by external authorities to control its affairs. There can at this time have been little sense of solidarity among the inhabitants, for the permanence of the settlement and the extent of the resources of the mines were still open to doubt. But already the Zacatecas strike had had deep effects on New Galicia, and the wealth of the mines was rapidly making itself felt further afield.

The rise of Zacatecas meant a shift in economic balance in New Galicia from west to east, which is reflected in the development of certain administrative arrangements in the province during the mid-century years. Guzmán had established Compostela as the capital of the province, from which all government had taken place, inasmuch as there was any government before 1536, the year of his departure. In Treasury matters the first recorded nomination is that of Cristóbal de Oñate to the office of *veedor de fundiciones* in 1531.[1] This must have been a somewhat speculative appointment, since at the time no precious metals had been found in New Galicia whose smelting might have demanded the supervision of a veedor. The first properly constituted local office of the Treasury – a *Real Caja* – appears in New Galicia in 1543, when one was established at Compostela; primarily, it seems, to collect silver taxes payable in the newly-discovered mines of Espíritu Santo.[2] Other mine discoveries followed in the south and west of the province to reinforce the need for the Caja. And in this form Treasury arrangements continued in New Galicia until 1549, in November of which year there went a letter from the Audiencia to the Emperor, referring to a petition made by the miners of Zacatecas that one Treasury official might reside in that town, to stamp and tax silver. The road from the mines to Compostela was long and dangerous, and the Audiencia emphasised the risk of evasion of Crown dues if silver were to be taken to Mexico City for taxation, as had indeed been happening.[3] This letter was the first shot in a long battle over the siting of the Caja; but inevitably the economic attraction of Zacatecas proved stronger in the end, and the Real Caja of New Galicia was eventually placed there, after a royal cédula was issued to that effect in 1552. The same cédula ordered that a smelting house (*casa de fundición*) should also be set up in Zacatecas (in which, it may be supposed, assay of silver could be carried out and the metal melted down into ingots of regular size). Silver

[1] BN Mexico MS. 9(72.32) OJE, 'Libro de Juan de Hojeda'; ff. 2v.–3, la Reina, La Coruña 25 January 1531, real provisión.
[2] Tello, *Crónica miscelánea*, pp. 518–19.
[3] AGI Guadalajara 51, ff. 7v.–8, Compostela 28 November 1549, Audiencia of New Galicia to Charles V.

gathered for the Crown in tax should be sent directly to Mexico City for immediate shipment to Spain. On no account were miners to be obliged to carry their silver to Compostela for taxation.[1] The Treasury officials duly moved to Zacatecas. It was, indeed, a move they had been advocating themselves for several years past; but hardly had they arrived when they began to find faults with the change. The mines in the west of New Galicia, they said, at Culiacán, Xocotlán and Guachinango, were richer than Zacatecas, and were not paying a peso in tax. Many Zacatecan miners were leaving to prospect at Xocotlán, taking their workers with them. Local ores were declining in richness and miners were disturbed by increasing unrest among the local Indians. The Caja should therefore be moved to Guadalajara.[2] No doubt the officials' misgivings were well founded, but it is hard to avoid the suspicion that the brusque change from the warm and luxuriant surroundings of Compostela to the barren aridity of Zacatecas had been too much for them. The Crown did not go back on its decision, however, and from then on the Caja remained in Zacatecas. Its establishment there was the symbol of the economic ascendancy of the east over the west of the province – an ascendancy which is reflected clearly in the move soon afterwards of the Audiencia itself from Compostela to Guadalajara, authorised by a royal order of 1560.[3] But even Guadalajara, in the following three-quarters of a century, was to be overshadowed by the mining city of the plateau to the east, surviving only as the seat of the Audiencia and as a local administrative centre of little importance.[4] It received a Treasury office, subsidiary to that of Zacatecas, in 1569.

Nor was the direct economic influence of Zacatecan silver slow to impress itself on distant regions to the south, on the already populated areas of New Spain and New Galicia. A primary need of the new town was a supply of food for its hordes of prospectors and labourers. The lands around Zacatecas were barren, and in any case fortune hunters were not yet prepared to divert their energies to the mundane tasks of agriculture

---

[1] BN Mexico MS. 9(72.32) OJE, f. 48v., Monzón 3 September 1552, el Príncipe to Treasury officials of New Galicia, real cédula.

[2] For these objections by the Treasury officials, see AGI Guadalajara 30, their información of 30 October 1553.

[3] CDHG, vol. I, p. 262, Toledo 10 May 1560, king to Audiencia of New Galicia, real cédula.

[4] In the mid-1570s there were actually proposals that the Audiencia should be moved to Zacatecas – a change advocated by the viceroy himself, on the grounds that Zacatecas was the centre of economic activity in the province, and that marauding Indians could be better controlled from there. The move was opposed by members of the Audiencia, and never came about. See, e.g. AGI Guadalajara 6, R. 1, Guadalajara 7 December 1577, Oidor Orozco to king.

and stock raising. So supplies were drawn to Zacatecas from the more fertile regions of southern New Galicia around Guadalajara, and from parts more distant still. (See ch. 4, below.)

Communication with the south was therefore an urgent need. The road to Guadalajara posed little problem, for it was by that route that Zacatecas had been discovered and settled. The way through the canyons of Tlaltenango, Juchipila and Nochistlán was clear in every sense. Only the crossing of the River Santiago presented any difficulty, for Indian resistance to the passage of men and goods had been largely eliminated by the defeat of the Caxcanes in the Mixton war. But Zacatecas also needed direct communication with Mexico City, the major source of prospectors in the rush of 1548 and 1549, and the source of returns on mining, for silver had to be carried there for minting. The opening of a route down the centre of New Spain was therefore the direct and inevitable result of the Zacatecas strike. The highway became known as the *Camino Real de la Tierra Adentro*, and later extended to link Mexico City with the remotenesses of New Mexico. But the first stretch was to Zacatecas, and that beginning was not easily achieved.

The sudden appearance of a township at Zacatecas, in the heart of an arid and hostile upland, is a remarkable event when compared with the slender results of more conservative advance in the lands immediately to the north of Mexico City. North of a line running roughly from Querétaro to Guadalajara, between the two Sierras Madre limiting the plateau to east and west, lay the country of the nomads, almost as impenetrable to the Spaniards, at first, as it had been for centuries to the higher indigenous cultures of central Mexico.[1] Not until the 1540s, after the failure of the Coronado expedition to reveal anything of importance in the furthest north, and after resolution of the difficulties of the Mixton war, did the slow advance of Spaniards into the borders of the wild tribes' hunting grounds begin. Progress was made with ranching and mission enterprises in the area that began to be identified as the province of the Chichimecas. Mendoza, recognising the danger of attack by the Indians of this region on communications and settlers further south, tried to consolidate control of the frontier by granting encomiendas and lands. The recipients of these *mercedes* were, of course, liable to military service in defence of their lands; and a number of distinguished land-owning military captains emerged on to the scene of the Chichimec frontier in the early 1540s. They fostered good relations with the well-disposed Otomí nation and slowly extended their cattle lands into Chichimec territory. At the same time, Augustinian and Franciscan missionaries ventured

[1] Powell, *Soldiers*, pp. 3-10.

deeper into the northern lands. And as Spanish pressure on the frontier increased, sedentary Indian settlers from the south moved up behind the outposts.

The exploratory movement resulting in the Zacatecas discovery had traced an arc far to the west of the Chichimec lands, describing a half-circle whose diameter was the direct route between the mines and Mexico City. This diameter now had to be ruled in. Up to the time of the Zacatecas strike, there had been little enough motive for subjugating the north, apart from the necessity of warding off attack. The cattle lands just spoken of were only beginning, in 1546, to provide an important part of the meat demanded by Mexico City and its surrounding towns; and in consequence the northern road had penetrated only a short way. There was a well-defined route as far as Querétaro.[1] From there the road to Zacatecas was gradually extended northwards to pass through San Felipe (splitting on the way, one branch going through San Miguel), then through Ojuelos, Encinillas, Las Bocas, Ciénaga Grande, Cuicillo, and finally to Zacatecas. This Camino Real was opened up between 1550 and 1555, and its early stages were supervised by Mendoza. The terrain can have offered little obstacle to establishing a route, since the plateau north of Mexico City consists of a series of smooth-floored basins separated by low ranges. From the beginning, the road appears to have been negotiable to the light two-wheeled *carretas* employed, but some preparation was necessary before heavier *carros* could be used. By 1555 it was passable to all traffic.

Feeder roads into the main highway soon became needed. Supplies for the north were also drawn from Michoacán, and in 1550 Mendoza set about improving communications from this region, trying to link Zitácuaro and Acámbaro with the highway. By the end of the 1550s supplies were moving from Michoacán to Zacatecas along at least two major routes. One, serving the Valladolid–Zitácuaro–Cuitzeo–Maravatío region, passed through Acámbaro, then struck directly north to San Miguel, where it joined a branch of the Camino Real. A second, serving an area further to the north-west, passed northward near the mines of Guanajuato, north-west through the Valle de Señora (later the site of León), and to the sites of the still-unfounded Lagos and Aguascalientes. Thence it moved straight north to Zacatecas, uniting with the Mexico City route at Cuicillo, some nine leagues south of the mines. The discovery of the Guanajuato silver deposits, in the mid-1550s, lying between the

---

[1] All information about roads is taken from Powell, *Soldiers*, pp. 16–31; and from P. W. Powell, 'The Forty-niners of Sixteenth-Century Mexico', *Pacific Historical Review*, vol. 19, 1950, pp. 235–49.

Discovery and Settlement

Camino Real and the second of the routes north from Michoacán, brought into existence a number of linking roads running east-west to join those already established.[1] (For these roads, see plan 3.)

Brief reference to routes between Guadalajara and Zacatecas has already been made. There were two principal roads. One went directly north through Juchipila, thereafter turning slightly east to reach Zacatecas as it passed up the valley of the River Juchipila. The other passed from Guadalajara north-east to Teocaltiche, from there to the later site of Aguascalientes, and so north to Zacatecas.

Inns were set up along the new roads. They served as resting places and shelters in the stretches of unpopulated country, sometimes being fortified and garrisoned for protection against highway attacks. They were run by Indians, land-owners and occasionally, religious houses. Grants of land and sites for inns were freely distributed by Mendoza in 1550. Cristóbal de Oñate, for example, received a licence for an inn on 2 May 1550, to be built on the new road to Zacatecas, five leagues beyond the inn granted to the Colegio San Miguel de los Chichimecas, for the 'advantage and utility of travellers'.[2] Viceroy Velasco continued Mendoza's policy of encouraging settlement along the route by distributing lands. Thus on 21 March 1551, one Juan de Jaso received, in a single grant, three *sitios de estancia* and three *caballerías de tierra*, all 'en términos de los Chichimecas' and along the River San Miguel.[3] In this way the road was gradually flanked by occupied land. Staging posts provided food and protection, when necessary.

Traffic along the roads at first mainly took the form of Indian carriers – the traditional *tamemes*. The practice of using human carriers still persisted, although it was constantly prohibited in legislation. For larger loads, the mule train was obviously more suitable. The mule-driver (*arriero*), a ubiquitous figure in Mexican history until long after Independence, was often Indian or *mestizo*. Indians took quickly to the life, frequently benefiting from the chance to become small time merchants as well. The carriage of the heaviest and bulkiest goods depended on wagon-trains, which were able to move over the Camino Real from 1551 or 1552.[4]

---

[1] It is said that Guanajuato was discovered in 1548 by prospectors (*gambusinos*) accompanying a convoy to Zacatecas. See Trinidad García, *Los mineros mexicanos*, México 1895, p. 121. But W. Jiménez Moreno claims documentary evidence for the discovery in 1552-3. See his 'La colonización y evangelización de Guanajuato en el siglo XVI', pp. 81 and 93 in *Estudios de Historia Colonial* (essays by the same author), México 1958.

[2] AGN Mercedes 3, f. 54-54v.

[3] AGN Mercedes 3, ff. 320v.-321v.

[4] There were two types of wagon. The carreta was a light, two-wheeled vehicle. The carro was a heavier covered wagon, also with two wheels. It was not introduced until the early 1950s. Powell, 'Forty-niners', p. 239.

Discovery and Settlement

Querétaro and San Miguel became the great centres of the wagon trade. The single most important commodity that the wagons carried was, at first, lead, which was fundamental to the smelting of silver ores. But from the late 1550s onwards, the wagon-loads of that dull and heavy metal were replaced by barrels of equally heavy mercury, the liquid metal essential to the new amalgamation process of silver refining, and scarcely less precious to miners than the silver bars that trains bore back to Mexico City on the return journey. Mercury was also sometimes freighted by mule train.

It was not to be expected that traffic along the new road would go unmolested by the nomadic tribes, as they saw Spaniards intruding on their hunting grounds. Their fighting ability and aggressiveness had been amply demonstrated in the Mixton war; and now, as their territory began to be occupied by Spanish settlers and stock raisers, they resisted the intrusion in the most obvious way open to them – assault on travellers and merchants using the road. So began the 'Guerra de los Chichimecas', the longest and most expensive conflict between Spaniards and the indigenous peoples of New Spain in the history of the colony. Its cost in cash and in men was to be far greater than that of Cortés' conquest of Anáhuac. The conflict was inevitable at some stage of the Spanish occupation of Mexico, since the nomads blocked the way to the north; but, inasmuch as it was the establishment of the Camino Real that sparked off the war, and inasmuch as Zacatecas was the reason for creating the road, it was Zacatecas that brought the matter to a head.

The Chichimecs were not slow in reacting to the presence of unwelcome strangers. In late 1550, Zacatecos Indians assaulted a group of Tarascans taking goods to Zacatecas, at a point between Tepezala and a place called Morcilique. (It has not proved possible to locate Morcilique.) A few days later, the same band of Zacatecos, emboldened by their massacre of the Tarascans, attacked mule trains belonging to Diego de Ibarra and Cristóbal de Oñate only three leagues south of Zacatecas itself.[1] Very soon after that, in their own territories further to the south and east, the Guachichiles and Guamares began their assaults on mule trains and wagons; and from that, it was only a short step to raids on estancias and livestock. The growing dangers of travel prompted merchants and other users of the road to group together for protection on the journey, sometimes taking escorts. But the Indians did not relax their offensive, and showed that both in bravery and in weapons they were a match for Spanish soldiers, as well as the warriors of the central Mexican peoples. And as the

[1] Gonzalo de las Casas, 'Guerra de los Chichimecas (1571–1585)', p. 170; in Hermann Trimborn, *Fuentes de la historia cultural de la América precolombina*, Madrid 1936, pp. 152–85.

22

Discovery and Settlement

attack on the road mounted, so did disturbances in the west begin to make themselves felt. The Caxcan Indians who had been overcome by the Spaniards in the early 1540s now began to appeal to their conquerors for protection against their northern neighbours, as the Zacatecos struck down the valleys to the north of Guadalajara. As the 1550s wore on, it became clear that all territory to the north of the Lerma–Santiago system was dangerous; and what had been 'tierra de Chichimecas' now became synonymous with 'tierra de guerra'. It was a vast area overrun by hostile, swiftly-moving Indians – the land of the surprise dawn attack and a horrible fate in the event of capture.

Yet Indian hostility was far from reaching its peak in the 1550s. It seems to have been concentrated in the area between Zacatecas and San Miguel. Here, spoils from assaults on merchants provided the basic motive for attack. There is no record of any direct attack on Zacatecas in this decade, nor does there seem to have been any check on explorations further to the north. These explorations may be considered at one and the same time the start of yet another phase of expansion and the mapping-out of the silver mining region of Zacatecas in its most important parts.

Once again, Juan de Tolosa appears to have been the moving spirit. In a letter to the king of August 1557, Dr Morones, oidor of the Audiencia of New Galicia, reported that Tolosa and Luis Cortés (his brother-in-law) had found the mineral deposits of San Martín.[1] This was the first strike in a rich mining district some 115 miles to the north-west of Zacatecas – a district which came to embrace the mines of Sombrerete, Chalchihuites and Nieves, as well as San Martín itself, and which was to outshine Zacatecas in the late seventeenth century. There is some suspicion that Ginés Vázquez del Mercado had found these deposits in 1552, while on his ill-fated expedition to the region of Durango in search of the fabled hill of silver. But, lured on by the prospect of readier wealth, he made no attempt to exploit San Martín even if he did locate it.[2] More reliable evidence comes from the alcalde mayor of Nombre de Dios, on the border of New Galicia and New Biscay, in 1570. He related that in 1554 'certain Spaniards' set out from Zacatecas and discovered San Martín; and that by 1556 it had been settled by thirty Spaniards and a priest. Working of the mines quickly began, supported by agriculture on fertile lands nearby (probably in the Valle de Súchil); and there was a double utility in the mineral deposits, for not only were they rich in silver, but also in lead, which was much in demand in Zacatecas at the time for use

[1] AGI Guadalajara 51, Compostela, 17 August 1557, Dr Morones to king.
[2] Amador, *Bosquejo histórico*, pp. 192–4; M. Othón de Mendizábal, 'Compendio histórico de Zacatecas', in *Obras Completas*, México 1946, vol. 5, pp. 85–271, here pp. 116–17.

Discovery and Settlement

in smelting.[1] From San Martín mining activity quickly extended to Sombrerete and Avino (probably by 1558) and to the smaller deposits of the area, where the *reales* of Chalchihuites, Ranchos, Santiago and Nieves grew up.[2] (See plan 2.) With the settlement of these townships by miners moving outwards from Zacatecas, the principal axis of the Zacatecas mining region, from the town itself to Sombrerete and San Martín, had been established. Other lesser discoveries were to follow over the next sixty years in the north and east, but the foundations of the region's wealth had been firmly laid. The mining expansion northwards went hand in hand with mission expansion, and it is claimed that a Franciscan hospice was in existence at Nombre de Dios, to the north of San Martín, by 1553.[3] Thereafter the spread of Franciscan mission houses in the north was at least as rapid as the expansion of mining. A pioneer Franciscan in the area was Gerónimo de Mendoza, nephew of the viceroy, who accompanied the early expeditions to San Martín.

So, as the first decade of Zacatecas' existence drew to a close, there was much achievement to be credited to the explorers and miners of the north. The most important mining area of New Spain had been encompassed and settled, within ten years of the first discovery of ore deposits. A foothold had been dug in the bleak territory of the plateau, in a land that was hostile both physically, in its barrenness, and militarily, in the aggressiveness of its hunter–gatherer nomadic population. Both these forms of hostility would have to be overcome. With the creation of channels of communication, and the subsequent flow of supplies and food from the south, the challenge of the land had to some extent been met.

[1] 'La villa de San Martín y Llerena e minas de Sombrerete', 6 February 1585, published in F. del Paso y Troncoso, *Papeles de Nueva España*, 2a serie, México 1905–48, 9 vols., vol. 8, México 1947, pp. 138–9. This document names fourteen men who left Zacatecas for San Martín in 1556. Tolosa is not one of them. But Tolosa's descendants in the 1594 *información* claimed that he discovered San Martín, Sombrerete and Avino on an expedition from Zacatecas, with forty armed horsemen. Witnesses stated that he spent six months on this expedition into the Tierra Adentro, which he undertook at his own cost, accompanied by Luis Cortés; and that on his return to Zacatecas he announced his discovery of the mines. The prospectors then left Zacatecas to settle them. See AGI Patronato 80, R. 1, No. 5, 'Información ... de Juanes de Tolosa', Guadalajara 2 May 1594, *passim* and especially f. 26v. and f. 61 (testimony of Pedro Gutiérrez). Mecham, in *Francisco de Ibarra*, pp. 68–70, maintains that the ores of Avino and San Martín were first discovered by Ibarra in 1554, and that Tolosa assumed credit for the find. The question has no answer, nor much importance.

[2] García, *Los mineros*, p. 129. For the foundation of Sombrerete, see pp. 156–8. There is evidence that Nieves was not discovered until 1574; see Paso y Troncoso, *Papeles*, 2a. serie, vol. 8, p. 163.

[3] Arlegui, *Crónica*, p. 58. Jiménez Moreno, in 'Los orígenes de la provincia franciscana de Zacatecas', p. 141, corrects this date to 1562. (For this article, see *Estudios de Historia Colonial*, pp. 135–50.) Mecham, *Francisco de Ibarra*, considers that some sort of settlement, created by Franciscans, existed at Nombre de Dios from 1558 onwards.

But the link was fragile. Its preservation was to be the result only of long and costly effort. That it was preserved, and that the effort was made, resulted from the strong financial interests of private citizens and public authority in the prosperity of mining. But as the decade of the 1560s began, prosperity was far from certain. Mere survival, indeed, appeared to be in doubt.

CHAPTER 2

CONSOLIDATION AND EXPANSION

Enthusiastic modern writers have dubbed Zacatecas 'mother' and 'civiliser' of the north of Mexico in their descriptions of the large contribution that the city made to the colonisation of the provinces of New Biscay, New León and New Mexico.[1] Zacatecas' part in the northward expansion of Spanish colonisation, both as a base for exploration and as a source of men, was indeed great. In the following pages some account will be given of the major movements to which it contributed. The detailed history of those movements lies outside the scope of this study; but before any local study of the city is undertaken, it may conveniently be fitted into the background of colonisation over the north as a whole.

As has been seen, expansion began very soon after the settling of the primitive mining camp under La Bufa, with discoveries of ores at mines in the area of Sombrerete. But even while this was taking place, the intensity of Indian hostility was increasing. The first concerted Chichimec campaign against established settlements came in 1561; the defeat of that campaign marked the true beginning of Spanish occupation of the north, and left the way clearer than before for exploration to continue. This campaign of allied Guachichil, Zacatecos and other Indians against Sombrerete, San Martín and estancias in that area in 1561 may have received more attention that it deserves, and hence appeared more serious than it was, because of the long and eloquent report given of it by Pedro de Ahumada Sámano, the leader of the force that put it down.[2] There seems little doubt, however, that a large force of Indians had united, for the first time, to launch a determined attack on the towns of Sombrerete and San Martín. By the time Ahumada was called in to combat them, they had burned and plundered a number of estancias and haciendas, and planned eventually to lay siege to Zacatecas itself. This

---

[1] W. Jiménez Moreno, 'Zacatecas, madre del norte', in *Estudios de historia colonial*, pp. 99–100; D. Kuri Breña, *Zacatecas, civilizadora del norte. Pequeña biografía de una rara ciudad.* México 1944.

[2] Pedro de Ahumada Sámano, 'Información acerca de la rebelión de los indios zacatecos y guachichiles a pedimento de Pedro de Ahumada Sámano', México 20 March 1562. In *Colección de documentos inéditos para la historia de Ibero-América*, ed. Santiago Montoto, vol. 1, Madrid 1927, pp. 237–368. Powell makes much of this report and of the danger of the threat in *Soldiers*, ch. 5. Ahumada was a resident miner of Zacatecas at the time and evidently an Indian campaigner of some note. He described himself as 'gobernador de la casa y estado del ilustrísimo Marqués del Valle'.

Consolidation and Expansion

threat was averted by Ahumada's prompt action; and having put down the trouble in the north, he then proceeded to harass other Indian marauders to the south of Zacatecas, who were cutting communication with Mexico City by threatening all traffic along the road. The Indian league against the Spaniards, he claimed, extended from San Miguel in the south to the Valley of Guadiana in the north – a distance of more than a hundred leagues.[1] For some time in 1561, Zacatecas was isolated and without supplies of food. The near-by woods and charcoal-making camps had to be abandoned, and lack of fuel in addition to lack of food meant that mining activity came to a halt. Spaniards were even reduced at times to eating the fruit of the prickly-pear, the *tuna* – a food-stuff dear to the nomads but despised by the settlers.[2]

To secure the roads, Ahumada placed garrisons at strategic points: one at Cuicillo, nine leagues south from Zacatecas, where the roads coming from Mexico City and from Michoacán converged; and another to the north, at the estancia of Saín, fifteen leagues from Zacatecas on the road to San Martín. With this protection, he said, travel had become safer, supplies had started to flow in again, and mining had recovered.[3] It is difficult to say just how much of a threat was offered to Zacatecas and the other towns in 1561. Ahumada had financed his expeditions himself, and was therefore understandably anxious to impress on the Crown both the seriousness of the situation and the importance of his own contribution in relieving it. But for all his talk about the collapse of mining, which is reinforced by the reports of the Treasury officials,[4] silver production was rather higher in 1561 than in the previous year; and production in the following years was not much greater than in 1561 (see Table 4). Most of the Chichimec war was characterised by this same pattern of sudden threat by the Indians, resulting in occasional sudden panic on the part of the Spaniards. But for long periods there was little action on either side; nor did the threat seem sufficiently grave at most times for any really determined effort, backed by all the financial and military power of New Spain, to be made against it.

Indian hostility certainly did not greatly curb exploration to the north after 1560, any more than it had done in the previous decade. Francisco de Ibarra, who at the age of sixteen had led his first expedition (*entrada*) north from Zacatecas in 1554 to the later site of Mazapil, to Avino, the

---

[1] 'Relación hecha por Don Pedro de Ahumada sobre la rebelión de los indios zacatecos y guachichiles y de la alteración en que pusieron el reino de la Galicia, 1562.' In *CDHG* vol. 5, No. 1, pp. 102–16; here p. 103.
[2] 'Relación hecha por Don Pedro de Ahumada', pp. 103–7.
[3] Ahumada, 'Información', p. 253, questions 14 and 15.
[4] AGI Guadalajara 51, f. 254v. Treasury officials to king, (?) February 1562.

Consolidation and Expansion

Guadiana Valley, and then possibly through the Sombrerete area back to Zacatecas, continued his explorations in the 1560s. As before, he was financed by his uncle, Diego de Ibarra, presumably out of the profits of mining.[1] By the early 1560s, Francisco was himself an important miner in the northern reales, above all at Avino, which he had been instrumental in settling. At San Martín, also, he played an important part as a miner, explorer and defender against Indians.[2] But it was not until 1562 that he undertook the expedition that resulted in the creation and settlement of the province of New Biscay. The suggestion for the expedition originated from Diego de Ibarra, who, in proposing it, revived a plan conceived by Viceroy Velasco in 1558 for the conquest of the regions of Copalá (later New Mexico). That project had had to be abandoned because of the need to divert forces to Florida at the time. But Diego de Ibarra later offered to undertake the task of his own cost. Francisco was to lead the force. Velasco agreed to the terms, and in 1562 appointed Francisco captain-general and governor of the lands he might take beyond San Martín and Avino. The resulting expedition was a truly Zacatecan one – financed with Diego de Ibarra's money, and made up of men recruited in the city itself. In late 1562 and early 1563, Ibarra passed through San Martín, Nombre de Dios and Avino, arriving in March in the Nazas valley. Topia was located in April of the same year, and, of more ultimate importance, in October and November 1563, Nombre de Dios and Durango were formally founded. Nombre de Dios had existed as a Franciscan foundation since 1558, and now Ibarra gave it a secular identity, appointing municipal officers, establishing the limits of the town and making grants of land to its inhabitants.[3] Durango, sited in the Guadiana valley, was a completely new foundation, a creation of Ibarra's; and he intended it from the first as the capital of his new province of New Biscay. He spent his own money on the construction of buildings; and in fact, conceded the whole output of one of his mines at Avino for the development of the city. The site was well chosen, being surrounded with good arable and pastoral land, as well as by silver deposits. The population in Ibarra's time was some 500.[4] Thereafter, he continued his explorations far to the north, ranging through Culiacán, Chiametla and Sinaloa, eventually reaching northern Chihuahua. But undoubtedly the most important of his achievements was the delineation of New Biscay and the founding of Durango in 1563, for these were solid

[1] For Ibarra's explorations in the 1550s, see Mecham, *Francisco de Ibarra*, pp. 59–69.
[2] Mecham, *Francisco de Ibarra*, p. 87.
[3] Mecham, *Francisco de Ibarra*, pp. 121–3.
[4] Mecham, *Francisco de Ibarra*, pp. 123–5.

Consolidation and Expansion

steps of colonisation in new areas of the plateau. Ibarra died in 1576.[1]

Ibarra's exploration was the last of the thrusting ventures to the north – in the tradition of Coronado and Vázquez del Mercado – until the New Mexico expedition of Juan de Oñate at the end of the century. Henceforth in New Galicia and New Biscay expansion was slower and steadier, being founded on the settlement of known deposits of silver ore and the occupation of the lands surrounding them. The decline in the pace of expansion no doubt had much to do with Indian hostility, but was probably also the result of the growing realisation among settlers that there was more advantage to be had from exploitation of known resources than from pursuit of ephemeral ones in the far north. The myth of Cíbola and the Gran Quivira had been long in fading, but now seemed to have lost most of its enchantment. So the decades of 1560 and 1570 show the settling and securing of a number of mining camps scattered over the region to the north of Zacatecas. Although not all of them fell into the jurisdiction of the Real Caja there, and so cannot be considered as belonging to the mining district of Zacatecas, all were founded directly from Zacatecas or from San Martín and Sombrerete, and form part of the movement of Zacatecan expansion. For that reason, some mention of them will be made here.

The journey from Zacatecas to San Martín took two days by cart or by pack-train. A common overnight stopping-place, about half-way along the road, was a spring some eight leagues to the north-west of Zacatecas, by which there grew a small ash tree. It was known that there were deposits of silver ore in the area, for Francisco de Ibarra had noted them in 1554; and perhaps two years later, a prominent miner and vecino of Zacatecas, Diego Hernández de Proaño, had located a hill containing silver veins. This 'cerro de Proaño' had been worked a little, but the ores were not rich enough to warrant much attention.[2] In 1566, however, four miners from Zacatecas again tried to find the hill, and in the attempt, discovered another one containing ore in the locality. This they named the 'cerro de San Demetrio', and began the extraction of ores. Encouraged by this success, others moved from Zacatecas, and restarted exploitation of Proaño's original find. A camp grew up around the spring and its ash tree, and was named, appropriately enough, El Fresnillo.[3] The cerro de Proaño ultimately proved far richer than the mines of San Demetrio,

---

[1] For the foundation of New Biscay in general, see Mecham, *Francisco de Ibarra*, pp. 101–33.
[2] 'Relación sobre las minas de Fresnillo', by Juan de Huidobro, Fresnillo 20 January 1582; in Paso y Troncoso, *Papeles, 2a. serie*, vol. 8, No. 6.
[3] For the foundation of Fresnillo, see the four 'Relaciones sobre las minas del Fresnillo' of 1585, in Paso y Troncoso, *Papeles, 2a. serie*, vol. 8.

and what is left of it is still being worked today. In 1568, Fresnillo assumed another rôle with the founding there of a fort (*presidio*) with garrison for the protection of traffic travelling to San Martín.[1]

The next mining settlements to be founded were much further to the north, and represented one of the final achievements of Francisco de Ibarra's efforts. In 1567, one of Ibarra's men, Rodrigo de Río de Losa, took an expedition to Indehé, to the north of Durango, where he established a mining camp; and pushing still further, he founded Santa Bárbara, for many years the northernmost Spanish settlement of any permanence. Although ores at Santa Bárbara were rich, isolation and difficulties in obtaining labour restricted production of silver; and it was not until the 1630s, when the wealth of the adjacent Parral mines was uncovered, that the Santa Bárbara district became important.[2] Santa Bárbara and Indehé, together with Avino, were in the jurisdiction of Ibarra's New Biscay. But the remainder of new discoveries made in the late 1560s and early 1570s belonged to Zacatecas, falling inside the boundaries of New Galicia. The most important of them was Mazapil, further east than any mine discovered to date. Whereas in other cases the effect of the Chichimec war had been to restrain or retard exploration for new mines, the opposite was the case with Mazapil, since its silver was found by soldiers on campaign against the Indians. Lying in a dreary and barren valley 140 miles north-east of Zacatecas, beyond an expanse of semi-desert, Mazapil might have remained long undiscovered if the Indian war had not led soldiers to its deposits. Nevertheless, once founded, it attracted a rush of prospectors, since its ores were of high quality. By 1569 there were more than 150 Spaniards on the site.[3]

Mazapil was the first mining strike to be made to the east of Zacatecas, and later discoveries were mostly in the same direction, although further south. All this land was occupied by the Guachichil people, who were rather more warlike and nomadic than their western neighbours, the Zacatecos.[4] Probably for that reason, the mining camps and townships in the east were more difficult to found and to sustain than those in the territory of the Zacatecos. Thus, although the minerals of Las Charcas were known about in 1572,[5] they were not exploited until 1574,[6] and

---

[1] Mecham, *Francisco de Ibarra*, p. 90.
[2] Mecham, *Francisco de Ibarra*, pp. 188–90, pp. 230–1.
[3] AGI Guadalajara 51, Guadalajara 25 February 1569, Dr Alarcón to king. Powell, *Soldiers*, p. 138. AGI Guadalajara 51, Mazapil 17 December 1568, Francisco Cano to Bishop Ayala of New Galicia.
[4] P. W. Powell, 'The Chichimecas: Scourge of the Silver Frontier in Sixteenth-Century Mexico', *HAHR*, vol. 25, 1945, pp. 315–38; here p. 325.
[5] AGI Guadalajara 5, Guadalajara 24 December 1572, Audiencia of New Galicia to king.
[6] AGI Guadalajara 5, Guadalajara 2 October 1574, Audiencia of New Galicia to king.

even five years later there was still difficulty in creating a permanent settlement.[1]

Similarly, the ore-bearing Cerro de San Pedro was discovered in 1583; but it was not until after the end of the Chichimec war that mines began to be worked in it and the town of San Luis Potosí was founded. The considerable deposits at Sierra de Pinos, between Zacatecas and San Luis, were not located until 1593; and those of Ramos, not until 1608. More will be said about San Luis, Pinos and Ramos in their place. But before developments at the end of the century can be recounted, the course and ending of the Chichimec war must be given some attention.

It has already been said that hostility was probably not continuous, and its intensity is indeed difficult to estimate. One possible index of the severity of attacks on towns and roads is the production of silver in the region. It might be expected that yearly production would vary widely with the pressure of Indian hostility, and that in years of exceptionally heavy attacks, production would slump. But no such thing happens. Variations in annual production from 1560 to 1590 are not great; certainly they are no greater than in the years of peace after the war. Nor does the graph depicting quinquennial totals show any drastic fluctuations during the period of the war. Output in the decade 1570 to 1580 was, indeed, higher than that in the decade 1590 to 1600, after the war was over (see Table 5). Economic causes quite separate from the war might be responsible for that, of course; temporary decline in the quality of ores, or shortage of certain raw materials are obvious possibilities. But, other things being equal, it would be reasonable to expect a rise in production once danger to towns and roads had been removed. The absence of such a rise suggests that mining suffered rather less from the effects of the war than the gloomy dispatches of the Audiencia of New Galicia and of miners would suggest; while at the same time it has to be admitted that it might have done better if there had been no Indian hostility – though how much better it is obviously impossible to say. The pattern of the war was one of the sudden surges of danger in long periods of relative calm. At times the threat to communications and to some of the mining towns was serious indeed, and at those times the complaints of settlers and administrators were shrill in demands for official action to be taken against the marauders; but the mere fact that the affair was allowed to drift on for forty years is an indication that the problem lacked urgency for much of the time.

After the planned attack on Sombrerete and San Martín of 1561 had been dissolved by the action of Pedro de Ahumada Sámano, danger to

[1] AGI Guadalajara 6, Guadalajara 22 March 1579, Dr Orozco to king.

the towns of the north seems to have abated for some years. But attacks on roads and isolated estancias continued, and by the middle of the decade there was again a threat to the towns north-west of Zacatecas.[1] In 1566, Viceroy Falces tried to achieve peace by negotiation with the Indians, but the attempt failed, and he adopted a policy of 'guerra a fuego y a sangre', which was to be the principal strategy of viceroys until the mid-1580s. In the circumstances he probably had little choice but to try and defeat the Indians militarily. But two major difficulties plagued his attempt, as they did similar attempts by his successors. The first was the nomadic way of life of the Chichimecs, and their guerilla style of warfare, both of which made successful campaigns against them difficult. The second was the absence of any agreed system for financing the war. This was partly the result of the Crown's hostility towards the institution of encomienda, for the military contributions available from encomenderos must have been greatly diminished as gradual suppression of the institution proceeded after the New Laws of 1542. As it was, much of the military effort of the early part of the war was thrown upon the encomenderos of New Spain and Michoacán. Exploration and conquest in the New World had always been carried out by private enterprise and this tradition may well have contributed to preventing the direct partic- ipation of the viceregal authorities, with Crown money, in the fight in the north. The Crown was slow to realise its interest in the prosperity of mining, even though that interest was constantly being pointed out to it by settlers. Thus pleas from miners, churchmen and others in the mid-1560s for more Crown action were answered with a cédula of 20 April 1567 proposing that the Audiencia of New Galicia should take steps to protect miners and roads, but that two-thirds of the cost should be paid by the settlers themselves, with the Treasury providing the other third. It seemed a dusty answer, and the pleas continued.[2] Funds were consequently short for most of the war. The most serious result of this was that soldiers were insufficiently paid, and sought to increase their income by taking Indian slaves whenever they could. Captains placed in charge of bands of soldiers undertook sorties (*entradas*) deep into Indian territory merely to provoke resistance, so that they could legally seize slaves in 'just war'. That this was happening was clearly seen by the oidores at Guadalajara,[3] but it was beyond their power to stop it. Slaving naturally incited the Chichimecas to further resistance and attacks. Thus a vicious circle was set up. As slaving, both legal and illegal, continued, Indian retaliation

---

[1] Powell, *Soldiers*, pp. 91–3.
[2] Powell, *Soldiers*, p. 99.
[3] E.g. AGI Guadalajara 5, 6 March 1576, Licenciado Santiago del Riego to king.

increased; and so the need for men to protect roads, form garrisons and make punitive expeditions grew. But recruits could be attracted only by the promise of slaving, for the salaries offered were meagre.[1] Regular recruiting of soldiers who should be paid by the Treasury had begun by the time of Enríquez's departure in 1580, and this system was improved after he left.[2] But the practice of slaving must have given rise to vast damage by then, and is to be considered one of the main causes of the hostility of the nomads to the Spaniards.

The reluctance of the viceregal authorities and of the Crown to finance efforts against the Indians in full, and their determination to rely whenever possible on private enterprise, is exemplified by the appointments made by Enríquez in the first half of his administration of special lieutenant captain-generals (*tenientes de capitán general*) to supervise military matters in New Spain and New Galicia. One such teniente was Vicente de Zaldívar, miner and citizen of Zacatecas, who held the office in New Galicia from 1570 to 1574. He eventually resigned his post because of the cost of financing the war effort privately. He claimed he had spent 100,000 pesos.[3] His successor was another miner of Zacatecas, no less than Baltasar de Bañuelos, founder of the city. He also quickly abandoned the post because of its cost.

Military forays against Indians by roving bands of soldiers proved to be of very little use, when they were not actively harmful through provocation and slaving. More useful was the policy of defence of roads and defensive settlement undertaken from the time of Viceroy Velasco onwards. The town of San Miguel was made into a Spanish settlement in 1555 by the placing there of fifty Spaniards, with grants of estancias for livestock and of plots for building. Several years later, in 1561 and 1562, San Felipe was created to protect peaceful Chichimecs living in its neighbourhood. These were not settlements made solely for the defence of the road, but rather frontier towns created as outposts in the wilderness.[4] They served, nevertheless, as precedents for the presidios and towns placed along the Camino Real and other roads by Enríquez and his successors for the protection of traffic. The first two presidios set up by Enríquez were at Ojuelos and Portezuelo, just north of San Felipe, in 1570. Beyond these on the road to Zacatecas came later Las Bocas, Ciénaga Grande and Palmillas.[5] Others, set up in the following years, protected access to Guanajuato (on the Santa Catalina river and at the

[1] For discussion of slaving, see Powell, *Soldiers*, pp. 106–11.
[2] Powell, *Soldiers*, p. 115.
[3] P. W. Powell, 'Spanish Warfare against the Chichimecas in the 1570's', *HAHR* vol. 24, 1944, pp. 580–604; here pp. 585–6.
[4] Powell, *Soldiers*, pp. 67–9.   [5] Powell, *Soldiers*, pp. 141–3.

rancho of Jaso). One was placed on the site of Aguascalientes, guarding one of the routes from Guadalajara to Zacatecas; and later still, the chain of presidios was extended beyond Zacatecas, and on to other routes in the north. Enríquez also continued Velasco's practice in founding defensive towns, such as Celaya, which was established in 1570 with a triple rôle as a centre of Indian settlement, protector of the road, and nucleus of an area of agriculture for the supply of the mines to the north. The Villa de León was likewise created in 1575 in the Valle de Señora. Aguascalientes, which existed already under the name of Villa de Asunción, was formally founded under Enríquez, even before he placed a presidio there. Jerez de la Frontera, to the south-west of Zacatecas, was founded in 1570 by order of the Audiencia of Guadalajara as part of the same programme of defence.[1] Examples could be multiplied. All these foundations could not prevent Chichimec raiding, but they did contribute to reducing attacks on roads, especially when Enríquez added to them armed escorts for convoys and other protective measures, such as blockhouses positioned along the way.

So the Chichimec war dragged on into the 1580s in stalemate. There seemed to be little likelihood that the miners and settlers of the north could be driven from the territory of the tribes, but there was even less chance of overcoming the latter militarily. The severity of attacks began to increase again, as the President of the Audiencia of New Galicia wrote to Spain in 1580. The Indians were stealing mules from Zacatecas; outnumbering and attacking soldiers; threatening the existence of Zacatecas itself, of Sombrerete and Mazapil. No-one dared to use the roads. The Indians had taken to using horses and firearms. There was a danger, Dr Orozco thought, of New Galicia's being completely overrun.[2] The response of the Council of the Indies to this dramatic report, as expressed in the comment of the *Fiscal*, was no more than 'Seen, and there is no need to reply' ('vista y no hay que responder'). The answer of the newly-arrived successor to Enríquez, the Conde de Coruña, was to increase military action against the Indians. By 1582 money was being paid out of the Real Caja of Zacatecas for the prosecution of the war, and the salaried soldiery was augmented. But, although this method of retaliation was approved in general by landowners and inhabitants of the north, who conceived of no other way of pacifying the Indians, it was obvious that it was not a final solution. Viceroy Villamanrique, from 1585, did all he could to remove the causes of conflict, by freeing captives and forbidding

[1] Powell, *Soldiers*, p. 155. All information on the founding of presidios and defensive towns is taken from Powell, *Soldiers*, ch. 8, and from P. W. Powell, 'Presidios and towns on the Silver Frontier of New Spain, 1550–1580', *HAHR* vol. 24, 1944, pp. 179–200.

[2] AGI Guadalajara 6, R. 2, Zacatecas 28 September 1580, Dr Orozco to king.

Consolidation and Expansion

slavery. He saw that by now the Spanish soldier himself was the major source of trouble. And, heeding the counsel of a number of men who had been advising such a course for many years, he abandoned the policy of aggression and attempted to obtain peace treaties with the Indians in return for supplies of food and clothing. Before 1590, he had started to eliminate presidios and reduce the number of soldiers. And soon hostility had ceased everywhere.[1] The success of his efforts towards peacemaking left the way open for the second Viceroy Velasco to develop the pacification scheme into a wide-scale system of distribution of supplies to Indians over a large area of New Galicia and New Biscay. Food, clothing and agricultural tools were sent to stores (almacenes) placed at intervals over the nomads' lands, and thence distributed to Indians. The central deposit in New Galicia was placed at Zacatecas, and from there local almacenes at Colotlán, Las Charcas, Mazapil and Chalchihuites were supplied. In time, the system was extended further to the north, with an almacén at Saltillo. Velasco also intensified the pacification campaign by encouraging mission activity and evangelisation among the Indians. Of major importance, also, was the situating of colonies of Indians from the sedentary cultures of central Mexico in parts of the north. It was hoped that they would set an example, in creating agricultural settlements, that would be followed by the Chichimecs. The most famous of these migrations was that of some 400 Tlaxcalan families in 1591. They were placed, under the direction of Rodrigo de Río de Losa (last mentioned here as the explorer responsible for the founding of Indehé and Santa Bárbara in 1567) at Asunción Tlaxcalilla, near San Luis Potosí, at San Miguel Mezquitic and at Agua del Venado; further north, they were the first citizens of the town of San Esteban de Nueva Tlaxcala; and in the west, they were placed at Colotlán and San Andrés. Within a few years, they had spread to other towns in New Galicia, such as Sierra de Pinos, Chalchihuites and San Jerónimo del Agua Hedionda. The first two of these were mining towns.[2] The Tlaxcalans obtained privileges separating them from contact with the Chichimecs; but in time, as had been hoped, there was at least some cultural integration between them and the nomads, so that from the end of the Chichimec war the latter began to lose their identity.[3]

Thus the decade 1590 to 1600 saw the end of the forty-year conflict between nomads and Spaniards in the area of the Gran Chichimeca. What were the lasting consequences of the war, and how was Zacatecas

[1] AGI Guadalajara 6, R. 3, Guadalajara 24 May 1590, Audiencia to king.
[2] C. Gibson, Tlaxcala in the Sixteenth Century, Yale University Press 1952, pp. 184–7.
[3] For the pacification schemes of Villamanrique and Velasco, see Powell, Soldiers, chs. 11 and 12 (pp. 184–223). For the integration of nomads into the more advanced cultures, see Powell, Soldiers, p. 159.

35

affected by it? Firstly, of course, the peace meant the creating of a large area free henceforth from Indian hostility. New Galicia was never again to be directly troubled by such conflict. Only in the inaccessible fastnesses of the sierras to east and west of the northern plateau did Indian resistance persist. But it remained far from the populated, economically important regions of New Galicia. Thus the Tepehuán revolt of 1617 in the sierra to the west of Durango caused little disturbance in Zacatecas and its neighbouring towns. Similarly, there was periodic warring in the Sierra Madre Oriental, beyond San Luis Potosí, Saltillo and Monterrey. But this also was far from the core of the north. A second result of the war was the establishment of a chain of towns along the Camino Real to the north. No doubt many such towns would have sprung up in the normal course of events, but the war hastened their foundation as the need for garrison posts and defensive colonisation became apparent. One of the foundations made by the first Velasco, San Miguel, remains an important town to the present day. Enríquez's Celaya is another example, with León. Jerez, established by the Audiencia of Guadalajara in 1570, is still the head of a municipality to the south-west of Zacatecas, and the centre of a small but important agricultural region. Even a few of the presidios survive in some form – for example, Palmillas and Cuicillo, a little south of Zacatecas, which are still identifiable as hamlets. Settlement in these defensive towns was encouraged by the granting of land for agriculture, stock-raising and building. Thus they became nuclei of farming regions which, in time, assumed importance in the supply of the north. So permanent settlements were created between central Mexico and the north, and the chain of continuous Spanish occupation of the land was strengthened.

A third effect of the war, of fundamental importance for the consolidation of the country, was the drawing to the north of large numbers of Indians from various parts of central Mexico. The example of the Tlaxcalans has been mentioned. But long before their migration in 1591, the drift had begun. There were in Zacatecas by 1550 people from Michoacán and the valley of Mexico. The prime agent in attracting sedentary Indians from their communities in the south was the use of Indian auxiliaries in warfare. Mendoza had used them in the Mixton campaign, and possibly some of the early Indian mine labourers at Zacatecas were remnants of his forces of 1541 and 1542. In the Chichimec conflict, Spaniards used mainly Mexicans, Tarascans and Otomíes; some were pressed into service, others bribed, and others regularly paid, or given exemption from tributes and personal services to Spaniards.[1]

[1] For the use of Indian auxiliaries see Powell, *Soldiers*, ch. 9, pp. 158-71.

Consolidation and Expansion

Many of these auxiliaries remained in New Galicia after the end of hostilities, and contributed greatly to forming the Indian population of the province. Zacatecas preserved all through the seventeenth century distinct townships around the periphery of the Spanish city, each one belonging to a different Indian group. Significantly, there was no Chichimec unit; the nomads very quickly lost their separate identity once they had submitted to Spanish control and to exposure to the sedentary culture of the newcomers from the south.

From these final results of the war – the freeing of New Galicia from hostility, the cementing of links with central Mexico, and the attraction of sedentary natives from the south – Zacatecas undoubtedly benefited. Its long period as a frontier town was over. While some benefits had undoubtedly come to certain parts of the citizenry from all the military activity for which Zacatecas served as a centre and headquarters, the disadvantages were certainly greater. While the town was too large to be in danger of capture by storm, it could easily be reduced to near siege by the cutting of communications and supplies. This led naturally to high prices for food and mining goods. Trade, which in the forty years after the war was scarcely less important to the prosperity of Zacatecas than silver, could not develop while contact with the south was uncertain, and while continued occupation of the regions to the north of the city was always in doubt. There was also a heavy and direct financial burden of the war on the citizens. Because of the unwillingness of the Crown to contribute to the expenses of the war for many years, and no doubt partly because of confusion over control of Treasury funds in New Galicia, the cost of the campaign devolved, up to 1580, largely on to wealthy men who would undertake military action as tenientes de capitán general. In such private financing of the war, much capital was lost that would more profitably have been invested in silver mining. Only after the mid-seventies did substantial payments start to be made from the funds of the Treasury, and it was not until 1581 that the first disbursements were issued from the Real Caja at Zacatecas.[1] Viceroy Villamanrique, writing to the king in November 1586, indicated how rapidly the Crown's contribution to the cost of war had risen in the previous six years. He stated that during the administration of Enríquez, yearly payments from the Real Caja in Mexico City had been less than 25,000 pesos, and from Zacatecas, about 30,000 pesos. But in 1586 the amounts

[1] AGI Contaduría 842A, Real Caja de Zacatecas, *Sumario de datas*, 1581. A payment of 4,000 pesos was made to Antonio López de Cepeda, on 30 September 1581, by order of Viceroy Coruña. López was supply officer to the troops ('proveedor de bienes'). In 1582, war costs paid by the Caja of Zacatecas had risen to 77,346 pesos (see same legajo, *sumario de descargos*, 1582).

had been 80,000 and 130,000 respectively.[1] The enormous increases probably reflect both the growth of the Crown's contribution and the growth of military activity during the administration of Coruña, in reply to serious Indian depredations in 1580 and 1581. Larger participation by the Crown was certainly desirable, since it meant that the load on private individuals in the north was lessened.

With the ending of the Chichimec war, the process of consolidation and expansion of the mining district of Zacatecas was almost complete. There were a few more mine discoveries and settlements. The ores of San Luis Potosí, found in the Cerro de San Pedro in 1583, were not exploited until after the end of the war, when the town of that name was founded in 1592. San Luis was never in the Zacatecas district, and indeed lay outside New Galicia altogether. But Zacatecas contributed some of its early miners, and to some extent this settlement can be seen as part of the Zacatecan expansion. Also, in the early 1590s were discovered the silver veins of Sierra de Pinos, and by 1603 there was a thriving camp there containing more than sixty miners. As happened at Fresnillo, the richness of the ores of Pinos was not appreciated for some time after the first discovery.[2] The next find was at Ojocaliente, 25 miles to the south-east of Zacatecas, in the last years of the century.[3] The deposits there were worked for a time, but were never important. In 1608 came the last of the major discoveries in the district. This was at Ramos, 40 miles due east of Zacatecas. With this discovery the mining district of Zacatecas was completed. There were, of course, in later years, many discoveries of rich deposits of ore in already known mines; and such *bonanzas* continued at intervals into the nineteenth century. But at the end of the sixteenth century, all the major areas of deposits had been located.

Although the fifty years after the first discovery of ores thus saw the complete delineation of Zacatecas' mining district, the city's part in the settlement of the northern lands was still not finished. The last few years of the sixteenth century witnessed the preparation and departure of the last major exploratory expedition that can be said to have originated in Zacatecas. In 1598 Don Juan de Oñate led his large force northwards to finally achieve the long-projected settlement of New Mexico. The lands

---

[1] AGI Mexico 20, R. 4, No. 135, México 15 November 1586, Villamanrique to king. Villamanrique was mistaken in thinking that any payments were made from Zacatecas in the time of Enríquez, before 1580. He was probably thinking of the early years of Coruña's administration.

[2] AGI Guadalajara 7, R. 3, an anonymous document 'Lo que resulta de los papeles de minas de la Nueva España'. It relates the visita made to the settlement in 1603 by the oidor of the Audiencia of New Galicia, Licenciado Gaspar de la Fuente.

[3] AA.Z, LC 2, f. 162-162v., Cabildo meeting of 7 September 1600. The mines of Ojocaliente were being worked by one Pablo González.

Consolidation and Expansion

to the north of the Río Bravo had been awaiting colonisation since they had first been crossed by the Coronado expedition more than sixty years before. Oñate was the son of Cristóbal de Oñate, the founder-citizen of Zacatecas. The vast quantities of supplies with which he provisioned and equipped his expedition doubtless derived largely from the family mines and lands in the surroundings of Zacatecas. He took with him many Zacatecan men.[1] Until 1607 Oñate was governor of New Mexico, thus adding his name to the list of Zacatecans who had held governorships in the north. Two illustrious names already on that list were those of Diego and Francisco de Ibarra, who had served as governors of New Biscay. And after 1626 another was added – that of Don Martín de Zavala, governor of New León from that year until 1659. He was the son of General Don Agustín de Zavala, wealthy miner and benefactor of religious houses in the city during the early years of the seventeenth century. The settlement of New León had formally begun in 1596 with the foundation of the town of Monterrey; but it was many years before a large and stable population grew up there. Zavala brought with him in 1626 from the region of Zacatecas many miners and relatives, who were largely responsible for the development of the small but locally important mining industry of the province.[2] A similar emigration of personnel skilled in mining occurred in the early 1630s to the district of Parral, where a silver boom was then taking place. So, long after its frontier days were over, Zacatecas continued to contribute to the development of the provinces of the north-east and north-west as a repository of men and technique. No less was it a centre of ecclesiastical effort. As the seat of a Franciscan province, it continued to serve as a source of missionary enterprise into the eighteenth century. A mission college (*colegio de propaganda fide*) was built by the Franciscans in the first years of that century at Guadalupe, a little to the east of the city. The Jesuits used Zacatecas as a centre for evangelisation from the end of the sixteenth century.[3]

After this survey of expansionary movements from Zacatecas and of the course of the Chichimec war, attention may now be turned to the

---

[1] See, for Oñate's provisions, G. P. Hammond and Agapito Rey, *Don Juan de Oñate, Coloniser of New Mexico, 1595–1628*, 2 vols., University of New Mexico Press 1953, vol. 1, p. 44. For a general muster of armed men on the expedition, see vol. 1, pp. 150–60.

[2] See Eugenio del Hoyo, 'Don Martín de Zavala y la minería en el Nuevo Reino de León', in *Humanitas. Anuario del centro de estudios humanísticos*, Universidad de Nuevo León, No. 4 1963, pp. 411–26; *passim* and especially pp. 411–12.

[3] See P. M. Dunne, S.J., *Pioneer Jesuits in Northern Mexico*, Berkeley and Los Angeles 1944. Chs. 4 and 5, pp. 20–43, describe the early Jesuit missions going from Zacatecas to the Laguna areas around Parras and to the Tepehuán lands in the Sierra Madre Occidental to the west of Durango, beginning in 1594.

Consolidation and Expansion

growth of the city and to its institutions. The effect of the pacification of the Indians and of the explorations that have been sketched in the preceding pages was to leave Zacatecas at the focal point of a vast and secure area of Spanish occupation on the plateau of north Mexico. Zacatecas was in its own right a rich city; its prosperity attracted men and trade; it became, if not the 'civiliser' of the north, the commercial gateway to the lands of New Biscay, New León and New Mexico.[1] Its citizens claimed it was the second city of New Spain. What was it like?

[1] AGI Guadalajara 7, 'Relación de las ciudades, villas y lugares, pueblos de españoles y indios ... que hay en el nuevo reino de Galicia'. Undated (*ca.* 1600–10). The text reads: 'puerto y escala de toda la Nueva España y Nueva Galicia para lo demás que por aquella parte resta de ella y de la provincia de la Bizcaya'.

CHAPTER 3

THE CITY

The authors of the Royal Ordinances of 1573 for the laying out of new towns would have been keenly disappointed if, transported to the Indies, they had been able to survey Zacatecas from the top of La Bufa.[1] Instead of the regular pattern of a grid-iron town provided for by the Ordinances, with judiciously spaced plazas, public buildings and churches, all placed in a fertile hinterland and set about with woodlands, they would have seen a straggling linear settlement, cramped between two hills in a narrow valley. This was the *cañada* of Zacatecas, a near gully cut by a stream which, for most of the year, ran with negligible current. Looking around, instead of rich arable land, they would have been faced on three sides by rocky hills, whose gently undulating heights displayed little more than sparse patches of thin grass, and as a final flourish of vegetation, stunted mezquite and huizache. On the slopes grew nopal and palmilla cactus to vary the scene. Only if they had looked to the west or to the south-east would they have seen land productive enough to meet the recommendations of the Ordinances, which advised siting new towns in fertile surroundings. On the plains to the west, they might have glimpsed herds of cattle and mules; and to the south-east of the town, along the banks of the stream, and especially on the alluvial flat where the monastery of Guadalupe was later built, orchards and vegetable gardens (*huertas*) would have met their gaze. Beyond these huertas more herds of cattle and mules might have been seen. But nowhere did there appear in the surrounding areas the Indian towns foreseen in the Ordinances as the source of *repartimiento* labour. And instead of the recommended easy access, there was a rocky road running partly in the bed of the stream, which flash floods in summer were liable to make impassable. Almost the only coincidence between the ideal site envisaged in the Ordinances and the actual site of Zacatecas was the healthiness of the place. High and cold, there was a certain resemblance between the Serranía de Zacatecas and some desolate upland of Old Castile. The asperity of the land around Zacatecas, contrasted with its vast mineral wealth, recalled to the

[1] For these Ordinances, consisting of clauses 110–37 of the *Ordenanzas para descubrimientos, nuevas poblaciones y pacificaciones*, San Lorenzo, 3 July 1573, see *HAHR* vol. 4, 1921, pp. 745–9.

The City

Franciscan chronicler Arlegui an old saying, that 'land abundant in crops is not well matched with mines of importance'.[1]

The settlement of Zacatecas began, of course, long before the promulgation of the Ordinances of 1573; but there was in existence before then a body of legislation dictating the form that new towns should take.[2] The reason why Zacatecas was so poorly sited was not wilful scorn by the founders of the existing orders – if, indeed they were aware of them – but the supposition that the mining camp would be only a transitory settlement. By the time it was realised that the deposits were far greater in extent and richer in content than had been believed at first, it was already too late to move. Mota y Escobar, writing at the beginning of the seventeenth century, put this forward as the principal cause of the bad siting of the town. 'The intention of the Spaniards who settled here at the beginning was never to remain on this site, but only to extract the largest amount of silver they could, and so they made their houses, or rather shacks, as if they were itinerants and merely passing by; but so much wealth has been put into this city that it will never be abandoned; so it has been left with its mean, single-storey houses and with its jumbled streets.'[3]

Doubtless the spirit of the rush to Zacatecas of the early days and the impermanency that characterises both the occupation of mining and the nature of the miner himself contributed greatly to the hasty and undesirable siting of the city. Another reason for its positioning may have been the need for defence. It is not known where Ibarra and Tolosa built their fortified houses to protect the young community from Indian attack; but a likely defensive position would have been in the throat of the gulley between the two *cerros* of La Bufa and El Grillo (see plan 1). There they would have been protected on two sides by the steep slopes of the hills, and the openings at the ends of the cañada would have been narrow enough to allow for relatively easy defence. This was not, though, the position of the earliest recorded building of which the site is definitely

[1] 'Que tierra abundante para cosechas no hace buen maridaje con minas de fundamento.' Arlegui, *Crónica . . . de Zacatecas*, p. 121. If the general situation of Zacatecas may be compared in its desolation with Castile, the form of the city is similar to that of many Basque towns, which also lay in deep and narrow valleys. The similarity between the street plan of Zacatecas and some of those illustrated by J. Caro Baroja in *Los vascos, etnología* (San Sebastián 1949), ch. 1, is striking. Such similarity is doubtless coincidental, since any settlement in a narrow valley is bound to adopt an elongated form. Basques among early settlers found themselves in somewhat familiar surroundings. For an enlightening discussion of the transfer of town plans and forms from Spain to the New World, see George M. Foster, *Culture and Conquest. America's Spanish Heritage*, Chicago 1960, ch. 4.

[2] For a brief survey of town-planning orders before 1573, see D. Stanislawski, 'Early Spanish Town Planning in the New World', *Geographical Review*, No. 37, 1947, pp. 94–105.

[3] Mota y Escobar, *Descripción*, p. 64.

known: a chapel built in 1549 at the place called El Bracho, rather to the north of the city towards the mass of the hills and the mines. But it seems unlikely that there was ever much building around El Bracho; especially since soon afterwards, a chapel was constructed at the foot of La Bufa on the site of the later parish churches and the present cathedral.[1] The area to the south of this primitive parish church became the main square (*plaza pública*) and market place of Zacatecas. A smaller plaza flanked the church on the north side. This formation of two plazas, divided by the parish church, became the nodal point of Zacatecas. It was both the centre of commerce and the elegant dwelling quarter of the city. Religious houses and churches of later foundation, arising during the second half of the sixteenth century, formed reference points away from the plaza pública and in some cases appear to have served, for a time, as limits to the expansion of the town. Thus the Capilla y Hospital de la Vera Cruz, erected soon after the foundation of Zacatecas well to the south of the parish church, appear to have represented the furthest extent of building in that direction for many years. The site was taken over in 1604 by the newly arrived Dominican friars for their house in Zacatecas.[2] Four years later came the first members of the Order of San Juan de Dios, who established themselves on a site further to the west, close by the brook that ran down from the area of La Quebradilla and Tonalá Chepinque to join the main stream in the southern part of the city. Their new monastery and hospital of San Juan de Dios, built in 1609, also functioned as a reference point and limit of the town to the south.[3] They lay under a small hill, which was known as the *loma de la Carnicería* for the good reason that the municipal abattoir was situated on it. Until the end of the seventeenth century little building seems to have taken place to the south of the hospital of San Juan; certainly no Spaniard lived in that part of the town.

In the absence of sixteenth-century notarial records, it is impossible to follow the course of construction and growth in the town in its first five or six decades. There is notice only of ecclesiastical building, and that from sources of only doubtful reliability. But since such building was of major importance, it is worthwhile tracing the outline of its development.

Five religious orders established houses in Zacatecas over the sixty years following the foundation. Their buildings were among the most prominent of the town, and as has been said, served as landmarks. The early evangel-

---

[1] José del Refugio Gasca, *Timbres y Laureles zacatecanos, o cantos a Zacatecas, con notas crítico-históricas, escritos por* ..., Zacatecas 1901, p. 87.

[2] Gasca, *Timbres*, p. 78.

[3] Gasca, *Timbres*, pp. 78–9.

isation of New Galicia was undertaken exclusively by the Franciscans, working mainly from their existing missions in Michoacán. It is said that Tolosa was accompanied on his exploratory trip to Zacatecas in 1546 by three Franciscans,[1] but there is no contemporary primary evidence for this. None of the *relaciones de méritos* referring to the discovery of Zacatecas mentions any such priests. Through most of the next decade there appears to have been a lack of religious in the city, apart from one or two secular clergy. The future of the northern mining settlements was still perhaps too uncertain to warrant the expense and effort of founding a permanent house in Zacatecas, although evangelisation of Indians further north was proceeding from a Franciscan house at Nombre de Dios.[2] But possibly as soon as the late 1550s, Franciscans had settled in Zacatecas, never to leave again during the colonial period. They came from the *custodia* of Michoacán to a decent lodging ('decente hospedaje') and moderate hospice ('moderado hospicio') provided by the grateful citizens, on the later site of the Augustinian monastery.[3] The subsequent history of Franciscan building is rather confused; but it is clear that by the late 1570s they possessed a more permanent residence consisting of church and monastery, probably on the site where the ruins of the Franciscan monastery now stand, about half-a-mile to the north of the plaza. This second house was built partly with funds donated by the citizens, and partly with money from the royal Treasury. A cédula of November 1569, directed to the Audiencia of New Galicia, instructed the oidores to go into the question of the construction of a Franciscan house in Zacatecas. The townspeople had reported that Franciscans, noting the continued wealth of the mines and the lack of ministers to care for the host of Spaniards, Indians and Negroes gathered there, had settled in the city and now wished to establish a monastery and a church. The city could not raise the 10,000 ducats necessary for the project, since it was already burdened with the con-

---

[1] Amador, *Bosquejo*, p. 191; and Gasca, *Timbres*, p. 159.

[2] The early history of Franciscan houses at Nombre de Dios is confused. A house of some sort existed there from 1558. See Mecham, *Francisco de Ibarra*, p. 121.

[3] Gasca, *Timbres*, p. 160. Amador, *Bosquejo*, p. 209. Arlegui, *Crónica*, p. 48, believes that a Franciscan hospice was founded in Zacatecas in 1564, but makes no mention of any earlier foundation. Jiménez Moreno finds no evidence of a Franciscan house in Zacatecas before 1567. See 'Los orígenes de la provincia . . .', p. 139. Certainly by 1570 there was a Franciscan building in Zacatecas locally referred to as a monastery (*monasterio*). See Rubén Villaseñor Bordes, *La inquisición en la Nueva Galicia (siglo XVI). Recopilación, introducción y notas por el Dr...*, Guadalajara 1959, pp. 54–5, proceedings against a vecino de Zacatecas, Alonso de Mancilla, in December 1570. Mancilla said of Fray Francisco de Rivera, a Franciscan of Zacatecas, 'Every night he sleeps outside the monastery, and I will catch him, though it cost me many a bad night, in the house of his mistress' (*manceba*). Mancilla accused another Franciscan, Fray Diego Valadés, of dancing sarabands with married women. Silver attracted fashion, among other things.

struction of a parish church and the upkeep of a priest (*cura*), sacristan and other officers. So a grant from the Crown was essential.[1] The response to the request was surprisingly fast; in May 1572 a payment was ordered from the *bienes de difuntos* (a fund consisting of the goods of those who had died intestate in the Indies) at the Casa de la Contratación in Seville. The amount was only 2,000 ducats, far short of the 10,000 applied for; but the Franciscan house was built.[2] Before it was finished, the mission's importance had been recognised by its elevation from the status of hospicio to that of head of a custodia, although still within the Province of San Pedro y San Pablo of Michoacán;[3] it embraced the four Franciscan foundations that now existed in the north, at Nombre de Dios, Zacatecas, Durango, and San Juan del Río. By 1600, the number of monasteries in the custodia had grown to seventeen, and there were plans for founding others. This increase in importance of the northern custodia of Zacatecas led in 1603 to the creation of a Province based on the city,[4] a token of the part played by Zacatecas in the evangelisation of northern New Spain. The idea had long been proposed; witness a letter of the Audiencia of New Galicia to the king in April 1583, suggesting that the creation of a Franciscan province centred on Zacatecas would greatly increase the efficacy of missionary activity among the Indians of the north, and so contribute to pacification.[5] There is little record of the fabric of the Franciscan monastery. Its church is known to have burned down in 1648, but was quickly rebuilt.[6] Nor is anything known about the provision of funds for the building, apart from the 2,000 ducats contributed by the Crown. The remainder is said to have come from citizens, but no details remain of gifts. The Franciscan monastery seems to have been regarded as the limit of the town proper to the north. The street leading to it from the central plaza was known simply as the 'calle de San Francisco'; and after it passed the monastery it became 'el camino de las minas'.

The Augustinians were the next to establish themselves in Zacatecas. After some initial dispute, they were granted in 1575 a site on the west

---

[1] AGI Guadalajara 230, Z 1, ff. 208–9, El Escorial, 9 November 1569, real cédula, king to Audiencia of New Galicia.

[2] AGI Guadalajara 230, Z 1, ff. 242v.–3, Madrid, 18 May 1572, real cédula, king to oficiales reales de la Casa de la Contratación.

[3] The date of the elevation was about 1574. Jiménez Moreno, 'Los orígenes de la provincia franciscana', p. 140.

[4] Fray Angel de los Dolores Tiscareño, *El colegio de Guadalupe desde su origen hasta nuestros días*, Zacatecas 1905–10, 4 vols., vol. I, ii, p. 15, quoting Arlegui, *Crónica*, no page reference. The papal bull authorising the creation of the Province was given on 10 April 1603.

[5] AGI Guadalajara 6, R. 2, 8 April 1585, Audiencia of New Galicia to Crown.

[6] I. M. Bustamante, *Descripción de la Serranía de Zacatecas, formada por* ..., *1828 y 1829*, Zacatecas 1889, pp. 15–16.

side of the plaza pública by the cabildo, where they built a church and monastery. This site was taken over in 1588 for the construction of the *casas de cabildo*, and the Augustinians were evicted to the now abandoned early house of the Franciscans. There they remained for many years, in cramped conditions, until in 1613 a wealthy and influential miner of the city, Agustín de Zavala, provided them with money to construct adequate buildings. These remained in use until the second half of the eighteenth century; in 1772 a new and sumptuous church, which still stands, was consecrated.[1]

The first Jesuits to arrive are said to have appeared in 1574 to combat 'idleness, drunkenness and dissolution'.[2] They were evidently quick to undertake their crusade of virtue, since the Society had arrived in New Spain but two years before. Father Hernando Suárez de la Concha, whose preaching one Good Friday in the parish church had been quite remarkably effective in improving the morals of Zacatecas, seems to have been resident in the city only intermittently during the succeeding years. Only in 1590 was a Jesuit house set up, with missionaries from Guadalajara. At first, as with the other Orders, the foundation was small; it contained only two priests, who evangelised other mining towns to the north. But in 1616 a grandiose Jesuit college was established, financed by an enormous endowment from the Maestre de Campo Vicente de Zaldívar and his wife, Doña Ana de Bañuelos. Of the 100,000 pesos they are said to have donated, only some 27,000 were used in the building of the college, and 8,000 in the church. Of the remainder of the capital much appears to have gone into land; of that, further mention will be made in due course. The College and the church were built on a site above, and to the west of, the parish church and the plaza pública, around what is now called the plaza de Santo Domingo. There is no mention of a plaza in the locality of the College in the seventeenth century; and from the present arrangement of buildings it is impossible to tell how the ground may have been laid out. The Jesuits rebuilt extensively in the mid-eighteenth century, and their severe, but elegant, monastery now stands on the upper and western side of the

---

[1] For Augustinian foundations: Tiscareño, *El colegio*, vol. 1, ii, pp. 265–6; S. Vidal, *Estudio histórico de la ciudad de Zacatecas*, Zacatecas 1955, p. 63; Gasca, *Timbres*, pp. 149–50; J. Ribera Bernárdez, *Compendio de las cosas más notables contenidas en los libros de cabildo de esta ciudad de Nuestra Señora de los Zacatecas, desde el año de su descubrimiento 1546 hasta 1730*, Zacatecas 1732, ed. used, México 194–, Biblioteca de la Academia mexicana de la historia, vol. 2, p. 10; Fray Diego Basalenque, *Historia de la Provincia de San Nicolás de Tolentino de Michoacán*, Editorial Jus, México 1963, pp. 204–5. The amount of Zavala's contribution to the building of the monastery is not known. He was a rich and powerful man in later years, father of Martín de Zavala, governor of New León. The church of 1772 has recently been restored, on the initiative and under the direction of Don Federico Sescosse.

[2] Amador, *Bosquejo*, p. 246.

The City

plaza de Santo Domingo. The Baroque church attached to the foundation was completed only a short time before the expulsion of the Society from the New World in 1767, and was occupied on their departure by the Dominicans; hence the present name of the plaza. It now serves as parish church.[1]

Of the arrival of Dominican friars at Zacatecas and the construction of their monastery, little is known, other than that they adopted the site and the building of the Hospital de la Vera Cruz in 1608 or 1609. They may have arrived four or five years earlier. The hospital and its church stood well to the south of the plaza pública, on the left bank of the stream, looking down towards Guadalupe. Care of the sick was the special task of the Order of San Juan de Dios, which, according to a consensus of opinion, took up residence in 1608; it may have arrived slightly earlier.[2] In any case, as has been said above, the monastery and hospital of San Juan de Dios were founded in 1609, some hundreds of yards to the west of Santo Domingo, under the slope of the loma de la Carnicería.[3]

Information on secular building in the sixteenth century is scant, apart from occasional references to public constructions such as the casas de cabildo, the prison, the treasury (casas reales) and bridges. In grouping public buildings together on the plaza the founders of Zacatecas acted in consonance with at least the spirit of the 1573 Ordinances, although the houses were a good deal longer in appearing than the planners would probably have liked; and when they did appear, they were far from being the elegant constructions designed to enhance the aspect of the well-proportioned plaza that the Ordinances provided for. It was many years before the town council had a permanent meeting place of its own. Whether an early house was really destroyed by fire, as has been suggested,[4] or whether there simply never was one, cannot be known. In 1575, assemblies were still taking place either in the sacristy of the parish church or in the house of the alcalde mayor;[5] and presumably this practice had

---

[1] For the history of the Jesuits, see Tiscareño, *El colegio*, vol. 1, ii, pp. 68–72; Amador, *Bosquejo*, pp. 246–7, pp. 315–16; Gasca, *Timbres*, pp. 156–7. Vicente de Zaldívar was a highly respected citizen of Zacatecas by this time, as well as being a miner of great wealth. He was son of the Tentente de Capitán General de Nueva Galicia Vicente de Zaldívar, 1 captain in the Chichimec war and a leading citizen in the late sixteenth century. He gained his title of Maestre de Campo during the conquest of New Mexico, serving under Juan de Oñate.

[2] Gasca, *Timbres*, p. 78.

[3] For the monasteries of Santo Domingo and San Juan de Dios, see: Gasca, *Timbres*, pp. 78–9; Vidal, *Estudio histórico*, p. 38.

[4] Suggested by J. L. Mecham, 'The real de minas as a political institution', *HAHR*, vol. 7, 1927, p. 64, note 47.

[5] Vidal, *Estudio histórico*, p. 53.

47

to continue for most of the next decade, for in 1587 the cabildo was still trying to raise money to build itself a hall. At the meeting of 7 December 1587, it decided to go to the extraordinary lengths of selling a small street, close to the existing prison (and therefore central) to Baltasar de Bañuelos for 200 pesos. With this money could be purchased a building to house the cabildo, the court (*audiencia*) and a new prison.[1] Some weeks later a house had been bought in the 'plaza de los frailes de San Agustín' for conversion into a casa de cabildo.[2] This first site of the monastery of San Agustín, it will be remembered, was on the west side of the plaza pública and there the casa de cabildo stayed henceforth. Under one roof stood the council chamber, the dwelling house of the *corregidor* and the prison. The cabildo records of the seventeenth century are full of complaints about the poor condition of the building, and repeatedly prophesy its imminent collapse. Indeed, one of the regular tasks of the town surveyor (*alarife*) seems to have been the inspecting of the casa de cabildo. In 1627 the council engaged a pair of master masons to survey the building; they concluded that the cheapest solution was to demolish it and rebuild.[3] But that was never done, and patching continued to be carried out. The weakness of the construction, of course, was that it was of adobe; which, while adequate enough for ten months of the Zacatecan year, would turn to mud in the prolonged heavy rain of July and August. (Even today there is the same problem. When there is exceptionally heavy rain in the summer, adobe houses, if not properly maintained, crumble away.) But even after there had been a hundred years' experience of building in the city, the repairers of the prison in 1688 still worked with adobe bricks – more than 6,000 of them.[4] Despite this effort, when, three years later, the alarife inspected the house of the *alcalde de sala*, the chapel, the upper torture chamber (*sala alta de tormento*), the old gaol (*calabozo viejo*), he found all in great ruin, with the bricks eaten away.[5]

Few houses in Zacatecas in the sixteenth and seventeenth centuries were stone-built. It seems quite likely that even the first parish church, erected during the 1570s, was of adobe, for it began to collapse in 1605 and had to be demolished soon thereafter. The reconstruction lasted from 1612 to 1625, often delayed by lack of funds. In 1621, to provide money for completing the structure, the bishop of New Galicia called on the nine

[1] AA.Z, LC 2, ff. 18v.–19v., cabildo of 7 December 1587.
[2] AA.Z, LC 2, f. 26, cabildo of 20 January 1588.
[3] AA.Z, LC 3, f. 176–176v., cabildo of 20 December 1627.
[4] AA.Z, LC 7, ff. 87–90, expenses of the Alférez Joseph Martínez de León in repairing the prison, 1688.
[5] AA.Z, LC, ff. 1v.–2, Zacatecas 18 May 1691, report on inspection of casas de cabildo and prison by alarife Juan Bautista and *maestro de albañilería* Juan Salbado.

The City

religious brotherhoods (*cofradías*) existing in the city to contribute a quarter or a fifth of their yearly incomes. These were not large, for the sum so raised was no more than 1,200 pesos per year. Payments were to be continued for six years.[1] Other contributions came from private benefactors, but it is not known who they were, nor how much the building finally cost. It was consecrated on 8 September 1625, and lasted for more than a century before being destroyed by fire.[2] But whether it was merely poor construction, or the use of adobe, that caused the threatened collapse and subsequent demolition of the tower in 1689 is difficult to say. Orders were given for it to be re-erected, using only charitable contributions for the task, and not any funds from the Treasury.[3]

Stone building, however, was not unknown in Zacatecas, even before the end of the sixteenth century. The soft pink stone that now characterises so much Zacatecan building was used even then, as is shown by a debate in the cabildo in May 1595 about the appropriation as city property ('propios de las ciudad') of a quarry of this same stone ('la cantera colorada de piedra') cut in a hill to the west of the town called the Cerro de los Carneros.[4] The first house sale that the surviving notarial records of Zacatecas reveal, is that in 1614 of a house opposite the Franciscan monastery, sold for 525 pesos while only partly completed. The contract declares that the price includes 'all the wood and stone that is in the said house with the red stone (*piedra colorada*) which is for finishing the said house ...'.[5] But, as Mota y Escobar noted at the beginning of the seventeenth century, such dwellings were rare. 'The houses of this city are generally of adobe and mud walls. All have an entresol (*entresuelo*); they are all of small capacity; some are built of stone, and a few have an upper storey ('*con altos*').'[6] The problems of maintaining adobe structures are again brought out by one Juan de Bermeo, who in 1635 claimed to have found a better material for roofing houses than the wooden shingles (*tlaxamaniles*) then in use. Sadly, he omits to describe his invention. He pointed to the fragility of these roofs and to the lack of durability of the earthen walls of most houses ('paredes poco permanentes de tierra muerta'). His invention, if such it was, cannot have been popular, for eighteenth-

---

[1] AA.Z, LC 3, ff. 77–78, Zacatecas 28 April 1621, meeting of corregidor, treasurer and bishop of New Galicia.

[2] For the parish churches of Zacatecas, see Gasca, *Timbres*, pp. 87–92.

[3] AGI Guadalajara 22, expediente on the tower of parish church at Zacatecas, beginning with real cédula, Madrid 12 June 1689, in AGI Guadalajara 21, Guadalajara 18 November 1689, president of New Galicia to king.

[4] AA.Z, LC 2, f. 112, cabildo of [6] May 1595.

[5] AN.Z, PC, 1614, f. 8v.

[6] Mota y Escobar, *Descripción*, p. 65.

century plans of Zacatecas show most buildings roofed with tlaxamaniles (see plate 2).[1]

The typical house of the poorer members of the community – the lesser tradesmen, white and mestizo, prospectors and unsuccessful miners, for instance – was a single storey adobe building containing a large living room (*sala*), a smaller room (*aposento*), a kitchen and a storeroom (*bodega*). It might also possess a yard (*corral*) with a well and some facilities for stabling.[2] Most houses had a domestic water supply in the form of a well and storage cistern for rain-water (*algibe*); drinking water was not normally drawn directly from the stream, which was polluted by effluent from mine reduction works, as well as by refuse and sewage. Wells seem generally to have been adequate, There are few complaints of lack of domestic drinking water. These single storey dwellings (*casas bajas*) predominated everywhere away from the centre of the town. A common transaction in notarial records is the sale of such houses combined with shops. The building would be rather larger, containing the living quarters mentioned above, together with a shop giving on to the street, and a back room (*trastienda*) for storage of merchandise.[3]

The centre of the city was graced with more substantial houses, many being of two floors (*casas altas*). The property of leading miners, merchants and officials, they were probably stone-built in the majority. A typical example of such a house was one sold in 1656 on the street leading from the plaza to San Francisco: two storeys, shop and storeroom, yard and fruit garden. The latter was rare in the centre of the town, where buildings stood in terrace fashion along the streets and filled the blocks between them. The price was 500 pesos.[4]

It is difficult to generalise about house prices and rents over the long term; partly because they were naturally affected by changes in the prosperity of the town, and partly because in the majority of contracts not enough detail is given about the quality of the property for useful comparisons and conclusions to be drawn. A casa baja could cost between 40 and 800 pesos, depending on its size and on whether it included a shop. Casas altas were naturally more expensive on average, ranging from 200 to 2,000 pesos. As an indication of the value of houses it may be noted that a slave cost between 200 and 600 pesos, according to sex, age and

[1] AA.Z, 5, no. 32, Juan de Bermeo, Zacatecas 2 May 1635.
[2] This description is taken specifically from the sale of a house by Diego Bernárdez de Valdés to Jusepe and Nicolás Marqués. AN.Z, FE 1671, ff. 156v.–7v., Zacatecas 22 September 1671.
[3] For example, lease of houses and shop by the convento de Santo Domingo to Juan Román, AN.Z, FE 1671, ff. 125–6v., Zacatecas 10 July 1671.
[4] AN.Z, FE 1656, ff. 83v.–4v., Zacatecas 20 April 1656.

The City

caste (that is, whether Negro, mulatto or *chino*). And for comparisons with incomes, it may be pointed out that the corregidor's official salary was some 1,650 pesos per year; while the wages of a master mason, if he were fully employed throughout the year, would have been around 450 pesos; and those of a building labourer similarly employed, some 165 pesos.[1] So the cost of a house of some variety was generally not prohibitive to an employed man.

Indeed, ownership of urban property appears to have been evenly distributed among the citizens. There were few landlords possessing many houses, and in general, miners' wealth did not go into town buildings; or if it did, changes in mining fortunes, and consequently in the wealth of families, ensured that property was sold or permanently leased. This happened to a large group of houses acquired by Baltasar de Bañuelos and preserved, as far as possible, by his heirs. These lay in the centre of the town; some in the plaza pública, some in the plaza to the north of the church, and some perhaps in the street sold to Bañuelos by the cabildo in 1588.[2] But such extensive town property was rare in one family. Holdings of comparable size belonged to Doña María de Cuadros, widow of one Captain Domingo de Arana, a rich merchant of the city. On remarrying she brought a dowry worth, according to her estimate, 68,000 pesos; of these, 20,000 consisted of dwellings, shops and casas bajas, widely scattered over the city.[3] Another large urban estate emerges from the will of one Leonor de Saldaña, who in 1659 owned a number of single storey and two storey houses and shops in the plaza pública and adjacent streets. These she had probably inherited in the course of her two marriages to miners, and on her death they were distributed among the eight surviving children of those marriages. The equal distribution of estates among children was one reason why large urban holdings rarely accumulated. This was certainly the case with mining property, as will be seen.[4]

The only owners whose property was free from division among heirs, and relatively resistant to changes in the fortunes of mining and trading, were the religious foundations. All five religious orders in Zacatecas

---

[1] These wages are given only for comparison. They are taken from 1688 and do not necessarily coincide with earlier wages, of which records are rare. AA.Z, 11, ff. 87–90. Expenses of the Alférez Joseph Martínez de León in repair of prison.

[2] Three of these houses were passed to the monastery of Santo Domingo by Doña Catalina Tremiño in her will in 1659. She held them on permanent lease (*censo perpetuo*) from Bañuelos' heirs. AN.Z, FE 1659, ff. 27v.–8v., testament of Doña Catalina Tremiño, Zacatecas 18 February 1659.

[3] AN.Z, FE 1656, ff. 207v.–14, Zacatecas 21 October 1656, dowry of Doña María de Cuadros.

[4] AN.Z, FE 1659, Zacatecas 15 November 1659, testament of Leonor de Saldaña.

engaged to some extent in leasing property acquired by them by one means or another. In many instances, houses were willed to them by owners in return for services rendered during the lifetime of the testator, or for the foundation of a *capellanía*. Under this last arrangement, in return for income derived from the lease of the property willed to it, the monastery undertook to say a number of masses every year for the deceased. The other means by which the Orders gathered property was the *censo*. A man wishing to raise money might obtain a loan from a monastery, giving as surety his house. The amount of the loan was generally the same as the value of the house; and interest of 5 per cent (*de veinte mil el millar*) was invariably charged on the principal. The censo could be redeemed only by total repayment of the principal; but, for a man who in effect had been forced to mortgage his home in the first place, repayment was often impossible. In fact, he was frequently unable to keep up with the interest payments; and when that happened the house eventually became the property of the monastery. In this way, urban property gradually accrued to the Orders in Zacatecas, and they became probably the largest individual owners in the city. Having acquired houses, they might then lease them, again on a contract called a censo, and again at the rate of 5 per cent of their value. Occasionally, the assessed value of a property would be reduced, on the condition that the tenant improve or rebuild it. The process of acquisition was inevitably a slow one, and the disappearance of the monasteries' archives hinders knowledge of the size of the holdings. But a fragment of a document of 1655 gives valuable information on the resources of the monastery of San Juan de Dios. The prior complained that income from houses and censos, over a period he unfortunately did not specify, had fallen from 2,250 to 1,500 pesos because of the general decline in the state of the city, and the consequent fall in rents.[1] Assuming that censos were yielding 5 per cent interest, the capital value of property owned by the Order thus dropped from 45,000 to 30,000 pesos. The other four Orders, except the Franciscans, engaged equally in the leasing of houses, so that a very rough figure for the value of town property belonging to the regular clergy before the depression of the mid-seventeenth century could be some 200,000 pesos, yielding to each monastery 2,000 or 3,000 pesos in rents each year. These figures are of interest in themselves, as they go some way towards

---

[1] AN.Z, loose document, the first folio of a lost expediente, 'Información de los Padres de San Juan de Dios', 4 February 1655. Income from rents had fallen from 2,150 pesos to 1,500 pesos. But the total income of the monastery had declined from 9,000 pesos to 2,000. This was mainly because receipts from a playhouse (*corral de comedias*) owned by the monastery had failed; so had those from an apothecary's shop (*botica*) belonging to it, previously worth over 2,000 pesos a year; charitable contributions (*limosnas*) had also lapsed.

revealing how the religious communities maintained themselves. But of more interest here is the size of the capital assets of the monasteries, and their rôle in the economic life of the city. In the eighteenth century the Orders, with vast accumulated wealth, functioned as banks and sources of credit in New Spain. But in Zacatecas in the seventeenth century, they did not play this part to any important degree. Some of their townhouses fell to them when the owner, having in effect mortgaged his property to an Order, defaulted on interest payments. The original principal of the mortgage paid to the owner was, of course, not recovered (or only partly recovered in interest), and may be regarded as a transfer of capital from the monastery to the citizen – in effect, a loan. But the monasteries of Zacatecas had not thus paid out all the 200,000 pesos postulated above as the value of their urban property; for many houses had come to them not through censos, but through gifts or bequests. And even 200,000 pesos would not have been a large amount of credit, when distributed over many years, in comparison with credit supplied by merchants and, indirectly, by the Treasury.[1]

Despite the relatively small value, in cash, of the houses owned by the monasteries in Zacatecas, their number was large. It is common to find in sales of property that a seller would locate his house by stating that it lay between dwellings owned by this or that monastery; and, if extrapolated, the figures given by the prior of San Juan for rents and incomes suggest that the total number of houses owned by the religious communities may have been between 90 and 130.[2] Mota y Escobar stated that in his time there were above 300 houses in Zacatecas.[3] So, if growth

---

[1] The crucial matter of credit will be fully discussed below. Discussion of censos is inevitably confused by the multifarious meanings of the word. Fundamentally a censo was any monetary transaction between two parties in which credit was transferred from one to the other (although in some instances the transfer was only notional). In return the second party undertook to pay interest, usually at 5 per cent of the amount transferred. See François Chevalier, *La formation des grands domaines au Mexique. Terre et société aux XVIe–XVIIe siècles*, Paris 1952, pp. 333–6, where he shows that the term censo embraced mortgages, rents, endowments; and, in effect straightforward loans at interest, which were still deplored as usurious.

[2] 'Información', 1655 (see note 1 on p. 52). The prior stated that income from rents to his monastery, before the depression of the mid-century, had been 2,250 pesos per year. Rents had been 6–8 pesos per month: i.e. 72 to 96 pesos per year, per house. Assuming that the other Orders enjoyed similar incomes from rents, and charged similar rates (but ignoring San Francisco, which had little property), the number of houses owned by the four monasteries of San Juan de Dios, San Agustín, Santo Domingo and the Society of Jesus lay between (2,250× 4)/96 and (2,250× 4)/72, i.e. between 94 and 125; or roughly, 90 and 130. Notarial records of leases of property by the Orders during the second half of the seventeenth century do suggest that all of them except the Franciscans, owned similar numbers of houses.

[3] Mota y Escobar, *Descripción*, p. 65.

The City

of the city is allowed for, a rough estimate would be that towards the middle of the seventeenth century the Orders owned a fourth or a fifth of the houses. Inasmuch as there was any pattern in the distribution of their property, the monasteries gathered it in their own parts of the town: thus the Dominicans predominated in the south-east, the friars of San Juan in the south-west, the Jesuits and Augustinians in the central area, and the Franciscans, with what little property they had, in the north. The abstention of the Franciscans from acquiring property was normal in New Spain. Chevalier suggests that they adhered more closely to their vows of poverty than other Orders, and were concerned only to secure sufficient income for the upkeep of their monasteries.[1]

The parish church was less fortunate in attracting benefactors and bequests than the regular foundations. This was one of the reasons why the construction of the second church took thirteen years, from 1612 to 1625. In 1621, the majordomo said that its income was a mere 500 pesos a year, bequeathed as a capellanía by one Pedro de Lorenzana.[2] The preference shown by the citizens for the Orders over the church may have originated in a feeling that it was an institution with a less easily recognisable and defined rôle than the monasteries, which, with their permanent bodies of friars, their mission activities and their property holdings, seemed more a part of the life of the city. The cofradías, to which citizens of all standings belonged, were usually associated with a particular monastery, in which they held their meetings and services; although some were attached to the parish church. Personal association with an Order may thus have been a motive for donating property to it. Again, the younger sons of many families entered religious communities, and later inherited property which in due course fell to their monastery. And while it is true that sons also entered the secular clergy, their inheritances often took the form of capellanías, which belonged to them personally as a cash income; and passed after their death, not to the church, but to another priest specified in the terms of the original capellanía, who was usually a member or descendant of their family. Thus the regular communities could preserve as their own the inheritances of their members, while the secular church had no such claim on the goods of its priests. These are some of the reasons why the parish church of Zacatecas fared so badly in its finances.

The cabildo was generally as bereft of money as the church. Demands

---

[1] Chevalier, *La formation*, pp. 309–11.

[2] AA.Z, LC 3, f. 77v., Zacatecas 1 May 1621. A statement of Diego de Sosa, mayordomo de la iglesia mayor. The majordomo was an official appointed annually by the cabildo to maintain the church and its possessions.

The City

on the city funds were not heavy, but a constant preoccupation was the state of roads and bridges within the limits of the town. Lying between steep slopes, accessible only along the floors of valleys roughly cut by streams, Zacatecas was not attractive to carters; and if the precarious roads were allowed to deteriorate, then, the cabildo feared, the amount of goods entering the city would fall. As it was, the entrance from the south-east (and Mexico City) was a road running in and along the bed of the stream. There was little difficulty for most of the year; but in the summer, sudden floods could cut away the banks, wash down boulders, and make the road impassable. The same floods destroyed bridges and swamped houses in the city. The first reference to a bridge is found in 1559, when the cabildo ordered that one should be built to connect the plaza pública with the Calle de Tacuba, the continuation inside the town of the road from the south.[1] This bridge, the first in Zacatecas, was the most important, as it carried goods into the market place. By 1592, there were two others, both in danger of collapse.[2] The Tacuba bridge had been built of wood, and by 1594 it had been carried away by the stream; so that in January of that year the cabildo agreed to have a stone structure erected. This project may have been carried out, for in later years there are frequent references to houses and shops standing on the Tacuba bridge, which appears to have become a massive stone culvert. A lighter wooden structure lay close by, and generally the stream was forded by carts. It would be tedious to go into all the plans and contracts for maintaining bridges and streets in the seventeenth century. Very gradually the number of bridges grew; in 1732 there were five.[3]

No general description of the city of Zacatecas exists for the sixteenth and seventeenth centuries, except the slight comments of Mota y Escobar, who noted with distaste the long straggle of the town. 'It has, for all its narrowness, four plazas and seven streets, six of them short and the long one that runs from end to end.'[4] The plan and the size of the city did not change greatly over the century after the bishop's visit. Even today, the long central street is the thoroughfare of Zacatecas, the site of shops and the course of the evening *paseo*. The four plazas may be identified as that lying to one side of the Franciscan monastery in the northern extremity of the town; the *plazuela* on the north side of the parish church, which up to the start of the seventeenth century had no name, but was

[1] Ribera Bernárdez, *Compendio*, p. 9.
[2] AA.Z, LC 2, f. 81, Cabildo of 6 April 1592.
[3] J. de Ribera Bernárdez, *Descripción breve de la muy noble y leal ciudad de Zacatecas*, México 1732. Published in *Testimonios de Zacatecas*, selección de Gabriel Salinas de la Torre, México 1946. In this 1946 edition, p. 59.
[4] Mota y Escobar, *Descripción*, p. 65.

55

then titled the 'plazuela del Maestre de Campo', in honour of the rich miner and explorer, Vicente de Zaldívar, who lived on its east side; the plaza pública, to the south of the church; and the plazuela de San Agustín, in front of the monastery of that Order. Around the plaza pública stood the casa de cabildo, the prison, fashionable houses and shops. There, also, were the buildings belonging to the Treasury, and that housing the royal chest itself (the Real Caja).[1] The plaza was used as market place from the earliest days. To the south-east of it flowed the main stream, dividing it from the important Calle de Tacuba, another centre of commerce and a residential street. Few other streets received names, except for those close to religious houses and some associated with guilds. Thus, the 'Calle de los Zapateros' led eastward from the plazuela de San Agustín to join Tacuba; and the 'Calle de los Gorreros' ran along the south side of the Hospital de San Juan de Dios.

What Mota y Escobar failed to mention was the growth of Indian townships around the Spanish core of the city. The date of their founding is not known, but some must have arisen in the very early days. Indians grouped themselves according to their 'nations', of which four were readily identifiable in Zacatecas. The Tlaxcalans formed a *barrio* called Tlacuitlapan to the north-west of San Francisco, in the valley of a tributary of the principal stream; the Mexica gathered in Mexicapan, near by; Indians from Texcoco occupied a barrio called El Niño Jesús, to the south of the town; and Tarascans formed two townships, San José and Tonalá Chepinque, to the west under the hills. As the seventeenth century proceeded, other barrios began to form. Thus the whole area behind the parish church, below La Bufa, was an Indian suburb. The area still known as El Pedregoso, to the west, begins to be mentioned in the mid-seventeenth century, peopled by both Spaniards and Indians.[2] But while these new quarters grew, the original Indian pueblos remained intact and distinct;[3] and the separation between them and the central area containing monasteries, dwelling houses, shops and municipal and Treasury buildings always remained clear.

Into this crowded setting was fitted the mining industry of Zacatecas.

[1] Requests by the Treasury officials for permission to build casas reales and a real caja begin in 1567; see AGI Guadalajara 230, Z 1, f. 182, Madrid 9 July 1567, real cédula, king to Audiencia of New Galicia. Houses for holding the Caja and Treasury archive had been bought by 1577 at a cost of more than 1,000 pesos; see AGI Guadalajara 6, R. 1, 7 March 1577, Licenciado Santiago del Riego to king.

[2] E.g. AN.Z, FE 1656, f. 138, refers to houses belonging to Petrona López, an Indian woman, in the barrio del Pedregoso.

[3] Evidence of this is that in 1682 there was still a distinguishable 'pueblo de Tlaxcala y Tonalá Chepinque' which elected a cabildo of six members annually. AA.Z. 10, No. 17.

The City

The haciendas de minas, with their long sheds, stables, houses and corrals, occupied most of the space along the banks of the streams passing through the city; and were strung out along the stream towards the mines in the north and down the valley to the south-east. They were the first and last cause of the city's existence, and would have been the first signs of habitation seen by the traveller approaching from north or south. Yet they were not the only source of employment nor of wealth in Zacatecas. And if the traveller, as is very likely, had been a merchant or the owner of a pack-train, he would have been less immediately interested in the slow processes of milling and refining ores than in one of the principal consequences of the silver makers' activities: the thriving markets and shops of Zacatecas.

CHAPTER 4

SUPPLIES AND DISTRIBUTION

'No measures are taken, nor is any necessary, to ensure that this city is well provided with all supplies; for there are many people who live by this trade, and they take great care to bring each thing in its season and to supply the city with all its needs.'[1] Thus the writer of a report on Zacatecas in 1608 explained how the city, with a permanent population of 1,500 Spaniards and 3,000 Indians, Negroes and mestizos managed to survive in surroundings largely useless for cultivation. Freighting with wagon trains was one of the earliest secondary occupations to grow up in the north as a result of the discovery of the silver of Zacatecas. Carretas and, soon afterwards, heavier carros had begun to roll over the rough tracks from central Mexico and Michoacán by 1550, carving themselves a permanent road within a few years. Despite the perils of Indian attack, the flow of goods into Zacatecas from the south was thereafter continuous; the lure of high prices made the risk and the hard journey worth while. Areas already producing food-stuffs quickly found themselves able to export to Zacatecas; and patterns of trade were set up which persisted beyond the end of the seventeenth century. The linking of the grain-producing areas of Michoacán with the Camino Real in 1550 is one example. Mendoza encouraged this, since he had been told that the inhabitants of Michoacán wished to cart supplies from the towns of Zitácuaro and Tajimaroa to Zacatecas, and to bring back ores to be refined in Zitácuaro. He therefore ordered that the road from Zitácuaro to Acámbaro should be repaired.[2] The extent to which Zacatecas had impinged on the economy of New Spain in a short period after its foundation is indicated by a statement of Baltasar de Bañuelos in 1562. He claimed that mine-owners had spent in the construction of their haciendas de minas more than 800,000 ducats (about 1,091,000 pesos). More silver was extracted in Zacatecas than in all other mines in New Spain, and the mines were of the greatest benefit to the whole country. This was shown by the flocking of traders to Zacatecas from every direction: from Culiacán and Colima in the west; from La Purificación, Guadalajara, Michoacán, Mexico City and Puebla in the south; and from many other

[1] DII, vol. 9, pp. 179–91, 'Relación de Nuestra Señora de los Zacatecas, sacada de la información que, por mandado del Consejo, en ella se hizo el año de 1608'; here, pp. 187–8.
[2] AGN Mercedes 3, f. 97v., México 21 June 1550, Mendoza to Governor of Michoacán; also f. 332, México 16 September 1550.

places.[1] Another enthusiastic inhabitant made a still more sweeping statement when he said of the mines of Zacatecas, San Martín and Avino, 'by means of them New Galicia and New Spain are sustained, and when the said mines decline, the effect is felt in all New Spain ...'.[2] This was more than the boast of a citizen extolling his *patria chica*. There was relatively little specie in circulation in New Spain at the time, and the release of 800,000 ducats into the economy, implied by Bañuelos' statement, together with later sums of similar size, inevitably drove prices upwards over a wide area, as will be seen (below, note 2 on p. 68).[3]

One of the most important food-stuffs imported into Zacatecas was maize; it was the traditional staple of Indians and an essential fodder for mules during the dry season in the absence of much pasture in the vicinity of the mines. The first clause of the first series of labour Ordinances issued in the city underlines the primacy of maize when it bids employers of free Indians to give them a *cuartillo* (about 2 lb. 5 oz.) per day, and a quantity of *frijoles* (kidney beans).[4] Hardly less important a cereal, though, was wheat, which was eaten by Spaniards and probably by many others who could afford it. Mota y Escobar noted the fine, white and tasty wheaten bread to be had in Zacatecas.[5]

Disappointingly little detailed information survives on imports of grain into Zacatecas, and what there is relates to the seventeenth century alone. Before that only a general description of sources can be given. Much grain arrived from distant regions. Michoacán has already been mentioned; the Bajío was another supplier. But there was cultivation of cereals closer at hand. Where conditions were favourable they could be raised on the high plateau. The most suitable sites were river valleys, where there was water for irrigation and some depth of alluvial soil. A rich area close to Zacatecas, for example, was Jerez, where the normal occupation of the inhabitants was maize growing for the mines.[6] Settlements in the area of Sombrerete drew their cereals largely from the two valleys of Súchil and Poanas, to the north-west. Fresnillo was well placed for agriculture, lying close to the Río Grande, along which stretched numerous wheat and maize farms (*labores de trigo y de maíz*).[7] The river

---

[1] Ahumada, 'Información' 1562, p. 296.
[2] Ahumada, 'Información' 1562, p. 274. Testimony of Jaime Delgado.
[3] See Chevalier, *La formation*, p. 150.
[4] AGI Guadalajara 5, 'Averiguaciones ... Contreras y Guevara ... 1570', f. 116. La Marcha's ordinances, 27 April 1550, clause 1.   [5] Mota y Escobar, *Descripción*, p. 67.
[6] See Paso y Troncoso, *Papeles, 2a. serie*, vol. 8, p. 204.
[7] Paso y Troncoso, *Papeles, 2a. serie*, vol. 8, p. 298, 'Relación de Fresnillo' 17 January 1585. According to the witness, Alonso Tabuya, not only were there maize and wheat, but also an abundance of squashes, chile, tomatoes, barley, beans, chick-peas, lentils, cabbage, lettuce and radishes.

Supplies and Distribution

was lined with farmsteads, of which the best-known was the hacienda of Trujillo, part of the property of the Ibarra y Velasco family. In the far north of the region, there were several major areas of cereal production: Saltillo, the hacienda of Patos, and the valley of Parras, all of which sent some quantities of wheat and maize to Zacatecas. To the south-west lay other producing districts. The hopefully named Valparaíso, in the distant and isolated western extreme of the region, lived up to its name in fertility, but its cultivation was restricted by Indian attacks in the sixteenth century. More useful sources were the valleys of the south, the deep river-eroded canyons with rich alluvial floors, sheltering the towns of Tlaltenango, Juchipila and Teocaltiche. Here crops of many varieties could be raised. Further east, the lands surrounding Lagos were fertile in grain.[1] In all these places, cereals were cultivated principally under irrigation, because rainfall in most of them was slight, and fell mainly in the late summer months when crops sown in the spring would be ripening. Consequently, it was common practice to sow winter crops in September or October, and to grow them under irrigation for harvesting in March and April.[2]

In greater or lesser quantities, grain arrived at Zacatecas from these areas in the sixteenth century, and continued to do so in the seventeenth. But it is not until 1635 that records are available showing the amounts derived from each region, and enabling a distinction to be made between wheat-producing and maize-producing districts. That year is the first for which there survives a book of declarations (manifestaciones) made of consignments of grain entering the exchange (alhóndiga) of Zacatecas. The information extracted from this libro de manifestaciones of 1635, and from later books of 1652 and 1675, is summarised in Table 1. Some clear patterns of cultivation emerge. It is evident that wheat-growing areas were largely distinct from those where maize was cultivated. The Bajío provides most of the wheat, whereas maize comes in large quantities from what has here been called the intermediate zone and from the canyon zone of the south. Michoacán and the north remit relatively little grain of either variety to Zacatecas. The predominance of the Bajío among wheat growers is striking: it provides between two-thirds and

[1] For cereal growing areas, see Mota y Escobar, Descripción, pp. 55–80, passim.
[2] For methods of crop farming in New Galicia, see Mota y Escobar, Descripción, p. 27, and Domingo Lázaro de Arregui, Descripción de la Nueva Galicia (Seville 1946), p. 19. Both authors concur in saying that irrigated crops (de riego) were sown in autumn and harvested in spring. Arregui states that crops to be grown without irrigation (de temporal) were sown in April and May, to be harvested in November and December. He enthused about crops grown de temporal, which he said were surer than irrigated ones. Mota y Escobar's observations contradict this rather surprising view. He says that 'non-irrigated wheat does not grow well, but black and shrivelled, whereas irrigated wheat grows marvellously'.

four-fifths of the wheat entering the alhóndiga. According to Chevalier, the rise of the Bajío as a region of wheat cultivation is a seventeenth-century phenomenon. He explains that by the early years of the century the process of formation of the great estates in the Bajío had advanced to a point where large tracts of land had fallen to ecclesiastical and private owners; the increasing size of holdings made possible extensive agriculture (including large irrigation projects), where less efficient methods had prevailed before. This may well be true, although a more elementary explanation might be that the removal of the Chichimec threat in the last years of the sixteenth century had released vast expanses of fertile land for agriculture. Chevalier believes that the northern silver mines declined from the beginning of the seventeenth century, so that his attempt to relate the rise of the Bajío in that period to demand from the mines is a little strained, and his chronology becomes vague.[1] But the problem is resolved if it is allowed that silver production at San Luis Potosí did not decline until after 1620, and at Parral until after 1635, as seems likely. Zacatecas, for certain, did not experience any decline until the late 1630s. The development of the Bajío can therefore be seen as a direct consequence of the prosperity of mining. Within the Bajío, the area of Celaya and Salvatierra predominated in exporting to Zacatecas. To the total export in 1635 of 4,304 cargas, this area contributed 2,710; in 1652, of 4,005 cargas, 1,840; and in 1675, of 3,674 cargas, 1,744.[2]

The fertility of the Bajío, and doubtless the efficiency of methods of farming used there, as suggested by Chevalier, is reflected in its great dominance in exports to Zacatecas over regions that were far closer to the mines, and which therefore had a lesser handicap in freight costs. (These, as a proportion of the total cost of grain at the mines, varied between a third and a half, according to distance.) Only a little wheat was raised in the vicinity of Zacatecas (including the lands of Jerez and those bordering the Río Grande, all locally renowned for their richness); while the fertile valleys of the north (Saltillo, Parras, Súchil and Poanas) contributed scarcely to Zacatecas' wheat supply. Much of their production was certainly absorbed by the more northerly mines of Sombrerete and Mazapil, leaving little margin for export to Zacatecas. What is more surprising is the relative poverty in wheat of the intermediate region, embracing Aguascalientes and Lagos. This may have been caused by lack of water for irrigation and a consequent turning towards the cultivation of maize, which was sent northwards in large quantities.

---

[1] For Chevalier's views on the Bajío, see *La formation*, pp. 76–8.
[2] A *carga* of grain equalled 5·15 bushels, or 228 lb. weight. It comprised 2 *fanegas*. M. Carrera Stampa, 'Evolution of Weights and Measures in New Spain', *HAHR* vol. 29, 1949, pp. 2–24.

Supplies and Distribution

Among the maize producers the prominence of the canyons is notable. In 1652, for example, they contributed almost half the maize entering the alhóndiga. Permanent streams flow along these fertile and alluvial valley floors, permitting extensive irrigation now as then. The Caxcán Indians had occupied the canyons before the Spanish conquest. They had advanced some way towards an agricultural and sedentary culture, and grew maize; so there was a basis of cultivation which could later be developed. The canyons were probably more suited to maize than to wheat (although wheat was grown in them) since their floors are low-lying and consequently offer warmer and more humid conditions for agriculture than the upland. Today they are extensively used for sugar-cane, which thrives in the conditions they present. Another major maize producing area was the intermediate region, stretching from Lagos north to Aguascalientes. And the considerable production of maize around Zacatecas itself shows that farmers managed to make something of the local lands. The libros de manifestaciones are not specific about the exact origins of this grain; it probably came mainly from Jerez and the haciendas and labores of the Río Grande.

All the above information has been drawn from the libros de manifestaciones of the alhóndiga at Zacatecas. These books are not a complete record of the amounts of grain entering the city, since, although declaration of consignments was obligatory, it would be foolish to think that all were in fact registered. Citizens no doubt brought in private supplies of grain for their own use or for sale, without declaring them. It would have been especially difficult to keep a check on grain carried into the town by miners who grew it on their own lands for consumption in the haciendas de minas. And furthermore, ecclesiastical producers were exempt from both alhóndiga and sales tax (alcabala) regulations, so that their large contributions to the supply passed in without record. Nevertheless, it is worth presenting the imports of grain as they appear in sporadic libros de manifestaciones during the second half of the seventeenth century, since it may be taken that the quantities indicated came, over the thirty years covered by the books, from the same type of producer (that is, the secular land-holdings in the areas described above); and that they are therefore representative of the total amounts arriving in the city.[1] (See table opposite.)

The general excess of wheat over maize in these figures is one characteristic of them worth noting. This excess may be taken as indicating the prevalence of Spanish over Indian culture in the town during these years.

[1] Figures are taken from libros de manifestaciones of the alhóndiga at Zacatecas for the years quoted. These books are in AA.Z, 7, 8 and 9.

Supplies and Distribution

That more wheat was being consumed than maize (and the disparity is exaggerated if it is recalled that maize was fed to mules) suggests either that the group in the population showing predominantly Indian culture had gone far towards abandoning its traditional staple, or that this Indian group was numerically small. Considering that the thirty years for which figures are here given embraced a period of depression of the local mines, it is quite possible that the size of the Indian–mestizo labour force was indeed small. Towards the end of the period, the mines

Year	Wheat (cargas)	Maize (cargas)
1655	5,278½	4,641
1656	4,096	1,781
1659	4,932	3,800
1661	4,978½	5,945
1663	5,227½	4,233
1664	4,516½	3,033
1667	6,094	4,715
1669	4,283	2,260
1671	5,502	2,093
1672	3,958	2,753
1675	3,674	2,594
1676	5,165	4,080
1677	4,973	3,102
1 Jan. 1678–20 May 1679	6,349	4,618
1680	4,425	4,377
1681	4,560½	3,969
1683	6,709	6,842
1686	6,622	4,273
1687	5,899	6,439

began to recover. A consequent growth in the labour force may perhaps be reflected in the maize figures for 1683 to 1687, which are higher than in previous years; they begin to exceed the wheat totals. An instructive comparison may be drawn with quantities of wheat and maize presented for declaration at the alhóndiga in 1732. 42,900 cargas of maize and 9,750 cargas of wheat arrived in that year. The consumption of wheat had almost doubled in comparison with 1687; but the consumption of maize had increased almost sevenfold. The mining boom of the early eighteenth century was taking place. And these increases in consumption probably reflect increases in the size of the Spanish and Indian sectors of the population. In times of mining prosperity, the number of Spaniards naturally rose considerably, but the number of Indian and mestizo labourers, who were the maize eaters, multiplied many times over.[1]

[1] Maize and wheat figures for 1732 are taken from Ribera Bernárdez, *Descripción breve*, p. 81.

63

Supplies and Distribution

What other sources supplied cereals, and in what quantities? The Church was an enthusiastic farmer, and its produce was not subject to normal regulations. From January 1688 to February 1689, 1,936 cargas of wheat and some 2,200 cargas of maize arrived in Zacatecas from ecclesiastical lands, mainly in the Bajío: from the monastery of Nuestra Señora del Carmen and the Carmelite monastery of San Angel, both at Salvatierra; from the Augustinian house at Celaya; and from the Augustinian monastery of San Nicolás in Michoacán. The secular clergy also contributed, by selling off grain yielded by tithes from Teocaltiche and Aguascalientes.[1] Unfortunately, this is the only year for which information has been found on grain coming from lands owned by the monastic Orders; but if the pattern observed in 1688–9 was that of earlier years, their contribution to the city's supply was high; a fifth or a sixth of wheat, and a third to a quarter of maize.

Perhaps the most striking feature of the process of grain supply to Zacatecas is the width over which the net was cast. It has already been remarked that the discovery of the Zacatecas deposits accelerated, and in some cases, directly caused, the settlement and utilisation of land far to the south of the mines; specie flowing out from Zacatecas into the important Bajío area must have contributed very largely to its occupation and cultivation. (The mines of Guanajuato exercised a similar effect.) The 4,000 cargas of wheat, for example, sent to Zacatecas from the Bajío in 1652 meant the injection into the economy of that region of some 60,000 pesos. Zacatecan silver was carried on homeward-bound carts and mules in literally every direction, finding its way, in payment for grain, to Saltillo in the North and to Puebla in the South. The geographical and geological accidents that made minerals and agriculture such incompatible partners in the Zacatecas district thus ensured that silver from this, the largest producing region of New Spain, should be distributed over the whole colony. Fluctuations in output at Zacatecas must indeed have been felt within months everywhere, as the testimony of Jaime Delgado in 1562 suggests (quoted in the first paragraph of this chapter).

Within the city the distribution and marketing of grain was controlled from the early years of the seventeenth century by the town council. Like their mediaeval predecessors in Spain (and Europe in general), cabildos in Spanish America attempted to supervise supplies of food within their jurisdictions. The agency for cereals was the alhóndiga, or grain market, to which all grain entering the city had to be taken before sale. The producer or carrier declared the size of the consignment he

[1] AA.Z, 10, No. 66.

Supplies and Distribution

brought before the supervisor (*fiel, diputado* or *alcaide*), paid an excise tax on it, and was then permitted to sell it at the alhóndiga, but nowhere else. The object was to control the retail price of grains by ensuring that all transactions took place under supervision; so reducing, it was hoped, possibilities of cornering the market and profiteering.

Zacatecas did not establish an alhóndiga until 1623, although the idea had been mooted as early as 1594, in response to the need for some central buying and selling point for cereals.[1] But a licence was not granted until 1623, by which time the motive was as much the securing of dues for the municipality as the control of prices and sales. By order of the president of the Audiencia of New Galicia the cabildo was empowered to build an alhóndiga and to operate it under the same ordinances as were applied to that of San Luis Potosí, set up in 1609.[2] (These were similar to those given for Mexico City in 1583.) Under them, the cabildo could charge a duty of two reales on each incoming carga of wheat flour and one real on each carga of maize. This tax was a valuable part of the municipality's income.[3] The delay in founding the alhóndiga, from 1594 to the 1620s, is puzzling. It can only be supposed that the town's need for revenue had grown in the intervening years, as public buildings, roads and bridges became more dilapidated. Possibly also the prosperity of the mines in the 1620s lifted prices to a height that could not be ignored, so that some attempt at control was eventually seen to be unavoidable. Thereafter the institution continued as a central part of the trading system of Zacatecas. Failure to declare grain was punished. Dues were always levied, except when shortages of grain tempted growers to seek more profitable markets; this happened in the early summer of 1634, and the cabildo abolished charges on wheat flour for three months in an attempt to attract supplies.[4] In the second half of the seventeenth century, instead of being administered directly by the cabildo, the alhóndiga was rented out and its income farmed. The contract was offered for auction.

[1] AA.Z, LC 2, f. 104, cabildo of 8 January 1594.
[2] AGI Guadalajara 30, Guadalajara 14 November 1623, Pedro de Otálora, auto.
[3] For alhóndigas and pertinent legislation see R. E. Lee, 'Grain Legislation in Colonial Mexico, 1575-1585', *HAHR* vol. 27, 1947, pp. 647-60. For the ordinances of the alhóndiga of Mexico City, founded in 1578, see *Recopilación* 1680, IV xiv 2-19. 1633 had been a poor year for grain. The growers of Tlaltenango and Lagos found it more profitable to sell their maize at Parral, which was at the height of a mining boom, and in other parts of New Biscay. Maize prices rose sharply in Zacatecas in the early months of 1634, and the cabildo commissioned an agent to go and buy grain for the city as far away as Toluca. They also took steps to obtain from the Audiencia a ban on the export of maize from Teocaltiche and Tlaltenango to New Biscay. See AA.Z, 5, No. 40; AA.Z, LC 3, ff. 287v., 294, 295v., 298-298v.
[4] AA.Z, LC 3, f. 302, cabildo of 31 August 1634.

Supplies and Distribution

Thus in 1696 one Juan Ignacio de Algarra y Loyola made a successful bid for two years' lease, with a promise to pay 1,400 pesos a year.[1] By this time a grain store (*pósito*) had been added. The alhóndiga was largely an exchange through which grain passed rapidly; its storage capacity was evidently small, for in September 1693 a week's lapse in arrivals of wheat left it empty.[2] But in the previous year the town had at long last learnt its lesson, as yet once again a sudden shortage of cereals had brought soaring prices in its train. It was decided to guard against further repetition of the circumstance by establishing a pósito. This was, as Florescano points out, something more than a mere store. It was also a depository of public or municipal capital, to be used for buying in grain when markets were most favourable, and distributing it at times of scarcity with the specific aim of suppressing prices to a level accessible to poorer members of the community. The initial working capital of the Zacatecas pósito was a loan of 6,100 pesos made by the corregidor and various important citizens. With this sum an alcalde ordinario was dispatched to buy maize in the Canyons and as far off as León and Lagos.[3]

The efficacy of the alhóndiga in regulating prices is unknowable. Its function was mainly that of a retail market – indeed, it was designed to prevent the resale of grain and flour anywhere in the city besides within its walls. But even if it did succeed in restraining the activities of regraters, the fundamental causes of price rises in grain were obviously beyond its reach – droughts, bad harvests and consequent scarcity. The pósito was a more ambitious institution, since it was intended to go some way towards combating market forces. But it is difficult to imagine that even its far larger stocks of grain, sold at reduced prices, would have been sufficient to influence wholesale prices for very long – at least, not without placing an unacceptable burden on the local community, which had in the long run, through taxes and loans, to provide cash for the purchase of the grain stocks of the pósito. And even once grain had legally passed through the alhóndiga, the story was not at an end; for since private stores of grain could legally be accumulated, providing the purchases had been made in the proper way, the possibility of regrating and profiteering still remained. No doubt speculators did buy in times of glut and low prices with a view to selling in lean months. On frequent occasions the cabildo exercised

[1] AA.Z, 11, No. 39, 'Arrendamiento de las alhóndigas por dos años que se cumplen el día 4 de septiembre de 1698', 4 September 1696.

[2] AA.Z, 11, No. 14, f. 7, Zacatecas 29 September 1693.

[3] AA.Z, 11, No. 24, 'Autos fechos sobre el pósito que se ha de hacer de harinas y maízes a Don Juan Rendón' (n.e.d.) 1692. See Enrique Florescano's informative article 'El abasto y la legislación de granos en el siglo XVI', *Historia Mexicana*, vol. 14, No. 4, pp. 567–630. For particular reference to pósito and alhóndiga, see pp. 611–24.

Supplies and Distribution

compulsory purchase of private reserves of grain when there was a shortage, going to the lengths of inspecting houses to discover hoards.

Most surviving information on prices derives from regulations issued by the cabildo, which referred to retail costs at the baker's, of wheat bread and bran. (Data on maize are so scarce as to be useless.) The weight of these to be sold for one real varied with the current wholesale price of wheat. Thus in 1663 the Corregidor set a sliding scale for bread and bran prices according to the cost of wheat.[1]

Price of wheat (pesos per carga)	oz. of bread	oz. of bran
7–8	28 per real	56 per real
9–10	26	54
11–13	24	52
14–16	22	50

Some wheat, bread and bran prices are given in Table 2. It is difficult to draw anything but the most general conclusion from them, since the cabildo issued regulations only when prices were exceptional and when control was urgently needed. Thus the bread prices are not necessarily representative of the normal state of affairs. Short-term fluctuations were wide: not only because of variations in production from year to year and from season to season, but also because a temporary halt in the supply to the city, which was without ample stocks and largely dependent on provisions from distant regions, could result in sudden scarcity and a leap in prices.[2] But even from these scant figures there emerges a notable stability in bread prices from the end of the sixteenth century to 1670.[3] Abundant production from the Bajío, made possible by the extensive methods of cultivation suggested by Chevalier, is probably responsible for this in part, together with the decline of the mines in the mid-century, which tended to depress all prices. Unfortunately, no information is available for the years of the first mining boom of Zacatecas during the 1620s, when a rise in prices might reasonably be expected. But the high

---

[1] AA.Z, 8, Zacatecas 18 July 1663, Corregidor Don García de Vargas Manrique.
[2] No complaints were found of conscious manipulation of the Zacatecas grain market through withholding of supplies by growers.
[3] Stability of maize prices obtained in Mexico City during the seventeenth century. A basic level of 10–12 reales per fanega was interrupted by only occasional sharp rises caused by temporary shortages. See C. L. Guthrie, 'Colonial Economy. Trade, Industry and Labor in Seventeenth Century Mexico City', *Revista de Historia de América*, No. 7, December 1939, pp. 103–34; here p. 114.

levels of 1693 and 1695 can be tentatively accounted for by the increasing mining prosperity of that time; there is also evidence of scarcity of all grains in those years.[1] Data for the sixteenth century are so poor that little commentary can be made on them. Prices were doubtless heavily influenced by Indian hostility in the form of attacks on farms, wagon-trains and pack-trains. For instance, the near isolation of Zacatecas in 1561 brought wheat to a price not to be equalled until the end of the seventeenth century; but the normal price in the 1560s was some $9\frac{1}{2}$ pesos per carga, a figure apparently not far below the normal levels of the seventeenth century.[2]

Zacatecas was obliged to draw its grain supplies from distant regions. But meat was available closer at hand. At the beginning of the seventeenth century Bishop Mota y Escobar observed that in all the 18 leagues that lay between Mecatabasco and Zacatecas, and over all the similar distance between Aguascalientes and Zacatecas, there was not so much as an Indian pueblo to be seen, nor any other settlement except numerous sheep and cattle ranches.[3] Zacatecas was indeed surrounded by ranching lands. The high steppe of the plateau made for poor farming, but the rough grass and scrub was pasture palatable enough to cattle and sheep. The traveller approaching the city from any side, even only a few years after the foundation, would have seen on his way numerous herds of cattle, and little other sign of life. The west was particularly rich in livestock. The banks of the Río Grande afforded fine pasture;[4] and it was here that the hacienda of Trujillo stood, the centre of a vast estate on which Diego de Ibarra branded in 1586 33,000 young steers (*novillos*). His northern neighbour, Rodrigo de Río de Losa, branded 42,000 head in the same year on his estates extending northwards from Sombrerete

---

[1] AA.Z, 11, No. 24. Again in 1693 the cabildo had to despatch an agent to buy maize in the south.

[2] Even this was more than seven times the price in Mexico City. See W. W. Borah and S. F. Cook, *Price Trends of Some Basic Commodities in Central Mexico, 1531–1570*, Ibero-Americana: 40, University of California Press, Berkeley and Los Angeles 1958, pp. 19–23. Chevalier, in *La formation*, p. 74, points out the extraordinary price of grain in Zacatecas in 1550, before adequate communications were developed. The price was more than sixty times what it had been in Guadalajara in 1547. Prices soared firstly because of scarcity of supply and secondly because of the flood of silver spreading outwards from Zacatecas. As early as 1551 there were complaints about high prices in Compostela. These were reiterated in 1560 by the oidores of New Galicia. See AGI Guadalajara 5, 13 January 1560, 'Información recibida de oficio por la Audiencia Real de su majestad del Nuevo Reino de Galicia sobre los gastos y costas que tienen, para suplicar a su majestad les acreciente el salario'. The high prices were attributed to Compostela's isolation; but were certainly caused in part by the increased circulation of silver.

[3] 'Estancias de ganados mayores y menores.' *Ganado mayor* comprised cattle, mules and horses; *ganado menor*, sheep, goats and pigs.

[4] Paso y Troncoso, *Papeles, 2a. serie*, vol. 8, p. 310, 'Relación de Fresnillo', 1585.

Supplies and Distribution

and Cuencamé.[1] Cattle and silver were commodities which the inhabitants of the Zacatecas district could produce in quantity.

In time, the cabildo of the city came to exercise a closer control over the supply of meat than it ever could over that of grain. The fact that production was local enabled it to draw up and supervise contracts (*asientos*) with breeders for provisioning the city over a specific period of time. Like all Spanish American towns, Zacatecas possessed an official abattoir (the *carnicería*, later known as the *rastro*) from an early date.[2] The first reference to it that has been found occurs in 1587.[3] At that time it was evidently functioning as a free meat market to which stock-raisers took their animals for slaughter and sale. No restrictions appear to have been placed on the sale of meat apart from the rule that transactions should take place in the carnicería. Some attempt had been made by this year to establish what later became the regular system of supply; the periodic auctioning of an asiento to a single breeder by which he was to provide meat at a fixed price. But efforts had not been successful, since in 1587 it was said that owners of mine haciendas were sending their workers every Saturday to kill cattle in the carnicería to secure the following week's meat for the labour forces (*cuadrillas*) of their mines and haciendas. This practice was forty years old, but was considered undesirable by some since it gave rise to riots and fights among Indian and Negro bands from different haciendas.[4] But there was no advance on this system until 1609, when a visitor-general to New Galicia, Licenciado Gaspar de la Fuente, reported that in the absence of a regular supply by contract, the indiscriminate slaughter of cattle by the inhabitants of Zacatecas was seriously diminishing the livestock of New Galicia.[5] The cabildo quickly produced a bidder for a contract, who promised to provide young beef (*carne de novillo*) at 8 lb. the real.[6] The first complete asiento to survive is that of 1612–13, drawn up with two citizens of Zacatecas, Juan González Hidalgo and Hernando Ortiz de Río, after competitive bidding. It took

---

[1] Basalenque, *Historia de la Provincia*, p. 364.
[2] The *Ordenanzas para . . . nuevas poblaciones* of 1573 (clause 122) advised siting the carnicería, fish market, tannery, and other establishments producing noisome waste, where this could easily be disposed of. In Zacatecas, the abattoir was outside the built-up area, to the south.
[3] An auto acordado of the Audiencia of New Spain in 1584 ordered the foundation of a carnicería in every Spanish town, to be run on a system of auction, as was later done in Zacatecas. E. B. Beleña, *Recopilación sumaria de todos los autos acordados de la Real Audiencia y Sala de Crimen de esta Nueva España y providencias de su superior gobierno*, México 1787, 2 vols., vol. 1, p. 24, No. xxxvii, 27 January 1584.
[4] AGI Guadalajara 35, No. 16, ff. 8, 30v., 'Baltasar Temiño de Bañuelos sobre que se le haga merced de un regimiento de los Zacatecas', (n.e.d.) 1587.
[5] AA.Z, LC 2, f. 231, Zacatecas 12 January 1609, 'Licenciado Gaspar de la Fuente, visitador general de la Nueva Galicia'.
[6] AA.Z, LC 2, f. 233, cabildo of 11 February 1609.

the form characteristic of its successors. The contractors undertook to supply, at fixed prices, beef and mutton, both on the hoof and as dressed carcases. Fixed prices were also proposed for offal, hides and tallow. A specified quantity of meat was to be sent each week to all the monasteries and to the prison; and bulls were to be provided for use in the ring on feast days two or three times a year (the normal stipulation was for the Shrovetide celebrations and for those of the birth of Our Lady in September). Finally, the successful bidder was to pay a cash sum (*prometido*) to the city. In return for these obligations he obtained a virtual monopoly of the meat supply to Zacatecas. The usual privileges attached to the contract were that no-one else was to be allowed to slaughter cattle, either for his own use or for sale. Nor might anyone sell tallow candles; this was a valuable concession, for the demand for candles to light the mines was always high. No other abattoir should be permitted in the city or in its jurisdiction. The only exceptions made to these conditions were that miners were normally allowed to buy cattle from stock-raisers other than the *asentista* and kill them for consumption in their own haciendas, providing that purchases were registered before the corregidor. Occasionally miners were also given permission to manufacture candles for their own use.[1]

This contractual system functioned adequately for most of the seventeenth century. The competitions for asientos were held every one or two years, according to the length of the contract. Sometimes there was difficulty in finding bidders; one such occasion was 1648, when two months of proclamations announcing the opening of bidding failed to produce any offers.[2] The mining depression of the mid-century, with its accompanying slump in prices, was doubtless responsible for the un-willingness of stock-raisers to commit themselves to what must often have been an enterprise of uncertain profitability. There was always difficulty in maintaining the monopoly; and where the representation of mining and land-owning interests on the cabildo was as great as it normally was in Zacatecas, it would be surprising if infringements were not sometimes ignored. (The valuable manufacture of candles, for example, was often too great a temptation for the townsfolk; asentistas constantly complained that illicit manufactures were undermining their sales.) There are many instances of unauthorised persons slaughtering cattle. Nevertheless, the asiento continued to operate, probably in favour

---

1 The first asiento, of 1612–13, is in AA.Z, 3, No. 8, *remate* of 19 January 1612. Other asientos are to be found in AA.Z, 3, 4, 5, 6, 7, 10 and 11. Surviving examples are rarer in the second half of the seventeenth century.
AA.Z, 6, No. 92, asiento of 1648, finally awarded to Diego de Salas, 6 October 1648.

Supplies and Distribution

of the citizens. The auctioning of the contract to the best bidder did at least assure a supply of meat at a fixed price, even if free-market prices might have from time to time been lower still. Bidding appears to have been conducted fairly by the cabildo, which showed itself active in seeking provisions. In 1687 it sent letters advertising opening of bidding in March of that year to Aguascalientes, San Miguel, Santa María de los Lagos and San Luis Potosí.[1] The purpose of the system of auction, according to an *auto acordado* of the Audiencia of Mexico in 1583, was to ensure a steady supply of meat, to control prices and weights and to submit the processes of slaughter and sale to the inspection of officers of justice.[2] On the whole, the operation of the asiento in Zacatecas seems to have fulfilled these objects.[3]

The asientos offer interesting information on prices of meat in the seventeenth century, which is presented in Table 3. Price data are also available for the sixteenth century, although not for the city itself. Graph 4 was drawn up from prices paid for novillos by the Crown officials who supervised the *salinas* of Peñol Blanco and Santa María, to the east of Zacatecas. These salt pans, from which the *saltierra* necessary for processing silver ore came, were worked until the late 1620s by Indians drawn from the canyons of the south. In 1629, extraction of salt was handed over to private contractors. Officials provided food for the workers at royal expense, buying cattle on the open market from stockraisers. Records of purchases survive in special account books kept for the salinas, but naturally stop at the time when direct management by the Crown was removed.

The progress of beef prices is shown clearly by the graph. After initial irregularities in the 1560s, the price settles at four pesos per animal for almost thirty years. From the beginning of the seventeenth century until the end of the record, it shows a steep but fluctuating rise. This rise is indicated similarly in the terms of the asientos, where the amount of beef given for one real falls steadily from 1612 to 1627. But by 1640, the price of a pound of beef, and also of a bullock hide, has fallen by a half. There is also a decrease, although not so pronounced, in the price of mutton and tallow. Levels then apparently rise quite slowly towards the end of the century; although the absence of information between 1652 and 1691 makes generalisation of little value.

[1] AA.Z, 10, No. 50, cabildo to 'General' of San Luis Potosí, Zacatecas 2 February 1687.
[2] Beleña, *Recopilación sumaria*, vol. 1, p. 24, No. xxxvi, auto of 19 October 1583.
[3] See W. H. Dusenberry, 'The Regulation of Meat Supply in Sixteenth Century Mexico City', *HAHR* vol. 28, 1948, pp. 38–52. The system functioning in Zacatecas was similar to that in Mexico City.

Supplies and Distribution

There are two principal reasons for this pattern of price changes, one general to New Spain and one particular to the Zacatecas district. The livestock explosion of sixteenth-century New Spain is one of the outstanding features of the history of the period.[1] And even in the north, troubled as it was by the Chichimecs, cattle and sheep proliferated; some idea of the size of Ibarra's and Río de Losa's herds has already been given. But towards the end of the century there came a tendency to stabilisation among the herds of the centre and south. Vast slaughter of animals for hides, a growing taste for meat among southern Indians, and, most important, exhaustion of pasture, seem to have been the reasons for the levelling off of the curve.[2] Exports of cattle from New Galicia to the south had always taken place, and increased in the last years of the sixteenth century and the early years of the seventeenth. This drawing-off of stock, combined with a fall in the size of herds in parts of New Galicia itself, caused an increase of price there in the early seventeenth century.[3] Slaughter of breeding cows for their hides and excessive exports to New Spain were the causes adduced by the Bishop and Chapter of Guadalajara in 1606 when they complained of diminution of the yield of their tithes resulting from scarcity of cattle.[4] Legislation controlling exports was difficult to enforce, and in any case, the damage was done. High prices attracted cattle southwards just as high prices attracted grain northwards. The first three decades of the seventeenth century also saw the first major boom of the mines of the Zacatecas district; the upward movement of beef prices coincides with the climb of the curve tracing the boom, as might be expected. Increased production of silver led to increases in prices. By 1640 production had fallen drastically, and beef prices in the city, as noted above, had slumped by a half. The coincidence in the remainder of the century between fluctuations in the production of silver and in the cost of beef is observable, but not exact. The data are insufficient; but it appears that prices began to rise slowly long before silver had recovered from its mid-century decline. Continued shortage of cattle is

---

[1] See L. B. Simpson, *Exploitation of Land in Central Mexico in the Sixteenth Century*, Ibero-Americana: 36, University of California Press, Berkeley and Los Angeles 1952; particularly the graph in the frontispiece. Simpson does not deal with New Galicia; but ranching grew as quickly there as in the south.

[2] Chevalier, *La formation*, pp. 128–30.

[3] AGI Guadalajara 7, R. 6, 17 April 1607, Licenciado Juan de Paz de Vallecillo to Crown. He stated that between 1594 and 1607 the number of yearling cattle (*becerros*) in the vicinity of Guadalajara had fallen from 23,000 to less than 5,000.

[4] AGI Guadalajara 236, AA, 1, f. 114–114v., Crown to Montesclaros, real cédula, Madrid 27 March 1606. Rodrigo de Río de Losa had on one occasion sold more than 60,000 head in Mexico City. Francisco de Urdiñola was another offender; with other breeders he exported over 20,000 head a year.

indicated by this; although not of sheep, for the cost of a *carnero* fell constantly from 1645 to 1691. But in the absence of information about trends in the livestock population of the whole of New Spain in the latter part of the seventeenth century, any speculation about movements of prices, even at a specific point such as Zacatecas, must be of very doubtful value. Nor is there any remaining record for the seventeenth century of the absolute and relative numbers of cattle and sheep consumed. This knowledge would be of the greatest value in an attempt to calculate the effect of changes in meat prices on the cost of living in the period.[1]

Supplementary to its basic needs of maize, wheat and meat, Zacatecas was supplied with a great variety of lesser foodstuffs, revealed by inventories of shops and by libros de manifestaciones. Perhaps the single most important item was wine. Some was imported from Spain, although much of the so-called *vino de Castilla* came from the vineyards of Parras, in the north of the Zacatecas district just over the border with New Biscay. Wine was one of the major sources of alcabalas and for a long time was also subject to a special excise tax (*sisa del vino*), which yielded a proportion of the municipality's income. Trade in wine was brisk and profitable, but caused misgivings among authorities responsible for public order. It was generally forbidden (and the prohibition was generally ignored) to sell grape wine to Indians, mulattos and Negroes, since their intoxication led to violent fights and to casualties. But no such ban was placed on the sale of alcoholic drinks derived from coconuts (*vino de cocos*) and from the maguey cactus (*vino de mescal*). These spirits contained more alcohol, but their effect on non-Spaniards was nevertheless considered less harmful than that of grape wine.[2] But while wine of any variety remained a good source of public and private income, it is hardly surprising that bans on its sale were lightly observed and sporadically enforced. Of sixty-six transactions recorded in a book of alcabalas for the first half of 1591, half were sales of wine. It was a thriving business.[3]

Other provisions were drawn, as ever, from a wide area. Libros de manifestaciones for the mid-seventeenth century show that sugar, largely

---

[1] In 1732, 40,000 sheep were consumed, 5,200 hogs and 4,000 cattle. See Ribera Bernárdez, *Descripción breve*, p. 81. The high proportion of sheep is significant, if it also obtained for the seventeenth century, since prices of mutton varied less than those of beef.

[2] Bans on the sale of vino de Castilla to Indians and castes throughout Spanish America were, of course, common. A Zacatecan example is that issued by Corregidor Don Juan de Cervantes Casaus, 17 June 1620, in AA.Z, 2, No. 2.

[3] AT.Z, Reales Oficiales 1, 'Testimonio que da Alonso de Avila León ... desde principio del año de mil y quinientos y noventa y un años', (n.e.d.) 1591.

Supplies and Distribution

in the crudely refined form known as *muscovado* (*chancaca* in New Spain) came mainly from Michoacán (specifically from Jacona, Pinsándaro and Pátzcuaro). Dried and cured meats (*cecina de puerco* and *jamones*) were produced in large quantities at Teocaltiche; again the southern canyons appear as Zacatecan horns of plenty. Sayula, in present-day Jalisco to the south of Lake Chapala, supplied vino de mescal. Parras was the source of grape wine; and Colima, on the Pacific coast, that of coconut wine. Cacao arrived from Caracas, Maracaibo and Guatemala, supplementing the supply of chocolate grown in New Spain.[1] Salt fish, a useful source of protein, was a product of Michoacán, with its many lakes and rivers. Salted catfish (*bagre*) was brought to Zacatecas from Chapala, Pinsándaro and La Barca. Chiametla, on the coast, contributed bass and shrimps. Cheese, another important protein food, arrived from Aguascalientes. Leguminous foods included frijoles (from Teocaltiche, Aguascalientes and Jalostotitlán), lentils (from Jacona and Zamora in Michoacán) and chick-peas (from along the Río Grande).[2]

Closer at hand lay the sources of fresh vegetables and fruit, which were grown in market gardens (*huertas*) occupying the bottom-lands of valleys around the city, and principally the main valley leading out to the south-east. Once again, Bishop Mota y Escobar, as ever an enthusiastic observer, is informative. 'The fruits of Castile all reach great ripeness. There are cherries, although they do not grow very well, peaches, figs and splendid grapes. But of all the fruits of Castile that grow here, the best are the apples and pears, which rival those of Ocaña and Nájera. Vegetables, greenstuffs and legumes of every sort grow well in the extreme. Some Spaniards own large gardens outside the city, cultivating vegetables and fruit and nopales, from which they derive much profit and have enriched themselves with their business.'[3] And, although allowance must be made for the Bishop's usual optimism, there is no doubt that the huertas were profitable undertakings; there was rarely difficulty in finding purchasers and tenants for them. One of the best known was the *huerta de abajo* (later called the *huerta de Melgar* after one of its owners in the early seventeenth century). It was situated at the end of the main valley, and

---

[1] For exports of cacao from Venezuela to New Spain in the seventeenth century, see E. Arcila Farías, *Comercio entre Venezuela y México en los siglos XVII y XVIII*, México 1950, especially pp. 52–5. In the seventeenth century New Spain took far more Venezuelan cacao than Spain.

[2] AT.Z, Reales Oficiales 14, Libro de manifestaciones for 1 January to 4 July 1655; AA.Z, 7, No. 55, manifestaciones of 4 September 1658; AA.Z, 8, No. 4, manifestaciones of March–April 1660; AT.Z, Reales Oficiales 24, 'Cuaderno donde se toma razón de las entradas de los arrieros que vienen de México y la Puebla con hacienda para vecinos de esta ciudad de Nuestra Señora de los Zacatecas', (n.e.d.) 1662.

[3] Mota y Escobar, *Descripción*, p. 67.

Supplies and Distribution

in the eighteenth century was incorporated into the grounds of the newly-built Franciscan Colegio de Guadalupe. A huerta formed a self-contained unit, with dwelling house, accommodation for workers, and perhaps a chapel. The all-important water supply normally came from a well with a bucket chain; water was stored in stone tanks. Mules and donkeys were kept to operate the *noria* and to carry produce. The selling price of a good huerta, even during the impoverished years of the mid-century, was high: examples in 1656 and 1659 were sold for 4,000 and 2,000 pesos each.[1]

Municipal regulations required that lesser food-stuffs (including huerta produce) should be registered before authority on arrival in the city, in the same way as grains and meat. Clause 23 of la Marcha's Ordinances of 27 April 1550 bids that anyone bringing goods for sale into Zacatecas should declare them before an officer of justice within three days, so that a price could be assessed for them.[2] Sale before declaration, or at a price higher than that fixed, was punishable. As with grain, the object was not so much to impose a permanent fixed price on goods, irrespective of the conditions of supply and demand; but rather to prevent profiteering. Indians selling their own produce were not subject to this provision, so long as they traded in the plaza pública or in one or two other specified places.[3] Among food-stuffs, Indian produce was the exception in not being liable to control. But goods other than foods, although they had to be declared and were naturally liable to alcabala, did not, in practice, undergo regulation of price. Some constantly recurring imports were textile goods (including blankets, clothes and hats as well as simple cloth) from Puebla, Campeche, Spain and China; soap, from Puebla; leather goods (especially shoes) from Michoacán and specifically from Sayula; earthenware from Guadalajara and Michoacán. From Mexico City there flowed in a variety of merchandise, including, of course, items imported into New Spain; two of the principal materials demanded by the mining

---

[1] AN.Z, FE 1656, ff. 69–70, sale of huerta by Bartolomé de Herrera to Captain Juan de Ugarte, 1 April 1656. AN.Z, FE 1659, ff. 235v.–7, sale of huerta de Melgar by Pedro Ruiz de Oliver to Juan de Salas, for 2,000 pesos, 6 November 1659.

[2] The principle of declaration of goods was common. See *Recopilación* 1680, IV ix 22; and la Marcha's ordinances, 27 April 1550, clause 23, in AGI Guadalajara 5, 'Averiguaciones ... Contreras y Guevara ... 1570', f. 118v.

[3] AGI Guadalajara 5, 'Averiguaciones ... Contreras y Guevara ... 1570', ff. 122–37, 'Este es un treslado bien y fielmente sacado de unas ordenanzas que hizo en las minas de los Zacatecas el Señor Licenciado Don Francisco de Mendiola, oidor alcalde mayor de la Real Audiencia de este reino de Galicia según que por ella parecía, su tenor del cual es éste que se sigue', Zacatecas 6 March 1568: here, clause 11 (ff. 123–4); and AGI Patronato 238, R. 2, No. 3, 'Ordenanzas hechas por el Licenciado Santiago del Riego, oidor de la Real Audiencia del nuevo reino de Galicia para el arreglo de las minas y real de Zacatecas y Pánuco', Zacatecas 10 August 1576 (n.f.).

industry, iron and steel, passed through the capital to Zacatecas.[1] But if it was not thought necessary to impose some retail price control on these durable goods, food was a different matter. The frequency with which orders requiring declaration is repeated shows how far they were disregarded, and how easily the isolated market of Zacatecas could be exploited.[2] A common practice was to intercept incoming traders on the road into the town, buy their goods, and thus prevent these from reaching the market-place and shops. This was strictly forbidden by an order of 1620, which reinforced the old rules calling for declaration of goods before sale. But merchants of the city continued to attempt to corner the market.[3] Some evidence that merchants heeded price regulations, however, at least at the end of the century, is afforded by a petition from a group of shopkeepers to the corregidor in 1684 for increases in assessed prices on certain goods. Here again, that price fixing by the civic authority applied to retail goods, and that assessments were adjusted according to current conditions, is shown by these merchants' complaint that wholesale prices of certain Castilian items were high, and profits had been consequently reduced. The merchants succinctly presented the trading situation of Zacatecas when, as their second reason for demanding higher prices, they commented that 'all the other goods [i.e. apart from those of Castile previously mentioned] that enter this city come in by cart, and the shortage or surfeit of them is what sets their prices, since no supplies grow in this city nor in its jurisdiction . . .'.[4]

Goods, once in Zacatecas, were distributed through the market in the plaza pública or through retail shops. The number of these varied in the seventeenth century with the prosperity of mining. Mota y Escobar provides the first count: he estimated the number at about fifty. By 1608 there were 'more than fifty', and by 1615, these had increased to eighty-one. The maximum in the period 1600–50, for which there are records,

---

[1] Sources as in note 2, p. 74. The supply of raw materials to mining will be discussed in ch. 6.

[2] See for example AGI Guadalajara 6, R. 4, 28 March 1600, Oidor Pinedo to Crown. He complains of the ubiquity of profiteering. 'The common judges (*jueces ordinarios*) are the biggest regraters, even of shoes and candles and the least things of all.' He is referring to the whole of New Galicia.

[3] AA.Z, 4, No. 38, 'Yo, Mateo de Herrera, escribano . . . doy fe que entre las ordenanzas que el doctor Antonio Roque del Cotero parece hizo siendo justicia de esta dicha ciudad para el buen gobierno de ella está la siguiente . . .'. The order refers in particular to 'those merchants [who] with particular care buy all the Castilian and native goods that arrive in this city, and other goods which are generally in short supply, in order to sell them at excessive prices, all to the great harm and disadvantage of the poor and the citizens . . .'. N.d., but certainly 1620.

[4] AA.Z, 10, No. 25, *gremio de mercaderes* to Corregidor Captain Don Tomás Freide de Somorrostro, (n.e.d.) February 1684.

was ninety-nine in 1621. Then came a gradual decline: ninety-eight (1622), eighty-one (1633), seventy (1644), sixty-eight (1650).[1] An analysis of 106 persons paying alcabalas in 1656–7 shows that sixty-one were keepers of shops of one sort or another. The most common was grocery store (*tienda de menudencias*) of which there were thirty-three; general stores selling mainly dry goods (*tiendas de mercadurías*) numbered twenty. Other shops dealt in clothes (three), cured meats (two), wax and candles (one), doublets (one); there was one master confectioner. The remaining payers of alcabalas were carters and sellers of wood and charcoal (sixteen), shoemakers (fifteen), vendors in the mines (three), owners of huertas (three), carters (two), persons slaughtering cattle in haciendas de minas (two), shopkeepers in Pánuco (two), and one tannery owner. One person's occupation is not described.[2] There are obviously notable omissions from the list. The absence of the numerous tailors of Zacatecas is conspicuous. But it is clear that at this time, as at others, there were far more merchants and shopkeepers in Zacatecas than owners of mines and of haciendas de minas. This is testimony to the city's importance as the trading centre. (The obvious fact that shopkeeping was less hazardous an occupation than mining must also be pointed out. Investment necessary for setting up a shop was far less than that required to enter mining, and gave a steadier return. When mining was at a low ebb, numerous shop-keepers went out of business, it is true; but a higher proportion of miners suffered bankruptcy.) In addition to these permanently established merchants of Zacatecas, there were also a large number of travellers, who sold where they could, carrying their goods on pack trains. Mota y Escobar reported a floating population of 100 to 200 traders and men of affairs at the beginning of the seventeenth century.[3] Doubtless, owners of pack-trains and wagons engaged in trading in their own right. In the lesser mining towns the travelling merchant was the prime source of goods; established shops seem to have been few, probably because of the difficulty of maintaining an adequate flow of stocks. The traveller was obviously at an advantage in such a situation, since he had quick access to wholesale markets.[4] Merchants in Zacatecas sometimes operated branches

[1] Mota y Escobar, *Descripción*, p. 66; *DII*, vol. 9, p. 187; AA.Z, 3, No. 9; AA.Z, 4, No. 8; AA.Z, 4, No. 16; AA.Z, 5, No. 27; AA.Z, 6, No. 106; AA.Z, 7, No. 1. These are inspections of shops (*visitas de tiendas*) undertaken by the cabildo in 1615, 1621, 1622, 1633, 1649 and 1650.

[2] AT.Z, Reales Oficiales 17, untitled book of alcabalas collected in Zacatecas from February 1656 to February 1657.

[3] Mota y Escobar, *Descripción*, p. 66.

[4] AT.Z, Reales Oficiales 17, book of alcabalas paid to Captain Domingo de Barreda y Cevallo. Of twenty-one recorded payments of alcabalas in Mazapil from April 1655 to February 1657, ten were made by *mercaderes viandantes*.

in smaller towns, run by partners or managers, to which they sent consignments of goods.[1] The same sort of simple company bound some merchants in Zacatecas itself to Mexico City. The unfortunate lack of notarial documents for the first half of the seventeenth century makes it impossible to say when such bonds began to form, but they were common in the later part of the century. The first contract of this sort that was found joined a merchant not of the capital, but of Puebla, to a citizen of Zacatecas. Martín Fernández de Colmedo, of Puebla, had provided capital to set up Sebastián Osorio in a retail business in Zacatecas. No details of the contract were given.[2] A contract going still further afield was that agreed between Captain Martín de la Mata and Don Juan de Mena in 1684. La Mata was a merchant and citizen of Seville, resident in Mexico City; he had delivered Castilian goods worth just over 5,000 pesos to Mena for sale in Zacatecas. There was difficulty in selling them, and Mena was obliged to return them.[3] This is the only known instance of such a direct link between Zacatecas and the sources of goods in Spain; normally goods would pass through the hands of middlemen in Mexico City. La Mata was evidently acting as his own agent there.[4] Simple shop companies were often set up between merchants in Zacatecas itself; one provided the capital and the other the labour. Profits were shared equally, or according to the participation of the partners. No discussion will be made at this point of the effects of this transference of capital from the south to Zacatecas; trading credit forms only a part of the large general movement of credit northwards in the second half of the seventeenth century, which was highly significant for the development of the mining industry. This larger issue will be discussed in its place.

In 1587, Baltasar de Bañuelos, writing to the king about Zacatecas' commercial importance, noted that trading northwards from the city extended more than 200 leagues into the 'inner lands' (the *tierra adentro*). From Zacatecas went goods to the mines of Santa Bárbara, Indehé, Avino and New León, to mention only a few destinations.[5] It was always

[1] For example, AN.Z, FE 1676 (n.f.), *obligación* of Francisco Serrano Carrasco to Juan de Retana, signed in Zacatecas, 25 November 1675. By this contract Serrano carried 5,000 pesos' worth of goods to Mazapil, for sale there. Retana supplied the goods, taking half the profit. The other half went to Serrano for his labour.

[2] AN.Z, FE 1653A, *poder* (power of attorney) of Martín Fernández de Colmedo to Captain Gregorio Gómez de Bustamante, Puebla 9 September 1652.

[3] AN.Z, JM 1684–5, f. 43–43v., Zacatecas 27 September 1648, obligación of Don Juan de Mena, resident and merchant of Zacatecas, to Captain Martín de la Mata, citizen and merchant of Seville.

[4] For a brief account of the normal distribution of European goods in New Spain in this period, see J. J. Real Díaz, *Las ferias de Jalapa*, Seville 1959, p. 10.

[5] AGI Guadalajara 20, Zacatecas 2 April 1587, Baltasar de Bañuelos to Crown.

the boast of the citizens that Zacatecas was the 'gateway to the north' – a point of exchange to which the carters of the south brought their goods, and to which the traders and settlers of the far north flocked to buy their supplies. The city's geographical position was largely responsible for its assuming this rôle; but its wealth and size also made it a good market in itself, a focal point for the whole of the north. As were all other aspects of Zacatecan life, this trading function was greatly altered after the collapse of the mining boom in the early 1630s. For the previous fifty years or more, Zacatecas had been the richest city in New Galicia, New Biscay and New León; but now, not only were its own sources of prosperity beginning to dry up, but a rival centre of attraction was developing in the north. This was Parral, where a rich silver strike was made in 1631. After this, it became worthwhile for traders from central Mexico to carry their goods further up into New Biscay, avoiding Zacatecas, which thus suffered a loss of income and consequence as a point of exchange. In 1652, a member of the cabildo could write that as a result of the Parral strike 'total ruin has afflicted this city, from emigration both of its citizens and of its mine workers; for the greater part of the population of Parral is drawn from this city; and this has not been the only evil, for this city was the gateway to all the cities, towns and mining reales of all the said kingdom of Biscay, and all the silver that was extracted there was traded here; this trading made up a large part of its [Zacatecas'] commerce. And all this has completely stopped, for all that kingdom, and the mines of Parral, is supplied with the abundant and plentiful goods that enter it on wagon-trains.'[1] The rise of Parral was only part of the reason for the decline of Zacatecas as an entrepôt. Certainly, by the mid-century, when the above report was made, the depression of Zacatecas, and indeed of the economy of New Spain in general, was largely to blame for the falling-off of trade. The situation improved towards the end of the century as mining prosperity returned to the city. A document of 1689 refers to the 'fat commerce' ('grueso comercio') of Zacatecas,[2] and in 1696 it was said that 40,000 pesos a year could be collected in alcabalas; which, if it was a true estimate, was more than the tax had ever been worth before. It was also reported that all goods for Sombrerete and New Biscay had to pass through Zacatecas, so that a return to the trading pattern of pre-Parral days appears to have taken place.[3] At least, the northward-bound traffic was passing through again, although perhaps the business of

---

[1] AA.Z, 7, No. 24, Zacatecas 4 June 1652, report of Nicolás de Gueycoichea, *depositario general*.

[2] AGI Guadalajara 21, Guadalajara 22 June 1689, Visitor Feijoo Centellas to Crown.

[3] AGI Guadalajara 232, Z 8, ff. 51v.–5v., Madrid 6 November 1696, letter from Crown to Viceroy Sarmiento de Valladares.

exchange was not being conducted as fruitfully as before. It is not true to say, of course, that Zacatecas had been, even at its height, the sole distribution point for all the settlements of the north; naturally, lesser towns, such as Sombrerete, served as local centres.[1] But the ultimate source of their stocks was Zacatecas. And it would not be an exaggeration to suggest that, up to the time of Parral, there was a 'beyond-the-line' feeling about the lands to the north of the city, the tierra adentro. The penetration of wagon-trains and mule-trains from central Mexico into the fastnesses of New Biscay after 1631 can only have served to dissipate this feeling. Zacatecas' position on this largely psychological frontier between southern civilisation and northern barbarism had helped it to develop as an entrepôt. It could never recover the same function once the 'frontier' had been dissolved, although, as the reports quoted above show, it still lay on the road to the north and received the benefits deriving from passing traffic.

The Zacatecas of the market place, the warehouse and the shop is not the one celebrated by modern writers on the city and by local singers of its colonial glory. Yet commerce was an activity second only to mining; and in the minds of the vecinos, wealth derived firstly from silver and then from trading with central Mexico and with the north. 'Among the noble vecinos', said Mota y Escobar, 'few are rich, and those are miners; but among the middling people there are many with fortunes of twenty, thirty and forty thousand pesos, and there may be three or four worth a hundred thousand, and all these are merchants with public shops ...'.[2] In these pages, some idea has been given of the vast extent and variety of the region over which Zacatecas cast its influence; it is obvious that the prosperity of wide agricultural areas of northern New Spain depended to a large extent on the mineral output and prosperity of Zacatecas and its district. Examination of these wider effects, however, lies outside the range of this study, which is concerned with the city and its region. The administration and government of these must now receive some attention.

---

[1] AT.Z, Reales Oficiales 2, Zacatecas 22 January 1604, *expediente* 'Los apuntamientos que dieron los mineros sobre lo del ensayar'. Para. 5 states that Sombrerete, with its officers of justice and other officials, served as a trading centre for mining towns in the north of the Zacatecas district: San Martín, Chalchihuites, Avino and El Peñol.

[2] Mota y Escobar, *Descripción*, p. 66.

CHAPTER 5

CORREGIDOR AND CABILDO

There is perhaps historiographical irony in the fact that the majority of the very considerable literature that exists on the administration of Spanish colonial towns in the sixteenth and seventeenth centuries is in many respects disappointing precisely because authors have drawn heavily for their information on the most obvious of sources – the *libros de cabildo*, or books of transactions of municipal councils. These volumes, which survive in appreciable numbers from an early date in many regions of Hispanic America, record faithfully every meeting of town councils, the number, names and offices of councilmen, their votes on many issues, their proposals and their executive orders in matters which they were competent to decide. The books, then, serve admirably as sources for the description of a cabildo's activities, and many such descriptions have been drawn from them by local and general historians of municipal life in the Spanish colonies.[1] But precisely because they are official records, compiled by the town council's scribe, they draw a veil across dissension and dispute within the cabildos, hiding almost completely from view the play of interests of whose existence the historian is frequently aware from other sources. The local politics of colonial towns, in short, cannot be followed from the libros de cabildo, and other sources for them are so sporadic that any account must contain a large element of surmise. This is certainly

[1] Two very full descriptions of cabildos are: Constantino Bayle, *Los cabildos seculares en la América española*, Madrid 1952, and John Preston Moore, *The Cabildo in Peru under the Hapsburgs*, Durham, North Carolina 1954. Moore describes cabildos in all parts of Spanish South America, taking 'Peru' to mean the viceroyalty of Peru in its widest sense. Uniformity of institutions in the Empire was such that his observations are almost entirely valid for New Spain as well. There appears to have been no activity of the cabildo of Zacatecas that did not have its counterpart in some South American cabildo. For general comments, see also W. W. Pierson, 'Some Reflections on the Cabildo as an Institution', *HAHR*, vol. 5, 1922, pp. 573–96. Articles by Fredrick B. Pike offer interesting suggestions on specific aspects of cabildo activities: 'Aspects of Cabildo Economic Regulations in Spanish America under the Hapsburgs', *Inter-American Economic Affairs*, vol. 13, 1959–60, pp. 67–86; 'The Cabildo and Colonial Loyalty to Hapsburg Rulers', *Journal of Inter-American Studies*, vol. 2, 1960, pp. 405–20; 'The Municipality and the System of Checks and Balances in Spanish American Colonial Administration', *The Americas*, vol. 15, 1958, pp. 139–58. The most sophisticated analysis of cabildos to appear so far, though for an earlier period than that considered here, and from a mainly juridical point of view, is that by Mario Góngora, in *El estado en el derecho indiano. Epoca de fundación, 1492–1570*, Santiago de Chile 1951, pp. 68–89.

true of Zacatecas, where most of the libros de cabildo for the period under study survive, with the exception of the first book, ending in 1586, and the fourth, covering the years 1639 to 1650. In view of this paucity of useful sources, it is not intended here to go far beyond a simple description of local administration in Zacatecas, such as is necessary for completeness' sake in a study of this sort, nor to suggest more than a few possible conclusions about those aspects of local politics that were related to the economic life of the town, and especially to mining.[1]

The libros de cabildo of Zacatecas do more, of course, than record the administrative decisions and practices of the cabildo itself. In them are recorded the orders and communications of the several administrative authorities that exercised control over the city's affairs: the town governor, the President and the Audiencia of New Galicia, the viceroy, sometimes acting in conjunction with the Audiencia of New Spain, and ultimately the Consejo de Indias and the king himself. These authorities acted generally in harmony to regulate government of the town, but frequently in disharmony. Their control was the framework within which the cabildo functioned, and some account must be given of them before the cabildo itself may be studied.

The supreme authority resident in the city was the governor. The post was held from 1549, the year of the first appointment of such an officer, until 1580, by a series of alcaldes mayores designated by the Audiencia of New Galicia. After 1580, the governor, with the title of corregidor, was appointed by the Crown. The powers of the alcalde mayor and corregidor were similar, although the prerogatives of office differed. As is stated by Parry, among others, Spanish colonial administration was characterised by a fusion of political and jurisdictional functions in a single office, and this fusion is exemplified in the office of city governor in Zacatecas.[2] The corregidor and alcalde mayor were, within the territorial jurisdiction of the city, senior executive administrators and senior judges in civil and

---

[1] It is a very obvious observation to say that if historians wish to escape from the largely descriptive accounts of cabildos that have hitherto prevailed, they must pay at least as much attention to the local history of towns in every aspect of their life as to the cabildos themselves. For example, knowledge of local personalities is clearly fundamental to the study of town politics; and knowledge of politics is essential to the resolution of certain perennial questions about cabildos which always occur in the standard descriptions. For example, who or what did cabildos represent? How far were the various economic controls at their disposal applied or effective? To what extent is it true that cabildos lost energy and power in the seventeenth century? Was this power transferred to informal groups acting outside any institutional framework? The local knowledge necessary to answer these questions can only come from studies of urban history based on research in notarial and municipal archives – and not on published series of cabildo transactions.

[2] J. H. Parry, *The Sale of Public Office in the Spanish Indies under the Hapsburgs*, Ibero-Americana: 37, University of California Press, Berkeley and Los Angeles 1953, p. 49.

Corregidor and Cabildo

criminal cases of the first instance (and also in cases on appeal from the judgements of the regular town magistrates, the alcaldes ordinarios).[1] The alcaldes mayores were appointed annually at a salary of 300 pesos a year, and as far as can be seen they were all residents of New Spain or New Galicia; indeed, some of them were vecinos of Zacatecas itself. Some held office several times. No explanation emerged in the course of research for the Crown's decision to choose the administrator of the city itself, from 1580 onwards; but this development can be considered characteristic of a tendency towards firmer control of the Empire from Spain. This is a feature of the period noted by several authors. Haring, for example, speaks of the tendency of the Crown to increase its share in the 'designation of all the more important provincial officers' after the 'earlier years of the Hapsburg era'.[2] Similarly, Miranda sees in the Crown appointment of corregidores to various towns a sign of growing absolutism, manifested in centralism.[3] In the case of Zacatecas, certainly, there may be truth in the observation. By 1580 the Crown had good reason to wish to extend its direct control over the city, which by that time was patently a mining centre of high importance. There would certainly have been an arguable case for breaking the local monopoly of direct control over the town. Possibilities of free play of personal interests among the President and oidores of Guadalajara might have seemed too great for safety as long as the Audiencia continued to appoint alcaldes mayores to Zacatecas. But there seems to be no documentary evidence giving the specific reason for the change; and even the direct effect on administration is difficult to gauge, in the unfortunate absence of the first libro de cabildo, which covers the period of the alcaldía mayor and which would provide a basis for comparison of administrative practices in the two periods. From the point of view of the Audiencia of New Galicia, of course, abrogation of the right to appoint the alcalde mayor must have meant that manipulation of the city's government through personal influence became more difficult; and possibly it is in this negative sense of depriving the Audiencia of control, rather than in the positive one of reinforcing the influence of the Crown, that a degree of centralisation was achieved.

Instructions given to early corregidores in their titles of office do not cast any further light on the question of the change from alcaldía mayor to

---

[1] For a full description of the powers of alcaldes mayores and corregidores see *Recopilación*, 1680, V ii 1–52; José Miranda, *Las ideas y las instituciones políticas mexicanas. Primera parte, 1521–1820*, México 1952, pp. 121–4; C. H. Haring, *The Spanish Empire in America*, New York 1947, ch. VIII (a); C. E. Castañeda, 'The Corregidor in Spanish Colonial Administration', *HAHR*, vol. 9, 1929, pp. 446–70.

[2] Haring, *The Spanish Empire*, p. 129.

[3] Miranda, *Las ideas*, p. 95.

corregimiento. Titles issued to corregidores did not even make clear to which authority in New Spain they were immediately responsible in administrative affairs: whether to the Audiencia of New Galicia and its President, or to that of New Spain and the viceroy; or whether the sole controlling authority was the Consejo de Indias.[1] A vagueness characteristic of much Spanish colonial legislation thus surrounded the jurisdiction of the corregidor – a vagueness increased by an equally characteristic appeal to custom in the assigning of powers to corregidores (at least, as far as these powers are set out in titles of office). The title of Juan Núñez, third corregidor of Zacatecas, issued in 1585, is typical in this respect. In it Núñez is authorised to appoint lieutenants to those places in his jurisdiction to which his predecessors have been accustomed to appoint them; he and his lieutenants may collect such fees (*derechos*) as corregidores customarily enjoy in Spain and the Indies; the viceroys, presidents of Audiencias and all justices of the Indies are bidden to treat Núñez with due respect, observing all the liberties, prerogatives and immunities 'which apply and ought to apply to my corregidores of the said cities of the Indies and of these said kingdoms'.[2] No doubt this appeal to custom in such titles is a stylistic device calculated to avoid the necessity of enumerating all the powers and prerogatives of the corregidor in all the situations which might arise. But the fact remains that not even a clear general statement of the corregidor's authority is to be found in these titles. And bearing in mind that Núñez was only the third corregidor of Zacatecas, and that his predecessors had had only five years to establish the customs of the office, it is clear that he could expect to enjoy wide freedom of action in exercising his authority.[3]

The corregidor did indeed enjoy a large measure of freedom of action, at certain times and in certain matters. His freedom varied, though, because the degree of control exercised on the city by external authorities, in the form of visitas (inspections by officers specially commissioned by the viceroy or by the President of New Galicia) and the imposition of Ordinances, depended to a surprising extent on his determination to resist such control and on the determination of the outside authority to overcome his resistance. A battle of wills between the local and the

---

[1] Parry, *The Audiencia*, states that the corregidor was responsible to the president of New Galicia; but *Recopilación* 1680, V ii 1, which he quotes, does not support this.

[2] AGI Guadalajara 236, AA, 1, ff. 2–3, Barcelona 27 May 1585, 'El Licenciado Núñez. Título de corregidor de la población de las minas de las Zacatecas de la Nueva España'.

[3] It is possible that the attributes of the corregidor's office were defined, if not by design, in effect, by the actions of the early corregidores themselves. An analogous example is pointed out by Góngora, when he refers to the creation, through custom, of certain faculties of colonial cabildos. See *El estado*, p. 86.

viceregal administration, rather than a reasoned debate over jurisdictions, might thus determine, for example, whether a visita should be imposed on Zacatecas. It is not out of place to give two examples of these conflicts, for in the first place the visita was the more direct and powerful instrument of outside interference in Zacatecas, and might bring serious consequences in its train for the town; and secondly, the stories of these visitas illustrate certain common and probably important features of Spanish colonial administration.

The first example took place in 1570, and is therefore drawn from the period of the alcaldía mayor; but the procedure of the alcalde mayor and the justices of the city in the affair is similar to that adopted by certain corregidores in later years. The matter, as it was related to the Crown by Bishop Mendiola of New Galicia, had insignificant beginnings.[1] A miner of Zacatecas, Pedro de Ahumada (almost certainly that same Ahumada who had defeated the Zacatecos and Guachichil Indians in 1561) had died in Michoacán, leaving his hacienda de minas tied to various charitable works (*obras pías*). But debts on his estate more than exceeded its value. An executor, one Venegas (probably Pedro Venegas, a miner in Zacatecas in these years) was administering the hacienda, which was to be finally inherited, after payment of debts, by Juan de Sámano, alguacil mayor of Mexico City. Sámano was impatient to gain control of the hacienda and had threatened Venegas in various ways to oblige him to hand it over, before outstanding debts were paid off. His impatience eventually led him to denounce Venegas before the Audiencia of New Spain, accusing him of defrauding the Crown of the *quinto*, the royal tax on the production of silver. The Audiencia, headed by its President, Viceroy Enríquez, decided to investigate the matter. They sent one Bachiller Martínez as *pesquisidor* to Zacatecas. According to a subsequent account of the affair by the Audiencia of New Galicia, Martínez arrived in Zacatecas, accompanied by an alguacil, on 21 December 1570.[2] He carried his staff of office, but did not bring, apparently, any document from the Crown or the Audiencia of New Spain conferring authority on him. The alguaciles of Zacatecas thereupon tried to seize the staffs of office from Martínez and his companion, who naturally resisted, a great commotion ensuing at the door of the parish church. Evidently the pesquisidor was overcome, for the alcalde mayor of Zacatecas, Juan de Rentería, imprisoned him in the casa real used for taxing silver – an ironically appropriate gaol, in view of Martínez' mission. There he remained for several days. On being

[1] AGI Guadalajara 55, Guadalajara 15 April 1572, the Bishop-Elect of New Galicia to Crown.
[2] AGI Guadalajara 46, R. 3, Guadalajara 28 December 1570, 'Testimonio de los autos hechos en la Audiencia Real del Nuevo Reino de Galicia contra el Bachiller Martínez'.

informed of what had happened, the Audiencia of New Galicia supported the local officials in Zacatecas, and issued an instruction that in future no provisión or order of the Audiencia of New Spain should be executed in Zacatecas until it had been approved in Guadalajara. The oidores of Guadalajara wrote soon afterwards to the Crown, complaining bitterly about this intrusion by the authorities of Mexico City into their jurisdiction. The viceroy should at least have informed them beforehand of his intentions. They recognised, however, although very grudgingly, that the viceroy had a right to send a first-instance judge into New Galicia to investigate grave affairs, on the authority of a royal provision which (in the oidores' chosen words) he was said to hold.[1] In the event, the viceroy's will prevailed. After a few days, Martínez managed to recover his authority and in his turn deprived local justices in Zacatecas of their staffs of office. There is no account of the outcome of this visita. But according to Bishop Mendiola's letter of 1572, the wishes of the central authorities were eventually realised. The Audiencia of New Spain obtained a royal order appointing another juez pesquisidor for Zacatecas. But it is noteworthy that this task was given by the Crown to Oidor Orozco of Guadalajara, and not to an official from Mexico City. The Crown does not seem to have been over-anxious to reinforce the viceroy's authority at the expense of the Audiencia of New Galicia.

The second example of a visita challenged by the local authorities of Zacatecas is taken from nearly a century later, and is at the same time a simpler and more important case. In 1662, the Viceroy Conde de Baños resolved to investigate the proceedings of the royal Treasury officials in Zacatecas. He appointed a visitor, Tomás de Alarcón, with several assistants. As soon as the cabildo of Zacatecas got wind of the viceroy's intentions, it appealed to the Audiencia of New Galicia, saying that the city was in a miserable condition and could not afford a visita. (It was the double misfortune of the subjects of these investigations that they had to pay not only the penalties that might be imposed, but also the salaries of the inspecting officials.) The Audiencia remitted the cabildo's protest to Mexico City, but Baños proceeded as he had planned. Alarcón duly arrived in Zacatecas, to have his commission seized by the corregidor and sent to Guadalajara. The corregidor quoted a provision of 1603 held by the city which exempted it from obeying any external justice without the assent of the local Audiencia. The fiscal of the Audiencia denied the validity of Alarcón's commission, asserting that it ought to have been issued from Guadalajara. The viceroy allowed himself to be overruled,

[1] AGI Guadalajara 51, Guadalajara 16 January 1571, Audiencia to Crown.

and the visita was suspended, never to take place. The Audiencia of New Galicia sought Crown confirmation for its action in the dispute.[1] These visitas raise a number of interesting questions about administration in New Spain. It should firstly be emphasised, though, that for Zacatecas these disputes, apparently arising from imprecision and clashes of jurisdiction, were not merely matters of local pride or pique. The cabildo in 1662 claimed that the city could not afford to pay the salaries of the inspecting officials. Yet this cannot have been its principal reason for fighting the proposed visita so fiercely. The ostensible object of the investigation, it may be noted, was not the city itself, its administration, or its economic activities (such as mining and commerce), but the officials of the royal Treasury. These were direct servants of the Crown, and therefore, on the face of it, a natural object of concern to the viceroy, the king's other self in the colony. But why should the corregidor and cabildo have been so anxious to relieve the local tax collectors of an enquiry into their affairs? The answer must be that the town had learned from the experience of several similar visitas which it had undergone in the 1640s and 1650s. In the last of these, in 1655, the visitador, Pedro de Oroz, had brought a number of charges against the Treasury officials, of which the most important can be reduced to the accusation that the officials had gone beyond their powers in distributing salt and mercury to miners on credit.[2] These two substances were essential ingredients of the process of silver reduction. Furthermore, earlier visitadores had, in compliance with their instructions, tried to collect the debts owed by miners to the Crown, as a result of the largesse of the Zacatecas Treasury officials, for salt and mercury. In so doing they had ruined many miners who, in these years of depression, were in any case on the edge of bankruptcy. Many haciendas de minas had been shut down, and subsequently crumbled to ruins.[3] Thus, in 1662, threatened with a repetition of former visitas, Zacatecas rushed to the defence of its Treasury officials, who, partly out of private interest and partly out of sympathy towards miners, continued to allow more than the official margin of credit on the salt and mercury they administered. The corregidor, in seizing the commission of the viceroy's investigator and invoking the help of the Audiencia of New Galicia, was thus directly protecting the vital

---

[1] AGI Guadalajara 11, '1662 años. Autos fechos en razón de lo pedido por parte del cabildo ... de Zacatecas ... sobre la comisión despachada por el ... Conde de Baños ... contra el Tesorero y demás oficiales reales de dicha ciudad'. Information used here is taken from the preliminary report of the Audiencia of New Galicia to the Crown, dated Guadalajara 17 April 1663.

[2] AGI Guadalajara 11, '1662 años. Autos fechos', ff. pp. 59–61.

[3] The causes and effects of the mining depression of the mid-century are discussed in ch. 8.

economic interests of the town. There was more at stake than political demarcation.

The Audiencia of New Galicia, it will be noted, gave invaluable support to the local authorities of Zacatecas in the two cases just quoted of resistance to viceregal investigations. Without the Audiencia's pretensions to authority in its own province, the alcalde mayor or corregidor could have had no legal support for his defiance of the visitador. And though it is not directly germane to the history of Zacatecas, a brief reference may be made here to the larger question that lay behind the Audiencia's support of Zacatecas in these instances: namely, the dispute over the possession of administrative authority (*gobierno*) in New Galicia. Did it belong to the viceroy or the President of the local Audiencia? The question was often raised but never firmly settled. There was no definitive royal pronouncement on the matter. A letter from the Crown to the viceroy in 1644, written to inform him that a certain degree of military authority in New Galicia and New Biscay was to be delegated to the President of those provinces, incidentally referred to letters and cédulas of 1574, 1577, 1578 and 1639 conferring total administrative and judicial authority in New Galicia on the President of the Audiencia.[1] On the other hand, a viceroy in search of precedents for claiming administrative control in New Galicia did not have far to look. He could refer back to the total control in matters military, fiscal and administrative claimed by Viceroy Villamanrique in the late 1580s, and the royal orders substantiating Villamanrique's claims.[2]

It would be straying too far from the theme here to enter into any lengthy general discussion of the intriguing topic of jurisdictional conflict in the Spanish Empire. A proper study of the subject is much needed. Conflicts of this type were so common that it is difficult to imagine that

[1] The letter of 21 April 1574 from the Crown to Dr Orozco, president of the Audiencia, is quoted in Diego de Encinas, *Cedulario Indiano, recopilado por* ..., facsimile edition, Madrid 1945–6, 4 vols., vol. 1, p. 243. The letter of 1644, dated Zaragoza 22 September, is in AGI Guadalajara 230, Z, 3, ff. 7v.–8.

[2] See AGI Mexico 22, R. 1, No. 2c, San Lorenzo 29 June 1588, real cédula to the Audiencia of New Galicia, ordering obedience to Villamanrique in 'gobierno, guerra y hacienda" The Audiencia refused to accept this order, and appealed to the king to revoke it, although with bad grace they submitted to the viceroy's authority in the interim. See Audiencia to Villamanrique, Guadalajara 4 November 1588, and Audiencia to Crown, Guadalajara 6 November 1588 – both letters in AGI Guadalajara 6, R. 3. For Villamanrique's conflict with the Audiencia, see Parry, *The Audiencia*, pp. 170–2. The dispute led to an invasion of New Galicia by troops under the viceroy's orders, an attempt to arrest the Audiencia, and rumours of civil war reaching Spain. It cost Villamanrique his viceregency. The political causes of the dispute are more serious than those given by Parry, and derive from the viceroy's strong-willed attempts to restrain the centrifugal tendencies in administration clearly apparent in New Spain by this time. Villamanrique wished to impose as strong a central control as possible from Mexico City in all aspects of the colony's administration.

Corregidor and Cabildo

their effects in all aspects of colonial life were not far-reaching. Some recent writers on Spanish colonial administration have used a Weberian argument in trying to account for the ubiquity of jurisdictional disputes. Sarfatti, for example, argues that jurisdictions were deliberately left vague by the central Spanish administration in order to stimulate conflict between authorities in the Indies and consequently oblige them to have frequent recourse to the Crown for the settling of disputes. This, the argument runs, emphasised the central power of the Crown.[1] This reasoning is hardly new, except in the emphasis placed on the conscious stimulation of conflict. In other respects it resembles the well-known 'checks and balances' argument advanced by many writers on Spanish colonial administration. According to this, the Crown felt unable to trust its servants at so great a distance, and therefore constructed an administrative system in which decisions could only be taken by several authorities acting in concert, in which any single authority might find itself being spied on by several others, and in which there was a good deal of control by inspection, in the form of residencias and visitas.[2] Góngora stresses the duty incumbent on all subjects of the Crown to provide information and counsel (pareceres) for the king.[3] The frequent reports and complaints sent by colonists of all ranks to the authorities in Spain certainly also constituted a means of keeping a watch on administrators at every level.

The question of how far the Crown consciously created disputes among its officials and how far it benefited or suffered from those disputes is one demanding further investigation. Interpretations of the findings are also likely to be very debatable. It is quite clear, though, that many purely jurisdictional conflicts arose naturally from the circumstances of the Empire. The Crown could not hope to legislate exactly at such a distance. Much discretion had to be left to local officials, and the effects of their decisions quite naturally often infringed the limits of another official's sphere of action. Again, the constant conversion of custom into law – a process whose importance Góngora has emphasised[4] – could not fail to produce clashes between authorities. The distribution of powers between them might change while they were not looking, as it were. If the example of Zacatecas is typical, then clearly the Crown often stood to lose by conflicts. A local administrator such as the corregidor, if he were suffici-

---

[1] Magali Sarfatti, *Spanish Bureaucratic-Patrimonialism in America*, Institute of International Studies, Berkeley, California 1966, p. 31.
[2] See, for example, Parry, *The Audiencia*, pp. 167–8; and for examples at local level, Pike, 'The Municipality'
[3] Góngora, *El estado*, pp. 168–9.
[4] Góngora, *El estado*, p. 10.

ently skilful, might easily play off superior authorities against each other and prevent, or indefinitely postpone, any action in the Crown's interest. This is not to suggest that Zacatecas escaped all outside interference or visitas.

If the corregidor thus gained independence for himself and the town by balancing the authority of the viceroy against that of the Audiencia, he was afforded yet greater freedom of action by being untrammelled with the residencia. From 1592 a newly-appointed corregidor always carried to Zacatecas with his title of office an order forbidding the Audencia of New Galicia to subject him to any enquiry in the form of a residencia.[1] The inspection was supposedly to be carried out by the succeeding corregidor, who rarely took the duty seriously. In this way the Audiencia was further excluded from investigation into the affairs of the town. The Crown probably had a double purpose in so legislating. The dignity of the corregimiento was enhanced. And the oidores of the Audiencia were denied access to the rich pickings to be had from the mining and commerce of the city. In other parts of New Galicia the oidores certainly used their authority to draw illegally on the wealth of the land, principally in stock-raising and agriculture.[2]

From the first, corregidores were appointed for five or six years at a salary of some 1,630 pesos (1,000 pesos de oro de minas). Their term was therefore far longer than that of the alcaldes mayores and their salary far greater, although not large. The post was one of some honour and it may well have been partly to hold in its gift the considerable patronage of the corregimiento of Zacatecas that the Crown began to appoint to the office. The only other town corregimientos in New Spain lying in the direct gift of the Crown were those of Mexico City and Veracruz – one the capital and the other the principal Gulf Coast port.[3] Corregidores were almost always *hombres de capa y espada*, as were most executive officers in the Empire, and not lawyers. Unlike the alcaldes mayores they were almost all appointed from posts in Spain. Of seven corregidores nominated between 1605 and 1632, only one had previously held office in New Spain: Don Juan de Cervantes Casaus, a former alcalde mayor of Puebla. He was in Zacatecas briefly in 1621, before proceeding to a distinguished

---

[1] Examples of such orders to the Audiencia of New Galicia are in AGI Guadalajara 236 AA, 1, f. 50–50v., Berlanga 10 December 1592, real cédula; f. 104v., Buitrago 19 May 1603, real cédula; f. 190, Evora 18 May 1619, real cédula.

[2] For the exploits of members of the Audiencia in agriculture and ranching, see Chevalier, *La formation*, pp. 209–16.

[3] Not even the major industrial and ecclesiastical centre of Puebla had been made a corregimiento at the time of the *Recopilación* of 1680. It was still an alcaldía mayor. See *Recopilación* 1680, V ii 1.

career in the Tribunal de Cuentas in Mexico City.[1] The other six nominees in this sample were either military men (typically of the rank of captain of infantry or galleon commander) or civil administrators (one had been governor of Modica in Sicily, and others had served as aldermen, or *veinticuatros*, in Seville or Granada).[2] The corregimiento of Zacatecas was a prize awarded for long service to the Crown and for some the culminating point of a career. For a few it was the final appointment. Death on the long journey from Cádiz to Zacatecas was not uncommon.

There was more to be gained, however, from the journey than the dignity of the office and a small salary. From the early years of the corregimiento, the Audiencia, perhaps with a note of sorrowful envy, complained to the Crown of the peculations of corregidores. They cared only to amass a fortune, it was reported in 1585; they considered themselves directly subordinate to the Consejo de Indias, ignored the Audiencia and feared no residencia.[3] Oidor Altamirano deplored the corregidor's devotion to business: 'The justice that is done in matters of business depends on the degree of friendship he has with the particular citizens who engage in it', he lamented.[4] The aldermen (*regidores*) complained of similar abuses by early corregidores.[5] Corregidores in the seventeenth century discovered an occupation that was both lucrative to them and acceptable to citizens – supplying credit to miners. At first they appear to have used their own funds,[6] but later they may frequently have acted as agents in Zacatecas for professional silver merchants (*mercaderes de plata*) from Mexico City, whose practice it was to buy silver at discount from miners in return for credit. A corregidor of the late seventeenth century, General Don Andrés de Estrada, indulged in this business. One of the few corregidores unfortunate enough to be submitted to a residencia, he was in 1683 accused of having illegally

[1] AGI Guadalajara 1, 14 September 1617, *consulta* of the Consejo de Indias, to Crown. The fact that the move from Puebla to Zacatecas was considered a promotion substantiates the claim of contemporary Zacatecans that their city was second in importance in New Spain only to the capital.

See AGI Guadalajara 1, 31 August 1605, consulta of Consejo de Indias to Crown; and similar consultas of 8 May 1630 and 21 February 1632.

[3] AGI Guadalajara 6, R. 2, Guadalajara 2 April 1585, Audiencia to Crown.

[4] AGI Guadalajara 6, R. 2, 6 November 1585, Licenciado Altamirano to Crown. He referred to Don Félix de Zúñiga y Avellaneda, the first corregidor.

[5] E.g. AGI Guadalajara 30, Zacatecas 18 November 1594, regimiento to Crown. They protested about the conduct of the recently-arrived corregidor, Don Antonio de Saavedra Guzmán, who used his authority to engage in trade at the expense of merchants. He also owned silver reduction works and illegally seized Indians to work in them.

[6] AGI Guadalajara 30, Zacatecas 28 January 1603, vecinos of Zacatecas to the president of the Consejo de Indias, on Don Fernando de Valdés, corregidor 1598–1605. They approved of his money-lending, commenting 'he is not very rich and has not taken advantage of his position' [presumably, to make money].

supplied miners with *avío* (goods on credit and cash loans). He made no attempt to deny the charge, but explained that he was acting for mercaderes de plata in the capital, and claimed that in arranging to provide credit he had done the mining industry of Zacatecas nothing but good.[1] Many miners would have agreed with him. Corregidores had long plied the same trade, evidently to their considerable profit, if the sums that certain of them were prepared to pay the Crown for the office are any indication of its value to them. Parry states that the sale of provincial governorships began in America after 1670,[2] and it is soon after then that the corregimiento was first exchanged for cash. A public auction was not held, a rather more discreet transaction being preferred. For example, Bernardo Zumbil y Echarri received the office in 1675 in return for his services to the Crown and for a gift (*donativo*) of 10,000 pesos.[3] Succeeding corregidores paid for their offices in the same indirect way. As will be seen, sale of office had long been common among the lesser posts in Zacatecas. The corregimiento remained unsold for so long because the Crown was reluctant to sell higher administrative posts, particularly because they carried with them heavy judicial responsibility. But corregidores were not necessarily of lower quality after 1670 because the office was sold. It had always been their custom to engage in illegal commercial activities. In selling the office, the Crown had in effect merely acknowledged that the abuse existed; and, once resigned to it, sought to take advantage of the evil by making corregidores pay for the opportunity to profit from mining and commerce in Zacatecas.

The corregidor, as was stated above, was the superior administrator and judge in the city. Unfortunately, very little record of his day-to-day activities either in government or in justice has come down in the manuscripts. It is not even clear, for example, whether he or the annually-elected alcaldes ordinarios actually heard cases in the first instance.[4] In his administrative capacity the corregidor might, and did, issue orders independently. Don Francisco Fernández Zapata, newly arrived in 1633, promulgated a series of thirty-five Ordinances dealing with various social and fiscal matters. A curfew was imposed from nine at night; citizens were forbidden to harbour Negro and Indian mine-workers who

---

[1] AGI Escribanía 389, 'Zacatecas, distrito de Guadalajara. Residencia del General Don Andrés de Estrada ... año de 1684. Juez, el Señor General Don Tomás Freyre de Somorrostro ... Año de 1683'. Foliated 1–370. *Passim*, and especially ff. 48v.–9, 80–80v.
[2] Parry, *The Sale of Public Office*, pp. 54–5.
[3] AGI Guadalajara 3, Madrid 17 June 1675, Crown to Conde de Medellín.
[4] The distinction between the jurisdiction of the alcaldes ordinarios and of the corregidor is not clear. The authorities quoted in previous footnotes here do not illuminate the question greatly. *Recopilación* 1680, V iii 19, declares that where the jurisdiction of alcaldes ordinarios is in doubt, previous custom shall be observed. So practice probably varied from place to place.

had fled from their employers; no-one should incite Indians to riot; the spring of drinking water on La Bufa should not be contaminated by the washing of clothes; goods entering the city should not be permitted to escape declaration before they were sold; various existing orders on mine labour should be observed.[1] Such series of orders may have been frequently issued by corregidores. Few were found in the archives of Zacatecas, but the survival of documents there is so sporadic that no accurate estimate of the commonness of a particular type of document can be made. Most of the orders for local government still to be found are written in the libros de cabildo, and were issued by the cabildo acting under the presidency of the corregidor. A parallel may be drawn with viceregal government, in which it was the practice for the viceroy and his Audiencia, acting in conjunction, to issue *autos acordados*, or joint executive orders. The limits of legislative and administrative authority between the corregidor and the cabildo were indistinct.[2] The laws incorporated in the *Recopilación* of 1680 gave little guidance. One of the few definite rulings was that the corregidor was forbidden to interfere in the voting of cabildo members. In Zacatecas, such interference was the source of certain contention.[3] In practice the corregidor or his lieutenant presided over all cabildo meetings. He held a casting vote in ballots.[4]

Further comment on the relationship between corregidor and cabildo soon becomes hypothetical speculation. It is perfectly clear, though, that on the state of that relationship, even at a personal level, might depend the distribution of authority between the governor and the council. It seems reasonable to suggest, for example, that any rift between the two would tend to be to the corregidor's disadvantage, since he would be deprived of the opportunity to exercise authority through the council members, who were mostly highly-respected and powerful men in the town in their own right. Obviously, personality had a large part to play in determining the ease of the relationship in particular cases. But there does also seem to be a general shift in attitudes from the sixteenth to the

---

[1] AA.Z, 5, No. 29, 'Autos de buen govierno fechos por el señor Don Francisco Fernández Zapata, corregidor de esta ciudad, pregonados en ella en 24 de octubre de 1633 años'.

[2] The relevant sections of *Recopilación* 1680 are V ii 1–52, 'De los gobernadores, corregidores, alcaldes mayores y sus tenientes y alguaciles'; and IV ix 1–23, 'De los cabildos y concejos'.

[3] *Recopilación* 1680, IV ix 9. The commonest form of interference was in the election of alcaldes and regidores. Corregidores were forbidden to so interfere; but nevertheless did so, to the cabildo's annoyance. See AA.Z, LC 2, ff. 3–3v., Guadalajara 22 November 1586 Audiencia to Corregidor Don Félix de Zúñiga y Avellaneda, real provisión.

[4] Of the authorities previously quoted, Bayle gives the account of corregidor-cabildo jurisdictional relationships most closely approaching the situation in Zacatecas. He states that the corregidor was not officially part of the cabildo, but dominated it by virtue of his supreme power in administration and justice. He presided over the council if he attended, and voted only when a casting vote was necessary. See *Los cabildos seculares*, p. 155.

seventeenth centuries, inasmuch as the cabildo's early complaints about the peculations of the early corregidores appear to cease. Similarly, the grievances of early corregidores over supposed infringements of their jurisdictions by members of the cabildo – Corregidor Juan Núñez in 1589 even protested at the election in that year of the statutory two alcaldes ordinarios[1] – largely cease to be heard, although corregidores apparently continued interfering in cabildo elections from time to time in the seventeenth century. This quieting of voices may merely mean that one party had become accustomed to the other, and also reflect the growing lassitude of the cabildo in the seventeenth century. But it may also mean that the corregidores had learned to shape their extra-official commercial activities in a way calculated not to disturb the cabildo or the town. If there is a turning point, it may well be Fernando de Valdés, corregidor from 1598 to 1605, referred to in note 6 on p. 91. He was possibly the first corregidor to act as aviador to the miners of the city. The vecinos, in their letter of January 1603 to the President of the Consejo de Indias, actually requested that Valdés be given another term of office and an increased salary. For not only had he maintained peace and justice, but had acted 'with such skill' that no haciendas de minas had ceased to operate during his term. This he seems to have achieved by protecting miners from merchants who had lent them money and who were prepared to suck an hacienda dry in order to recover it.[2] No doubt the curbing of merchant aviadores suited Valdés' own credit-supplying activities very well. And after him most corregidores were also aviadores, as far as can be told. Thus an accommodation can be said to have been reached between the corregidor and the cabildo, which was directly representative of the powerful economic interests of the town. The corregidor 'sold' the cabildo his political cooperation for a share in the mining wealth of the town, and the town 'bought' his cooperation by allowing him to operate as an aviador without protest. In this way, the interests of the town and the corregidor came to coincide very closely. And the corregidor was as much protecting his own livelihood as that of the citizens when he used his authority to quash outside interference in the governing of the city, in the way that has been described above. If, then, the Crown's intention in first replacing alcaldes mayores in Zacatecas by a corregidor was in some way to improve probity in the government of the town, the object was soon lost, as was predictable, by

---

[1] AGI Guadalajara 236 AA, 1, f. 34–34v., Madrid 1 March 1589, real cédula to Villamanrique, referring to a letter from Juan Núñez to the Crown.

[2] AGI Guadalajara 30, Zacatecas 28 January 1603, vecinos to president of the Consejo de Indias.

the corregidor's 'selling-out' to local interests. This is not to say that there was no upright and dedicated corregidor in Zacatecas in the seventeenth century. He may have existed, but in the absence of records, justice cannot be done by him.

In his dealings with the cabildo, what nature of body did the corregidor face? It is not a wholly anachronistic question to ask how far the cabildo was representative of the citizens, for early American towns recovered some of the democratic procedures which Peninsula towns had lost, although those procedures were eroded away in the course of the later sixteenth century.[1] Did the activity of the cabildo vary in type or intensity from one time to another, perhaps with changes in its composition? And was it actively useful in furthering the interests of the town? These questions are closely interconnected, and, with the evidence available, are debatable. But some pointers can be clearly seen.

Like any other incorporated town in Spanish America at the time, Zacatecas had a cabildo consisting basically of two types of official: aldermen (*regidores*) and magistrates (*alcaldes ordinarios*). These were the voting members. As first a town (*villa*) and then a city, Zacatecas was legally enabled to maintain a cabildo of two alcaldes ordinarios and up to six regidores.[2] It is impossible to know when the cabildo was established, because the first book of minutes has gone; but long before the start of the second libro de cabildo in 1587 the council evidently existed with two alcaldes and a number of regidores. The alcaldes were co-opted from among the citizens by the cabildo, for yearly terms. Some of the regidores were selected in the same way. But three *regimientos* were by this time permanently occupied by officials of the Treasury in Zacatecas, who held them *ex officio*. They were on the council ostensibly to protect the interests of the Treasury; but their presence might also be seen as the intrusion by the Crown of its agents into local government. There are indeed other signs of the progressive quashing of local autonomy by the Crown – the most obvious being, of course, the nomination of the corregidores after 1580. Nor were the Treasury officials the only *ex officio* regidores placed on the cabildo by the Crown. In 1587 – for the first time, as far as can be seen – an alguacil mayor was appointed to Zacatecas by the king with the privilege of voting on the cabildo.[3] Ten years later

[1] See Góngora, *El estado*, pp. 69–90.   [2] *Recopilación* 1680, IV x 1–2.
[3] The alguacil mayor was the constable of the town, chief executive officer of justice, and entitled to bear the royal staff of justice. The position was one of great dignity and prestige. See AGI Guadalajara 230, Z, 1, ff. 332v.–8, San Lorenzo 25 January 1578, for the permanent appointment of Juan de Somorrostro to the alguacilazgo mayor of Zacatecas, in recognition of his services to the Crown. He was authorised to appoint two lieutenants. He was an *ex officio* regidor with voting rights in the cabildo. In council assemblies he took precedence over normal regidores, and was junior only to the alcalde mayor and the Treasury officials.

the first *depositaría general* of the city was sold.[1] This office also carried voting membership of the council. The effect of these intrusions of permanent officials with the status of regidores on the structure of the cabildo in, say, 1590, can be appreciated from a listing of the full council of that year. The voting members were: the corregidor (non-elected), two alcaldes ordinarios (annually elected), three Treasury officials (non-elected), one alguacil mayor (non-elected), one depositario general (non-elected) and three regidores (annually elected). So six voting members held proprietary offices and five members were annually co-opted.[2] Even this minority of co-opted members was soon to be reduced.

The decade of the 1580s brought various changes to the status and institutions of Zacatecas. It began with the arrival of the first corregidor. 1585 saw the granting of the title of City, and 1587 the conferring of arms on the new city.[3] These honours were certainly a reflection of the growing size and importance of the town. The enhanced status and prosperity of Zacatecas made it a profitable market for the sale of offices. Certain positions began to appear lucrative. Several notarial posts were sold in the mid-1580s,[4] and the sale of the depositaría general in 1588 has already been noted. This was the first sale of a voting office on the cabildo. Regimientos, which in other parts of the Empire had begun to be sold in small numbers before 1554,[5] were not so disposed of in Zacatecas until the 1620s. But regidores ceased to be chosen annually long before that. As had happened in Mexico City as early as 1524, the Crown began appointing proprietary regidores in Zacatecas.[6] It did so at the city's request; for in 1586 the cabildo, in what in modern light appears a determined effort to undermine its own democratic procedures, sought permission to choose six or eight permanent regidores to replace those who were currently being selected by annual co-optation.[7] The cabildo gave no reason for its wish to abandon annual elections. Perhaps it preferred to be relieved of the bother of the procedure; perhaps members

---

[1] The *depositario general* was the custodian of goods embargoed by the justices during litigation and also of the goods of people dying intestate. The sale of the office referred to here is recorded in AA.Z, LC 2, ff. 41–50, Guadalajara 1 September 1588. The post went to Diego Machón de Urrutia for 4,800 pesos.

[2] See AA.Z, LC 2, f. 61.

[3] AGI Guadalajara 30, San Lorenzo 20 July 1588, 'Escudo de armas a la ciudad de Zacatecas'.

[4] See Parry, *The Sale of Public Office*, pp. 6–20, for an account of sales of notarial offices in Spanish America. They began in 1559.

[5] Parry, *The Sale of Public Office*, p. 37.

[6] For early appointments of regidores in New Spain, see Parry, *The Sale of Public Office*, p. 35.

[7] AGI Guadalajara 236, AA, 1, ff. 75–6, 'en el campo' 16 November 1596, Crown to the president of New Galicia, real cédula.

sitting in 1586 hoped that they themselves would be selected for a proprietary office; or perhaps they merely thought it fitting that the newly-created city should have a permanent council composed of its most illustrious citizens. Whatever the reason, the proposal coincided with the Crown's policy of creating permanent regimientos, and was approved. Owing to administrative delay and difficulty in finding the right men, the first proprietary regidor did not appear until 1594, and only in 1602 did the second take his seat.[1] The number of permanent regidores never reached the eight suggested by the cabildo in 1586. Such a number would perhaps have made the council unwieldy. Even as it was, the number of voting members in the early years of the seventeenth century was larger than ever before or after. At a full cabildo held in May 1612, there sat twelve members with votes: the corregidor, two alcaldes ordinarios, three Treasury officials, three proprietary regidores, the *alférez real*, the alguacil mayor and the depositario general.[2]

Regimientos, having been made proprietary in the 1590s, were made saleable in the 1620s. This was the only change in methods of recruitment to the cabildo to come about in the seventeenth century. It happened when the Treasury officials lost their *ex officio* seats in 1620, ostensibly because their presence to safeguard Treasury affairs was no longer necessary;[3] but more probably to release for sale the seats that fell vacant. Sold some of them were – one in 1622 and another in 1624. But there was no rush of purchasers.[4] No more proprietary regimientos were granted by the Crown; a regidor now of necessity bought his office.[5] A regimiento seems to have been worth little in cash to its holder and few people were willing to pay for the mere status of the position. The cabildo therefore shrank. By the late 1620s only six to eight voting members attended

---

[1] AA.Z, LC 2, f. 107v. The name of Cristóbal Martínez, first proprietary regidor, appears in the list of cabildo members meeting on 1 January 1595. Juan de Monroy, the second permanent regidor, first appears in 1603.

[2] AA.Z, LC 2, f. 282, cabildo, Zacatecas 4 May 1612. The meeting was held to discuss the honours to be performed on the death of Margaret of Austria. The alférez real was the bearer of the royal standard in civic ceremonies, a dignitary of importance. The office was never disposed of gratis in Zacatecas. The first recorded sale of it there was in 1608. See AA.Z, LC 2, ff. 222v.–6. Juan Cortés Tolosa Moctezuma, a grandson of Hernán Cortés and vecino of Zacatecas, bought the office for 2,050 pesos.

[3] AA.Z, LC 3, ff. 94–5, Madrid 14 June 1620, Crown to Audiencia of New Galicia, real cédula.

[4] AA.Z, LC 3, ff. 127v.–9, Guadalajara 31 December 1622, title of regidor to Pedro de Enciso Zorrilla, vecino of Zacatecas. Enciso paid 1,000 pesos. AA.Z, LC 3, ff. 247v.–52, Guadalajara 22 February 1624, title of regidor to Martín Sánchez de Vera. He paid 1,050 pesos.

[5] Parry, *The Sale of Public Office*, p. 45, states that the Crown ceased granting regimiento after 1606. In 1620 it was forbidden to elect regidores (*Recopilación* 1680, VIII xx 7).

meetings. It remained at about this size until the last two decades of the century, when attendance increased to nine or more.[1] Thus the extension of sale to nearly all offices of the cabildo was a direct cause of the reduction in its size.

The effect of, first, granting regimientos and then selling them was, of course, to fix the composition of the cabildo and to reduce greatly the number of citizens who could hope to hold office. From the last years of the sixteenth century the two alcaldes ordinarios were the only members replaced annually. This progressive hardening of the composition of cabildos was common to all towns in Spanish America, and the reasons for it were much the same as those which have just been outlined for Zacatecas. It happened rather later in Zacatecas than in the towns of central Mexico – partly because Zacatecas was a newer foundation, and perhaps partly because its position on the periphery of settlement prevented its way of life from falling into the fixed patterns that imposed themselves on towns far from the troubled conditions of the frontier. The petition of the city to be granted permanent regimientos, it may be noted, coincided in the late 1580s with the closing period of the Chichimec war. Peace brought stability to the life of the town: a stability which was reflected in the increasingly static composition of the cabildo.

This is a convenient point at which to comment on the representativeness of the cabildo. What effects did the increasing inflexibility of the selection system have on the recruitment of council members? It is arguable that the effects were less serious than might at first be thought. Records of voting members show that, apart from the Treasury officials, who retained their *ex officio* regimientos up to 1622, miners completely dominated the cabildo. The alcaldes ordinarios and the regidores (the latter no matter whether co-opted, proprietary or purchasers of office) were nearly always miners before the middle of the seventeenth century. This is what would be expected, since regidores and alcaldes were chosen from the most prosperous and respected section of the community, and that section in Zacatecas comprised the miners. Historians of the cabildo in America have frequently argued that the effect of grants and sales of regimientos was to turn the councils into small and irresponsible hierarchies, often uninterested in the welfare of their towns. Members, it is said, were chiefly concerned to gain social status and to benefit financially from their positions. The cabildo became even more closed, it is said, after 1606, when permission was given for regidores to renounce and sell their offices. Since regimientos could thereafter be passed from father to son, or to other relations, they tended to become the property of a

[1] AA.Z, LC 7, *passim.*

small number of families in each town.[1] Was this true of Zacatecas? To an extent, the peculiarities of the mining society appear to have curbed the process there. Such were the fluctuations of mining that few families dependent on the industry retained their wealth for more than a generation. The composition of the mine-owning group therefore varied quite quickly. Given the tendency of cabildo offices to fall to the rich and powerful of the day, the opportunities for passing offices between relatives were consequently reduced, although some such passing did occur. It is possible that these peculiar circumstances in which the cabildo of Zacatecas existed made it, in a limited sense, more democratic. Compared with the system of election of regidores by full suffrage of vecinos that had originally been set out for America in 1523,[2] there was, of course, little democracy in the co-optation of regidores by the sitting cabildo, as was the practice in Zacatecas in the sixteenth century. There was still less of democracy in the purchasing and granting of offices. But at least Zacatecas was spared a hereditary cabildo, and enjoyed circumstances which permitted membership to change. At any particular time, the mining group of the city was represented on the cabildo by members of the prosperous mining families of the moment;[3] and when, in the mid-seventeenth century certain merchants began to play an important financial rôle by supplying credit to miners, their names were not long in appearing on the council.[4] It is, indeed, almost a truism to say that the cabildo of Zacatecas was representative of the town and of its interests, since its interests were so firmly centred on mining, and the cabildo consisted almost by definition of miners together with those merchants who were intimately connected with mining. Because Zacatecas was so specialised a community, depending so heavily on mining for its prosperity, it is also a truism to say that what was good for the plutocracy of miners and merchants was probably good, in general terms, for the populace as a whole. Of course, from what has been said it will be quite clear that the portions of the citizenry of lesser economic power and lesser social

---

[1] Parry, *The Sale of Public Office*, pp. 44–5; Moore, *The Cabildo in Peru*, p. 266.

[2] Haring, *The Spanish Empire*, p. 152.

[3] In 1630, for example, the alguacil mayor, Antonio de León Covarrubias, and the alférez real, Lorenzo Tostado, were both heads of mining families and important miners themselves.

[4] Of particular interest is the appearance of Captain Joseph de Villarreal as alguacil mayor in 1654. He was a dealer in silver, buying unminted silver from miners at a discount and giving them credit. By the time of his death in 1680, Villarreal was owed debts of some 140,000 pesos. See his will, AN.Z, JL 1676–80, ff. 246–50v., Zacatecas 7 April 1680. Villarreal was probably the first merchant to hold a seat on the cabildo. He was joined in 1660 by Captain Joseph de Arroyo Santerbáez. References to both merchants are scattered through AN.Z, LC 5. In law a merchant could not hold a regimiento, since the cabildo had extensive control over local commerce. See *Recopilación* 1680, IV x 11–12.

standing had no representation on the cabildo, nor any say in selecting its members. Yet, when the cabildo purported, as it often did, to be speaking on behalf of the city, it was probably telling the truth to a surprising degree. And to judge the effectiveness of the cabildo's efforts in the city's interests, it is obviously necessary to know what it did.

Moore has resumed the powers of town councils in America under three headings.[1] They had political authority in their right to select certain municipal officers, in their right to send representatives (*procuradores*) to the royal and viceregal courts, and in their ability to convene a *cabildo abierto* (an open meeting of vecinos to debate matters of general concern). They held economic authority in their power to make land grants and issue regulatory Ordinances for trade and business. And they had social authority of various sorts: they could improve the conditions of the poor, encourage education by fostering schools, and sponsor fiestas in celebration of important events. The libros de cabildo of Zacatecas record that the council there did, at various times, perform these functions and enjoy these powers.[2]

It would be tedious and unilluminating to give a list of examples of these powers in detail. But the range of activity of the council may be gathered from the number and variety of lesser officials who were selected from the citizenry by the regidores each year. On 15 January 1628, for example, the voting members of the cabildo met to choose the following officials: the *procurador general de la república* (a city attorney, almost an ombudsman, who presented citizens' grievances before the cabildo), the *obrero mayor de la ciudad* (clerk of the works), the *mayordomo de la ciudad* (custodian of municipal property), the *alcaide de la alhóndiga* (supervising and registering arriving loads of grain), the *letrado de la ciudad* (possibly the corregidor's legal adviser), the *escribano de la alhóndiga* (secretary and scribe thereof), the *procurador de pobres y defensor de indios* (a lawyer available to Indians and the poor), the *depositario y mayordomo de la fábrica de la iglesia mayor* (responsible for the funds and the fabric of the parish church), the *veedor y fiel de la carnicería* (inspector of the city abattoir, enforcing sanitary conditions and checking weights), the *fiel de pesos y romanas* (inspector of weights and balances in shops and market place), the *fiel de medidas de madera y barro* (inspector of measuring rods and liquid measures), the *portero del cabildo*, the *veedor de cera labrada* (inspector of candle making, checking weights and watching for adulteration of wax candles with tallow), the *alarife* (town surveyor), the *agente y procurador de la ciudad en la Corte de Su Magestad* (the city's representative in Spain,

---

[1] Moore, *The Cabildo in Peru*, p. 75.
[2] With the exception that no instance of a cabildo abierto was found.

with a stipend of one hundred pesos a year), the letrado (legal representative) of the city in the Audiencia of New Galicia; and lastly, another
procurador, of uncertain function.[1] In later years there appears to be a
special inspector for every important guild: the hat makers, carpenters,
blacksmiths and gunsmiths. There was also for many years an official
appointed to care for the town clock.

It is readily apparent that the functions of most of these officials were
of a regulatory and inspecting sort. Few records remain, unfortunately, of
the operation of these regulations, apart from lists of shops visited during
the inspection of measures; but the exercise of these various controls was
one of the major responsibilities of the cabildo, and one that could not
be ignored.

There was, in fact, an undercurrent of cabildo activity which could
never cease while the town still existed. A typical part of this activity was
the raising of municipal funds to pay the salaries of various minor officials,
to finance the repair of roads, bridges and public buildings, and to provide
for the fiestas regularly sponsored by the municipality. The sources of
income were threefold. Part came from an excise tax on wine, the
sisa del vino, which had originally been imposed by Viceroy Enríquez in
1576 to raise funds for the defence of the city against Indian attacks;[2]
after many petitions the city was finally allowed in 1607 to take half for
its own use.[3] The second source was the periodic auction of the meat
contract (see above, ch. 4), which produced an annual sum (*prometido*)
for the cabildo. And thirdly, after the creation of the alhóndiga in 1623,
there was additional income from dues levied on incoming grain. They
were worth, in the early 1630s, some 2,000 to 2,500 pesos a year.[4] The
total annual income of the town in these years, from the three sources
mentioned, approached 4,000 pesos a year.[5] Economic decline on all
fronts reduced it greatly in the middle years of the century. In 1672 the
total was 2,533½ pesos, on which the largest debit, including 600 pesos
spent on feasts in celebration of the arrival of a new corregidor, was
1,393½ pesos paid for fiestas of various sorts; salaries took another 580

---

[1] From AA.Z, LC 3, ff. 177v.–8, cabildo, Zacatecas 15 January 1628.
[2] AGI Guadalajara 5, Guadalajara 6 March 1576, Audiencia of New Galicia to Crown.
[3] AA.Z, Cédulas 4, f. 178, Guadalajara 12 August 1608. The president of the Audiencia,
Don Juan de Villela, granted half the sisa to Zacatecas for four years in the first instance.
Appropriation of the *media sisa* was never a statutory right of the city, and the licence was
periodically renewed in the seventeenth century.
[4] AA.Z, Cédulas 2, ff. 114v.–16, Madrid 30 July 1631, real cédula to cabildo of Zacatecas;
ff. 119–20v., Madrid 3 March 1637, real cédula to cabildo.
[5] AA.Z, 5, No. 1, account taken of Nicolás de Gueycoichea for his term as mayordomo of
the propios of the city, 1634. Total income in that year was 3,718 pesos 3 tomines; in 1635,
3,285 pesos 1 tomín.

pesos; repairs, 300 pesos, and minor expenses, 255 pesos.[1] The disproportionate expenditure on fiestas seems frivolous; but it was common to all cabildos in Spanish America, and such celebrations may well have usefully reinforced social cohesion.[2] In law a cabildo was not allowed to make extraordinary disbursements from its funds above some eleven pesos (3,000 maravedís) without the permission of the local Audiencia or provincial governor; but this regulation was never observed in Zacatecas and only one attempt to enforce it was found.[3]

Such preoccupations formed the basic work of the cabildo within the city; enforcement of price controls on retail goods, the elementary regulations for buying and selling, the gathering of certain taxes, the upkeep of the fabric of the town – without these municipal life would have been disordered. The procedures were those common to medieval towns in Europe, and so firmly had they become embedded in the institutional structure of towns in Spanish America that they operated almost without supervision. Even in the difficult years of the mid-century, when, as will be seen, the cabildo was less active, these basic functions continued.

Before any attempt is made here to show in what ways, if at all, the activity of the cabildo decreased in the seventeenth century, another of its essential tasks must be examined. The preceding paragraphs have dealt with what might be called the internal rôle of the council: local town administration. It was also responsible for representing the interests of the town before outside authorities. There were numerous occasions on which it might do this – when petitioning for the title of City, for example, protesting against a proposed visita, or complaining of outside interference in city elections. But possibly the longest and most illustrative of these representations was that conducted during the first forty years of the seventeenth century over sales tax (*alcabalas*).

The alcabala, having long been levied in Castile at a nominal rate of

1 Pike, in 'The Cabildo and Colonial Loyalty', pp. 411–18, suggests an explanation for the ubiquitous high spending of cabildos on celebrations. As the providers and organisers of important local celebrations, cabildo members found compensation for their lack of political power. The Crown's toleration of high spending on frivolities thus tended to increase the loyalty of holders of cabildo offices. Their dignity was satisfied, though they had little power. This article makes useful suggestions about the values attached to holding cabildo offices, although, for the sake of the argument, it plays down excessively the political functions of the councils.
2 AA.Z, 9, No. 15, account of city funds for 1675.
3 Haring, in *The Spanish Empire*, p. 159, points out the regulation. In 1690 the Audiencia of New Galicia tried to force the cabildo to repay 585½ pesos which it had spent on festivities in excess of the approved 3,000 maravedís. AA.Z, 11, No. 2, ff. 3v.–4, Guadalajara 6 June 1690, real provisión of the Audiencia.

10 per cent, was introduced in New Spain in 1574,[1] as an impost of 2 per cent on sales of many varieties of goods.[2] In the district of the Treasury office of Zacatecas it was administered from that date by the Treasury officials. Collection was lax and the accounts now remaining are too incomplete to be of any use as records of commerce. Possibly because of this inefficiency the viceregal authorities approved a request by the cabildo in 1603 to be allowed to collect the alcabala within the city.[3] This was, in effect a farm (*encabezonamiento*) of the tax such as had been undertaken by the cabildo of Mexico City in 1602.[4] The agreed value of the alcabala in Zacatecas was 4,000 pesos a year; the sum was first collected and paid to the Treasury in 1607.[5] The same rate appears to have been maintained until 1622, when the town's petition for renewal of the farm at the slightly increased value of 5,000 pesos was refused by the recently arrived new viceroy, Gelves. He ordered that a public auction of the tax should be held, seeing, in all likelihood, that in the boom that Zacatecas was by then enjoying, far more than 5,000 pesos could be extracted each year from the city's commerce. The cabildo protested, saying that to entrust collection of the tax to the private citizen who bid most for it would lead to excessive pressure of taxation on traders and would probably discourage carters from bringing goods to the city for sale.[6] It was an admission that the previous farm of 4,000 pesos was less than the tax had been worth. But Gelves prevailed. In July 1622 the alcabala was auctioned to four merchants of the city for 9,240 pesos a year.[7] This was the first major increase in the alcabala revenue – the beginning of a steep rise in the yield of the tax which the cabildo was constantly to fight. In 1627 the council accepted a farm of 10,000 pesos proposed by Viceroy Cerralvo,[8] glad to free the town from the avaricious grasp of private tax gatherers. A heavy blow came five years later. In 1632 Zacatecas felt for the first

[1] *Recopilación* 1680, VIII xiii 1. For alcabalas in Castile in the sixteenth century, see R. Carande, *Carlos V y sus banqueros*, (3 vols., Madrid 1943–68), vol. 2, *La Hacienda Real de Castilla*, Ch. 5; and especially 230 ff., where it is shown that although alcabala in Castile was levied at a nominal 10 per cent, farming of the tax progressively reduced its yield to less than 2 per cent.

[2] *Recopilación* 1680, VIII xiii 14. The precise conditions of the imposition, the goods on which it was levied, and exemptions, are not important to this discussion. For details, see R. S. Smith, 'Sales Taxes in New Spain, 1575–1770', *HAHR*, vol. 28, 1948, pp. 2–37; and also F. de Fonseca and C. de Urrutia, *Historia general de real hacienda, escrita por orden del virrey Conde de Revillagigedo*, México 1845–53, 6 vols., vol. 2, pp. 5–22.

[3] AA.Z, LC 2, f. 172–172v., cabildo, Zacatecas 4 April 1603.

[4] The cabildo of Mexico City hoped that by assuming the encabezonamiento it would relieve pressure of taxation on small shopkeepers. Smith, 'Sales Taxes', p. 5.

[5] AA.Z, Cédulas 2, cabildo, Zacatecas 29 October 1640.

[6] AA.Z, LC 3, f. 100–100v., cabildo, Zacatecas 15 June 1622.

[7] AA.Z, LC 3, f. 103, cabildo, Zacatecas 20 July 1622.

[8] AA.Z, LC 3, f. 174, cabildo, Zacatecas 13 December 1627.

time the consequences of the increment of 2 per cent that had been added to the alcabala in 1627 for the *derecho de Unión de Armas* – a special duty intended to raise 250,000 pesos a year in New Spain for the support of galleons guarding the Atlantic trade route.[1] The alcabala expected of the city was now doubled to 20,000 pesos. The cabildo would not undertake to raise this sum and again the tax was auctioned.[2] In the succeeding years there was sometimes difficulty in finding bidders and the cabildo continued from time to time to voice its opposition to the auctioning of the farm. It was a time of incipient decline in mining and commerce, and in 1637 the merchants of the city declared they could no longer assume the collection of the tax. With the diversion of trade to Parral, commerce had so diminished in Zacatecas that the 20,000 pesos currently being demanded could no longer be raised.[3] 1639 presented the greatest trial of all. Zacatecas had then to contend with a further 2 per cent imposed in 1636 for the upkeep of the Armada de Barlovento, the fleet created to guard the Windward Islands. The rate of taxation now stood at 6 per cent and the product demanded of the encabezonamiento correspondingly at 30,000 pesos. The cabildo had little choice but to try to raise the sum, for it had proved impossible to farm the tax privately in 1638. But by the beginning of 1640 only 10,000 pesos of the 30,000 demanded had been gathered. The cabildo explained that mercury necessary for the processing of ores had not arrived, so that production of silver had been low and trade consequently depressed; furthermore, no slaves or wine, sales of which were the most fruitful source of alcabalas, had arrived in 1639; and, as a final blow, the billetting of three companies of soldiers on the town had scared away carters. Shopkeepers were abandoning Zacatecas for Parral, where mining was more prosperous and where, best of all, there was no alcabala.[4] The city could not, it said, accept an encabezonamiento for 1640 of more than 15,000 pesos. The viceroy offered 28,000.[5] In the event the alcabala for 1640 had to be collected by the Treasury officials, who were also obliged to gather, over several years, the arrears remaining from 1639. The cabildo had undertaken to produce 30,000 pesos and had not done so. Its members, therefore, were responsible for making up the deficit. Since it had long been obligatory for them to find guarantors

[1] Haring, *The Spanish Empire*, p. 269.
[2] AA.Z, LC 3, f. 235–235v., cabildo, Zacatecas 14 January 1632.
[3] AA.Z, LC 3, f. 341v., cabildo, Zacatecas 18 March 1637; f. 342v., cabildo, Zacatecas 16 April 1637.
[4] Alcabalas were not introduced in New Biscay until 1686. For the cabildo's report, see AA.Z, Cédulas 2, f. 53, cabildo, Zacatecas 11 January 1640.
[5] AA.Z, Cédulas 2, f. 69, México 31 January 1640, *mandamiento* of Cadereita to the Treasury officials; ff. 70–1, cabildo, Zacatecas 24 February 1640.

(*fiadores*) when they accepted an encabezonamiento, and since local merchants normally were called on to serve in that capacity, the load of the 1639 alcabala was spread over a large part of the commercial section of the community. Owing to the difficult trading conditions of the time, most merchants were no longer as prosperous as in earlier years, and so in 1641 various fiadores suffered confiscation of their goods when they found themselves unable to pay the sums they had guaranteed in 1639.[1] It was a further blow to the already weakened merchant community. Surviving records do not show whether the full 30,000 pesos were ever collected, nor how much alcabala was gathered in 1640 by the Treasury officials. But it is clear that 1639 was the year that finally discouraged the cabildo from struggling to collect the tax in the city and that destroyed its determination to prevent the farm falling into private and extortionate hands.

For the sake of completeness, the history of the alcabala in Zacatecas up to the end of the century may be sketched out. Until the end of 1645, it was under the direct control of the viceroy, whose appointed officer took nearly 18,000 pesos a year from 1641.[2] But even this fell short of the sum demanded and he owed over 28,000 pesos to the Treasury at the end of his term. In 1648 and 1651 the farm was auctioned to citizens of Zacatecas, who were unable to pay what they had promised.[3] In 1652, the city complained to the Crown about the inhibitory level of taxation, saying that renters of the tax and their guarantors in the previous few years had all suffered bankruptcy.[4] There was little change until the recovery of mining at Zacatecas in the last two decades of the century. Alcabalas were administered by the Treasury officials or were farmed to groups of merchants in the town. In 1682 the tax yielded over 18,000 pesos, still at 6 per cent; and in 1696, it was said to be worth some 40,000, although far less than that was actually reaching the Treasury.[5]

This narrative raises points worthy of comment. The first is the

[1] AA.Z, 6, No. 5, Zacatecas 20 June 1641, Treasury officials to cabildo.

[2] AT.Z, Reales Oficiales 9, México 10 December 1640, Viceroy Villena, 'Comisión a Pedro de los Ríos Proaño de juez administrador de las reales alcabalas'; AT.Z, Reales Oficiales 11, México 30 March 1648, Viceroy Salvatierra to Treasury officials of Zacatecas.

[3] AT.Z, Reales Oficiales 14, Zacatecas 3 February 1653, Treasury officials to viceroy. The contractor in 1648, Diego López de Inoso, had promised 17,000 pesos a year, but was unable to raise that sum in his first two years together. The farm in 1651 went to a wealthy merchant of the city, Captain Domingo de Arana, who offered 12,000 pesos.

[4] AGI Guadalajara 230, Z, 3, ff. 151v.–2v., Buen Retiro 20 February 1653, real cédula of Crown to Viceroy Alba de Aliste.

[5] AGI Guadalajara 21, Guadalajara 22 June 1689, Visitor Feijoo Centellas to Crown. AGI Guadalajara 232, Z, 8, ff. 51v.–5v., Madrid 6 November 1696, Crown to Viceroy Sarmiento de Valladares.

obviously damaging effect of the increased tax demand made of Zacatecas in the 1630s. The latter part of the decade was a time of waning silver production; and the decline seriously reduced the volume of commerce in the city and discouraged merchants from trading there. The added prospect of heavy tax levies made selling at Zacatecas still less attractive. Secondly, it is worth considering why the cabildo should have wished to assume collection of the tax. The farming of alcabalas was common in the towns of New Spain in the seventeenth century, and had initial advantages for all parties. It relieved the Treasury officials of work, guaranteed a regular income to the Crown, and enabled a town to bargain for a quota that it was able to pay. It was only when the Crown began to demand sums nearer the true value of the tax than it had at first received, and then increased the rate of taxation to finance defence projects, that the disadvantages of the encabezonamiento for the towns became apparent. It became necessary for cabildos to delegate collection of the tax to private individuals or groups – who, in Mexico City as in Zacatecas, were normally merchants.[1] This was done unwillingly, and the cabildo of Zacatecas was no doubt genuinely concerned to prevent its happening; for the principal object that private citizens could have in accepting the farm was to profit from it. Moreover, it would be ingenuous to suppose that, in retaining collection of the alcabala for itself, the cabildo did not seek, and did not gain, advantages for itself. It is true that in the period when the council was campaigning most vigorously for the reduction of alcabalas, during the 1630s, it was composed almost entirely of miners, and that these would not have benefited more than any other normal purchaser of goods in the city from lower taxes. Miners, it might be thought, had no special interest in keeping the alcabala down. But behind the miner was always the aviador, normally a local merchant, on whose supply of goods on credit the miner depended. It is only possible to guess at the personal pressures put on mining councilmen by their aviadores, but they were doubtless great. The aviador, as a merchant, had good cause to worry when alcabalas rose, cutting into his sales and profits.[2] And if the cabildo,

---

[1] See Smith, 'Sales Taxes', *passim*.

[2] Against this argument, admittedly based on hypothesis, that aviadores (i.e. merchants) exerted pressure on miners to reduce levies of sales taxes, there is an objection that raises still more hypothetical questions: why, if merchants really thought that they could achieve their purpose through the cabildo, did they sometimes assume collection of the tax themselves? The answer that most readily suggests itself is mere impatience, and a desire to make up, with the profits of collection, the losses caused by increased taxation – or merely to avoid paying altogether. These would obviously be good reasons for the cabildo's wishing to retain collection of the tax. The play of interests between cabildo and the merchant group, and within that group, must have been complex; but is, sadly, totally beyond the range of available documentation.

Corregidor and Cabildo

a body of miners, complained that high taxes were driving merchants to Parral, then very possibly it was loss of avío that it feared, as much as the decline of the city's prosperity. Not that it was unconcerned about the general health of Zacatecas – for the many complaints flowing from it about invidious tax rates have an altruistic air about them which may reflect a local patriotism typical of Spanish and Mexican towns to this day. And since, as has been said, what was good for mining was, on the whole, good for Zacatecas at large, it is probably true to say that in this case a cabildo was fulfilling one of its proper functions – that of protecting the interests and the privileges of its community from external threats.

The purpose of giving this account of the internal and external doings of the cabildo has been to illustrate the range of its activity and to provide a base from which to assess its development in the seventeenth century. In the discussion of selection of cabildo officers, the reduced rate of change in membership resulting from sales and grants of proprietary office was noted. Did the fact that the cabildo was thereafter composed largely of regidores who might, and often did, hold office for twenty years mean that the council inevitably became less active – as Parry, for one, has said commonly happened in Spanish American towns?[1] In Zacatecas, as far as can be seen, there was no immediate lapse of activity. No irresistible process led the long-term official towards stagnation, although the danger of his falling into fixed ways cannot be denied. But, as at any place and time, experience may have counted as much as freshness. And there was a large element of chance in the matter, for if a particularly energetic individual gained a place on the council he could goad it into action. For example, the cabildo might have acquiesced more easily in the interference of the Audiencia in municipal elections from 1611 onwards, if it had not been for the constant efforts of one proprietary regidor, Juan de Monroy; who, as legal spokesman for the city in many years, contested the Audiencia's right to practise such interference.[2] It is, of course, difficult to measure the activity of the cabildo in any objective or conclusive way. It would be easy to read into the decrease in frequency of council meetings and the increase in attention to protocol observable from the early years of the seventeenth century a decline in the council's

[1] Parry, *The Sale of Public Office*, pp. 44–5.
[2] Monroy was procurador general of the city for many years in the early seventeenth century. He claimed to have been in the service of the Crown for forty-seven years, fighting Indians, serving as alcalde mayor of Aguascalientes and Lagos and prospecting for mines. He was a proprietary regidor of Zacatecas from 1603 to 1632. AA.Z, LC 3, ff. 215–16v., 'Testimonio de los papeles y nobleza del Capitán Juan de Monroy y de sus servicios' (final date, Guadalajara 1 October 1629).

concern for local government. But such signs of stagnation were not necessarily representative of the total activity of the cabildo, and the argument that they were could be countered by citing the cabildo's long campaign over alcabalas. Indeed, it is after that campaign, in the 1650s, that the libros de cabildo begin to lose interest and are filled with little more than copies of titles of officials, records of sales of offices, and accounts of elections of alcaldes and minor officials. This is not a coincidence. The cabildo finally abandoned the task of administering the city's alcabala because the decline in trade meant that the tax could no longer be collected at the assessed rate. By 1640, Zacatecas was well on the way to economic depression, and with the decline of mining, a shadow came across the remainder of the city's life. Trade had departed, rents had fallen. It was a time when few miners died solvent and when the impetus had largely disappeared from the prospecting and working of mines. Many families suffered poverty; many of the illustrious names of the early century disappeared. It was in these years of gloom that the cabildo appears finally to have abandoned its watch over the interests of Zacatecas and to have lapsed into the squabbles of protocol and precedence that have often been presented as characteristic of administrative bodies in New Spain in the seventeenth century.[1]

There was, indeed, less for it to do. The reason may partly have been, as Moore suggests, that with the further encroachment of royal control over towns the councils were less active in an advisory rôle to the local governor (here the corregidor) than they had formerly been.[2] But in Zacatecas a particular reason for a decrease in activity was that outside bodies took less interest in the city in the mid-seventeenth century than in its prosperous days. An instance of this is the meddling of the Audiencia of New Galicia in elections of alcaldes ordinarios, which has been occasionally alluded to above. It was the custom in Zacatecas, as in other towns in the Empire, for the cabildo to select on the first of January two alcaldes from the vecinos to serve for the coming year.[3] This the cabildo was entitled to do, free from outside interference, by law.[4] The Audiencia was obliged, however, to confirm these elections[5] and frequently used this faculty as an instrument for controlling the elections in the first place. Its interventions were sometimes justified, as, for example, when it

---

[1] See, for example, Moore, *The Cabildo in Peru*, p. 269.
[2] Moore, *The Cabildo in Peru*, p. 268.
[3] *Recopilación* 1680, V iii 1, provides for the annual election of alcaldes ordinarios. Election on New Year's day seems to have been common, but was not legally obligatory.
[4] *Recopilación* 1680, V iii 2.
[5] *Recopilación* 1680, V iii 10.

suspected that the election had been irregularly conducted, or when an appointee seemed unsuitable for some other reason.[1] On other occasions its motives were less clear; perhaps it merely wished to demonstrate that it had some influence over the affairs of Zacatecas, after its power there had been diminished by the installation of the corregidores; or perhaps the oidores wished to insinuate themselves into the affairs and the wealth of the town through the justices they had placed. Whatever the reason, the cabildo deeply resented the interference, without being able to do more than protest. In 1611 the Audiencia ordered that alcaldes should be elected thirty days before the New Year and that their names should be submitted for approval. The cabildo yielded.[2] Two years later the Audiencia went further. It demanded that the cabildo should send it a list of six candidates fifteen days before the New Year, from whom the President would select two. Again the cabildo acquiesced, on the condition that in future the city's rights of election should be restored.[3] But they were not, and elections were interfered with frequently in the 1620s and occasionally in the 1630s. After that, however, the Audiencia ceased to concern itself with the matter, either because there were no more valuable pickings to be had in Zacatecas, or because its own activity and efficiency declined. In the second half of the century, confirmation of alcaldes ordinarios seems to have been given automatically.[4] So contests with the Audiencia no longer bothered the cabildo on this score by the mid-seventeenth century. And, without such goads to action, it did little more than maintain the essential municipal controls and regulations that have already been described.

If there has been much discussion in this chapter of conflicts of interests and jurisdictions in the local government of Zacatecas, it is not because the cabildo was a body particularly strife-torn within itself, nor particularly fractious in its relations with higher authorities. It is merely that the only parts of local political life that can be seen through extant documentary evidence are those revealed when official, rather than private, clashes of interest arose. And, as was stated at the beginning, it is the political life of colonial municipalities which offer the interesting challenge to the historian of Spanish American towns. For the rest, the cabildo, governor and local Audiencia acted and reacted in much the same way

---

[1] See, for example, AA.Z, LC 2, f. 199, cabildo, Zacatecas 23 January 1607. The Audiencia disputed the election of Cristóbal de Zaldívar and Francisco de Zaldívar in this year, because they were cousins.

[2] AA.Z, LC 2, f. 275, cabildo, Zacatecas 1 December 1611.

[3] AA.Z, LC 2, ff. 313–15, cabildo, Zacatecas 14 December 1613.

[4] See AA.Z, LC 6, f. 145, for a rare case of annulment of an election by the Audiencia, in January 1681.

as did cabildos, governors and local Audiencias all over the American Empire. The normal course of daily government was smooth enough. The corregidor issued his ordinances for the town, the alcaldes tried their cases, the cabildo maintained its various social and economic activities – regulated prices, raised funds, repaired roads, saw that the clock was wound – and over all this the Audiencia presided with equanimity. Only when an extraordinary event or an extraordinary personality intruded on the scene did the calm dissolve and the quarrels irrupt.

The disputes of Zacatecas attracted the attention of Guadalajara and Mexico City for the obvious reason that Zacatecas was rich. But that wealth was concentrated in a small area. The territorial jurisdiction of the cabildo and corregidor was surprisingly restricted. Its practical limit to the north was the mining village of Pánuco, which was two leagues from Zacatecas. The limit to the south was a source of dispute in the last years of the sixteenth century and the early years of the seventeenth between the cabildo and the Audiencia.[1] After various adjustments, the jurisdiction of the town in the seventeenth century extended to a radius of five leagues to the south and east, embracing Cieneguillas and Los Tlacotes. This southern area, and the northern district of Pánuco, were normally administered by lieutenants (*tenientes de corregidor*) whom the corregidor was authorised to appoint. The tenientes were primarily constables with power to arrest criminals, referring them and their cases to the corregidor himself.[2] There was one other class of judicial officer in the city – the Indian alcaldes of the townships around Zacatecas. From 1610 an alcalde was elected yearly for each of the barrios of Tonalá and Tlacuitlapan; and after 1689 the barrio of San Joseph, adjacent to Tonalá, also received an

---

[1] See AA.Z, LC 2, f. 162–162v., cabildo, Zacatecas 7 September 1600. The cabildo claimed that it had previously had jurisdiction over Juchipila, Teocaltiche and Tlaltenango in the south, but that these were now administered by alcaldes mayores sent from Guadalajara. The city had also had jurisdiction for six leagues to the south over an area called Monte Grande, from which it drew supplies of wood and charcoal. The Audiencia, in retaliation for its loss of control over Zacatecas with the appointment of corregidores, had reduced this jurisdiction by placing an alcalde mayor only three leagues from the city at the fuerte del Malpaso. (For this, see AGI Guadalajara 35, Zacatecas 10 May 1596, Antonio de Saavedra to the president of the Consejo de Indias.) The cabildo was piqued at its consequent loss of jurisdiction over much of the Monte Grande and in 1600 decided to petition for restoration of this area and extension of jurisdiction to Fresnillo in the north and Aguascalientes in the south. It appears to have recovered some of the Monte Grande, but gained nothing else.

[2] See AA.Z, Cédulas 2, f. 134, Zacatecas 11 February 1641, the title of teniente issued by Corregidor Don Sancho de Avila y Guevara to Alonso Bravo, vecino of Zacatecas. Bravo's jurisdiction was to extend five leagues from the huertas of Zacatecas to a limit one league beyond Los Tlacotes, embracing all the intervening homesteads and ranches ('estancias y ranchos') of woodcutters and mule breeders.

Corregidor and Cabildo

alcalde.[1] Candidates were chosen by the Indians of each barrio at the beginning of the year, and the cabildo selected one for office. No record remains of the activities of these alcaldes; they evidently served mainly as magistrates in petty cases.[2]

Beyond the jurisdiction of Zacatecas, an enclave of the corregidor's power, lay lands in the direct administration of the Audiencia of New Galicia. The remaining mining towns of the province, and some other large settlements, were the heads of alcaldías mayores. At the beginning of the seventeenth century the alcaldías of the Zacatecas district were those of Fresnillo, Monte Grande, Jerez, Lagos, Mazapil, Sombrerete and San Martín, and Sierra de Pinos. Juchipila and the mines of Tepec also formed an alcaldía, which embraced the corregimiento of Nochistlán.[3] The alcaldes mayores had much the same judicial and administrative authority as the corregidor of Zacatecas; but since they were appointed by the Audiencia of New Galicia, they did not enjoy his independence. In country districts beyond the reach of the alcaldes mayores, the supervision of justice and the pursuit of criminals were entrusted to officials of the Santa Hermandad, a volunteer rural constabulary.[4]

In its task of keeping the peace the Hermandad was complemented by the military organisation of New Galicia. There was no standing army in the province after the end of the Chichimec war, but provision existed for raising militia in time of emergency. Indian revolt was the main danger envisaged; but militia could also be used for the pursuit of criminals. The command of military operations was given to a teniente de capitán general of New Galicia – a rank created, it will be remembered, during the Chichimec conflict. In the seventeenth century, the post was usually held by a leading vecino of Zacatecas[1] and was often given to the

---

[1] See AA.Z, LC 2, f. 256-256v., cabildo, Zacatecas 1 January 1610. The order for the selection of Indian alcaldes was given by Licenciado Gaspar de la Fuente in 1603. In the early years of the elections, the townships were known as the barrio de San Francisco and the barrio de San Augustín. The latter first was attributed the name of Tonalá in 1618 (see AA.Z, LC 3, f. 20v., cabildo, 1 January 1618); the name of Tlacuitlapan for the former does not appear until 1631 (see AA.Z, LC 3, f. 220v., cabildo, Zacatecas 1 January 1631).

[2] For the duties of Indian alcaldes in the valley of Mexico, see C. Gibson, *The Aztecs under Spanish Rule. A History of the Indians of the Valley of Mexico, 1519–1810*, (Stanford, California and London 1964), 180. Indian alcaldes regularly heard civil and criminal cases in which Indians were involved. In the absence of particular information for Zacatecas, it is reasonable to assume that alcaldes had the same function there. *Recopilación* 1680, VI iii 16, indicates the constabulary rôle of Indian alcaldes.

[3] For these alcaldías, see AGI Guadalajara 7, R. 6, 'Recaudos para la verificación del primer capítulo' (of a letter of 19 April 1607 from the Audiencia of New Galicia to the Crown).

[4] See Parry, *The Sale of Public Office*, pp. 29–30. The Hermandad was created in New Spain by the first Viceroy Velasco.

Corregidor and Cabildo

corregidor himself. The seventeenth century also saw a proliferation of lesser military offices – captains, sergeants and ensigns – which were sought for the social standing they conferred on their holders. The duties attached to these offices were of the lightest, and they were eagerly taken by many miners and merchants of Zacatecas, especially in the second half of the century.

In this chapter and those preceding it a description has been given of the development of Zacatecas from a primitive and transitory agglomeration of huts in 1548 to a complex mining and trading city in the seventeenth century. The movement of expansion to north, east and west has been sketched out. Zacatecas distributed its men and expertise to the new mining areas, and its missionaries to the plains and the mountains. The physical growth of the town has been followed. The central street sprang from the nucleus of the plaza pública and parish church, serving, as it extended to north and south, as an axis around which the town assumed its form. The religious houses were built in the last thirty years of the sixteenth century, symbols of the established importance of the city and auguries of its permanence. Indian communities, containing groups of distinct regional origins, encircled the Spanish centre. And as the town grew in size, the essential structures of supply and commerce developed. Roads were cut to link the new market of the north with the grain lands of the Bajío and Michoacán. Distribution of wheat, maize and meat was supervised. Traders took advantage of Zacatecas' geographical position to set up there an exchange market with the people of the northern provinces. A new economic circuit was established, as wealth began to flood from Zacatecas and its northern neighbours. The administration of the city was modified to deal with its burgeoning prosperity and increasing financial value to the Crown. The appointment of the first corregidor secured the city from the self-interest of the Audiencia of New Galicia and created more direct links of control with Mexico City, and thence with the Consejo de Indias.

No part of the story of Zacatecas can be far from the story of its mines. Allusions have been frequent in earlier pages to the consequence of booms and slumps in the various aspects of the life of the city that have been described. Monasteries were rebuilt in the early seventeenth century with silver given by miners prosperous on the upswing of the first great

<hr>

[1] See, for example, in AT.Z, Reales Oficiales 5, a document bearing a final date of Zacatecas 10 December 1638: 'Al General Agustín de Zavala para la conducción de los soldados que su excelencia el Señor Marqués de Cadereita mandó se levantasen en esta ciudad de Zacatecas ...' Zavala's title is included here. It was issued by Viceroy Cerralvo, in Mexico City, 12 April 1625.

boom. Prices of beef rose at the same time. So did the number of shop-keepers selling in the city. Reversal of the direction of the curve brought depression to trade, falling rents, an apathetic cabildo and demoralisation of the citizenry. Zacatecas had no reason for existence beyond its silver mines; commerce, though lucrative in periods of plentiful silver, dwindled as mines were abandoned. It is to the mining industry, the mainspring of the city's life, that the following chapters will be devoted.

CHAPTER 6

THE CIRCUMSTANCES OF MINING

This chapter is basically descriptive. It sets out to account for some of the more interesting institutions that were imposed on, and developed by, the miners of Zacatecas and its district in their efforts to extract the mineral wealth of their region, and to show the circumstances in which they worked. It is concerned, therefore, with what a French historian would undoubtedly call the *structures* of mining – for example, the connection between mining and land-ownership; systems of labour; mining technique; and the supply of raw materials. These subjects will be dealt with as discrete topics, and it is hoped that the inevitable ensuing loss of continuity will be compensated for by a gain in clarity. A preliminary qualification about the range of the discussion must also be made. What follows is intended to be an account of mining in the whole district of Zacatecas – that is, embracing both the city and the various lesser mining towns for which it acted as a centre. But to a large extent, specific reference will be made only to Zacatecas itself, and its mines and miners. The basic reason for thus limiting the view is simply that little information is available about the smaller towns. In any case, it is fairly clear that concentration on Zacatecas itself can lead to observations and conclusions which are valid for the whole region, merely because the evidence that *is* available indicates that conditions in the city (with certain exceptions, which will be obvious) were representative of those obtaining in the surrounding smaller towns. And furthermore, Zacatecas so far outstripped its lesser neighbours in wealth and silver output that the history of mining in the district during the sixteenth and seventeenth centuries is largely the history of a few square miles of the Serranía lying to the north of the city, containing assorted major silver veins, the Veta Grande and the village of Pánuco. Fresnillo, Sierra de Pinos, Chalchihuites, Mazapil, Nieves, Río Grande, Charcas and Ramos, *reales de minas* all, counted for little beside the mines of the Serranía. The only true challenge to Zacatecas' dominance in silver output came from Sombrerete, in a few decades of glory in the late seventeenth century. It then relapsed into the obscurity of earlier days.

The large and continuous supplies of food – basically grain – demanded by Zacatecas were drawn in great part from distant lands to the south, from estates in Michoacán and the Bajío on which miners had no claims of ownership. But miners did not lack interest in land. Land-ownership was probably, as historians have frequently pointed out, a source of social status in New Spain. But even the miner with the humblest social pretensions would have wanted access to land in order to ensure the supply of grain to his own hacienda de minas and its workers, to breed cattle for slaughter, and mules for turning his machinery. So a few pages on the miner as land-owner will not be out of place here. The intention is not to give a full description of the growth and decline of rural estates in Zacatecas during the sixteenth and seventeeth centuries. A separate investigation would be needed to achieve that – and a laborious investigation, for of all the many types of document surviving from colonial Spanish America it is surely land-titles that are most consuming of a historian's effort for least result. In any case, the master of the art of dealing with land documents – Chevalier – has already gone far towards providing such a full description in a chapter of his work on Mexican estates entitled 'Le Nord: "Les hommes riches et puissants" ',[1] to which the reader may be safely referred. In it he gives an outline of the processes by which certain miners became the owners of large estates in New Galicia and New Biscay. A look at the particular case of Zacatecas enables the outline to be filled in and modified to a degree.

As Chevalier demonstrates, the second half of the sixteenth century found miners engaged in the accumulation of land. Territory was easily obtained through grants (*mercedes*), by purchase, and by simple occupation of unclaimed areas. It may be supposed that the prosperous miners of Zacatecas took care to secure grazing and agricultural land where it was available. There is little documentary record to show how they did so; but doubtless there were many imitators of Diego de Ibarra, who gathered land to form his vast estate centred on the hacienda of Trujillo, west of Fresnillo. Ibarra made a *mayorazgo* of these lands (an entailed estate) and, after the death of his son Luis in 1576, the estate passed to his daughter Mariana, who later married Hipólito de Velasco, Marqués de Salinas, and sometime governor of New Biscay. Since alienation of lands in such a mayorazgo was generally restricted, it is probable that when Velasco presented the title of the estate for ratification before the President of New Galicia in 1611, the lands were much as Ibarra had left them. There were eighty-four titles to *sitios*, representing a total area of some 365,000 acres.[2] Only a few of the names of the sitios can now be placed;

---

[1] Chevalier, *La formation*, pp. 195–241.

[2] AGN Tierras 700, ff. 414v.–16, Guadalajara 17 May 1611, mandamiento given by the President of the Audiencia, Don Juan de Villela, in consolidation of the titles of the estate. A *sitio* had two possible areas. If it was de ganado mayor it measured 5,000 varas square, or 4,338 acres; if *de ganado menor*, 3,333 varas square, or 1,928 acres. This document does not

but from those that can, it is clear that the mayorazgo embraced land from south of Zacatecas as far north as Sombrerete and as far west as Valparaíso: a vast area filling the centre of the Zacatecas district. Even if the sitios were not contiguous, the effective domain of the Velasco family no doubt included the gaps, and overflowed the borders. It would be of fundamental interest to the history of the area to trace this estate through the seventeenth century; but no further notice of it appeared in the documents examined – so easily may a land-holding of even this size disappear from view.

For the accumulation of such large estates, political power as well as money was required. Diego de Ibarra was governor of New Biscay. Holders of that office generally managed to do well for themselves in land. Perhaps the process was cumulative – they first became eligible for office because they were land-owners, and then authority enabled them to build up their domains still further. A sixteenth-century governor after Ibarra, Rodrigo de Río de Losa, acquired great tracts of country to the north of Sombrerete; and an early seventeenth-century holder of the same office, Francisco de Urdiñola, had a vast hacienda at Patos, just over the northern border of New Galicia, which stretched eastwards as far as Saltillo. But these estates, although they dominated the rural scene, were not typical of the pattern of land-holding in New Galicia. Indeed, they could hardly have been so, for there was no space for more than a few holdings of such size. They belonged to Chevalier's rich and powerful men. As far as can be seen, hardly any vecinos and miners of Zacatecas owned so much land. The limits to land acquisition by the miner without high political authority were probably reached by a man like the Maestre de Campo Don Vicente de Zaldívar Mendoza, a prosperous and distinguished miner in Zacatecas in the early seventeenth century. He gathered or inherited a considerable estate in the fertile Súchil valley, to the west of Sombrerete, centred on the hacienda de San Pedro. There he bred cattle and horses, and cultivated grain, doubtless for the supply of his mines at nearby San Martín.[1] The possession of land in association with mines was common; but few miners owned an estate even as large as Zaldívar's, let alone anything to compare with the holdings of Ibarra, Río de Losa and Urdiñola.

---

specify which type of sitio is referred to in it. Grants of sitios de ganado mayor were perhaps more common. It is doubtful, in any case, whether legal measures were followed in practice.

[1] AN.Z, FE 1656, f. 244, Zacatecas 28 November 1656, lease of various lands in the Súchil valley by Doña María de Oñate Cortés, widow of Vicente de Zaldívar, to the Sargento Mayor Don Alonso Ramírez de Prado, alcalde mayor of Aguascalientes.

The Circumstances of Mining

A miner of moderate prosperity often possessed a small stock ranch, an *estancia de ganado mayor*, consisting usually of up to a dozen sitios, and thus ranging in size from, say, 10,000 to 50,000 acres. At first sight, such a holding appears far from small; but given the general infertility of land in the area, it was no more than was necessary for breeding and pasturing mules used in reduction works, and for cultivating a certain amount of maize to feed them and the workers of the mines. An example is an *estancia de ganado mayor y menor* called Buena Vista, the property of one Martín de Chirriaga, owner of an hacienda de minas with three molinos in Zacatecas. As it was described in his will, drawn up in 1659, Buena Vista supported 200 cattle, 200 sheep and 1,000 mares (*yeguas*). His hacienda de minas in Zacatecas was normally stocked with 100 mules.[1]

Numerous examples of similar land holdings by miners could be given. Chirriaga perhaps raised more stock than many others, some of it possibly for sale. Not all land in the vicinity of Zacatecas was owned by miners. There were many small farmers and stock breeders not directly connected with mining. A man of this sort was Captain Juan Avila Carrillo, a vecino of Jerez in the first half of the seventeenth century. He owned a quarter share in two sitios, which had a total area of 42 caballerías, or about 4,500 acres.[2] On his part of the land, a little more than 1,000 acres, he cultivated maize, and pastured, in 1644, 108 cattle; 585 sheep; 96 horses, mules and donkeys; 118 draught oxen and 47 pigs.[3] In the area to the south and south-west of Zacatecas (embracing Los Tlacotes, Palmillas, Malpaso and Jerez) there were many small farmers like Avila Carrillo, making a modest living from the land, farming for their own subsistence and for the Zacatecas market.

Chevalier suggests that the decline in mining in the seventeenth century provoked what might be called an 'introversion' of some of the haciendas of the north.[4] As demand from mines for mules, leather and food decreased, the haciendas became closed units, more self-sufficient and isolated than they had ever been. This is an interesting argument, but Chevalier does not support it adequately with examples. If he had followed the history of Ibarra's hacienda de Trujillo, or Urdiñola's lands around

---

[1] AN.Z, FE 1659, ff. 152–5v., Zacatecas 1 August 1659, will of Captain Martín de Chirriaga, vecino and miner of Zacatecas. The site of Buena Vista is not described in this document. There is a modern settlement called El Bordo de Buenavista about 18 miles north-east of Zacatecas.

[2] A *caballería* measured 1,104 by 552 varas – the equivalent in area of some 106 acres.

[3] AN.Z, FE 1664, Zacatecas 2 July 1664, will of Captain Juan Avila Carrillo, vecino of Jerez.

[4] Chevalier, *La formation*, especially 'Le repli des mineurs et le cas du Nouveau-León', pp. 234–41. Chevalier places the decline in mining twenty years too early, in the first decade of the seventeenth century. But this mistake does not affect the nature of his argument.

Patos, through the seventeenth century, much light would have been thrown on the matter. As it is, it appears that the seventeenth century, far from being a period of formation or even static consolidation of the estates, was for many of them a period of dissolution. There were special reasons why lands owned in association with mines were difficult to hold together. Most miners contracted large debts to the Crown for mercury. When it became apparent that they were unable to pay them, the Treasury could, and often did, confiscate their possessions: mines, houses, reduction works and lands. These, after a time, were often sold by auction. Miners, therefore, who possessed land were not only often obliged to sell or lease it in order to pay off debts; they might simply lose it directly to the Treasury. And owners of holdings large and small saw them sold or confiscated. The decline of mining in the mid-seventeenth century therefore brought about extensive changes in land-ownership in New Galicia. The recovery of mining in the second half of the century was, on the other hand, the reason for the re-formation of estates. A new order emerged from the flux of the middle years.

As brief illustrations of these two processes of dissolution and re-formation of estates, the lands of the Zaldívar family in the valley of Súchil and those of the Bravo family between Jerez and Juchipila may be mentioned. By the middle of the seventeenth century there was evidently considerable pressure on the Zaldívar estate. The widow of the Maestre de Campo Don Vicente de Zaldívar, Doña María Oñate Cortés, leased a large part of the land at Súchil in 1656, excepting only the sitio of San Pedro itself – the centre of the hacienda. The lease was renewed in 1664 by her son, this time to include all the family's lands at Súchil. The son, el Adelantado Don Nicolás de Zaldívar y Oñate, was a miner in Zacatecas, as Don Vicente had been. In his will, of 1679, he complained of his great poverty; all his goods had been confiscated by the Treasury for his debts; all his lands had been leased, also by the Treasury. (Most of the rent went to the Crown; in such cases the debtor was permitted to retain only a meagre living allowance.) The debt owing on the family estate was more than 300,000 pesos; much of the land at Súchil had been sold; and the rent from the rest did not cover the income due to censos and capellanías imposed on it.[1] The wealth of the Maestre de Campo had thus been completely dissipated, as a result of the family's failure in mining.

While the Zaldívar's were losing land, the Bravo family was gathering it. Scattered notarial records show that first Bartolomé Bravo de Acuña, an innovating and enterprising miner at Veta Grande, and then his son,

[1] See AN.Z, JL 1676–80, ff. 185v.–8v., Zacatecas 28 March 1679, will of Don Nicolás de Zaldívar Oñate, adelantado of New Mexico.

The Circumstances of Mining

Don Juan Bravo de Medrano, were buying land from the early 1650s onwards between Jerez and Juchipila. Don Juan was as successful a miner as his father; and in 1691 he purchased the vacant Spanish title of Conde de Santa Rosa, becoming the first Zacatecan to possess a title of nobility, and starting what is still called in the city 'la época de los Condes'.[1] The Condado de Santa Rosa was composed of the lands he and his father had together collected. The case of the Bravo's is not isolated. In the later years of the seventeenth century, other miners of the city acquired estates to rival in size those of a hundred years before. Don Joseph de Quesada, a miner who had come to Zacatecas in the second half of the century after having been a member of the consulado de México and a dealer in silver, died in 1685 the owner of 30,000 head of sheep on land lying to the north of Nieves. In the following year his widow, Doña Francisca de Lezcano, bought additional lands for the estate, so that it comprised, in 1686, 130 sitios de ganado mayor, 114 caballerías and 31 sitios de ganado menor. This land extended into New Biscay as far as Avino, Indehé and Durango. It is interesting to note, and illustrative of the argument for the re-formation of estates in the late seventeenth century, that many of the titles to the land bought by Doña Francisca dated from the last decades of the sixteenth century, and some indeed had originally been granted to Rodrigo de Río de Losa, whose domains had covered the region where the new estate was arising. The available documents unfortunately do not relate the no doubt intricate story of these land titles through the seventeenth century.[2]

It is of interest to see that some of the land acquired by Don Juan Bravo de Medrano had originally belonged to a convent in Querétaro, the Convento de Religiosas de Santa Clara de Jesús.[3] He did not, however, buy any of the rural property of the religious houses of Zacatecas. This property was, in any case, small, if the records of it surviving in local

[1] See AN.Z, FE 1653A (n.f.), Zacatecas 4 April 1653; AA.Z, 10, No. 52, Zacatecas 19 January 1667; Zacatecas 20 March 1667; Zacatecas 25 February 1687. All are purchases of land by Don Bartolomé and Don Juan Bravo.

[2] AN.Z, IG 1685, ff. 17–27, Zacatecas 7 January 1685, will of Don Joseph de Quesada, vecino and miner of Zacatecas, drawn up by his widow, Doña Francisca de Lezcano; AN.Z, IG 1686, ff. 102v.–5, Zacatecas 8 March 1686, 'Poder para tomar dinero a censo' of Doña Francisca de Lezcano to Captain Don Joseph de Aldabalde; and AN.Z, DV 1687, ff. 2v.–8v., Zacatecas 2 May 1687, foundation of a capellanía by Doña Francisca de Lezcano in favour of her son Don Francisco de Quesada, clérigo de menores órdenes.

[3] AA.Z, 10, No. 52, Zacatecas 25 February 1687, traspaso de tierras by Diego García de Belaustegui, vecino of Zacatecas, to Captain Don Juan Bravo de Medrano. How this land, containing the four sitios of La Quemada, Los Edificios, El Cuicillo and El Arenal, had become part of the domain of the nuns of Querétaro, is not known. La Quemada still exists as an hacienda, close to Los Edificios, a popular name given to the archaeological remains of Chicomóztoc.

archives are a true guide to its extent. As in other parts of New Spain, the leading ecclesiastical land-owner in Zacatecas was the Society of Jesus. The Jesuits submitted the titles of four sitios for ratification (*composición*) in 1645. This land, which had been either sold or donated to them, was used to support an hacienda de minas owned by the Society in the 'Cañada de Abajo' – presumably the valley between Zacatecas and Guadalupe.[1] For a period of unknown length before 1653, the Society also possessed a sizeable hacienda two leagues from Aguascalientes, with irrigated land on which wheat and maize were grown. This hacienda, called San Nicolás Chapultepec, was sold in 1653 to one Miguel de León, a merchant of Zacatecas, for 8,900 pesos. León actually paid only 900 pesos, the balance being divided into two censos: one of 3,000 pesos in favour of the Zacatecas Jesuits, and one of 5,000 pesos in favour of the heirs of Juana de Rivera, wife of the vecino of Aguascalientes from whom the Society had originally purchased the hacienda. Income from the censos, at the standard rate of 5 per cent, would have brought 150 pesos per year to the Jesuits and 250 to Rivera's descendants. It was perhaps as a result of the economic difficulties of these years that the College in Zacatecas ceased to work the hacienda directly, preferring a fixed income from its land. Or possibly that land was simply no longer productive, for only four months later León resold it for a mere 200 pesos in cash, transferring the 8,000 pesos of principal on which the censos were payable.[2] The Jesuits were nevertheless far from landless at this time, for they retained an hacienda called La Cieneguilla, which lay adjacent to San Nicolás. And later in the decade they began to purchase agricultural and grazing land in the area of Saín Alto, Río Grande and Sombrerete.[3]

It was in this same northern area that the Augustinians held the only land which records show they possessed. This was the hacienda of La Pastelera, originally of the property of Don Francisco de Pinedo, who, upon entering the Order as a novice in 1607, and being without heir, bequeathed it to his monastery. At the beginning of the eighteenth

---

[1] AA.Z, 6, No. 61, Zacatecas 5 December 1645. The titles were presented for composition by the Rector of the College, Padre Antonio del Castillo.

[2] For these two transactions, see AN.Z, FE 1653A (n.f.), Zacatecas 22 January 1653, sale of hacienda of San Nicolás Chapultepec by Padre Lorenzo López to Miguel de León; and AN.Z, FE 1653A, Zacatecas 13 May 1653, sale of hacienda de labor San Nicolás Chapultepec by Miguel de León to Pedro Enríquez de Erquijo, vecino of Zacatecas.

[3] See AN.Z, FE 1659, ff. 218v.–19v., Zacatecas 30 October 1659, sale by Alonso Centeno, vecino of Zacatecas, in name of Diego Romero, vecino of Celaya, to the Society of Jesus in Zacatecas, of one sitio and three caballerías called El Cansalejo, for 400 pesos; and AN.Z, FE 1659 (folio number unknown) Zacatecas 20 December 1659, sale by Nicolás López Trujillo, vecino of Llerena, to the Society of Jesus in Zacatecas, of two sitios de ganado within 3 leagues of Sombrerete, for 350 pesos.

The Circumstances of Mining

century, La Pastelera comprised 5¼ sitios de ganado mayor, 2 sitios de ganado menor, 17½ caballerías. In the seventeenth century the land appears to have been generally leased.[1] Of the other religious houses established in Zacatecas, only the Hospital de San Juan de Dios appears to have owned land. In 1664 there is a record of a lease made by the Hospital to one Antonio Núñez of an hacienda called San Nicolás in the jurisdiction of Jerez. This was purely a stock holding with 38 horses, 64 cattle, 56 goats and a flock of 400 sheep.[2] For their part, the Dominicans had, apparently, no land to their name; nor did the Franciscans. It has been pointed out before, in reference to their lack of urban property in Zacatecas, that the Friars Minor in New Spain were the least given to the pursuit of goods among all the Orders established in the colony. It is therefore of little surprise that the Franciscans of Zacatecas were apparently as little concerned with rural as they were with urban property. It has to be said, as a general comment on this brief survey of ecclesiastical land ownership in the Zacatecas region, that the documentary sources in which information on the subject was sought were hardly likely to give a complete picture. If the archives of Zacatecan monasteries could be located, they might show that the Orders owned far more than has been suggested here. Nevertheless, it is probably true that their holdings did not compare with the larger private estates; nor, probably, with the estates owned by several of the Orders in central and southern New Spain. The land of the Zacatecas district was generally unsuitable for grain, the cultivation of which was the great occupation of the Orders in their southern domains.

The land occupied by the estates of the Zacatecas district had not supported, before the Spaniards arrived, any permanent Indian settlements; its only inhabitants had been the nomadic Zacatecos, Guachichiles and Tepehuanes. This fact to a large extent determined the nature of the labour systems by which mines and haciendas de minas would be worked; for where there were no permanent Indian towns or villages, there could be no encomienda and no repartimiento.[3] In the mines of New Spain proper, repartimiento was a very frequently employed means of using

---

[1] AA.Z, Propiedades 3, No. 27 (n.f.), dealing with La Pastelera from 1607 to 1704. And AA.Z, Propiedades 3, No. 24 (n.f.), which gives the original titles of the land, dating from as early as 1565.

[2] See AN.Z, FE 1664, ff. 98–9v., Zacatecas 1 September 1664, lease by the Hospital de San Juan de Dios to Antonio Núñez, of the hacienda San Nicolás, for five years at 90 pesos a year.

[3] For repartimiento – forced, but salaried, labour – see in general L. B. Simpson, *Studies in the Administration of the Indians in New Spain, III, The Repartimiento System of Native Labour in New Spain and Guatemala*, Ibero-Americana: 13, University of California Press, Berkeley and Los Angeles 1938.

Indian labour; but in those of New Galicia, for lack of Indians on whom to draw, it was almost unknown.[1] Zacatecas was, therefore, obliged to rely on two systems only: slavery and free wage-labour. Slaves were either Indian or Negro (and mulatto). Only in the sixteenth century do Indian slaves appear to have been numerous. The Chichimec campaigns gave soldiers the chance of taking slaves in 'just war', and some of these were put to work in mines.[2] But the unfortunate Indians of the Sierras did not escape slavery even in the late seventeenth century. Sixty-two of them were found in Zacatecas in 1672; by that time it had long been illegal to take them.[3]

Negro slavery was considered quite legitimate, and was well established in New Spain long before Zacatecas was settled. Negro slaves were among the first inhabitants of the town. La Marcha's labour Ordinances of 1550 refer quite distinctly to them.[4] Nor were mulattos long in appearing. And with the passage of time, freedmen and freedwomen, both Negro and mulatto, became numerous. Mota y Escobar found a number of them in Zacatecas; they hired themselves out for work on ranches, on farms and in mines. Of Negroes and mulattos in general he said '... commonly they are bad and vicious, both the free and the slaves; but the saying is there [in Zacatecas], "Bad to have them, but much worse not to have them" '. He counted about 800 Negro and mulatto slaves of both sexes.[5] Sales of slaves, the cabildo said on occasion, were, together with sales of wine, the most lucrative source of alcabalas. The price of slaves, as of goods, increased northwards, which probably explains why many slaves were sold to Zacatecas from Mexico City and Puebla (and occasion-

---

[1] There also appears to have been a statutory prohibition of repartimiento labour in the mines of New Galicia, although repeated searches have not brought the Ordinance to light. This prohibition was the subject of several complaints from Zacatecan miners in the seventeenth century. An early reference comes from an oidor of Guadalajara in 1583 (AGI Guadalajara 6, R. 2, 6 April 1583, Licenciado Pinedo to Crown), who noted that a previous (unspecified) cédula banning repartimiento in all mines of the colony had been rescinded for New Spain itself five or six years before, but was still observed in New Galicia. The ban was thus perhaps by default.

[2] Regulations in 1575 allowed Chichimecs captured in war to be enslaved for twenty years, provided they were males over the age of twenty. Many of the slaves taken were sold further south, since it was thought best to keep them away from the frontier. See Powell, *Soldiers*, pp. 110–11.

[3] AGI Guadalajara 12, Guadalajara 20 March 1672, Fiscal to the Queen Regent. The Chichimecs, Sinaloes and the natives of New León and New Mexico, he said, were still often enslaved. At Parral 202 of them had recently been freed.

[4] La Marcha's Ordinances of 27 April 1550, clause 11, in AGI Guadalajara 5, 'Averiguaciones ... Contreras y Guevara ... 1570', f. 117v. La Marcha spoke of 'esclavos' in distinction to free Indians and workers in mine cuadrillas. Indian slaves were normally referred to specifically as 'esclavos indios '; Negro slaves, being more common, were 'esclavos' without further qualification.

[5] Mota y Escobar, *Descripción*, p. 66.

ally from as far south as Oaxaca). Records of sales exist only in the notarial books of the city, which means that hardly any can be found referring to the sixteenth century and the first half of the seventeenth. After then it is possible to compile full lists of sales for some years. Typical years in which there were numerous sales were 1656 and 1685.[1] The transactions can be summarised as in the table.

Slave	Average age at sale	Average price in pesos	Number in sample	Total number bought
		1656		
Negro	24	305	17	18
Negra	29	268	16	19
Mulato	23	284	12	18
Mulata	24	225	11	12
Chino	40	200	1	1
				—
				68
		1685		
Negro	22	309	9	9
Negra	27	350	3	8
Mulato	24	302	12	16
Mulata	24	313	12	14
				—
				47

In both these years only twenty-three of the slaves sold were imported into Zacatecas, the remaining transactions being between sellers and buyers resident in the city. These figures are given merely to show prices in two more or less representative years and not in an attempt to demonstrate a trend, for which they are manifestly inadequate. The apparent general increase in prices in 1685 in comparison with 1656 is not confirmed by figures from later years. In general it appears that Negroes and Negresses fetched slightly higher prices than mulattos; this being, perhaps, the consequence of Spanish prejudices against half-castes of any sort. Mulattos also tended to be sold at a lower age than Negroes, which might have been another result of the same prejudice. An owner would perhaps keep the pure-blooded children of his Negro slaves while selling any mulatto children he might possess. The *chino* who appears in 1656 was by no means alone in Zacatecas in the seventeenth century.

[1] AN.Z, FE 1656, *passim*; AN.Z, JM 1684–5; AN.Z, IG 1685. In calculating averages, only slaves whose age and price are both known have been included. Since these details are not always given in full, the total number of slaves included in the sample is not the same as the total number sold.

The Circumstances of Mining

There were always a few of these slaves from the Philippines in the city.

If it may be taken that the 800 Negro and mulatto slaves seen by Mota y Escobar were men and women in roughly equal numbers, then these slaves constituted a fifth of the mine labour force at that time; for he estimated that there were 1,500 Indian workers in Zacatecas. (Female slaves were employed in domestic service by miners and non-miners.) Slaves were valued not because they worked better than Indians, but because they were a permanent force. Unlike Indians, they could not easily abandon Zacatecas if news came of a rich strike in some other mines. Mota y Escobar pointed out that they were of little use below the ground because they succumbed so easily to the cold and humidity of the mines. They were employed, then, as labourers in the haciendas de minas, moving ore from *molinos* to *incorporadero* to *lavadero*.[1]

It was the Indians who made up the largest and most useful part of the labour force. From the beginning they streamed into Zacatecas from the south. These people were *naborías* – roughly speaking, free workers. In 1550 la Marcha prohibited the justices of the city from trying to assign to miners those Indians who came of their own free will to the city; they should be allowed to hire themselves out to anyone they pleased.[2] There was evidently an established contractual form for engaging labour, although no example of any contract was found during research. In 1568 the visiting oidor of New Galicia, Francisco de Mendiola, ordered that no-one should attempt to hire a free worker, whether Negro, mulatto or Indian, who was already engaged, for pay, by another employer ('... que tubiere con otro asoldada la jornal'). The *jornal* seems to have been extended beyond its precise meaning of one day's labour, for the order goes on to say that workers may be hired only when they have 'fulfilled the time and the work for which they were contracted by the first employer'.[3] The particular form of contract common in mining was the *tequío*, a word whose literal meaning was the specific amount of ore that the mine worker was obliged to produce in a day.

---

[1] Mota y Escobar, *Descripción*, pp. 66–8. Occasionally, inventories of haciendas include a Negro or mulatto barretero, but in general Mota y Escobar's statement is true for the seventeenth century.

[2] La Marcha's Ordinances, Zacatecas 27 April 1550, clause 16, in AGI Guadalajara 5, 'Averiguaciones ... Contreras y Guevara ... 1570', f. 118.

[3] For Mendiola's Ordinances, dated Zacatecas 6 March 1568, see AGI Guadalajara 5, 'Averiguaciones ... Contreras y Guevara ... 1570', ff. 122–37, 'Este es un traslado bien y fielmente sacado de unas ordenanzas que hizo en las minas de los Zacatecas el Señor Licenciado Don Francisco de Mendiola, oidor alcalde mayor de la real audiencia de este reino de Galicia según que por ellas parecía, su tenor del cual es éste que sigue ...'; reference here is to clause 6 (f. 123).

The Circumstances of Mining

The first mention of this also comes in 1568; but no precise account of how the contracts worked in practice ever appears. Presumably the amount of the tequío was variable from mine to mine.[1]

Most of a miner's workers lived within the hacienda de minas, forming his *cuadrilla*, or labour gang. The cuadrilla is first mentioned in 1550 by la Marcha, and was doubtless an institution imported into Zacatecas from mines in the south.[2] Information on wage rates is very scarce, and wages quoted in cash are, in any case, as poor an indication of what the Indian really earned as they are of the true cost of labour to the miner. This is because of the difficulty of assigning a cash value to the benefits in kind received by many workers – notably ores, food and housing. La Marcha imposed a statutory maximum wage of four reales a week. Fifty years later Mota y Escobar found that *barreteros* were earning five to eight pesos a month; 'but', he said, 'for these Indians, salary is the least important thing, because of the stones containing rich ore that they extract from the common ore [*la gruesa*], and which they call among themselves *pepena* ...'.[3] The pepena was a bagful of high quality ore suitable for smelting, which the mine-workers were permitted to collect for themselves once they had fulfilled the day's tequío. They then sold it to the highest bidder, who was usually the owner of a small smelting plant. Occasionally, though, a mine-owner might himself buy the pepena from his own workers; or the Indian might reduce the ore himself and sell or spend the silver. The pepena was undoubtedly worth far more to the Indian than his pay. And although it meant that the miner lost a part of the ores in his mine, it also meant that Indians were always anxious to explore and extend mines to their own, and incidentally the miner's, advantage. Pepena could therefore be seen as a primitive productivity bonus. It brought certain disadvantages, naturally. Workers had no compunction about cutting away supporting pillars left in mines, if they contained good ores. And Indians went where pepenas were richest; so that if a mine was going through a lean spell, it was likely to lose its labour force. Both official and unofficial measures were often taken to prevent Indians from abandoning one employer in favour of another. Miners were found to be locking their workers up in private prisons; and there was voluminous legislation from the middle of the sixteenth century onwards, controlling the practice of labour 'poaching'

[1] See Clause 9 of Mendiola's Ordinances, in AGI Guadalajara 5, 'Averiguaciones ... Contreras y Guevara ... 1570', f. 123v.

[2] Clause 11 of la Marcha's Ordinances, Zacatecas 27 April 1550, in AGI Guadalajara 5, 'Averiguaciones ... Contreras y Guevara ... 1570', f. 117v.

[3] Clause 19 of la Marcha's Ordinances, in AGI Guadalajara 5, 'Averiguaciones ... Contreras y Guevara ... 1570', f. 118v.; and Mota y Escobar, *Descripción*, p. 69.

The Circumstances of Mining

(*sonsaque*), by which one employer tempted another's workers away with payments of cash.[1]

The retention of labour was, of course, a problem to be found wherever Indians were employed. A common solution was debt peonage. This first appeared in Zacatecas in the last quarter of the sixteenth century, and was the subject of extensive legislation, which aimed to reduce the amount of advance payment to four, or sometimes eight months' wages.[2] It would be wrong to think, however, that debt peonage was practised without exception by all miners. Wills of owners of haciendas de minas in the seventeenth century show that miners were often owed nothing by their workers. The Indian was probably more firmly attached to his employer by the pepena, and by the material advantages of being a member of a cuadrilla. He lived, with his family, in the hacienda de minas, where he received free supplies of meat and maize. While living conditions in the haciendas obviously cannot be idealised, and inevitably would have varied from employer to employer, they were probably at least as good as those to be had in the Indian barrios of the city. The hacienda was perhaps the only distinctive social institution of the mining industry. As a dwelling unit for the miner and his workers, it was to some extent self-contained. It held within its wall the house (*casa de morada*) of the owner, quarters (*aposentos*) for workers and their families, and a chapel. It also had stables for horses and mules, and the sheds and rooms necessary to hold machinery and stores. Most of the haciendas in Zacatecas lay within the town, along the sides of the stream, into which they discharged water used in the washing processes essential to refining silver. Some, though, were built by other streams and water-courses in the Serranía, several miles from the city. Workers may well have developed certain loyalties to their haciendas and the owners. There is evidence for this in occasional reports of brawls between cuadrillas from different haciendas. The ties, and workers' corporate feelings, were probably not strong – not strong enough, anyway, to prevent Indians from abandoning employers if there were prospects of higher earnings elsewhere. But even so, the hacienda may have served, incidentally to its main purpose as a refining plant, as a stabilising influence on the labour force.

There is no continuous information on the number of Indians employed in the mining industry. The Fiscal of Guadalajara reported that the great

---

[1] For imprisonment of Indian workers, see AGI Guadalajara 7, R. 6, 15 April 1607, Licenciado Gaspar de la Fuente to Crown. For sonsaque, see MA Mexico, Zacatecas microfilm, reel 7, 'archivo del ayuntamiento' (film of an unidentified volume), f. 405–405v., Guadalajara 16 December 1615, mandamiento of Dr Alonso Pérez Merchán.

[2] See, e.g., MA Mexico, Zacatecas microfilm, reel 7, ff. 402v.–3, México 11 October 1595, mandamiento of Velasco II limiting advance wages to eight months.

The Circumstances of Mining

matlazahuatl (probably typhus) epidemic of 1576–7 killed more than 2,000 mine workers at Zacatecas. He was referring only to Indians.[1] But this figure seems exaggerated when Mota y Escobar's estimate that the total force in 1602–5 was 1,500 Indians is remembered. Francisco de Villarreal, visitor to Zacatecas in 1625, is a more reliable witness. In the ninety-five haciendas de minas that he found in the whole district, 1,300 Indians were employed. 730 of these were at Zacatecas and Pánuco.[2] Villarreal refers only to those Indians actually working in haciendas, and not to those employed in mines, who could have been another 1,000,[3] making a total Indian labour force of some 1,700 or more. There is precise, but limited, information on the numbers of workers employed in 1622, when a census was made of Indians in the administration of the Franciscan monastery of Zacatecas. The Franciscans shared parish duties in the city with the secular clergy of the Iglesia Mayor, and their jurisdiction embraced the whole of the barrio of Tlacuitlapan. The barrio had a population of 240 adult Indians of both sexes. Fourteen haciendas de minas also fell within the Franciscans' area, at the northern end of the town, and these held a total of 664 adult men and women, of whom 280 formed the cuadrillas of the haciendas themselves and 384 those of the mines.[4] (That is the form in which the census is expressed. There is no suggestion here or in other documents that women worked in mines or even in the reduction process in the haciendas. If they worked at all it was probably in domestic service.) The number of Indians employed by individual miners ranged from the eighty-five attributed to Don Juan de Oñate down to the eighteen working in the mines and hacienda of Mateo de Herrera. The compiler of this census, Fray Pedro de Aguilar, the vicar of the monastery, adds an interesting qualification to his figures at the end of the document. He emphasises that the 904 Indians counted are those resident in April 1622. But the same part of the town sometimes contains upward of 2,000 Indians, when there are rich pepenas to be had

---

[1] AGI Guadalajara 6, R. 1, Guadalajara 6 March 1577, Licenciado Martínez to Crown.

[2] AGI Guadalajara 33, (Zacatecas?) 28 January 1626, 'Puntos esenciales a que se redujo la visita de minas que hizo el Contador Francisco de Villarreal en el distrito de la Real Caja de Zacatecas. (Ojo. Conviene mucho leerlos para entender el estado de estas minas)' (n.f.). This is 'No. 4' of Villarreal's report on his visit. Workers were distributed among the other towns of the district thus: Ramos and Pinos, 220; Fresnillo, 130; Sombrerete, San Martín and Súchil, 130; the remaining smaller towns, 90.
For the derivation of this figure, see note 4 below.

[4] BNM Archivo de la Provincia del Santo Evangelio de México, Caja 58, folder 1160, No. 2: Zacatecas 23 April 1622, 'Indios de las haciendas y minas sujetos a la administración parroquial del Convento de San Francisco de los Zacatecas'. (Reference from note 3 above: the ratio between hacienda and mine-workers in this census is 280:384, or about 1:1·4. Villarreal's number of 730 hacienda workers may therefore be multiplied by 1·4 to give a rough estimate of the number of mine-workers at his time. The result is about 1,000.)

in the mines. This confirms statements by other observers that Zacatecas had a very large floating population (see Appendix II), as well as demonstrating the power of the mines to attract voluntary labour. It cannot be said whether the distribution of Indians between haciendas and town shown in this census was typical of the whole of Zacatecas; but it is at least apparent that a very large part of the Indian population was in the direct and permanent employ of mine-owners, living in accommodation belonging to them: here, 664 out of 904 (about 73 per cent).

Indians flocked to the north at the time of the Zacatecas strike from various regions of central Mexico. There came Aztecs, Tlaxcalans, Cholultecans and Otomíes. Very soon immigrants arrived also from Michoacán and the Pueblos de Avalos. While the lure of riches lasted there was no faltering in this stream of voluntary labourers. The influx is neatly demonstrated by another document from the Franciscan monastery in Zacatecas, a register of births, confirmations and marriages occurring in the northern part of the town cared for by the Franciscans, during the years 1616–20.[1] In that period, forty-six marriages took place in which the origin of at least one partner is recorded. In thirty cases the husband was definitely not a native of Zacatecas or Pánuco; and in eighteen the wife was not Zacatecas born. Michoacán was the birthplace of most of the new arrivals. This was a time of increasing silver output, when Zacatecas must have offered good prospects. There were certainly, from time to time, shortages of labour, caused by disasters such as the epidemic of 1576 and lesser visitations of disease in later years; but the numbers were in general quickly made up again, even though the hundred years from 1550 to 1650 saw a continuation of the calamitous decrease in aboriginal population that had begun with the conquest of New Spain. The total Indian labour force in the district during the sixteenth and seventeenth centuries can never have exceeded 5,000 at the very most, if Villarreal's figures for hacienda employees in the mid-1620s are accurate. It is therefore unlikely that even a drastic decline in the total aboriginal population could have caused a serious shortage of labour in the mines of Zacatecas. There would always have been a large enough pool from which to draw workers to maintain such a small force. It is arguable, therefore, that if miners in Zacatecas complained of shortage of labour, as they undeniably did now and again, that shortage should be attributed to lack of attractions in mining itself – that is, low wages or poor expectations of pepenas – rather than to the general demographic situation of New

---

[1] The register, which is a vellum-bound book, is preserved in the Biblioteca Pública del Estado in Zacatecas. The title page is unfortunately destroyed, but the record obviously refers to the Indian barrios in the administration of the Franciscans.

The Circumstances of Mining

Spain. It is also possible that at times when the demand for labour rose very suddenly, as in the case of a major new discovery of ore, the normal system of increasing labour supply – spread of news of the strike attracting voluntary labour from a distance – proved so slow in operating that temporary shortages occurred. But Zacatecan miners clamouring for repartimiento Indians would have had to agree with Dr Juan González de Peñafiel, Fiscal of the Audiencia of New Spain, who observed in 1633, as the clinching point of a long series of impassioned arguments condemning repartimiento as a scourge of Indians, that 'The reales of Zacatecas and San Luis [Potosí] are the richest and most prosperous of the Kingdom, and they are without repartimientos, and they alone are worth almost as much as all the other [mines] which have them [repartimientos] ...'.[1] Generally speaking, the institutions of voluntary Indian labour (reinforced sometimes with debt peonage) and Negro slavery, which had taken root in Zacatecas from the beginning, were adequate to provide the labour needed by mining.

The mineral wealth sought by Spanish miners and Indian labourers alike lay concentrated in narrow rock fissures within the Serranía de Zacatecas, close by the city. The road that still winds its way past the Convento de San Francisco, along the rising course of the stream, and then over three or four miles of bare slopes to Veta Grande, crosses vein after vein of silver ore in its short extent. The exposed outcrops (crestones) of the steeply tilted vetas cut across the hills at frequent intervals, and are so clearly visible to even the casual walker that it seems astonishing that early settlers took so long to locate the richest veins. The veta de San Bernabé, between Zacatecas and Veta Grande, la Albarrada (part of the Veta Grande itself) and the veins of Pánuco were not found until 1548, two years after prospectors first came to Zacatecas. The weathered ores of these crestones were of vast richness; in later years, with what nostalgia and wishful thinking cannot be known, it was said that they had contained half rock, half silver.[2]

The accuracy of such statements, among many other doubtful and interesting questions, would be more easily verifiable if there existed

[1] AGI Mexico 75, R. 2, (México?) 24 March 1633, 'Carta a su majestad del Dr Peñafiel, fiscal de México, de 24 de marzo de 1633 con decreto que lo vea el señor fiscal en 11 de agosto, sobre la vara del Alguacil Mayor', f. 15–15v.

[2] See AGI Guadalajara 230, Z, 1, f. 183, real provisión, Madrid 3 August 1567. This provisión refers to a statement of the miners of Zacatecas about the increasing cost of extracting silver. They claimed, incidentally to their argument, that the common yield of one quintal of ore (100 lb.) was 100 marks of silver (50 lb.). The continued presence of such rich ores nearly twenty years after the discovery is very surprising. Perhaps the original document was badly transcribed at some point, so that 100 ounces should be read for 100 marks. That would still be an enormous yield by later standards.

The Circumstances of Mining

some contemporary work on mining in New Spain during the first two centuries of Spanish occupation. But the colony regrettably failed to produce a mineralogist and mining technologist to compare with Alvaro Alonso Barba – the man who, after years of residence at Potosí in Upper Peru, produced in 1640 his renowned treatise, *Arte de los metales*. This work describes mining practice in Peru at the time, and is specially informative in its accounts of various types of silver ore and of reduction methods appropriate to each of them.[1] In the absence of such a full contemporary work on mining in colonial Mexico, little can be said of the mineralogical knowledge of miners in New Spain in the sixteenth and seventeenth centuries. Zacatecan miners undoubtedly had considerable ability to recognise in practice the several varieties of ore found in their district, and knew by which process they could best be worked. Ores were judged by their colour. The basic distinction was between black and red (*negros* and *colorados*), a distinction which later observers have explained in chemical terms. Colorados were found in the upper part of the fissure veins in which the mineral deposits lay. They derived their colour from the iron oxide which was mixed with the various silver compounds present in the gangue. Negros came from the lower levels of the vein. They had a high content of lead sulphide (galena) and lacked the iron oxide that so distinctively coloured ores nearer the surface. The main silver minerals present in the veins were sulphides and oxides, both of which might be very rich. There was much native silver also.[2]

Both silver sulphides and silver oxides could easily be reduced by the amalgamation method that was widely employed in Zacatecas. Miners therefore came to be more interested in the yield of the ores than in their intrinsic nature. Only when an ore proved resistant to amalgamation did they begin to question its composition. It was known, for instance, that ores containing antimony could not be worked with mercury, and demanded smelting. In general, however, a mine was judged by the richness of its ores, not by their type. The exposed crestones of the veins were undoubtedly the richest portion of all, possibly because weathering removed much of the dross from the gangue, leaving ores in high concentration. It was the fabulous richness of these crestones that drew fortune hunters to Zacatecas in the 1550s. But these surface ores were soon removed and miners had to follow veins downwards into regions of

---

[1] Alvaro Alonso Barba, *Arte de los Metales*, Madrid 1640. The English translation by R. E. Douglass and E. P. Mathewson (New York 1923) is particularly useful in that it provides modern English equivalents of seventeenth-century Spanish mining terms.

[2] See J. Burkart, 'Du filon et des mines de Veta-Grande, près de la ville de Zacatecas, dans l'état du même nom, au Mexique', *Annales des Mines*, troisième série, vol. 8, Paris 1835; pp. 55–87, and especially pp. 65–8.

The Circumstances of Mining

lower yield. By the late 1550s there were complaints of declining quality of ore. Whereas in the first years richness had been measured in marks of silver extracted from a quintal of ore, now it was measured in ounces.[1] But in reality this was only the end of the beginning of Zacatecan mining. The deposits of deeper ores that were laid open once the crestones had been removed were still of sufficiently high quality to be profitably worked by contemporary methods of extraction and reduction. And so vast were they that Zacatecas remained an important silver producer for three and a half centuries. An exact figure for the yield of these ores cannot be given; but the colorados, which might extend down to a depth of over 400 feet, were generally of good quality. R. C. West, in his study of the Parral district, explains the relevant mineralogy: 'A peculiar characteristic of silver ore deposits is the occurrence of a pronounced zone of mineral enrichment above the ground water table, which, in the eastern foothills of the Sierra Madre Occidental, ranges from 200 to 400 feet; below the altered zone, low grade sulphides prevail.' This enrichment was produced by the action of descending surface water.[2] The enriched, oxidised zone corresponds to the colorados; the low-grade sulphides below the water table are the negros. The water table at Zacatecas lies within the same limits as those given by West for the Parral district. Within the colorados there was no consistency of quality. Not only did one vein vary in yield from the next, but rich pockets of ore occurred at random at all depths in a single vein. So it is not true to say of Zacatecas, as has sometimes been said of the silver mines of the New World in general, that yields decreased with depth.[3] Flores, whose study of the Zacatecas deposits appears to have been thoroughly made, concluded that there was no general pattern of distribution of types or quality of ore within the veins; the only reliable prediction that could be made was that rich pockets would occur where two veins intersected.[4]

The methods used for extracting ores from veins were primitive. In the beginning the crestones could, of course, be merely cut away on the surface; while ores at slightly greater depth were extracted easily by

---

[1] T. Flores, *Etude minière du district de Zacatecas*, México 1906, pp. 21-2.

[2] Robert C. West, *The Mining Community of Northern New Spain: the Parral Mining District*, Ibero-Americana: 30, University of California Press, Berkeley and Los Angeles 1949, pp. 17-18.

[3] There was apparently a belief among local miners, though in much later times, that ores improved with depth. A company formed in 1829 to work a promising mine called Las Bolsas, explained its subsequent failure by saying that contrary to the normal pattern in Zacatecas, the mine had lost quality as it went deeper. *Memoria en que el gobierno del Estado Libre de los Zacatecas da cuenta de los Ramos de su Administración al Congreso del Mismo Estado*, Zacatecas 1831, p. 21.

[4] Flores, *Etude minière*, p. 22.

open-cast mining. Gashes left in the tops of hills where veins run across them are to be seen everywhere in the Serranía. A shallow trough still remains where the Veta de San Bernabé was obviously thus worked *a tajo abierto*. It soon became necessary, however, to tunnel in the pursuit of ores. Underground technique was clearly elementary. It consisted mainly of following the course of the vein in the hope of striking good ores. The workings that resulted from this practice were obviously haphazard in arrangement and ultimately inefficient. It was simple to carry ores to the surface from a shallow depth through these unplanned tunnels. But once the mines went deeper, the lack of any properly thought-out system of workings made for severe difficulties of extraction, drainage and ventilation.

The ease with which veins could be followed by tunnelling into them from hillsides and the chance of quick rewards probably discouraged miners from taking the trouble to dig logically designed workings. But sooner or later the need to lift ground water out of the mines meant that vertical shafts had to be sunk; for the whim (*malacate*) that was used for drainage operated best in such a shaft (although it could be used to drag objects up a sloping tunnel). By 1567 miners were complaining that the deeper mines were flooded.[1] It cannot be known how they went about solving the problem at that time. A possible answer, if the flooded mines were those cut into hillsides, would have been to cut *socavones* (sloping drainage adits) from the flooded levels to the exterior. But socavones were never a popular remedy for flooding among miners of New Spain. To construct a long tunnel merely for the purpose of letting out water seemed a waste of money and effort.[2] In any case it is unlikely that mines sunk into the hills of the Serranía would have reached the water table by 1567; the flooded mines were more probably those sunk in parts of the veins running through the lower slopes and along the valley floors, where the use of socavones was not possible in any case. Drainage in later years was carried out with pumps and whims, but no firm date can be given for their introduction in Zacatecas. In 1583, it was suggested that one Bartolomé de Gálvez, a miner of Temascaltepec who had invented an apparatus (*ingenio*) for drawing out water, might go to Zacatecas to give help in the problem of drainage.[3] But what manner of

---

[1] AGI Guadalajara 230, Z, 1, f. 183, real provisión, Madrid 3 August 1567.

[2] Only where workings were very closely concentrated, which they were not in Zacatecas, was it worth opening an adit for drainage. One such case in New Spain was the famous Cerro de San Pedro of San Luis Potosí, in which a socavón was built to great advantage in the early years of the seventeenth century. W. W. Borah, 'Un gobierno provincial de frontera en San Luis Potosí 1612–1620', in *Historia Mexicana*, vol. 13, No. 4, April–June 1964, pp. 532–50.

AGI Guadalajara 30, México 17 May 1583, petition of Alonso de Oñate to Viceroy Coruña

The Circumstances of Mining

ingenio this might have been is a mystery. The first reference to actual pumps and whims comes in the early seventeenth century. Sometime shortly after 1609 a pump (*bomba*) was placed in a mine called El Terno, one of a number of workings on La Albarrada. The same mine was also equipped, before 1607, with a bucket chain and whim (*noria*); installation of this apparatus meant that the shaft had to be lined with wood (*encajonado*), presumably to reduce friction and wear on the leather bags used to draw out the water.[1] Some years later, nine pumps were being used in the mine La Palmilla on the Veta Grande, raising water from the lowest workings to the surface ('desde la lengua de la agua hasta la boca de la mina').[2] Later in the century there were numerous contracts between miners for the deepening and lining of shafts, with the aim of facilitating drainage.[3]

In the archives investigated for this study little indication was to be found of the precise design of the machinery used in mines. There is, however, preserved in the Public Library of Zacatecas a copy of the first edition of Agricola's *De Re Metallica*, published in 1556, which contains full instructions for the building of various sorts of pumps, windlasses and whims for use in mines.[4] The book is annotated in what appears to be a seventeenth-century hand, so there is a possibility that Agricola may have at least provided the local mining community with some ideas for the design of machinery. He gives detailed woodcut illustrations of a number of lift-pumps, constructed from hollowed treetrunks. One illustration shows a series of pumps being used to raise water from a great depth.[5] It was perhaps a series fashioned on this model that was installed in La Palmilla in 1625, although the pumps in that mine were worked by Negro slaves and not by the horses or mules that Agricola

[1] See AGI Escribanía 380B, '1614 años. Ciudad de Guadalajara. Año de 1618. Francisco de Zaldívar Lequeitío contra Doña Antonia Ramírez, mujer que fue de Felipe de Lezcano ... sobre el engaño que hubo en la venta de la hacienda de minas ...'. This suit has a total of 822 ff.; see especially ff. 84v., 128v., 139v.

[2] AGI Guadalajara 33, Zacatecas 30 May 1626, 'Testimonio y relación de los autos que hizo el Contador de Cuentas Francisco de Villarreal tocante al desagüe de las minas principales de Zacatecas' (n.f.). This is 'No. 3' of Villarreal's visit.

[3] For example, AN.Z, FE 1679 (n.f.), Zacatecas 5 April 1679. Sebastián Gómez Rendón, majority owner of a mine called San Joseph on the veta de San Bernabé, contracted with Don Salvador Sarmiento Rendón, a miner of Zacatecas, for him to install at his own cost a whim (*malacate de rueda y lanternilla*) in the mouth of the shaft (*en la boca del tiro*). Sarmiento was also obliged to deepen the shaft sufficiently for the mine to be drained (that is, probably, by means of a sump in which water would collect, to be lifted out with the whim). In return for these services he was to receive a share of a third of the mine.

[4] *Georgii Agricolae De Re Metallica Libri XII ... Basileae MDLVI*. Georgius Agricola, *De Re Metallica*. Translated from the first Latin edition of 1556 by Herbert Clark Hoover and Lou Henry Hoover, London 1912. See book 6 for illustrations of machinery.

[5] See Agricola, *De Re Metallica*, (English translation) p. 185.

recommended.[1] He also describes several cog mechanisms suitable for driving bucket chains. It is possible that Agricola had some influence on the design of the malacate in general use in Zacatecas in the seventeenth century; although the noria, which the mining whim probably resembled, had long been in use in Spain. Whims may have been powered by mules or by men, according to their size. Mules were certainly used long before the beginning of the seventeenth century to drive stamp mills in the mine reduction works in Zacatecas, their energy being transmitted through a series of cogs, pinions and cams; so that miners undoubtedly possessed the technical knowledge necessary to harness animals to whims. It is probable that the use of animals in mine drainage depended on the severity of flooding; in workings where drainage was only occasionally necessary, human energy would have been sufficient. Pumps, which, unlike malacates, could easily be installed underground, were necessarily man-powered when used inside workings. There is no evidence that animals were ever used anywhere but on the surface.

Humboldt, at the beginning of the nineteenth century, was impressed by the crudeness of mining technique in New Spain. He thought that the practices that had been carried to America from the Basque provinces and Germany (and possibly, it may be added, from Andalucía) in the seventeenth century had scarcely developed at all in the colonies since that time.[2] It is, indeed, very likely that some Basque, Asturian and Andalusian immigrants to Zacatecas in the seventeenth century brought with them mining skills from their homes in Spain, although there is no certain example. Humboldt's main criticism was that there was little communication between the various levels and working of mines – a defect which made the extraction of ore with trolleys and animals impossible. In Zacatecas during the sixteenth and seventeenth centuries, as at Guanajuato and elsewhere in Humboldt's day, ores were carried underground on the backs of human workers, who bore heavy loads in hide bags (*tenates*). Humboldt was astonished that Indians engaged in this labour (*tenateros*) could shoulder loads of 225 to 350 pounds for six hours at a time, clambering to the surface with their bags of ore up several hundred feet of narrow ladders.[3] Mota y Escobar commented that 'the hardest task in the mines is to go down into them, for they are now very deep in many places, to dig, to cut the ore with crowbars and to carry it out. This job is done by Indians, not by Negro slaves, for it is known from experience that if the

---

[1] AGI Guadalajara 33, Zacatecas 30 May 1626, 'Testimonio y relación de los autos que hizo el Contador de Cuentas Francisco de Villarreal ...'.

[2] Alexander von Humboldt, *Ensayo político sobre el reino de la Nueva España*, edition of México 1966, p. 366 (book IV, ch. 11).

[3] Humboldt, *Ensayo político*, p. 368 (book IV, ch. 11).

The Circumstances of Mining

latter are in the mines but for a short time, they are filled with a thousand illnesses by the great cold and dampness that are found in the centre of the mines'.[1]

The Bishop is misleading in giving the impression that ores were cut and carried by the same men. There were, in fact, even in his day (the first years of the seventeenth century) two distinct classes of underground worker: barreteros (who used the *barra*, or crowbar) and tenateros. In the mine El Terno, a total of thirty to forty workers of one class and the other were normally employed in the years 1605 to 1610.[2] The lot of the tenateros may have become less arduous as the seventeenth century progressed and certain technical advances begin to appear in some mines. In 1653 the owners of a new working in a hill called the Cerro de Buenavista agreed to share the cost of installing a malacate over the mouth of the shaft to extract slag (*tepetate*).[3] Useless rock from the gangue was normally left underground until it so hindered the working of the mine that it had to be cleared; presumably it was removed, in the normal course of events, by the tenateros: an immense task. A technical advance of possibly greater importance, and of much interest in the light of Humboldt's remarks about the lack of connection between underground workings, was achieved in the 1640s by an enterprising Zacatecan miner, Don Bartolomé Bravo de Acuña. Bravo acquired on the Veta Grande a group of four adjacent mines, which had been long abandoned because of flooding. He sank a completely new shaft to a depth of some 112 feet, cleared the existing mouth of one of the mines, and connected it with his new shaft at a depth of 60 feet. It is not clear exactly how the modified workings were designed, but it was thought that Bravo had greatly improved the mines by linking them together; and in due course he made a fortune from them.[4]

Although improvements of the sort made by Bravo were adopted in due course by other miners in Zacatecas, it is clear from Humboldt's comments and criticisms that they were far from widespread in New Spain even a century and a half later. Humboldt might well have found

---

[1] Mota y Escobar, *Descripción*, p. 68.
[2] AGI Escribanía 380B, 'Francisco de Zaldívar Lequeitío contra Doña Antonia Ramírez', f. 130v.
[3] AN.Z, FE 1653A (n.f.), Zacatecas 23 January 1653. The owner of the mine, Martín de Uraga, engaged Diego Bautista Inostrosa and Francisco [Núñez], vecinos and miners of Zacatecas, to sink a trial shaft (*cata a pique*) 2½ varas square and 7 escaleras deep (about 7½ feet square by 125 feet deep), which they should line with wood if necessary, to meet the vein. They were to install the malacate over this shaft.
[4] AT.Z, Reales Oficiales 20, containing a book of titles and viceregal orders, 1657 to 1663. See ff. 65–7v., 'Título de Teniente de Capitán General de las Provincias de la Nueva Galicia en el Capitán Bartolomé Bravo de Acuña', México 6 August 1661.

an explanation for the lack of planning he observed in Mexican mines in article 23 of the Ordenanzas de Minas of 1584. It was there laid down that the discoverer of a vein might stake out a claim on it measuring 160 by 80 *varas* (a vara being a little less than a yard); later claims should measure only 120 by 60 varas. Article 31 established that the discoverer could stake as many claims as he wished; late-comers, apparently, had to be content with one.[1] The effect of these orders was to produce a great number of small claims, or individual mines, along a vein. It was hardly worth the owner's while to plan exploitation of his mine with much care. The worth of a new claim could not be known until a trial shaft (*cata*) had been sunk, and if the mine then appeared good, it could be worked from that shaft. So small, arbitrary workings proliferated. Moreover, such was the rivalry and suspicion between neighbours on a vein that a concerted effort to plan the sinking of shafts and the cutting of levels in a reasonable way was rarely achieved. Visitor Villarreal found, in 1625, the greatest difficulty in persuading a group of leading miners in Zacatecas to cooperate in pumping water from a section of the Veta Grande in which they all had mines. Pumps were placed in La Palmilla, but the miners failed to supply the slaves they had promised to send to operate them. Suspicion that the other party to any agreement would gain more from it than he would seems to have prevented the Zacatecan miner from joining with his neighbours in drainage and tunnelling projects for most of the seventeenth century. Only in the later years did a change in attitude come. Companies of several miners began to be formed more frequently; neighbours agreed to extract ores from both their mines through the shaft of one of them.[2]

The ore, once extracted from the mine, was carried by mules to the hacienda de minas, or reduction works. The silver-bearing mineral (usually called simply *metal*) had already been separated from the useless part of the veinstone; that operation was carried out by hand, with hammers. The ore, once at the hacienda, was crushed in a stamp-mill. This machine, the molino, was the centre of the hacienda and indeed of the

---

[1] For these articles, see H. W. Halleck (ed. and translator), *A Collection of Mining Laws of Spain and Mexico*, San Francisco 1859, pp. 79–80 and 84–5. Halleck gives a complete translation of the series of mining ordinances issued at San Lorenzo, 22 August 1584, which were called by Francisco Xavier de Gamboa, 'Las ordenanzas del Nuevo Cuaderno'. See Gamboa, *Comentarios a las ordenanzas de minas, dedicados al católico rey, nuestro señor, Don Carlos III*, Madrid 1761.

[2] For example, AN.Z, JL 1681, ff. 6–7v., Zacatecas 5 January 1681. Bernabé López de Mesa and Antonio de la Ribilla combined three different mines in which they had interests: La Virgen del Buen Suceso, San Antonio, and La Cruz. They formed a company to sink a shaft (*tiro*) to serve all three mines, and also constructed a ventilation shaft (*lumbrera*) and a communication shaft (*barreno*) between the various workings.

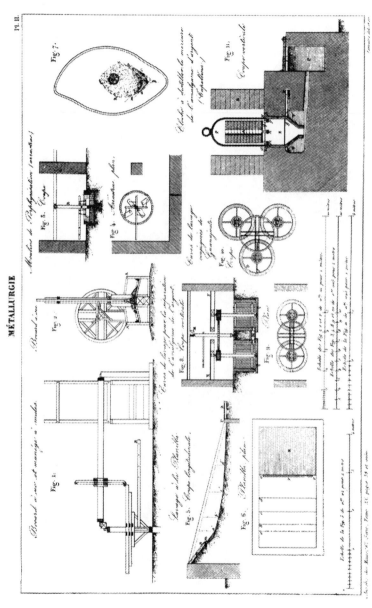

Plate 1. Illustrations of mining machinery, by P. Laur

(*facing page 136*)

Plate 2. Zacatecas in 1795, by Bernardo Portugal

The Circumstances of Mining

whole mining process. The selling price of an hacienda depended on the number and condition of its molinos. The basic construction of the mill can be seen from the accompanying nineteenth-century illustration by Laur.[1] (As far as can be seen from inventories of seventeenth-century haciendas, the design and construction of molinos did not change very much over the succeeding two centuries.) Power was provided by mules, two or three to each machine. They were harnessed to the bar marked *B* (Plate 1, fig. 1) and, walking or trotting in a circle, caused a large, horizontal, toothed wheel to rotate. This in turn drove a vertical wheel attached to a long horizontal shaft. As the cross-sectional view (Plate 1, fig. 2) shows, simple cams were attached to this shaft. For reasons which are obvious from the diagram, they were known as *triángulos*. As the shaft rotated, the teeth of the cams lifted tappets attached to long vertical rods, which were shod at their base with the stamp-shoe (marked *P*). The whole vertical assembly, consisting of the sliding rod and shoe, was the *mazo*. The shoe itself was the *almadaneta*: a block of iron weighing some 70 lb. when new. Wear on the iron components of the molino actually in contact with ore was naturally rapid. An almadaneta seems to have been discarded when its weight fell below 25 lb. The ore was crushed between the descending almadaneta and a fixed iron block, known as the *chapa*. This block fitted into a heavy wooden frame resting on the ground. The whole assembly of block and frame was the *mortero*. A typical molino of the seventeenth century had ten mazos; and an hacienda might have up to four molinos, although it was unusual for all of them to be in running order at one time. The prosperity of a miner was popularly judged by the number of mazos he owned, although there was not necessarily any relationship between his wealth and the capacity of his plant.

The crushed ore fell on to a hide stretched and pierced to form a sieve. The smaller particles fell through, to be gathered from below, while the coarser lumps were replaced under the stamps. In seventeenth-century Zacatecas, the process of trituration of ores took place solely in the stamp-mill. Laur illustrates a machine for further grinding of the ore, which he calls an *arrastra*. This device appears to have been used in other parts of New Spain during the period being considered, but no reference to it has been found in any document from or about Zacatecas. It was certainly used there in the eighteenth century, under the name *tahona*. This was an eminently simple apparatus, consisting of four heavy stones tied to a rotating beam, and moving over a stone base. The already-

[1] P. Laur, 'De la métallurgie de l'argent au Mexique', *Annales des Mines*, sixième série, vol. 20, Paris 1871, pp. 38–317; Plate II.

crushed ore was thrown on to the base, while the heavy stones were pulled around and over it by mules. The ore was thus ground very fine. Perhaps seventeenth-century miners in Zacatecas did not realise the advantage of obtaining a very finely powdered ore – which lay in the fact that the chemical process of amalgamation with mercury, by which ores were usually processed, took place the more readily the finer the ore was crushed; for the surface area of the particles of silver salts exposed to contact with mercury was thus increased. But if miners observed any improvement in the speed or completeness of amalgamation when they ground their ores more finely than usual, they evidently did not think the extra effort worth the result.

Amalgamation was the method of ore reduction used in almost all haciendas de minas in Zacatecas. The process first appeared in New Spain in the mid-1550s, having been developed there, it is generally thought, by one Bartolomé de Medina. Exactly how amalgamation reached New Spain is a question of some curiosity but of little practical importance.[1] Once there, it spread rapidly. In August 1557, Dr Morones, an oidor of Guadalajara, wrote to the Crown saying that the mines of Zacatecas would be worked permanently now that processing by mercury had begun.[2] By 1563 most ores were being reduced with mercury.[3] Amalgamation was, indeed, a technical innovation with dramatic results.[4] It enormously extended the range of ores that could be profitably worked. By the smelting process previously used, it was possible to work only small quantities of high grade ore. Amalgamation meant that vast amounts of ore yielding as little as an ounce and a half of silver per quintal could be reduced economically. The rapid diffusion of the process and the quick development of milling techniques, demanding an enormous investment in machines and haciendas de minas, form a largely unnoticed chapter in the economic history of Latin America. A witness claimed that by 1562 miners in Zacatecas had spent more than 800,000 pesos on buildings and ingenios alone.[5] And cost was only one difficulty to be overcome, as the following figures suggest. They show the number of water-powered and

---

[1] The clearest statement of the problems surrounding the introduction of amalgamation in New Spain is Silvio Zavala's 'La amalgamación en la minería de Nueva España', *Historia Mexicana* vol. 11, No. 3 January–March 1962, pp. 416–21.

[2] AGI Guadalajara 51, f. 103, Compostela 17 August 1557, Dr Morones to Crown.

[3] AGI Guadalajara 51, Zacatecas 10 February 1563, Treasury officials of New Galicia to Crown.

[4] See Alvaro Jara, *Tres ensayos sobre economia minera hispanoamericana*, Universidad de Chile, Santiago de Chile, 1966; p. 112, graph 2. The leap in Peruvian silver production in the late 1570s, after the introduction of amalgamation at the beginning of the decade, is enormous. Production quadrupled from the quinquennium 1570 to 1574 to that of 1575 to 1579.

[5] In Ahumada, 'Información', p. 260, testimony of Gonzalo de Avila.

The Circumstances of Mining

animal-powered stamp mills in the principal mines of New Spain in 1597.[1]

Mining town	Water-powered mills	Animal-powered mills	Total
Pachuca	59	23	82
Tasco	36	45	81
Zacatecas	0	65	65
Guanajuato	2	44	46
Sultepec	17	23	40
Cuautla	3	23	26
Zacualpa	23	3	26
Tlalpujahua	6	13	19
Temascaltepec	17	0	17
Ocumutla	4	0	4
	167	239	406

From the figures in the table it is clear that miners were basically reliant on animal power for grinding their ores. Only Pachuca, of the major mines of this date, had water enough to make hydraulic power important to its industry. Zacatecas and Guanajuato were all but entirely dependent on the energy of horses and mules, being situated as they were in the semi-desert altiplanicie of the north (in contrast with the mining towns with most water-driven mills in the above list, which were in central Mexico). Miners of Zacatecas and Guanajuato maintained 800 and 700 mules respectively. San Luis Potosí, Sombrerete and Parral, major mines of the seventeenth century, do not figure here because they had not yet attained any importance. But they also lay in arid regions of the north, suffering the same problems as Zacatecas and Guanajuato. Lack of water not only meant lack of cheap motive power for machinery: it also presented a serious difficulty in the washing operations essential to the refining of silver. It is a tribute to the ingenuity and determination of the northern miners – the important miners of the seventeenth and eighteenth centuries – that they managed to overcome these problems posed by Nature. The reader of Agricola's *De Re Metallica* is struck by the many

[1] These figures are from 'El estado que tienen las haciendas de minas de esta Nueva España que por comisiones particulares se han visitado hasta fin del mes de febrero del año pasado de 1597 años' – a valuable cross-sectional view of silver mining in New Spain at the end of the sixteenth century. It contains much information besides that presented here. It forms part of 'Relación del estado que tienen las minas de esta Nueva España y las de Zacatecas . . .', an anonymous and undated document accompanying AGI Mexico 24, R. 1, No. 7a, México 24 April 1598, Monterrey to Crown.

illustrations of water-wheels; and rushing mountain streams are expertly diverted through strakes and buddles to sift and wash ores. Miners in Zacatecas must have looked enviously at these woodcuts. But they and their companions in similar towns were successful in inventing what could be called a 'dry technique' of mining. This technique, coupled with that of amalgamation, was at the origin of most of the 'American Treasure' reaching Europe from New Spain.[1]

The crushed ore (*harina*) was taken from the mill on to a large and open stone-paved yard. The usual name for this in New Spain was the *patio* (hence Medina's process is commonly known as the *beneficio de patio*); but in Zacatecas it was usually called the *incorporadero* (the place where mercury was 'incorporated' with the ore). The harina was piled into heaps (*montones*) of between twenty and forty quintales (2,000 to 4,000 lb.), and water was added until a thick slime was produced. Common salt was mixed in, at the rate of two and a half to three pounds per quintal of ore. *Incorporo* of mercury followed. Some ten to twelve lb. were sprinkled on to the montón through the mesh of a coarsely woven cloth bag. (The amount of mercury varied, naturally, with the size of the montón and the richness of the ore.) The montón was then spread out to form a thin *torta*; this might be made from several montones combined. The semi-liquid mixture was contained by a temporary circular curb of wood or stone, and was thoroughly agitated. This was done by men treading the torta and turning it over with shovels; or possibly by teams of mules being driven through the slime. The treading process was known as *repaso*, and would be continued several times a day, until the mercury was thought to be thoroughly amalgamated with the silver. More mercury might be added if it was thought necessary. The critical task of assessing when the silver was fully *incorporada* was undertaken by the *azoguero*: a man of heavy responsibility in an hacienda de minas, since he had to ensure that the maximum amount of silver was extracted from the ore with the minimum wastage of quicksilver. The process of incorporo

---

[1] It should be said that the amalgamation process had certainly been known in Europe since Roman times. Biringuccio (in *The Pirotechnia of Vannoccio Biringuccio*, English translation from the Italian by C. S. Smith and Martha T. Gnudi, New York 1942, p. 384) gives an account of an amalgamation process under the heading 'The method of extracting every particle of gold from slags of ores, or sweepings of mints, gold beaters and goldsmiths; also that contained in certain ores'. His method was suitable for recovering small quantities of gold, silver or copper. The description is technically inadequate. Biringuccio's account of amalgamation is not included in Agricola's *De Re Metallica*, although Agricola does describe a method of recovering metallic gold from ores with mercury (English translation, pp. 295–8). It is a long way from Biringuccio's small-scale process to amalgamation as it was practised in New Spain. Medina may still be given the credit for having turned an interesting but evidently unusual method into a major industrial process.

might last two or three months. The time varied with the nature of the ore and with the season. A cold winter naturally retarded the chemical reactions of the process. When it was thought that the full silver content of the ore had been 'taken up' by the mercury, the torta was removed little by little in barrows to the washing vats, or *tinas*. These were tubs fitted with paddles rotated by mules. Water was added to the mixture, and under agitation the heavier particles (consisting of silver and mercury amalgam) sank, while the lighter earthy part of the torta formed a thin mud in the water and was drawn off as *lama*. Some of the amalgam (or *pella*) was inevitably carried off with the lama. To recover it, the waste was run through settling troughs. Mechanical losses of mercury and amalgam were thus reduced to a minimum. The pella was removed from the tina in a more or less liquid state. It was poured into canvas bags and there compressed in such a way that the free mercury was squeezed out through the weave of the cloth, leaving a near-solid mass of amalgam. This was beaten in moulds into triangular sections, which were piled together into a conical mass known as the *piña* and placed under a bell-shaped metal hood, called the *capellina*. With the application of heat from below, the mercury was distilled as vapour out of the amalgam, to condense on the walls of the capellina, run down to the base, and be recovered. The silver left in the piña was of almost perfect fineness. It only remained to melt it down into bars of standard size (in practice, of about 130 marks). This was generally done in the seventeenth century by an assayer employed by the Treasury.[1] (For the chemistry of amalgamation, see note 1 on p. 144.)

Humboldt remarked on the great simplicity of the patio process. It required, he said, nothing but a few animals to drive the mills, and an open space, if necessary in the middle of the desert, on which to work the torta.[2] The process may have appeared simple in comparison with practice in European silver mines of the late eighteenth century. But in the two preceding centuries American amalgamation and its related processes doubtless seemed complex enough. And they were, it may be repeated, considerable technical achievements; all the more so in that the technique of trituration (except for the use of the tahona), amalgamation

---

[1] This account of the amalgamation process is taken from Modesto Bargalló, *La minería y la metalurgia en la América española durante la época colonial*, México 1955, p. 128. Bargalló's description is supplemented in some details from G. F. Lyon, *Journal of a Residence and Tour in the Republic of Mexico in the year 1826*, London 1828, 2 vols., vol. 2, pp. 275–95 (Appendix 2), 'Notes of the process of amalgamation at the hacienda of La Sauceda, Vetagrande, Zacatecas'; and from seventeenth-century sources from Zacatecas. In essentials the process changed little between the seventeenth century and Lyon's day.

[2] Humboldt, *Ensayo político*, 381–3 (book IV, ch. 11).

and washing seems to have been established within fifty years or so of the first appearance of Medina's invention. Two technical advances in particular may be singled out, one mechanical and the other chemical.

An essential part of amalgamation was the separating of the 'incorporated' pella from the non-metallic part of the torta. This could only be done by washing; or more precisely, by flotation. The vat, or tina, was evidently developed very quickly to perform this function. (Only two vats were used per machine in Zacatecas in the seventeenth century; the triple-tubbed device (Plate 1, fig. 10) was a later, more sophisticated development.) The machine was powered by mules, which, harnessed to a beam, walked in circles on the floor above the vats. (In some seventeenth-century haciendas, the vats were merely sunk into the ground.) As they did so, they rotated a central shaft running down through a large horizontal cog-wheel. This wheel in turn drove two smaller pinions, which rotated paddles in the tubs, separating particles of amalgam from the waste material. It may be assumed that there were outlets from a point on the wall of the tina and from its base, through which the lama and the pella could be run off respectively (see Appendix I). Was this machine a native product of America? It cannot be known. But again Agricola may have provided the germ of an idea for its design. *De Re Metallica* contains description and illustration of a powered washing vat, which was sometimes used, according to Agricola, for separating amalgam of gold from waste rock and earth. This device employed a continuous stream of water to carry off lighter matter in suspension.[1] But in Zacatecas there could be no such prodigality with water, for the supply to the haciendas was generally drawn from wells by bucket-chains, and stored in tanks. It is remarkable that a sufficiently large and constant flow could be obtained in this way to wash the tons of ore contained in a torta. Perhaps the process was made more efficient, and the consumption of water thus decreased, by rotating the paddles of the tina at a very high speed, as Lyon observed was the custom in the nineteenth century.[2] Whatever the details of the method, it was undoubtedly possible to wash ores in tinas in the large quantities necessary. There was never any complaint from miners about difficulties in this stage of working their ores. If a special Mexican 'dry' technique of ore processing can be considered to have existed, then the tina was central to it. One of its characteristics was that it drew its power, like the stamp-mills, from animals and not from water-wheels. Now although the substitution of animals for

[1] Agricola, *De Re Metallica* (English translation), p. 299.
[2] Lyon, *Journal, 1826*, vol. 2, p. 286.

hydraulic power clearly cannot be claimed as a sweeping innovation discovered by the New World, there were obvious problems of cost and supply inherent in so great a dependence on mules and horses as Zacatecas was forced to accept. And in making it possible to wash the very large quantities of ore passing through the haciendas de minas – it is worth recalling that only an ounce and a half of silver was extracted from a hundred pounds of ore – the tina *was* the 'dry' technique. It is difficult to see how large-scale amalgamation processing could have been carried out in arid regions without the powered washing-vat. If the miners of northern Mexico developed the apparatus independently, then their invention is worthy of recognition: if they merely adapted a design illustrated by Agricola, or perhaps brought over by some German miner to America, then at least they deserve credit for seeing its possibilities – indeed, its necessity – in the circumstances of New Spain.

The second innovation in mining to be noted here was probably the last one of consequence to be made in the patio process during the colonial period. Mota y Escobar, on his journey through New Biscay, wrote that the hills there were rich in silver, but that they 'abounded in a type of ore which is called antimony [*antimonia*], from which it was not known up to now how to extract silver; [but] the method of reducing it has been found; it is to mix it with other ores called *magistrales*, which, being soft and copperish [*cobrizos*], reduce [*rinden*] the hardness and roughness of antimonial ores in such a way that all the silver is easily extracted from them; and with this method the miners of this kingdom of Biscay and [those of] Zacatecas have been revived; for their haciendas have been much depressed up to now because they did not know this method'.[1] The Bishop's observation was, it seems, accurate. Shortly afterwards, reports went from Zacatecas to the Crown that, with the discovery of the substance called 'magistral', ores that had previously been unworkable, from mines long abandoned, were being processed. The number of haciendas de minas was growing rapidly.[2] Magistral was simply copper pyrites (that is, copper sulphide); or, more probably in practice, a mixture of copper and iron pyrites. Its precise chemical action in the reduction process appears to be rather complicated. But there is no doubt that it became an indispensable reagent, allowing silver to amalgamate more easily with mercury. It was used, once discovered, in all amalgamation, no matter what variety of silver ore was to be processed.

[1] Mota y Escobar, *Descripción*, p. 83.
[2] See AGI Guadalajara 236, AA. 1, f. 124v., Madrid 3 October 1607, real cédula to viceroy and Audiencia of New Spain, referring to a report of one Alonso de Aíbar, made on behalf of the citizens of Zacatecas.

The Circumstances of Mining

The importance that was attributed to it is indicated by its name.[1] There is no clue about how its use was discovered. There was continuous and largely fruitless experimentation with the patio process; recognition of the value of magistral may have been the result of such trials and errors. Or perhaps some miner, working silver ores containing pyrites, was percipient enough to guess the cause of an increased yield.

Amalgamation was the method of reduction chosen by the majority of professional miners in Zacatecas. Most local ores were suitable for the process. There were, however, many people in the city who engaged in mining as a secondary occupation; and these people had neither the desire nor the means to construct the machinery and buildings essential for amalgamation. Provided they could obtain, legally or otherwise, ores of adequate quality, smelting offered good profits. And in certain other mining towns of the district, ores were nearly always smelted – especially those with a high content of lead. Sombrerete, in the second part of the seventeenth century, experienced a long bonanza derived mainly, it seems, from smelting ores (*metales de fuego* or *de fundición*). A little space may therefore be devoted to smelting practice.

There was, of course, advanced knowledge of smelting in Europe by the beginning of the sixteenth century, and the skills reached America quickly. German miners were at work in the Caribbean in the early years of the century; and some reached New Spain in 1536, settling possibly at Sultepec.[2] Basque and Andalusian miners emigrating to America doubtless contributed to a growing fund of mining knowledge. There was, therefore, little originality in the smelting technique used in New Spain. It employed blast furnaces in all essentials similar to those described by Agricola and Biringuccio. In Peru and New Spain the furnace commonly in use was known as the Castilian furnace (*horno castellano*), which was basically a hollow vertical column, pierced appropriately to allow charging, extraction of slag and metal, and introduction of the nozzle of

---

[1] Bargalló, a metallurgist, advances with some hesitancy a set of basic equations for the patio with magistral. The reagents are the ore, silver sulphide (Ag_2S), common salt ($NaCl$), mercury (Hg), and magistral, which he takes to be copper sulphate ($CuSO_4$) rather than copper sulphide (Cu_2S). They are said to react as follows:

$$CuSO_4 + 2NaCl \rightarrow CuCl_2 + Na_2SO_4$$
$$CuCl_2 + Ag_2S \rightarrow 2AgCl + CuS$$
$$2AgCl + nHg \rightarrow Hg_{n-2}Ag(amalgam) + Hg_2Cl_2$$

These equations must be regarded with caution, since the exact chemical processes of amalgamation are apparently improperly understood. Doubt also arises over Bargalló's transformation of magistral from copper sulphide into copper sulphate; it is generally thought to have been the sulphide. Chemists consulted by the author declared that the substances were not interchangeable in the reaction. For the equations, Bargalló, *La minería*, p. 194.
[2] Bargalló, *La minería*, pp. 94–5.

the bellows. It might be three to six feet high. It could be used for smelting stone containing native silver, or almost any type of ore having a high silver content. The most frequently smelted ores in the Zacatecas district belonged to the galena class. This is basically a lead ore occurring in association with silver ores and often containing some silver itself. It could be cheaply and easily extracted by smelting since the natural lead that the galena contained acted as a flux, and there was consequently no need to add metallic lead as a flux. Where it was wished to smelt ores that did not contain lead naturally, flux, of course, became necessary. The Castilian furnace could, if required, be used for separating by cupellation the mixture of lead and silver that emerged from the primary smelting of the ore; but the furnace had to be specially prepared for this purpose, and it was generally found simpler to maintain a second furnace, of the reverberatory type, for cupellation and the refining of silver.[1]

One of the earliest descriptions of an hacienda de minas to be found in the archives of Zacatecas is that of a smelting works leased near Fresnillo in 1608.[2] It had four Castilian furnaces, stone built (*de piedra y cal*), but with chimneys of adobe. The furnaces were housed in the usual shed, or *galera*, which also contained machinery for operating the bellows, and the bellows themselves. Power was provided by mules, turning a mechanism similar in design to that used in stamp mills. The bellows were pumped by means of a system of cams mounted on a horizontal shaft. In addition to the smelting furnaces, there was a cupellation furnace with its bellows and operating machinery (*una rueda de afinar*). And although the inventory is not entirely clear, it appears, from references to morteros, mazos and chapas, that there was also a stamp mill of some sort in the hacienda. Its presence suggests that ore was crushed before smelting. If this were really done, it indicates fairly advanced technique, for crushed ores fed into the furnace were more efficiently reduced than pieces of ore taken directly from the mine, or roughly broken up by hand. Charcoal used for firing the furnace was stored in a separate shed.

Smelting plants of this sort may have been common in some of the mining towns of the district, in particular at Fresnillo, Charcas, Ramos and Sombrerete. But there were few in Zacatecas itself; and records of those few show that they were generally small and dilapidated affairs.

---

[1] For furnaces, Bargalló, *La minería*, pp. 93–4.
[2] AA.Z, 2, No. 11, Zacatecas 30 March 1608, lease of the hacienda de San Pedro del Río Grande, in the jurisdiction of Fresnillo, by Doña Margarita de Covarrubias to Andrés Pereira. The inventory runs from ff. 4–5v.

This is not to say, though, that many inhabitants of the city did not engage in smelting in a small way. Ores could be bought or stolen; and a great advantage of smelting as a technique was that it required little capital outlay. There was no need to build banks of furnaces equipped with machine-driven bellows. A small stone furnace and a pair of hand bellows were adequate for reducing good ores in small quantities; and the slopes surrounding the city were littered with these small furnaces, known as *paradas de fuelles*. Indian mine-workers built them near the mines and city shopkeepers ran them in their back yards. In 1622 it was reported that in Zacatecas and Pánuco there were more than ninety paradas de fuelles; Viceroy Gelves had them banned.[1] Many were closed down for a time, but then sprang up again. The amount of silver produced by this small-scale smelting was not great in comparison with the regular output of the haciendas de minas; but it was an essential form of income to Indians and Negro mine-workers, and became a useful secondary source of wealth to many merchants.

Both the amalgamation and the smelting process demanded a number of essential raw materials. Charcoal was the principal necessity for smelting. Wood in the immediate surroundings of Zacatecas was cleared in the very early years of mining, before the amalgamation process was known. The barren slopes of the hills can never have been heavily forested in the first place (although, of course, removal of the trees would have caused erosion of soil from the slopes and made them still more barren than they had been to start with). In 1568 Oidor Mendiola found it necessary to issue orders controlling the cutting of trees for firewood. He specifically mentioned the *encina* (holm-oak) as a tree occurring in the vicinity.[2] There was doubtless also mezquite, as there still is. Both these trees, being of hardwood, were a source of good charcoal. By 1568, Mendiola's restrictions on felling timber may well have been unnecessary, since demand for charcoal was much reduced once amalgamation was widely adopted. Small amounts were still needed for the process of removing mercury from the amalgam by distillation; and in the seventeenth century, for roasting magistral before use, as was commonly done. But supplies were clearly adequate, for miners never complained about lack of wood or charcoal. There was probably enough, too, for domestic use and for the small furnaces belonging to Indians and merchants. The canyons of the south held vast resources of timber, both hard and soft,

---

[1] AT.Z/VO, México 30 December 1622, mandamiento of Gelves to the Treasury officials of Zacatecas.
[2] AGI Guadalajara 5, clause 26 of Mendiola's Ordinances, Zacatecas 6 March 1568, in 'Averiguaciones ... Contreras y Guevara ... 1570', f. 126v.

from which most of Zacatecas' charcoal probably came.[1] Wood, of course, had several uses beside serving as raw material for charcoal. It was the basic material for constructing machinery, for which purpose the hard timber of the mezquite served well. And roofing was usually of wooden shingles, or tlajamaniles; these were always in plentiful supply. Many miners held stocks of tens of thousands. There was not much call for timber underground. The country rock in which mineral veins occur is compact in the Serranía, so workings required little shoring.[2] At Sombrerete, wood and charcoal for smelting were certainly drawn from the nearby eastern slopes of the Sierra Madre Occidental, which are heavily forested with pine and oak.

Only one mineral raw material was essential to smelting – lead in some usable form. The two common lead-based substances employed in the Zacatecas district were *greta* and *cendrada*. Greta was litharge, or lead monoxide; it was in demand as a flux. Cendrada could perform the same function, being 'hearth lead', the crushed remains of used cupels (the tightly-packed ash lining of a refining furnace).[3] A flux of some sort was necessary in the smelting of ores with a low natural lead content; such ores were said to be 'dry'. Pure lead could be used for the purpose, but was expensive. In the early years of mining at Zacatecas litharge was imported from the mines of Izmiquilpan, which lay 75 miles to the east of Querétaro and some 250 miles (80 leagues) from Zacatecas. In the seventeenth century, New León proved an abundant source of lead, and supplied the needs of the Zacatecas district.[4]

The raw materials demanded by the amalgamation process were more numerous. There were abundant local supplies of two of them: magistral and salt. Magistral came from Tepezala, between Aguascalientes and Zacatecas. There were also mines producing it in the Serranía itself. No complaint was ever made about shortages.[5] Salt was required in larger

[1] See AN.Z, PC 1614, f. 54v., Zacatecas 17 March 1614, for an example of imports of timber from the canyons to Zacatecas. A contract was made by one Diego Santillán, 'aserrador de maderas en el monte de Juan de la Torre, jurisdicción de Tlaltenango', with Diego Pérez de Espinas, vecino of Zacatecas. He undertook to supply 223 sawn planks and 52 *cuartones* (sawn timber of unspecified size) from the yard (*astillero*) of Juan de la Torre at Tlaltenango. The price was 1 peso a plank (*tabla*) and 5 reales a cuartón.

[2] Señor Pascual García, present owner of the mine La Purísima, provided this information.

[3] West, *The Parral Mining District*, p. 29.

[4] See del Hoyo, 'Don Martín de Zavala', p. 414.

[5] See AA.Z, 6, No. 40, ff. 1–9, Zacatecas 20 November 1653; an agreement between Cristóbal Ramírez de la Campana and Rodrigo de Rentería to work two magistral mines called La Sauceda and San Bernabé 'en el paraje de la sauceda de Lucas Ruiz'. (There are several places called La Sauceda in the neighbourhood of Zacatecas. The best known was about two miles east of Veta Grande.) Magistral was also taken from the Cerro de Gil, two miles to the north-west of Zacatecas.

quantities. But again the supply was abundant. It came from the two salt-pans (or series of salt-pans) of Santa María and Peñol Blanco, some 55 miles east of Zacatecas. The salina of Santa María was known to miners of the region from the beginning. They took salt freely from it until 1562, when the Audiencia of New Galicia, seeing the profit available to the Crown if salt were sold, placed the salina under official control.[1] Miners thenceforth bought salt (or rather, *saltierra*, a crude mixture of salt and earth) at half a peso the fanega (2·58 bushels). The price remained unaltered throughout the sixteenth and seventeenth centuries. The salina at Peñol Blanco was discovered and first exploited in the late 1560s. It was evidently very close to Santa María, though its exact position is not clear.[2] The salinas continued to be administered by the Audiencia, which appointed an alcalde mayor and lesser officials at each, until 1629. The 'harvest' (*cosecha*) of salt took place in the spring, from January to May. The summer rains followed, from June to late September. Water then penetrated the surface of the salina, saturating the earth to some depth. In the autumn and winter it gradually evaporated, carrying salt to the surface and depositing it there as a crust, which could be removed by careful scraping and shovelling. If rain fell during the harvest, much salt was lost. By the 1570s a yearly average of 60,000 fanegas could be obtained, which was far more than the miners needed. The excess was bought by private dealers who took it to New Spain to be sold in the mines of the south.[3] Labour at the salinas was provided by Indians from the Canyons, who were obliged by the Audiencia to lend their services each spring. Until 1596 they were paid at half a real a day, and thereafter at one real;[4] sustenance, in the form of maize and beef, was provided at the Treasury's expense. In 1629, perhaps because of the rising price of food, and the consequently higher cost of feeding workers, the Audiencia relinquished control of the salinas. Asientos were drawn up with private contractors every ten years for the remainder of the century.[5] These contracts were generally for the supply of some 30,000 fanegas a year for sale in Zacatecas. Any excess which the contractors might produce could be sold by them for their own gain. Since the capacity of the

---

[1] AGI Guadalajara 5, 'Averiguaciones ... Contreras y Guevara... 1570', f. 100v., contains a real cédula, dated Segovia 22 September 1562, approving the Audiencia's action.

[2] Accounts of sales of salt, and of expenditure, at Peñol Blanco, appear for the first time in 1570. See AGI Contaduría, 841.

[3] For descriptions of the salinas, and production and methods of removing salt, see: AGI Guadalajara 6, Guadalajara 6 March 1577, Licenciado Martínez to Crown; AGI Guadalajara 31, 8 March 1577, Bernardo Ramírez de Vargas to Consejo de Indias.

[4] See AGI Contaduría, 841, 842A, 842B, 858 *passim*.

[5] The first asiento was auctioned in Mexico City to Captain Pedro Serrano de Arriaga. AGI Guadalajara 9, R. 2, Guadalajara 10 January 1630, president of Audiencia to Crown.

The Circumstances of Mining

salinas was far greater than 30,000 fanegas a year, asentistas might make a handsome profit.[1]

The use of machinery in both processes of ore reduction created a demand for iron; bearings and journals, cams, stamp shoes and mortar blocks were necessarily made of metal, or at least had metal working surfaces. Most iron was imported from Spain, for in the seventeenth century Mexico's own considerable deposits were not much exploited.[2] Copper, used in various mining utensils, was produced in New Spain in small quantities, which were perhaps sufficient for needs.[3] No complaints were found in the course of research about shortages or excessive prices of these two metals. This is sufficient evidence that supplies of them were adequate, for the miners of Zacatecas never let slip a chance to complain about anything they thought detrimental to their prosperity. Consequently, the major source of their concern and complaints was the last and vital raw material essential to amalgamation – mercury. But the question of mercury is so central to silver mining that it merits a separate chapter.

---

[1] AGI Mexico 267, 'Autos contra José de Villarreal, alguacil mayor de Zacatecas, sobre haber sacado plata sin pagar los derechos. 1671', f. 107–107v., testimony of Don Diego de Medrano, in the real cárcel de México, 6 November 1663. Medrano said that the asentista of 1651 to 1661, Mateo Díaz de la Madriz, had contracted to produce 30,000 fanegas of saltierra a year for sale in Zacatecas by the Treasury officials. In fact, he extracted from the salinas more than 200,000 fanegas a year, selling the excess at one peso the fanega, or more. It is not clear where Díaz sold this salt. It would hardly have been possible to do so in Zacatecas at that price, since the official price of ½ peso a fanega was certainly maintained there all through the seventeenth century.

[2] Bargalló, *La minería*, p. 251.

For sources of copper in New Spain, see Bargalló, *La minería*, p. 213.

CHAPTER 7

MERCURY

In 1609 the second Viceroy Luis de Velasco, now an old and sober man in his second term of office in New Spain, began a letter to a councillor of the Indies thus: 'It is indeed as your worship judges it, that the most important business that exists today in the Indies is the matter of quicksilver, for it is their principal support ...'.[1] And some fifty years before, when Viceroy Enríquez in September 1572 had placed the distribution of mercury in New Spain under Crown control, he reported some reactions to his reform to the king. The friars, he said, had objected, 'saying that to prohibit [free traffic in] mercury and to place it under monopoly (*estanco*) is like placing a monopoly on bread or meat, for it is understood that the sustenance (*sustento*) of this land depends on the mines of silver, and they cannot be maintained without mercury ...'.[2] These were typical comments, of which thousand-fold repetition can be found in Spanish colonial documents of the sixteenth and seventeenth centuries. And given the current equation, for all practical purposes unchallenged, of bullion and wealth, it was natural that comments of this sort should be constantly made. For where there was no chance of refining silver ores by smelting, because they were not rich enough or were otherwise unsuitable, mining depended entirely on mercury. No mercury meant no silver. No silver meant that the motive force was removed from the economy of the colonies. The large part of internal commerce that depended on the use of silver as an exchange medium would decline; external trade would be still more seriously reduced, since silver constituted the great majority of exports. The Crown would suffer grave losses of revenue from taxation – not only from direct taxation on silver produced, but an incalculable sum deriving from (and paid in) silver, such as sales taxes, tributes, customs dues (*almojarifazgos*) and all other levies whose yield varied, in the last analysis, with the prosperity of the colonies. It is difficult to overemphasise the importance of quicksilver to the economies of the Spanish colonies in America, and it was a topic constantly in the minds of the Consejo de Indias and the Consejo de Hacienda in Castile, though not so constantly as many colonial governors would have liked. It was the task

[1] BM Add. MS. 13,992, ff. 511–12. México 1609 (n.e.d.) Velasco II to councillor Aguiar y Acuña.
[2] AGI Mexico 19, R. 3, 1572 (n.e.d.) Enríquez to Crown.

Mercury

of these two councils to provide an adequate supply to the Indies, seeking mercury from widely separate sources and arranging for its collection, dispatch and distribution. This work began in March 1559, when the Crown, quick to recognise the importance of the amalgamation process recently adopted by miners in New Spain, assumed control of all exports of mercury from Spain to America. And although it is the aim here, ultimately, to account for the supply of mercury to Zacatecas, it is impossible to avoid a wider description of the question of mercury. The subject is intrinsically fascinating, since quicksilver was in a scarcely figurative sense the other side of the silver coin; but apart from that, no satisfactory account can be given of the mercury supply to a single place unless more general questions are considered. This will become clear, and be the justification for what must appear, at first sight, a long digression. It is proposed to begin with an account of the general problems of the supply of mercury to the mines of Spanish America; then to show how mercury was distributed in New Spain; and lastly to attend to mercury in Zacatecas.

Three useful sources of mercury were available to Spain in the period under discussion. Two were in Spanish lands. Almadén, a mercury mine known in Roman times and still being exploited today, lies about 65 miles due north of Córdoba, in southern Spain.[1] Huancavelica, in central Peru, and long employed by the Incas as a source of vermilion (extracted from cinnabar), which they used for cosmetic and ceremonial purposes, became known to Spaniards only in 1564.[2] The third source also lay in Hapsburg lands, but in those of the Austrian branch of the family. It was at Idria, at the head of the Adriatic, in present-day Yugoslavia. Generally speaking, mercury produced at Huancavelica was consumed in Peruvian silver mines, while the product of Almadén was exported to New Spain. Idria was drawn upon only in the period 1620 to 1645, when its mercury was sent to both viceroyalties. Attempts were made in the course of the seventeenth century to exploit at least two other sources. Deposits of mercury ore in New Spain, mainly in Michoacán, constituted one of these. Enterprising citizens of New Spain made several efforts during the second third of the century to work these deposits, and viceroys were even persuaded on occasion to lend financial help to the projects. But the ores proved too poor to be economic, as one commentator sardonically pointed out in 1662 – 'for to extract a thousand quintales of mercury at

[1] See, in general, A. Matilla Tascón, *Historia de las minas de Almadén. Vol. I. (Desde la época romana hasta el año 1645)*, Madrid 1958.
[2] G. Lohmann Villena, *Las minas de Huancavelica en los siglos XVI y XVII*, Seville 1949, here, ch. 2.

Mercury

ten ounces a quintal [of ore], a hundred and sixty thousand quintales of ore would be needed, an amount which would probably not go into the cathedral church of this city ...'.[1] (A quintal weighed 100 lb.) More interesting, and more consistently pursued, were the possibilities of importing mercury from China, via Manila. Whenever a shortage of mercury from other sources threatened, Chinese mercury was remembered. The first suggestion for using this source seems to have come in 1601 from Viceroy Velasco in Peru. His purpose in seeking Chinese mercury was to reduce production at Huancavelica, and thus relieve the hardships of *mita* Indian labourers in that mine. From an unspecified source of information he learned that Chinese mercury could be placed in Manila in large quantities and at low prices.[2] Four years later information of the same sort reached Montesclaros in Mexico. The resources of the East seemed boundless. No less than 100,000 quintales could be placed in Canton. And Montesclaros was hopeful that 1,000 to 1,500 quintales could be imported into New Spain every year, at a cost price of 45 pesos 5 reales each, a price only half that of Spanish mercury sold in New Spain in these years.[3] The prospects of either a reduction in selling price or an increased Crown profit on the sale of mercury therefore seemed good. But this proved to be wishful thinking, as Velasco the younger admitted in 1609. The Audiencia of Manila had declared it impossible to collect even 20 quintales.[4] The cause of the difficulty is not mentioned. But it obviously continued to be insuperable in practice, for only samples of Chinese quicksilver appear to have reached New Spain in the seventeenth century. Thirty-six quintales and 36 lb. came in the Manila galleon of 1615.[5] Another small consignment seems to have arrived in 1644,[6] and there were possibly others, though since they do not appear in any mercury account, it is unlikely they amounted to large quantities. And besides, whatever the practical difficulties of actually procuring mercury in the East, Spanish official opinion was not united on the wisdom of seeking it there. The kind of objection that was to become typical was first voiced in 1608, in opposition to a scheme advanced by a Portuguese for shipping Chinese mercury to Acapulco. It was said that this commerce would mean a drain of cash to the Philippines and China. Furthermore, the Portuguese,

[1] AGI Mexico 611, México 10 March 1662, Martín de Murga Eguiluz to Viceroy Baños, f. IV., in Baños to Crown, México 21 December 1662.

[2] AGI Mexico 27, Peru (Lima?) 2 May 1601, Velasco II to Crown.

[3] AGI Mexico 27, México 28 October 1605, Montesclaros to Crown.

[4] BM Add. MS. 13,992, ff. 511–12. México 1609 (n.e.d.) Velasco II to councillor Aguiar y Acuña.

[5] AGI Mexico 28, R. 3, 'Lo que viene en la nao Capitana de Filipinas que surgió en este Puerto de Acapulco a 2 de enero de 1615'.

[6] AGI Mexico 35, R. 3, México 20 September 1644, Salvatierra to Crown, 'No. 4'.

taking advantage of the 'hidden means and trade' they had with merchants in the islands, would doubtless bring other goods to New Spain along with the mercury, to the detriment of that colony and the Philippines, 'and everything become full of Portuguese' ('y llenarse todo de portugueses'). Worse still, the Portuguese were of doubtful faith.[1]

The escape of silver to China remained the principal official objection to buying mercury there. It was an argument particularly favoured by the Consejo de Hacienda, trying in vain to prevent leaks of bullion from the riddled vessel of the Empire. In 1630 the Consejo de Indias raised the very reasonable counter-argument that much more silver would be produced with the mercury that was acquired than would be lost in buying it. And if spending silver in China on silks and other unproductive items was permitted, then how much more reason there was to spend on mercury.[2] Cerralvo, two years later, made an equally reasonable point when he said if silver had to leave the lands of the Spanish Crown, nowhere could the loss do less harm than in China.[3] This argument would doubtless have failed to sway the Fiscal of the Audiencia of Mexico in 1662, when he commented on a current Chinese mercury scheme. The danger of sending money to the Philippines was serious, he said, because of the proximity of Macao, 'and the easy passage [of silver] to England, and once money went to those parts it would go to enrich foreign and enemy nations, without a real's passing to Spain ...'.[4] It may have been this unwillingness to provide the governor of the Philippines with sufficient cash to buy mercury, rather than lack of supplies of the metal in the Orient, that led to the failure of the several projects set up in the seventeenth century for purchasing Chinese quicksilver. The last of these appears to have been in 1692 and 1693, when the viceroy of New Spain did actually remit 12,000 pesos to be spent on mercury. In June 1693 the governor of the Philippines reported the return from Canton of the sampan (*champán*) in which he had sent off the silver. It carried 53 quintales and 42 lb. of good quality mercury, costing 3,222½ pesos. This was a negligible quantity, but the viceroy had asked for only 100 quintales in any case.[5]

---

[1] AGI Mexico 27, 1608 (n.e.d.), various 'personas inteligentes' formerly resident in the Philippines to Crown; 'Sobre el asiento que pretende hacer fulano de Baeza para traer azogue de las Filipinas'.

[2] AGI Indiferente General 1777, Madrid 25 September 1630, consulta of Consejo de Indias.

[3] AGI Mexico 31, R. 1, México 20 March 1632, Cerralvo to Crown '3° duplicado de materias de hacienda'.

[4] AGI Mexico 611, México 13 March 1662, 'Respuesta del Fiscal', in Martín de Murga Eguiluz to Baños, México 10 March 1662 – all in México 21 December 1662, Baños to Crown.

[5] AGI Mexico 612, Manila 1 December 1692, Don Fausto Cruzat y Góngora to Crown (and his 'añadido' of Manila 10 June 1693).

Mercury

The cost of this mercury, 60 pesos the quintal, was only some 30 pesos less than the current selling price in New Spain. With the addition of trans-Pacific freight and carting within New Spain, the cost price to the Crown would have risen to a level so high that little, if any, profit would have remained.

The failure of the experimental sources to provide useful quantities of mercury thus threw responsibility for supplying America on to Almadén and Huancavelica. Almadén was worked under asiento by the Augsburg bankers, the Fuggers. They were first granted exploitation of the mine in 1525 by Charles V, as part repayment of debts owed to them by the Spanish Crown. They worked the deposits continuously from the early 1550s to 1645.[1] Huancavelica was exploited under a similar asiento system from the time of Viceroy Toledo. When the immense value of mercury for reducing the ores of nearby Potosí became apparent, he took the mines out of the hands of the miners who had hitherto worked them, and made a Crown monopoly of them. The asentistas were the same miners as before, but they were now obliged to sell their product to the Crown, for distribution by the royal Treasury.[2] The first asiento was drawn up in 1573, for three years. Later asientos were for a similar or slightly longer period, although in the second half of the seventeenth century they became very much longer.

In general, these two mines appear to have given an adequate supply of mercury to American silver mines until the end of the sixteenth century. The Fuggers achieved a slight but continuous increase in production during the last quarter of the century. Average annual output during the asiento of 1573 to 1581 was 2,511 quintales; and in that of 1595 to 1604, 2,860 quintales.[3] (See Table 10b.) This mercury was consigned entirely to New Spain, where deficiencies appear to have been made up by imports from Peru. There was an order for the annual remittance of 2,000 quintales thence to New Spain at the end of the sixteenth century,[4] and doubtless private remittances added to this figure. Production at Huancavelica rose rapidly from a yearly average of 1,968 quintales in 1571 to 1574, to 8,083 quintales in 1590 to 1594.[5] (See Table 10b.)

The final years of the century, however, witnessed the end of Huancavelica's early productiveness. 1591 was the last year in the sixteenth or seventeenth centuries in which production in quintales reached five figures; and average yearly output in the final five years of the century

---

[1] Matilla Tascón, Historia ... de Almadén, pp. 37, 53–64.
[2] Lohmann Villena, Las minas de Huancavelica, ch. 4.
[3] Matilla Tascón, Historia ... de Almadén, pp. 107, 121.
[4] Mentioned in AGI Guadalajara 8, R. 10, Madrid 28 June 1606, real cédula to Montesclaros.
[5] Lohmann Villena, Las minas de Huancavelica, pp. 452–3.

fell to only 5,741 quintales.[1] This decline, it is true, was in part the result of conscious efforts to reduce production to a level closer to demand. By 1595 there were in store some 25,000 quintales.[2] But it also derived from intrinsic difficulties in the mine which now began to appear and which were to become constantly greater in the succeeding century. These difficulties would upset the satisfactory system of mercury supply to the American mines that had previously existed, and lead on occasion to frenetic and expensive searches for mercury by the relevant Councils in Spain. Up to the end of the sixteenth century, Huancavelica was worked mostly as an open-cast mine. But by the late 1590s the principal layer of ore, La Descubridora, was dipping too deep for the safe use of this method, in view of the loose nature of the country rock, which was sandstone. Miners therefore began to use subterranean workings which, without proper general supervision, soon became labyrinthine. This not only added to the difficulties of extracting ore, but gave rise to grave health hazards to Indian mine labourers. To the poor ventilation typical of ill-planned workings was added the danger of toxic dust from the mercury ores, which attacked the lungs. The terrible working conditions of the mita Indians brought protests from priests and Indian *caciques*, which eventually led Viceroy Velasco in 1604 to prohibit all but open-cast working. In a new asiento of 1 March of that year, this was a basic condition; and an additional order in favour of the Indians was a reduction of the mita from 1,750 to 1,600 labourers a year.

Despite these problems, the stock of mercury in Peru at the end of Velasco's term in 1604 stood at 17,000 quintales, enough to meet demand for three years.[3] But only 800 quintales were produced in 1604. This gave the new viceroy, Monterrey, much cause for concern, which he communicated to the Consejo de Indias. Consequently, in 1606 a cédula went to Viceroy Montesclaros in New Spain, telling him that Monterrey had reported from Peru that the annual shipment of 2,000 quintales to New Spain could no longer be continued, because of the difficulties of Huancavelica. Indeed, the direction of the flow was to be reversed. Monterrey required 6,000 quintales over the years 1607 and 1608 from New Spain. This was in fact an impossible request, since the total amount being shipped from Almadén to New Spain hardly reached 3,000 quintales a year. (See Table 10a.) The Consejo de Indias recognised this, and merely urged Montesclaros to send at least 1,000 quintales to Peru.[4]

---

[1] Lohmann Villena, *Las minas de Huancavelica*, p. 453. 1591 output was 11,522 quintales.
[2] Lohmann Villena, *Las minas de Huancavelica*, pp. 155–6.
[3] Lohmann Villena, *Las minas de Huancavelica*, ch. 10, *passim*.
[4] AGI Guadalajara 8, R. 10, Madrid 28 June 1606, real cédula to Montesclaros.

Mercury

This seems to have been the first occasion on which there was competition between the two viceroyalties for scarce supplies of mercury. In the event, it was largely a false alarm, caused to a considerable extent by the slowness with which information (often inadequate) reached Spain from Peru. Montesclaros did take 1,000 of the 3,700 quintales reaching New Spain in 1606 with him when he left as newly-appointed viceroy of Peru in 1607. But Velasco, now back in Mexico for his second turn, was prevented only by time from stopping this export, since he knew from personal experience that adequate stocks still existed in Peru. He, in turn, was apprehensive about the sufficiency of future supplies to New Spain, especially in view of the prosperous state of the Zacatecas mines, which only lacked mercury to yield more silver.[1]

Once again, apprehension about the mercury supply seems to have been largely unwarranted. There is no evidence of gross shortage in the first twenty years of the seventeenth century. At Almadén the Fuggers maintained a slow but constant increase in production. The annual average remitted to Seville during the asiento of 1605 to 1614 was 3,595 quintales, and in that of 1615 to 1624, 4,793 quintales.[2] The Fuggers appear to have had no difficulty in achieving this increase, and they consistently exceeded the output promised in their asientos with the Crown. The introduction of an improved type of reverberatory furnace in 1609 undoubtedly tended to improve production.[3] At Huancavelica, the century began badly, as has been seen, but then came a recovery. The quinquennium 1605 to 1609 was disastrous. Bans on entering subterranean workings were only gradually relaxed, and deep galleries, closed since 1604, were in any case found to be full of poisonous gases. Then in 1607 occurred what Lohmann Villena considers one of the greatest misfortunes to befall the mine. Surface workings had by this time penetrated the roof of an old gallery, into which heavy rain washed a deluge of tailings and detritus, filling the gallery and adjacent workings, and blocking the main entrance to all underground workings. Consequently, 1607 saw the production of only 1,617 quintales of quicksilver. Another subsidence occurred in February of 1608, killing various labourers. Average annual production in this quinquennium was only 2,888 quintales, and only the existence of large stocks saved the day.[4] But after 1610, improvement came rapidly. A team of experts had arrived from Almadén in 1609, under whose supervision ventilation shafts were cut to the deeper levels, making

---

[1] AGI Mexico 27, México 29 August 1607, Velasco to Crown, 'Real Hacienda y minas'.
[2] Matilla Tascón, *Historia ... de Almadén*, pp. 122, 137.
[3] Matilla Tascón, *Historia ... de Almadén*, p. 124.
[4] Lohmann Villena, *Las minas de Huancavelica*, pp. 199–205, 453.

previously gas-filled galleries available for exploitation. Registered production in the decade 1610 to 1619 ran at above 6,000 quintales a year.[1] There was a growing supply of voluntary labour to make up the deficiencies of the mita.

Mercury from Huancavelica was now entirely consumed in Peru; no further inter-colonial remittances were made until the last third of the century. And Almadén production, although rising, was not enough to meet the demands of New Spain as fully as the Mexican authorities would have wished. In a joint consulta of April 1621, the Consejos de Indias and de Hacienda stated that a constant effort had been made to send 5,000 quintales a year to New Spain. (In fact, current production at Almadén was falling only very slightly short of that.) They referred to an attempt made in 1614 to negotiate an asiento with one Carlos Albertineli, *alemán*, for the supply of 3,000 quintales from Idria in that year, and 2,500 quintales for nine years thereafter. But Albertineli had not found the conditions suitable, and had withdrawn. Now, however, in 1621, another asiento had been arranged, this time with Federico Oberolz, for the supply of 16,000 quintales over four years. This mercury was likewise from Idria, and was to be cheaper than that of the previous, abandoned asiento – 54 pesos (40 ducats) instead of 69 pesos (50 ducats) the quintal, including freight to Seville or Cadiz.[2] The Consejos also gave as a reason for pursuing this asiento the decline of Huancavelica, where, they had heard, the mines were deep and the Indians dying for lack of air. This was a chronic problem at Huancavelica in the seventeenth century, and it is not clear why authorities in Spain should have seized on it at this moment. It is true that registered production at Huancavelica had declined from previous high levels of over 7,000 quintales a year (in 1615–16) to below 5,000 (1618–19).[3]

The Oberolz contract was the first of a series of asientos for the supply of mercury to America from Idria to be drawn up over the next twenty-five years. In this period there was a noticeable, though not drastic, decline in quicksilver production from the two traditional sources, and the asientos, of course, made up the deficiency. But they were also a response to increased demand from the American silver mines. And when silver production figures for those mines are finally and fully known, it

---

[1] Lohmann Villena, *Las minas de Huancavelica*, ch. 13, *passim*.
[2] AGI Indiferente General 1777, Madrid 24 April 1621, consulta of Consejo de Indias and de Hacienda. In the same legajo is a copy of the Oberolz contract, 'Asiento que se tomó con Federico Oberolz en 29 de abril de 621 sobre la provisión de 16,000 quintales de azogue para las Indias en cuatro años. Madrid, 29 abril 1621'. Oberolz rented the Emperor's mercury mine at Idria.
[3] Lohmann Villena, *Las minas de Huancavelica*, p. 453.

is likely that this period will appear as a long and important boom. Reference to Graph 1 and Table 4 will show that this was true of Zacatecas, at least up to 1635.[1]

Most of the mercury from this asiento was sent to Peru,[2] as a supplement to the production of Huancavelica and a consequent alleviation of the mitayos' burden. In accordance with instructions from the Consejo de Indias, Viceroy Guadalcázar drew up in February 1623 a new agreement with the miners of Huancavelica, under which the number of mita Indians assigned to the mine was reduced from 2,200 to 1,400 a year, and expected output from 6,600 to 4,200 quintales. A further instruction of the Consejo was that the mine should be maintained in a state suitable for heavier exploitation later, if the need arose.[3] This running-down of Huancavelica was doubtless responsible to a large extent for the need of another asiento with Oberolz, which was negotiated to run from 1626 to 1628, at 4,000 quintales a year.[4] Certainly the quinquennium 1625 to 1629 was very unproductive at Huancavelica. Output fell to an average of only 2,689 quintales a year, a figure lower than at any time since the early 1570s. The labour restrictions imposed by Guadalcázar reduced production in 1628 and 1629 to around 2,000 quintales a year. Moreover, stocks of mercury were low. Viceroy Chinchón, on arrival in 1628, found only 2,800 quintales awaiting him.[5]

Chinchón's arrival marks the beginning of the most interesting chapter in the history of mercury supply to America in this century. Demands and interests that had hitherto been only vaguely defined now became clearly delineated, and entered into conflict. Chinchón brought with him from Spain 4,000 quintales of mercury, which no doubt gave him breathing space while he considered how the clearly unpromising condition of Huancavelica could be improved. He saw that the mine was deep and that there was insufficient labour, partly because the mita

---

[1] Some evidence of high silver production in Peru in the 1630s and 1640s is provided by Carmen Báncora Cañero in 'Las remesas de metales preciosos desde el Callao a España en la primera mitad del siglo XVII' (*Revista de Indias*, año XIX, No. 75, pp. 35–88). Silver remittances are high from 1634 to 1644 (see p. 86). But Treasury remittances naturally reflect silver output only distantly.

[2] AGI Contratación 4324, 'Contratación de Sevilla. Libros de cargo y data de azogues recibidos y entregados por los Factores. En 4 números'. Here, Nos. 2 and 3.

[3] Lohmann Villena, *Las minas de Huancavelica*, p. 266; and AGI Indiferente General 1777, Lima 30 April 1624, Guadalcázar to Crown. The philanthropic aims of the Consejo de Indias in establishing the first Oberolz asiento are referred to in a later consulta of that council, dated 24 April 1630, in AGI Indiferente General 1777. The Consejo was perturbed, basically, by the general decline of Indian population in Peru.

[4] AGI Indiferente General 1777, Genoa 25 September 1626, asiento with Federico Oberolz. The price of the mercury to the Crown was again forty ducats.

[5] Lohmann Villena, *Las minas de Huancavelica*, pp. 269, 454.

had been officially reduced and partly because the corregidores of the districts from which the labourers were drawn were negligent and corrupt in gathering together their quotas of Indians.[1] This was, in the event, far from displeasing to Chinchón, since he proved to be one of the most ardent defenders of Indians among seventeenth-century American viceroys. His desire to spare the mitayos the perils of working at Huancavelica clashed with his knowledge that high production at the mine was economically necessary. To consider the question of labour there, he set up a special junta in September 1629; but this body, like the viceroy, fell prey to conflicting opinions, and in 1630 Chinchón, still hesitant, was obliged to refer the matter to Madrid for resolution.[2] Writing to the king in February 1630, he said, 'I assure your majesty that it is a most terrible matter ('materia terriblísima'), for free, innocent, defenceless, poor and afflicted people are condemned to well-known risk of death, as is to be seen from those who have perished and from the lack of people that there is, and the fear they have of this sort of servitude ...'.[3] This was undoubtedly something of an exaggeration, in view of the large numbers of voluntary Indian workers who are said to have chosen to dig at Huancavelica.[4] But protests in this vein from high officials in the Indies were always likely to trouble the tender conscience of the more humane of administrators in Spain – a tender conscience that had perhaps been no more than soothed by pro-Indian legislation in the sixteenth and early seventeenth centuries. Judging by the number of consultas on Chinchón's problem flowing from the Consejo de Indias in 1630, the viceroy found a number of allies in that body. And a further note of urgency was added to the dispute by the fact that Oberolz had not delivered all the mercury due under the 1626 asiento. He had become bankrupt before handing over perhaps half the 12,000 quintales promised between 1626 and 1628. His creditors had bought up the portion of that quantity that had remained in Venice, awaiting shipment to Spain; and then tried to arrange with the Imperial government that future production at Idria should be restricted, presumably with the aim of creating a shortage and artificially raising the price.[5] Careful diplomacy would therefore be needed to preserve the supply of German mercury. This was not an encouraging prospect,

---

[1] Lohmann Villena, *Las minas de Huancavelica*, pp. 269–70.

[2] Lohmann Villena, *Las minas de Huancavelica*, pp. 273–9.

[3] AGI Indiferente 1777, Lima 2 February 1630, Chinchón to Crown, 'Gobierno y Hacienda No. 38'.

[4] See Lohmann Villena, *Las minas de Huancavelica*, e.g. pp. 258–9. Voluntary workers received double or treble the wage of mitayos.

[5] AGI Indiferente General 1777, undated letter of Don Cristóbal de Benavente y Benavides, with consulta of Consejo de Indias, 24 April 1630.

especially when Chinchón was saying that with the current low mita at Huancavelica, still only 1,400 Indians a year, the mine would supply only a third of the mercury needed in Peru.[1]

For a time the Consejo appears to have unquestioningly accepted the burden of Chinchón's letters – that Huancavelica was beyond retrieval, except by increasing the labour force of mitayos, which was inadmissible. Thus a consulta of August 1630 proposed that no more should be done than prevent the mine falling into disrepair, while other resources of mercury should be fully exploited. The mercury left at Venice should be recovered, new asientos should be arranged for German mercury, the possibilities of the Chinese source should be explored yet again, and the Fuggers should be urged to increase production at Almadén.[2] Another consulta, of late November 1630, shows that the conflict of humanity to Indians with economic need was still exercising and dividing the Consejo after nearly a year's deliberation. Juan de Solórzano Pereira, perhaps the councillor best qualified to judge the matter, since he had been visitor and governor of Huancavelica from 1616 to 1618, was representative in his opinions of the pro-Indian members of the Consejo. He advised the king that in view of the reported state of the mine and the decline of Indian population in the surrounding provinces, no further mita Indians could be obtained, nor the old ones imposed on too much, without heavy burden on the conscience ('sin muy grave cargo de consciencia'). The king should therefore be content with the mercury produced by voluntary labour – and possibly, in the future, criminal labour – in the mine. This consulta consists of separate statements by the councillors on the question of Huancavelica; roughly half agreed with Solórzano. So the matter finally went to the king for adjudication, after baffling the viceroy, his special junta, and the Consejo de Indias. Philip IV's scrawled marginal note on the consulta was decisive. Almadén should be worked to capacity; a new asiento for German mercury should be negotiated; mercury should be sought in China; criminals should be assigned to Almadén; and Chinchón should be instructed to extend the mita at Huancavelica, bringing new provinces into the catchment area if necessary. The king expressed his infinite desire to relieve the Indians of work in the mine, but to excuse them 'would appear to be neglecting the universal well-being and the maintenance not only of my Kingdoms but of the Catholic

[1] AGI Indiferente General 1777, Lima 27 May 1630, Chinchón to Crown, 'Hacienda Real No. 41'.
[2] AGI Indiferente General 1777, 22 August 1630, consulta of Consejo de Indias, entitled on verso 'Lo que ha parecido se debe y conviene ordenar para acudir al reparo de la falta de azogue que el Virrey del Perú escribe hay en aquellas provincias para el beneficio de las minas'.

religion ...'.[1] Only three and a half years had passed since the State bankruptcy of 1627, during which time Spain had suffered the expense of the Mantuan war, and the loss of the treasure-bearing fleet from New Spain to the Dutch in 1628. The newest threat was the possible intervention of France in Flanders.[2] The Indians of central Peru must have seemed very distant to the king.

In spite of this clear directive from Spain, Chinchón nevertheless continued to raise objections to the further use of Indians. Where, he asked in November 1631, should they be drawn from? To increase the area of the mita would drain workers from other occupations. And, in any case, mercury from Huancavelica was as dear in Peru as that from Almadén or Germany.[3] (It was not the first time he had commented on the high cost of quicksilver from Huancavelica. But since he did not substantiate the claim, it is difficult to say whether it really had any weight as an argument against working that mine.) But events moved to take the urgent edge from his worries, since, for reasons which are not clear, production at Huancavelica rose sharply after 1631 to over 4,000 quintales a year, giving a final average production in the quinquennium 1630 to 1634 of 4,328 quintales a year.[4] This was certainly not enough to meet the demands of Peru's silver mines; but help soon became available from a new asiento for mercury from Idria, drawn up with Antonio Balbi, a member of the Milanese banking company, on 31 August 1631. This provided for the supply of 6,000 quintales from 1632 to 1634.[5] In late 1636 the contract with Balbi was renewed and enlarged. He undertook to supply 16,000 quintales from 1637 to 1641.[6] The price of mercury to the Crown, as placed in Cadiz, was 54 pesos (40 ducats) in both these contracts. The mercury was duly delivered, though sometimes late, as Balbi delayed consignments until he was paid for previous shipments. In the second asiento he insisted on being paid in silver (as opposed to

---

[1] AGI Indiferente General 1777, Madrid 26 November 1630, consulta of Consejo de Indias.

[2] A. Domínguez Ortiz, *Política y hacienda de Felipe IV*, Madrid 1960, Part I, ch. 3.

[3] AGI Indiferente General 1777, Lima (?) 13 November 1631, Chinchón to Crown.

[4] Lohmann Villena attributes the improvement to the administrative skill of a new governor of Huancavelica, Licenciado Fernando de Saavedra. See *Las minas de Huancavelica*, p. 294; for production, p. 454.

[5] This contract is mentioned, for example, in AGI Indiferente General 1777, Madrid 18 April 1633, consulta of Consejo de Indias.

[6] The asiento was signed on 31 December 1636. A draft of it, dated Madrid 25 March 1636, is to be found in AGI Indiferente General 1777, with a consulta of the Consejo de Indias of 22 June 1636: 'El asiento de los azogues que se ha tratado entre Antonio Balbi y Juan de Quesada Sotomayor con intervención del Excelentísimo Señor Conde de Castrillo, Presidente del Real Consejo de las Indias, está efectuado en la forma siguiente ...'.

vellón), to be drawn on the Treasury office of Panamá, through which all bullion from Peru passed on its way to Spain.[1]
In securing this supply of mercury from Idria, the king and the Councils of the Indies and Hacienda had been preoccupied almost entirely with the unsatisfied demand of the Peruvian silver mines. Their neglect of New Spain is reflected in the scarcity of references to the northern viceroyalty in the preceding pages of this chapter. Peru was beyond doubt the major silver producer in the Empire, as councillors of the Indies and Hacienda reminded the king in September 1634. It was essential to send mercury to the Indies, 'particularly to Peru and Tierra Firme, since from it [i.e. the dispatch of mercury] derives the return of silver in which your majesty is the principal interested party, both in public and private [remittances] ...'.[2] The predominance of Peru in the minds of administrators in Madrid during these years is shown in the figures for exports of mercury for Spain to the two American viceroyalties. For the sake of completeness and contrast, exports are given here from the beginning of the seventeenth century. The totals are quinquennial, and the units quintales.

	To New Spain[3]	To Peru
1600–4	15,340	none
1605–9	15,062	3,031
1610–14	16,655	1,000
1615–19	24,014	none
1620–4	21,747	10,502
1625–9	23,884	9,006
1630–4	12,999	13,051
1635–9	unknown	18,276
1640–4	18,624	16,740

[1] For information on these asientos, and their financing, see various consultas of the Consejo de Indias in AGI Indiferente General 1777; e.g. 9 September 1634 (a junta, in fact, of the Consejos de Indias y de Hacienda), 24 November 1634, 22 June 1636; and a *membrete* of Secretary Juan de Otálora Guevara of the Consejo de Hacienda to the Conde de Castrillo, dated Madrid 8 May 1640. A consulta of the Consejo de Hacienda, dated Madrid 1 January 1635, also in AGI Indiferente General 1777, refers to an asiento with Balbi for the supply of 8,300 quintales in the years 1635–7. But absence of later references to this contract suggests that it was never enacted.

[2] AGI Indiferente General 1777, Madrid 9 September 1634, junta of Consejos de Indias y de Hacienda.

[3] For the source of these figures, see notes to Table 10a. There is one minor difference in sources. Whereas all exports to New Spain are taken here from AGI Contratación 4324, figures shown in Table 10a for exports to New Spain in the period 1624–34 are taken from AGI Mexico 31, as noted in notes 1 and 4 of that table. AGI Mexico 31 shows mercury actually received in New Spain. This accounts for discrepancies between quantities shown here and those in the Table.

Mercury

The figures in the table tell their own story. The first major export to Peru came in 1622 with the remittance of 4,177 quintales from the first Oberolz asiento. The origin of two further consignments in 1623 and 1624 is not known, but it is likely that they were also from Idria, since three further remittances in 1625, 1628 and 1629 certainly were. Up to this point, New Spain received the bulk of the export, and the totality of Almadén's production. But then the situation was reversed, as a direct result of Chinchón's representations from Lima. In a consulta of 22 August 1630, the Consejo de Indias suggested that, in view of the reported acute shortage of mercury in Peru, it might be necessary to divert part of Almadén's output from New Spain to Peru.[1] Although research has not revealed the executive order for this transfer, it undoubtedly took place, as the above figures show. In the quinquennium 1630 to 1634, for the first time, more European mercury was directed to Peru than to New Spain. Of the 13,051 quintales dispatched to Peru in these years, 9,465 were certainly mined at Almadén. The origin of the remaining 3,586 quintales is not specified in the document.[2] The only certain export of German mercury is a shipment in 1632 of 2,276 quintales to New Spain. It therefore appears that Peru had been assigned the traditionally safe supply of mercury from Almadén, and New Spain relegated to dependence on the insecure, *ad hoc*, source, Idria. It seems likely that Peru continued to take the majority of exports in the quinquennium 1635 to 1639. It was certainly assigned more than ever before, at 18,276 quintales – a figure which, considering the preceding and succeeding exports, would seem likely at least to equal the amount dispatched to New Spain in that time, although that amount is unfortunately unknown. In the early 1640s, New Spain regained a narrow majority of the export. And thereafter Peru's share dwindled rapidly, although figures for the late 1640s are not known. But from 1651 to 1658, New Spain took 20,097 quintales, against Peru's 4,358.[3]

A summary at this point will clarify the argument. In the 1620s, for the first time, Peru received large consignments of mercury from Europe, to enable the viceroy to reduce the number of mita Indians working at Huancavelica. This mercury came from the mines of Idria, while the whole output of Almadén continued to be directed to New Spain. In the 1630s Peru was assigned yet more European mercury, its quota probably exceeding that of New Spain. In the first half of the decade, the large majority of the mercury sent to Peru was from Almadén.

[1] AGI Indiferente General 1777, 22 August 1630, consulta of Consejo de Indias.
[2] AGI Contratación 4324, No. 3. For full reference, see note 1 of Table 10a.
[3] AGI Contaduría 404, No. 3. For full reference, see note 1 of Table 10a.

Mercury

The origin of mercury dispatched to Peru in the second part of the decade is not known. Possibly some came still from Almadén, but some was almost certainly supplied under the large second Balbi asiento of 1637 to 1641. The initial reason for the diversion of a large part of Almadén's output from New Spain to Peru was the uneasy conscience of Viceroy Chinchón and part of the Consejo de Indias over the sufferings of Indian labourers at Huancavelica. A further reason was the clearly unproductive state of Huancavelica in the late 1620s and the early 1630s. But even when Huancavelica recovered, as it did from 1631 onwards, large consignments were still sent to Peru, at the expense of New Spain. This was probably because the Consejos de Indias and de Hacienda considered Peru to be the traditional major source of silver in the Empire, and therefore potentially a more profitable recipient of mercury than New Spain. (Whether the second part of this supposition was well-founded can only be decided by investigation of Peruvian silver mining in the seventeenth century.) From 1640 to 1644, exports to Peru continued at a high level, though New Spain recovered a narrow lead. Again, the European origins of the mercury are not known; but this was the period of a third and final asiento with Antonio Balbi, which provided 16,000 quintales in these years.[1] This asiento could have yielded almost the total quantity sent to Peru.

The silver mines of Peru presumably benefited from this large supplement to their normal supply of mercury. Those of New Spain correspondingly suffered, as will be seen in due course in the particular case of Zacatecas. The protests of Mexican viceroys in the mid-1630s were loud. In 1636 Cadereita complained that he had received only 634 quintales in that year's fleet, when he needed 6,000; '... and from its lack there has fallen such a great frost ("tan gran hielo") on commerce as cannot be described to your majesty'.[2] Two years later he noted a two-fifths' decline in silver remittances to Mexico City from Zacatecas, Guadiana and Guadalajara, attributable to scarcity of mercury.[3] In its ability to direct supplies of mercury to one viceroyalty or the other, the administration in Spain possessed a powerful economic regulator – just how powerful, it did not perhaps realise.

[1] The terms of the 1640 asiento may be found in a membrete of Secretary Juan de Otálora Guevara to Don Gabriel de Ocaña y Alarcón, dated Madrid 18 February 1644, in AGI Indiferente General 1777. 2,000 quintales were to be delivered in 1641; 12,000 from 1642 to 1644; and 2,000 in 1645. The price to the Crown was, as before, 40 ducats. And payment was to be made to Balbi in silver, from the Treasury at Panamá. The silver was to be remitted on the same galleons as carried the mercury out.

[2] AGI Mexico 31, Cuaderno 1, f. 131–131v., México 15 June 1636, Cadereita to Crown, 'Gobierno'.

[3] AGI Mexico 34, Cuaderno, f. 81–2, México 12 July 1638, Cadereita to Crown, 'Hacienda Real'.

Mercury

There remains to be shown one further aspect of the supply of mercury to the American colonies during the period 1620 to 1640, when quicksilver for the first time became a truly scarce commodity. For reasons which will be explained below (at least in the case of New Spain), and by schemes which will also be described, the Crown, from the last quarter of the sixteenth century onwards, had distributed mercury to silver miners on credit. By the 1620s, miners had run up very considerable debts to the royal Treasury. For example, in Zacatecas and its district alone miners owed, in October 1620, some 356,000 pesos.[1] In Potosí, in June 1626, the mercury debt was some 2,977,000 pesos (1,800,000 pesos ensayados) and still rising.[2] In earlier years attempts had, of course, been made to collect these debts and to sell mercury under some scheme which would prevent their accumulating. But miners could always make out a good case for being provided with mercury on credit, and there were always administrators who argued that it was more profitable to the Crown to distribute mercury on credit and obtain silver in return than to restrict the amount of mercury available and thereby diminish output of silver. It is apparent, however, that by the early 1630s the Spanish Treasury's need for ready cash was becoming so urgent that such arguments were no longer accepted. In September 1630 the Consejo de Indias noted that the Consejo de Hacienda was becoming preoccupied with this question of mercury debts, and hastened to assure the king that in Peru Chinchón was attending to the matter closely.[3] But evidently not closely enough; for in September 1634 there went strict orders ('ordenes apretadísimas', said the Consejo de Indias) to both viceroys in America, instructing them to collect the debt at once and sell mercury henceforth for spot cash only.[4] Neither of the two instructions proved immediately practicable. But over the following years, stringent efforts were made to collect the debt. The effect on silver mining was dire, as will be seen in the case of Zacatecas.

Financial pressure on the Crown is a constant theme running through

[1] AGI Mexico 74, R. 2, Zacatecas 26 November 1620, Don Juan de Cervantes Casaus, 'Relación por mayor de las deudas que se debían a la Real Caja de esta ciudad de Nuestra Señora de los Zacatecas de todo género de Real Hacienda hasta postrero de octubre de este presente año de mil y seiscientos y veinte ...'.

[2] AGI Indiferente General 1777, in an anonymous, undated document, 'Lo que se ha escrito sobre ponerse cobro en las deudas que se deben en las cajas de Potosí, Huancavelica, Castrovirreina y Oruro', para. 3, the report of Dr Juan Gutiérrez, visitor of the Audiencia of Lima, 11 March 1627.

[3] AGI Indiferente General 1777, Madrid 25 September 1630, consulta of the Consejo de Indias.

[4] The order to Cerralvo, in New Spain, is in AGI Mexico 35, Cuaderno 2, f. 32, Madrid 9 September 1634, real cédula.

correspondence and reports about mercury during the rest of the century. One of its first consequences, in the matter of mercury, was to cause the Fuggers to abandon in 1645 their working of Almadén, after holding the asiento for 120 years almost continuously. Almadén was for many years one of their most profitable enterprises in Spain. Matilla Tascón estimates that their profits in the period 1609 to 1614 amounted to nearly 73 per cent.[1] This was the high point of their gain, though, for increasing costs cut the profit to some 35 per cent in the next asiento.[2] And this rate of decline persisted into the succeeding asiento (1625 to 1635) so that the previous earnings completely disappeared. In 1629 the cost to the Fuggers of each of the 5,112 quintales produced was 10,766 maravedís, and the selling price to the Crown, 11,000. These were years of rising labour prices in Spain, from which the Fuggers doubtless suffered.[3] But the technical costs of mining and extraction of ore also appear to have risen, for which the most plausible reason seems to be neglect of the mine. And this in turn reflects the general deterioration of the Fuggers' position in Spain. The debt owed to them by the Crown for previous loans amounted, in October 1633, to a balance of over 4,713,000 pesos (3,420,231 ducats). It seems that, although earnings were rapidly falling even there, Almadén was the Fuggers' last profitable enterprise in Spain, and that they extracted all the gain possible from it, at the expense of the proper upkeep of the mine.[4] The tenacity with which work was pursued there is remarkable, in view of the Crown's dilatoriness in paying for the mercury produced. The motives were, perhaps, a mixture of strange loyalty to the Crown and rather desperate hope of improved returns. In 1634 the Fuggers' administrator at Almadén pointed out that all the 45,000 quintales promised under the asiento of 1625 to 1634 had been delivered to Seville, indeed with an excess of 800 quintales. This had been achieved despite the fact that no payment had been received for part of 1630's mercury, and none for any of the deliveries of 1631, 1632 and 1633. And now the king had ordered that payment should be made in vellón, with a premium of 20 per cent. As the administrator rather wistfully complained, 'this delay and late and doubtful payment is not [calculated] to give to my superiors or their factors the encouragement they desire'.[5]

[1] Matilla Tascón, *Historia ... de Almadén*, p. 123. In this period 22,323 quintales were produced, at a unit cost of 5,493 maravedís (about 20 pesos); the selling price to the Crown was 9,500 maravedís (about 35 pesos).   [2] Matilla Tascón, *Historia ... de Almadén*, pp. 137-8.
[3] Matilla Tascón, *Historia ... de Almadén*, pp. 170-1.
[4] Matilla Tascón, *Historia ... de Almadén*, p. 176. For the decline of the Fuggers' fortunes in Spain at this time, see Domínguez Ortiz, *Política y Hacienda*, Part II, ch. 4.
[5] AGI Indiferente General 1777, Almadén (?) 24 June 1634, Juan Cristóbal Eberlin to Señor Don Gabriel de Ocaña y Alarcón.

Mercury

Nevertheless, a further asiento was undertaken, providing for 4,500 quintales a year between 1636 and 1645. Output was in reality to fall far below this figure. Remittances to Seville in the decade amounted to only 25,345 quintales; and, if Matilla Tascón's calculations are correct, the Fuggers suffered disastrous losses on this contract. The existing penury of the house meant still further deterioration of the mine – a process that was hastened by an underground fire in 1637.[1] The result is summed up by a report of the Consejo de Indias in April 1639, saying that up to then the Fuggers had failed to deliver 10,000 quintales due under the 1636 asiento. The bankers' agent in Spain had explained that he had no funds with which to work the mine. The Consejo de Hacienda said that it had no resources that could be applied to Almadén. The merchants of Seville had been sounded for a 40,000 ducat loan, but would not cooperate.[2] By 1645, no financial improvement had come about, nor was foreseeable. The Consejo de Indias reported to the king that the Fuggers were abandoning Almadén, 'since no money owed for mercury has been provided by the Consejo de Hacienda, whose task it is'.[3] So the vicious circle finally closed round the Crown. For lack of money, mercury could not be mined; for lack of mercury, silver could not be refined; and for lack of silver, the Treasury's income fell.

1645 marks the end of direct foreign participation in the mining of mercury for, and in, Spain. The third Balbi asiento, which ended in 1644, was not renewed, perhaps for the same reasons of State insolvency as led to the Fuggers' leaving Almadén.[4] Henceforth Almadén, like Huancavelica, was worked under the direct administration of the Crown. Since mercury was obtained from no other source in Europe up to the end of the century, and little was consumed in Spain itself, exports from Spain to America, as shown in Table 10a, closely represent the output of Almadén in the following years. Levels of production compare quite favourably with those of the last quarter of the sixteenth century, but poorly with those of the best years of the Fugger asientos, the first three decades of the seventeenth. Distribution of mercury from Almadén returned to the pattern dominant before 1620: the great majority was sent

---

[1] Matilla Tascón, Historia ... de Almadén, pp. 181–3. According to Matilla, in 1637 the cost price of one quintal, placed in Seville, was 20,397 maravedís (75 pesos), while the selling price to the Crown remained, apparently, at 11,000 maravedís (40 pesos). In 1642 the selling price was raised to 14,000 maravedís (51 pesos). It is difficult to believe that 1637's prices were typical of the whole decade.

[2] AGI Indiferente General 1780, Madrid 8 April 1639, consulta of Consejo de Indias.

[3] AGI Indiferente General 1780, Madrid (?) February 1645, consulta of Consejo de Hacienda.

[4] AGI Indiferente General 1777, Madrid 14 December 1646, decreto of king to the Conde de Castrillo, referring to a memorial from the Imperial ambassador in which it was enquired whether the Balbi contract was to be renewed.

to New Spain. In the absence of the promised, but not yet executed, second volume of Matilla Tascón's history of Almadén, the further story of the mine can be traced here only from a few papers of the Consejo de Indias to be found in the Archivo General de Indias. These refer almost exclusively to the need for funds. The subject was a source of some dispute between the Consejo de Indias and the Consejo de Hacienda – the one, the body with administrative control of the mine, and with immediate interest in seeing America well supplied with mercury; the other, the provider of money to create such a supply. In May 1659 the Consejo de Hacienda complained that it could not be expected to finance Almadén if payments for previous mercury were not sent back from the Indies – and on a separate account. It should not be necessary to support Almadén from other sources of income. The Consejo de Indias retorted that orders existed for keeping separate mercury accounts in New Spain, and that this was normally done. But even if it were not, it was to be supposed that the total remittance of Crown silver from America included payments for mercury. And furthermore – rather petulantly, this – either confidence should be placed in the viceroys and other officials in America, or it should not; and if it were not, why should they be entrusted with so much responsibility?[1] The continuing lack of funds for Almadén led to the negotiation of a cash asiento with Ventura de Onís in 1661, which provided for 87,500 pesos (50,000 escudos) over six months, beginning in March of that year. Further asientos were made with Onís in the following years, giving 175,000 pesos (100,000 escudos) in 1662 and another 175,000 in 1663.[2] But this injection of cash apparently helped little, for exports from Almadén were unusually low in the first half of the 1660s. Thereafter, until the end of the century, the mine was rather more productive; and if problems of finance again became grave, they had also become so commonplace as not even to merit a consulta from the Consejo de Indias. Little further reference was found to the question in manuscripts consulted in the Archivo General de Indias.

Production at Huancavelica, as shown by Lohmann Villena, remained at a steady and adequate level from the 1640s until the end of the century.[3] There were both technical and financial reasons for this generally satisfactory state of affairs. First came an improved system of extracting

---

[1] AGI Indiferente General 1778, Madrid 19 May 1659, consulta of the Consejo de Hacienda; Madrid 9 June 1659, consulta of the Consejo de Indias, 'No. 1'.

[2] AGI Indiferente General 1778, Madrid 26 February 1661, consulta of Junta of the Consejos de Indias y de Hacienda; and consultas of the Consejo de Indias, Madrid 31 January 1663, 10 May 1663, 5 March 1664. These documents do not give any indication of how Onís was to be repaid for his loans.

[3] Lohmann Villena, *Las minas de Huancavelica*, pp. 454–5.

mercury from the ore, invented by one Lope de Saavedra Barba, and generally adopted at Huancavelica by the late 1630s.[1] This system, employing a series of water-cooled condensers, made possible the use of low grade ores, reduced emission of toxic fumes, and brought about great savings in labour and fuel. A second fundamental technical improvement came in 1642 with the completion, after thirty-six years of frequently interrupted work, of a long adit reaching the deepest galleries of the mine.[2] This socavón, 520 metres long, improved ventilation of the deeper levels enormously; but its more dramatic effect was to facilitate extraction of ore. Where carriers had previously been able to make only one journey from the workings to the surface each day, they could now make forty. The socavón, named Nuestra Señora de Belén, also gave access to hitherto unexploited deposits. These improvements were sufficient to carry the mine over a difficulty encountered in 1648 – the loss of the principal vein or layer of ore, on account of a geological fault.[3] The vein was not rediscovered for a century; but the loss appears to have had little appreciable long-term effect on production. Indeed, output was considerably higher in the 1650s than in the previous decade.

It was about this time, according to Lohmann Villena, that a distinct change began to make itself felt in the financing of Huancavelica. The Treasury had always been slow to pay miners for mercury produced. By 1650, this tardiness had led to the Crown's owing a large debt to the miners. It was some 495,000 pesos (300,000 pesos ensayados); and because of constant demand from Spain for specie, it could not be prevented from rising. By the end of the 1650s, despite efforts by Viceroy Alba de Liste, it had risen to 538,000 pesos (325,350 pesos ensayados).[4] Further efforts by various viceroys in the later part of the century similarly failed to eliminate it. At times it reached a million pesos ensayados; at other times viceroys contrived to keep up with payments for current production, but could never pay off the backlog. How, then, did miners profit from the extraction of mercury? The most plausible answer is that they became dependent on merchants – the ubiquitous aviadores of Spanish American mining – for credit. To these merchants they also sold a large part of the mercury they produced. These sales were strictly illegal, since all mercury was the Crown's to distribute. Lohmann Villena implies that by the mid-1660s, illegal sales were so large that officially registered production bore little relation to actual output.[5] Since large Crown

[1] Lohmann Villena, *Las minas de Huancavelica*, pp. 301–4.
[2] Lohmann Villena, *Las minas de Huancavelica*, pp. 311–13.
[3] Lohmann Villena, *Las minas de Huancavelica*, p. 337.
[4] Lohmann Villena, *Las minas de Huancavelica*, pp. 350–60.
[5] Lohmann Villena, *Las minas de Huancavelica*, p. 371.

Mercury

debts to miners are said to have first arisen around the mid-century, it seems likely that Huancavelica was producing far more mercury in the second half of the century than that recorded in official figures. This would explain how there came to be a surplus that could be exported to New Spain, as first began to happen in 1670. Without further investigation, it is impossible to say exactly how much mercury passed from Peru to the northern viceroyalty; but there were certainly shipments of 3,000 quintales in 1670, 3,000 in 1683, and 3,005 in 1694.[1] As will be shown, this intrusion of merchants into mining was not limited to Peru, nor to mercury. The mid-century in New Spain saw a similar and thorough infiltration by merchants of silver mining. In both viceroyalties it was the inability of the Crown to continue supplying adequate credit to mining that gave rise to the extensive use of private capital. It is hardly necessary to point out that private capital was careful to secure its private profits, and that the Crown's lack of money caused it further financial losses. Crown monopolies could only be maintained when the Crown was financially strong, as had long been realised in the Carrera de Indias.

After this sketch of the sources and problems of mercury supply to the American colonies, it is possible to begin the return towards the central theme of this book, with an account of mercury in New Spain.[2] Quicksilver was generally shipped from Spain to Veracruz on the annual fleets to New Spain. Occasionally, in years when there was no fleet, it was put into mail boats (*avisos*) or carried in the Armada bound for Porto Belo. In the latter case, it would be transhipped for Veracruz at some point in the Caribbean. Still more rarely, special mercury boats were dispatched. But this was very expensive. In general, freight rates were remarkably low. Matilla Tascón gives the freight cost of a ton (20 quintales) of mercury from Sanlúcar de Barrameda to Veracruz in 1568 as 44 pesos (32 ducats). The cost per quintal was thus only a little over 2 pesos. In the mid-1630s the cost was but a little higher, at 3·08 pesos a quintal. These were charges for shipment in the fleet. But when two ships were specially fitted out in 1637 to carry 2,000 quintales to New Spain, freight rose to over 19 pesos a quintal.[3]

---

[1] AGI Indiferente General 1778, México 19 January 1671, General Don Francisco de Paz Granado to Queen Regent; AGI Mexico 612, México 8 August 1683, Viceroy Paredes to Crown, with 'Testimonio de los autos tocantes a los azogues que vinieron de los reinos del Perú por abril del año de 1683 en la nao nombrada Nuestra Señora del Pópulo en que trajo 3,000 quintales de cuenta de Su Majestad'; AGI Mexico 612, México 8 April 1694, Viceroy Galve to Crown, 'No. 1'.

[2] This topic is the subject of a Ph.D. dissertation being prepared by Mr M. F. Lang of the University of Salford.

[3] Matilla Tascón, *Historia ... de Almadén*, p. 222. AGI Mexico 35, R. 1, 'Del gobierno de la Nueva España. 1639. Para la carta del Virrey, No. 19, "Testimonio de los autos sobre el

Mercury

Mercury from Almadén arrived in New Spain packed in wooden casks or boxes, containing one quintal, or sometimes one and a half. In each cask were two or three leather bags, made of three layers of hide, and each holding two *arrobas* (50 lb.) of mercury.[1] From Veracruz to Mexico City, and from Mexico City to the mining towns, mercury was carried on mule trains or wagon-trains, still packed in its casks. Overland freight costs were naturally, distance for distance, far higher than shipping costs. Auctions were held for the carriage of individual consignments, the contract being awarded, obviously enough, to the lowest bidder. Freight from Mexico City to Zacatecas alone, in the 1620s, cost 3 to 4 pesos a quintal; from Veracruz to Mexico City, in 1637, the charge was 5·2 pesos per quintal. Freight costs were paid, until 1679, directly by the Crown, being considered as one component of the final selling price charged to miners.

The price of mercury fell, overall, from the mid-sixteenth century to the end of the seventeenth. When, in March 1559, the Crown assumed control of all exports of mercury from Spain to America, the Treasury officials of Mexico City were instructed to sell it for the greatest possible profit.[2] The Crown was evidently not only concerned to supply New Spain with essential raw material for amalgamation, but also anxious for the maximum gain from this substance of newly-discovered utility. The Fuggers were paid 75 pesos (55 ducats) for a quintal from Almadén; and in 1560 a quintal was auctioned in Mexico City for 215 pesos (131 pesos de oro de minas). Later in that decade the auction price reached 310 pesos (in November 1565 and July 1568).[3] The Crown's profit was therefore enormous. But by the early 1570s, the market was becoming glutted. Imports began to pour in from Peru, where Huancavelica was now able to produce in quantity, but where amalgamation had not yet been introduced to absorb its output. This mercury was bought by merchants in New Spain and sold to miners at prices undercutting those charged by the Crown. In 1572, Viceroy Enríquez, to prevent merchants profiteering in mercury at the Crown's expense, assumed control of all imports of the metal, whether from Spain or Peru, and devised the first of many schemes for distributing it to miners, as will shortly be shown. Mercury was to be sold for the highest price reached on the free market

---

repartimiento de los azogues que el año de 637 vinieron a cargo del Capitán Don Baltasar de Torres y el Marqués de Cardenosa" '. Final date, Madrid 5 September 1639, ff. 1–13, 41.

[1] Matilla Tascón, *Historia ... de Almadén*, p. 221.

[2] AGI Contaduría 669, Valladolid 4 March 1559, real cédula to Treasury officials of New Spain.

[3] AGI Contaduría 669 has accounts of remates of mercury in Mexico City, 1560–8.

Mercury

in 1572 – 180 pesos (110 pesos de oro de minas).[1] The price remained at this level until 1591, when it was reduced to about 165 pesos (100 pesos de oro de minas); further reductions came in 1597 (to 110 pesos, or 80 ducats); in 1602 (to about 95 pesos, or 70 ducats) and in 1608 (to cost price, which was estimated at 60 pesos). This, the lowest price in all the period under consideration, lasted until 1617, when it was suggested that 60 pesos were, in fact, less than the cost price; and sale price was raised to 60 ducats (82 pesos, 5 tomines, 9 granos) the quintal. Not until 1670 was any further change made.[2] Price reductions appear to have been the result of continuous pressure by miners and their spokesmen in New Spain. And it was a common opinion among government officials that, although income from mercury sales would obviously fall if the price were lowered, sales would increase in volume and lead to higher production of silver. This would mean, in turn, higher income from silver taxation, which would more than balance loss of revenue from decreased mercury prices. This was a reasonable point of view to take while the Crown had ever-increasing supplies of mercury available, as it did until the 1630s. After then, when supplies became rapidly scarcer, mining declined, for reasons which will be shown, and there were consequently obvious objections to an increase in mercury prices. Not until the first arrivals in the seventeenth century of Peruvian mercury, in the late 1660s, did the price again rise. In 1670 Peruvian mercury was being sold at Zacatecas for 110 pesos the quintal. Its dearness was caused in part by high production costs at Huancavelica; but rather more by high freight costs. The combined production and freight costs of this mercury, placed at Acapulco in 1679, were nearly 93 pesos the quintal; and carriage to Mexico City, alone, cost 10 pesos the quintal. The relatively high selling price of Peruvian quicksilver in New Spain in these years seem to have pulled the price of Spanish mercury upwards; for, after remaining steady at just over 82 pesos until 1677 or 1678, it rose (at Zacatecas, in any case) to fluctuate between 90 and 100 pesos in the 1680s.[3] Part of the increase came from miners' having to pay

---

[1] AGI Mexico 19, R. 3, No. 74, f. 23v., México 22 September 1572, *relación* of Enríquez' letter to Crown.

[2] For mercury prices: AGI Mexico 19, R. 3, No. 74, f. 23v., México 22 September 1572, relación of Enríquez' letter to Crown; AGI Mexico 22, R. 2, México 30 October 1591, Velasco II to Crown, para. 2; AGI Mexico 23, R. 4, México 16 November 1597, Monterrey to Crown; AGI Mexico 29, R. 1, Ventosilla 17 October 1617, real cédula to Guadalcázar; and *Recopilación 1680*, VIII xxiii 8.

[3] For the import of Peruvian mercury in 1679, and current prices, see AGI Mexico 612, México 7 February 1679, Archbishop Payo to Crown, 'No. 18'; especially the '1° Testimonio' of Don Francisco Fernández Marmolejo, dated México 9 January 1679. For Zacatecas prices, see AT.Z, Reales Oficiales 26, 'Relaciones declaradas' by the Treasury officials of mercury distributed in Zacatecas from 1667 to 1679.

freight costs separately, whereas before they had been included in the global price. It should be emphasised that these prices were those charged by the Treasury for the mercury it distributed. The Treasury in theory held total monopolistic control of the metal until it passed into the miners' hands. But when quicksilver became scarce, in the second third of the seventeenth century, the monopoly obviously tended to become ever less complete, and black marketing developed. Merchants bought mercury from miners who, for one reason or another, preferred selling it to using it. Resale prices to other miners, according to reports about Zacatecas in the mid-1660s, reached 220 to 230 pesos (160 to 170 ducats) the quintal.[1]

Almost a century had passed since Enríquez had first introduced legislation with the precise aim of excluding merchants from traffic in mercury. To show how the full circle had been turned, some account must be given of Enríquez' scheme for mercury distribution and those of his successors. The circumstances these schemes gave rise to influenced the development of silver mining in New Spain in more than merely institutional ways. They basically affected its economic progress. In 1572, Enríquez was faced with the need for wide reforms, if control of mercury were really to pass from private hands into the power of the Crown. If the Crown wished to assume control of sales in such a way that private traffic stopped, then it had to organise the whole process of distribution, leaving no loopholes through which mercury could slip out, nor merchants in. The selling price had to be high enough to ensure that at least part of the Crown's former profit was preserved; but it could not be so high as to drive a substantial number of miners out of business, or into the arms of merchants. Merchants dealing in quicksilver had given extensive credit; the Crown had to follow suit. Enríquez therefore decided to find out the mercury consumption of every mining town or district. To the local alcalde mayor should be sent, at frequent intervals, enough mercury to meet the town's demands. The alcalde should give extensive guarantees for the metal in his care (the amount of the guarantee being prescribed by the Treasury officials of Mexico City); and he should distribute it to the miners, who would have up to a year to pay for each consignment they received. In this way, Enríquez thought, miners would always have mercury available, and would therefore be able to work continuously. The price was to be 180 pesos.[2] In New Galicia, the Treasury officials of Zacatecas were to have charge of distribution. Mercury was to be dis-

---

[1] AGI Mexico 611, México 17 February 1665, Don Cristóbal de Calancha to Crown.
[2] These arrangements are described in AGI Mexico 19, R. 3, México 1572 (exact date unknown) Enríquez to Crown.

patched from Mexico City to a store (*amalcén*) in Zacatecas, from which it should be sent out to the smaller towns, apparently for distribution in them by their alcaldes mayores. The basic price of 180 pesos was to be increased to cover freight costs to the north.[1]

Enríquez' arrangements of 1572 form the basis of the many series of mercury Ordinances that were to be issued by viceroys during the last quarter of the sixteenth century. Some of these were ingenious, but a full account of them and their development would be long-winded. They all sought to resolve conflicts between the interests of miners, as consumers of mercury, and the Crown, as supplier. Miners naturally wished mercury to be as cheap and as plentiful as possible. The Crown, in general, wished the miners to have sufficient stocks of mercury in hand, or at least sufficiently easy access to supplies, for them to produce silver continuously and in the greatest quantities possible; but at the same time, the mercury had to be paid for. Miners insisted, and the Crown sometimes agreed, that mining was a hazardous profession; they could not always pay for mercury on the spot; nor, indeed, over any particular period. The Crown was therefore obliged to recognise, within a few years of taking control of mercury, that there would always be a heavy and largely bad debt owed by miners.[2] Successive viceroys, according to their judgement of the difficulties and needs of the industry, extended or restricted credit, now handing out large grants of mercury on loan (*depósitos*), now insisting that nothing but spot cash would be tolerated in future. And as the debt grew, an attempt was made to recover at least part of it by taking from the miner a small proportion of each batch of silver he brought to the Treasury office of his local town, or to his local alcalde mayor, for registration, assay and taxing. The proportion varied from time to time in the sixteenth century between a quarter and a twentieth.

All schemes were subject to defects of administration. Several were abandoned, or greatly modified, because the officials in charge of them, particularly the local officials, embezzled funds. The alcaldes mayores employed by Enríquez were discovered to be using the money they collected in payment for quicksilver for their own commercial activities. It was also found that a miner, if in need of ready cash, would sell part of

---

[1] AGI Mexico 19, R. 3, México 10 October 1572, Enríquez to Crown, para. 24. The carter who carried the mercury from Mexico City to Zacatecas had to provide guarantees for it during the journey, and paid for any losses (*mermas*) suffered en route. The selling price in Zacatecas in 1575 was approximately 188 pesos a quintal (115 pesos 5 reales de oro de minas). See AT.Z, 'Register of disbursements of mercury used for mining operations in the province of Zacatecas, 1574–84'.

[2] See AGI Mexico 20, R. 3, México 18 November 1586, Villamanrique to Crown, para. 7. He stated that by 1586 the unpaid debt owed to the Crown by miners for mercury exceeded a million pesos.

Mercury

the mercury he held in stock (*en depósito*), with a two-fold result: the amount of silver he could produce was reduced; and this, in turn, meant that he was less able to repay the Crown for the depósito that had been credited to him. He might sell either to other miners or to merchants. It was inevitable that in the supply and distribution of such an essential and valuable commodity as mercury, especially when credit was so extensively given, fraud would creep in. The authorities recognised this, and that losses to the Treasury from fraud and default on credit had to be balanced against the gains in silver taxes that would come from a liberal policy of mercury distribution. Miners were never slow to claim that the Crown would benefit far more in the end from dealing mercury out generously and cheaply than from relentlessly trying to recover the mercury debt.[1]

By the end of the sixteenth century the two principal methods by which mercury was distributed through the Treasury had been determined and put into effect. The first was the already mentioned depósito: a substantial loan of mercury, for which the miner made running payments consisting of a small percentage of the silver he refined. The second method operated to ensure that the depósito did not become depleted. It was a procedure known as *consumido*, started by Viceroy Coruña in 1582. A miner, when bringing a batch of silver to the Treasury or local alcalde mayor to have it registered, was to be charged, in silver, for the amount of mercury he said he had used in producing that batch. The declared quantity was then to be restored to him, and his depósito thus made up to its former level. The disadvantage of this scheme, as it subsequently transpired, was that the miner, in order to avoid paying, naturally understated the quantity of mercury he had used. This difficulty was overcome by Archbishop Contreras, when acting-viceroy, with an order that a miner should receive one pound of mercury for each mark of silver he presented.[2]

[1] The development of systems of mercury distribution in New Spain in the sixteenth century is traced by numerous viceregal letters in AGI Mexico 19, 20, 22 and 23. See especially Enríquez' correspondence of September to October 1572 (in AGI Mexico 19, R. 3); Villamanrique's correspondence of May 1586 to February 1587 (in AGI Mexico 20, R. 3 and 4); and particularly the letter dated México 14 February 1587, which includes 'Copia de la instrucción que dió el Virrey Marqués de Villamanrique a los alcaldes mayores de minas para la nueva administración de los azogues y para que se vayan cobrando los depósitos de ellos sin pesadumbre de los mineros'. AGI Mexico 22, R. 1, contains Villamanrique's 'Memoria de las cosas que me ha parecido advertir al Señor Virrey Don Luis de Velasco ...', dated México 14 February 1590, in which he gives a long summary of mercury legislation from 1572, pointing out the faults of each system that had been tried.

[2] AGI Mexico 20, R. 4, No. 136, México 18 November 1586, Villamanrique to Crown, para. 7. He refers to Coruña's order for consumido of June 1582, and to Contreras' order (not dated by him).

Mercury

This was in accordance with the common estimate that a quintal of mercury was consumed in the production of 100 marks of silver.

Depósito and consumido were devices arrived at after a long search for systems of mercury distribution that would reconcile and satisfy the demands of Crown and miner. But nothing could stop debts arising as long as the administration continued to be basically liberal with mercury. Viceroys frequently found themselves with a difficult choice to make. If there was mercury available in the storehouses, should it be dealt out freely to miners, thus certainly causing the mercury debt to grow, but also certainly increasing production of silver and with it general Treasury income from all tax sources? Or should mercury be regarded as a commercial proposition, and be at least made to pay for itself? In the event, as long as mercury was available in large quantities, viceroys generally chose to be liberal. This was the course taken in 1619 by Guadalcázar, who appears to have made the last large and general depósito throughout the mines of New Spain. In the previous two years, he explained, the supply of mercury from Spain had been much increased. The Treasury officials of Zacatecas had reported that they held in store a full thousand quintales, which they could not distribute because existing regulations required miners to pay spot cash for mercury. The miners, for their part, said that without quicksilver they could not produce silver with which to buy more quicksilver. (The individual depósitos they had previously held had been allowed to run down.) In view of all this, Guadalcázar said, in an *acuerdo de hacienda* of 3 July 1619, it had been decided to order the Treasury officials of Zacatecas to visit all refining works there, determine their capacity, and issue a new depósito in accordance with the needs of each one. This new depósito should be paid for by a levy of one fifteenth (*el quinceno*) on silver produced by miners, and be maintained by consumido. Similar orders were given soon afterwards to alcaldes mayores of mining towns in the jurisdiction of the Audiencia of New Spain, where depósitos were also to be made. Guadalcázar's report does not say how much mercury was actually issued. But there were in store at the time 3,322 quintales, including the 1,000 quintales at Zacatecas, but not including unspecified amounts at Guadalajara and Durango.[1] If all these had been distributed to miners, the debt immediately incurred to the Crown, at the current selling price of 82 pesos 5 tomines 9 granos a quintal, would have been over 270,000 pesos.

Viceroy Gelves, a forceful defender of the king's interest, criticised Guadalcázar for this disbursement of mercury when he surveyed the state

---

[1] AGI Mexico 29, R. 2, 'Copia de lo probeído cerca de volver a poner los depósitos de azogues en las minas citadas en el capítulo 9 de la carta de hacienda de 27 de septiembre 1619'.

of mining in 1622. It had given rise to great debts. Moreover, miners, being frequently unable to pay these debts, were tempted not to present their silver for registration. In this way the Crown lost tax income on silver produced, and silver was illegally exported from New Spain, often to fall directly into the hands of foreigners.[1] Such arguments came to have ever greater weight. There appears to have been no further massive issue of mercury by any viceroy after Guadalcázar. And as the general financial situation of the Crown progressively deteriorated in the late 1620s and the 1630s, there was increasing reluctance in Spain to tolerate the mercury debt. Up to this time, viceroys had been given a free hand in judging how mercury was best to be administered in the Crown's interest. But in 1634 came the order direct from Madrid, previously referred to, stating that henceforth miners should receive mercury against spot cash, or not at all. Existing debts were to be collected and the cash remitted to Spain on the first boat.[2] The instant collection of the debt was impossible, of course, for miners did not have the wherewithal to pay. But the order marks a turning point in the Crown's attitude towards silver mining, and in particular a change in its policy of supplying mercury to the industry. If before, as seems clear, mercury had usually been regarded as a mere adjunct to silver production – a necessary condition of increased general prosperity, but not a good to be considered of economic import-ance in itself – now it became a valuable commodity in its own right. It should therefore be made to pay. (This was a consequence both of its increasing scarcity and of the Crown's increasing penury.) The official price of mercury was not raised; perhaps this was a concession to the recognised difficulties of silver miners. But quicksilver tended to be distributed much more selectively. In the late 1650s and early 1660s, Viceroys Alburquerque and Baños began to sell mercury directly from Mexico City to individual miners in silver towns, thus cutting across the traditional and rather cumbersome system of distribution through local administrators or Treasury officials. This innovation brought dangers of new varieties of fraud, but at least the miners paid in cash.[3] And, as was mentioned above and will be shown more fully in discussing silver production in Zacatecas itself, the second half of the century saw a deep infiltration of mining by merchants, on whose credit miners came to rely. These aviadores naturally supplied money only to reliable clients. Mercury thus tended increasingly to go to more efficient miners. The Crown's purposes in changing its policy on mercury in the 1630s seem to have been

---

[1] AGI Mexico 29, R. 5, México 13 June 1622, Gelves to Crown 'Sobre los azogues y minas'. See especially in this, México 22 April 1622, Gaspar Vello de Acuña to Gelves.

[2] AGI Mexico 35, Cuaderno 2, f. 32, Madrid 9 September 1634, real cédula to Cerralvo.

[3] AGI Mexico 68, México 17 February 1665, Don Cristóbal de Calancha to Crown.

achieved to an extent. Few long-term mercury debts were incurred after 1650.[1] But this result was obtained only at high cost to the mining industry; for the insistence on making mercury pay put many miners out of business.

And so, at length, to Zacatecas. The quantities of mercury arriving in the city during the seventeenth century are shown in Table 9a and illustrated in Graph 2. From the Graph it will be seen that Zacatecas received a high proportion of the total mercury import to New Spain – often between a third and a half, or even more. The size of Zacatecas' share is confirmed in Table 9b, where for specific years and periods, individual distributions of mercury to the city and to the mines of New Spain in general are shown. From the almacén the Treasury officials sold mercury directly to the miners of the city and its surroundings, and sent it to subordinate officials (*receptores de azogues*) in some of the lesser towns of the district. In 1625 there were receptores at Sierra de Pinos, Ramos, Fresnillo, Sombrerete and Avino, each issuing mercury and collecting payment for it in his immediate area. In most cases the receptores were the local alcaldes mayores. Despite their known bent for peculation, it had proved impossible to dispense with them at local level in the distribution system, and they continued to administer mercury laxly, sometimes fraudulently, as they had done from the 1570s.[2] They did, however, generally produce some sort of accounts of what they sold, sending them to Zacatecas, where the Treasury officials compiled a full record of the mercury ramo. Regrettably, the officials did not begin to do this until 1608, so there remains no useful information about consumption of mercury in the Zacatecas district in the sixteenth century. Nor, in fact, is there any continuous record of arrivals of mercury in the district until the seventeenth century.

The opening of the new century not only brought better accounting, but also the introduction of the first system of mercury distribution and payment that was to prove permanently workable in Zacatecas. At the end of August 1603, the Treasury officials and Francisco de Quintana Dueñas, visitor to the Treasury of New Galicia, drew up a new scheme, at the behest of Viceroy Monterrey.[3] All existing debts owed to the

---

[1] AGI Mexico 611. An untitled expediente of mercury accounts and related documents referring to receipts of mercury in New Spain from 1650 to 1669; foliated 2–426. Here, ff. 189v.–239, 'Data y distribución de dicho azogue'.

[2] See AGI Guadalajara 33, Zacatecas 22 January 1626, report of Francisco de Villarreal on his visits to the Treasury at Zacatecas – section 'Depósitos de azogues'.

[3] AGI Guadalajara 33, Zacatecas 31 August 1603, 'Copia del acuerdo que se tomó en 31 de agosto de 1603 de los mineros de lo que debían a su magestad hasta este día por pasado como por deudas viejas y nuevas'.

Mercury

Treasury for salt and mercury were to be compounded, no matter under what credit system they had been incurred. The total debt owed by each miner was to be paid off by him with one fifteenth of the silver he produced – the quinceno. A fifteenth was a reasonable fraction; it gave the Crown, in effect, a considerable interest on its loans of mercury, and was not too heavy a burden on the miner. The granting of further mercury to miners 'en depósito' was not ruled out. Such mercury should also be paid for by quinceno.

One major division of Zacatecas quicksilver accounts in the seventeenth century on the credit side (*cargo*) was therefore the *orden del quinceno*, by which payment was made for mercury distributed on credit. The other major division was the *orden del consumido*, which recorded the cash-down payments made by miners when replenishing their stocks. It will be remembered that 'consumido' signified the amount of mercury supposedly consumed by a miner in producing a specified quantity of silver. Since it was generally assumed that the ratio (*correspondencia*) of mercury consumed to silver produced was one pound to one mark, the orden del consumido thus also functioned as a useful guarantee that the miner would, in fact, submit all his silver for registration and subsequent taxation. Let it be assumed, for the sake of illustration, that a miner held no depósito, and that when he registered a certain batch of silver before the local authority, he had exhausted his supplies of mercury. If he had produced, for example, 100 marks of silver, and possessed ores from which, with sufficient mercury, he could produce a further 100 marks, than he was obliged to present before the officials the total of his first 100 in order to receive, according to the orden del consumido, a quintal of mercury with which to produce his second 100. If he presented less than his first 100 marks, he received less than a quintal, and was thus unable to refine his second 100 – unless he possessed stocks of mercury on which to draw, which the present imaginary miner did not. But even if he did have stocks, persistent understatement of his production led to their being depleted in the end. The orden del consumido depended on the calculated ratio of mercury consumption to silver production being accurate; in fact, it was often slightly favourable to miners – and certainly so at Zacatecas. With even moderately good ores, 110 or 115 marks could be refined with a quintal of mercury. The miner then had a choice: either he could present all his silver, and receive (and pay for) more mercury than he had consumed; or he could present only enough silver to receive the amount of mercury he needed to maintain his silver output at its current level. The decision depended on his financial circumstances and the amount of mercury he needed at a particular time. If he failed to present all his silver for registration and taxation, he was, naturally, defrauding the Treasury. Fraud, in its various guises, is a topic apart, which will be given attention at the beginning of the next chapter.

Not even the most comprehensive of accounting systems, nor the most upright of officials could, of course, prevent mercury debts arising at Zacatecas. But discussion of those debts belongs properly to the story of silver production at Zacatecas; and after briefly considering the validity of the output figures that have been extracted from Treasury accounts, and the related topic of silver taxation, it is to the production of silver that attention will now be turned.

CHAPTER 8

THE PRODUCTION OF SILVER

Registered production of silver in the districts of Zacatecas and Sombrerete is shown in Tables 4 and 7. As notes to those tables indicate, production figures are taken from accounts of the royal Treasury offices in the two towns. These accounts, of which the essential purpose was to record the amount of tax paid by the miners on the silver they produced, are the only source of continuous information on output. And since the purpose of this chapter is to account for the observable variations in silver output, it will be as well to see if the Treasury records are a reliable indicator of production. What was the rate of taxation? How were accounts drawn up? And – the fundamental question – how far was the Crown defrauded of its dues on silver?

In Spain and the Empire, subsoil rights belonged to the Crown. But it was obviously impossible for the Crown to organise mining as a state concern, so that in practice all subjects were free to prospect for mines and work them to their own advantage, provided they paid a proportion of their output to the Crown. The proportion varied in time and place; but in New Galicia during the period of this study it was a tenth – *el diezmo*.[1] The tax was collected by the Treasury officials at the Real Caja. The practice was as follows: the miner, having produced pure silver in his hacienda by distilling off the mercury contained in the amalgam, took it to the assay office (*casa de afinación*), where its fineness was examined, and where it was melted down into ingots (*barras*) of some 130 marks; he then carried his ingots to the Real Caja, where the silver was taxed; a tenth was taken for the Crown, and 1 per cent to pay the salaries of officials and other administrative costs; the total levy thus came to 10·9 per cent; and when this proportion of silver had been cut away from the ingots, the remainder was returned to the miner, stamped with the royal arms to show that it had been *dezmada*.[2] After this, the miner could sell or trade with his silver as he wished.

At Zacatecas itself taxation was levied in this uncomplicated way. But arranging and ensuring taxation of silver produced at the other towns and

---

[1] By a real provisión of Valladolid 17 September 1548, the tax rate was reduced for six years from one eighth to one tenth. The concession was extended several times, and eventually became the unquestioned rate of tax. See AGI Guadalajara 33, Valladolid 11 August 1559, real provisión extending the *merced del diezmo* for seven further years. See articles 57–9 of the *Ordenanzas l l nuevo cuaderno*, 1584.

The Production of Silver

mines of the district was more difficult, since there was no Real Caja outside the city. It was hardly to be expected that miners from distant towns would bring their silver to the Caja, at great trouble and expense, merely to pay the diezmo. The solution was to install a receiver (*receptor*) at each important centre.[1] Silver was to be taken to him as it was produced. He should place on it a special stamp (*la marca del diezmo*) indicating that it had not been taxed, but that it had been legitimately produced by a miner, and was therefore liable to the diezmo. The stamp carried the name of the town in which the receiver officiated. At times, instructions were given that the name of the miner should also be placed on the bars and ingots he brought to be marked; but these instructions were not always observed. Silver thus *marcada del diezmo* could circulate freely, although still untaxed. Until then, it changed hands at a reduced value.

The diezmo was, in fact, a permanent concession granted to miners, since the basic rate of tax on precious metals was a fifth (or *quinto*). In theory, the distinction between silver to be taxed at a tenth and that to be taxed at a fifth was clear: only silver produced by a *bona fide* miner in his own hacienda de minas, with ores from his own mines, was to be considered *plata del diezmo*; on any other silver, not produced directly by a miner, a quinto was to be levied. What sort of silver could be considered *del quinto*? Primarily, it was *plata del rescate*, or silver that had been bought. Into this class fell metal that had been produced from pepena ores bought from Indians. Merchants buying ore and smelting it in a parada de fuelles, or buying rough smelted silver from Indian mine-workers, were therefore liable to pay a fifth. Indeed, silver produced by Indians from their own pepenas, though not strictly de rescate, was also taxed at a fifth, since it was not the produce of a proper miner; that is, the owner of mines and a refining plant.

This, in outline, was how tax on silver was collected. One means of avoiding tax (apart from declining to present silver at all) will already be obvious. The producer of silver from bought ores could avoid paying half the legal levy by pretending that his plata del rescate was really silver produced by a miner. He might achieve this by persuading or forcing a miner to take the *rescate* silver to the Treasury and swear that it came from his own hacienda. He would then pay a tenth instead of a fifth. The possibility of this deception clearly arose as soon as differential tax rates were instituted, and there are complaints about this type of fraud in Zacatecas as early as 1562. The Treasury officials found it difficult to distinguish between plata del rescate and plata del diezmo. Miners almost

[1] The receiver was normally also the man in charge of collecting debts on mercury, and alcabalas.

182

The Production of Silver

always paid merchants for goods in unminted silver. Very often the merchant was paid in silver that had not been taxed. When he presented this silver for taxation, how were the Treasury officials to know whether some of it came originally not from a miner but from the furnace of the merchant himself? Even if the ingots carried the marca del diezmo, indicating that a miner had registered them before a receiver in a town somewhere in the district, might not the stamp be false? Or might not the receiver have been bribed? No adequate system of checks was ever devised to defeat the ingenuity of merchants and dealers in silver who wished to avoid paying the fifth. The entries in the Zacatecas accounts for plata del quinto are in general insignificant in comparison with those for plata del diezmo. It is to be expected that they would be small, because the amount of silver produced in back-yard furnaces was far less than that refined in haciendas de minas; but they were far smaller than the administration thought they should be. That was why there were periodic attempts to do away with the many small furnaces in and around Zacatecas. They disappeared for a short while, only to spring up again as numerous as ever.

The officers of the Treasury were naturally worried about this escape of royal revenue. But for the immediate purpose here of assessing the reliability of Treasury accounts as a source of information on silver production, it is important to note that most silver, whether produced in the standard way in a refining works, or in an illegal furnace, was taxed at one rate or the other. One basic reason for this was the difficulty in trading in untaxed metal, which would serve only in certain transactions. A merchant might take untaxed silver in payment of goods from a miner. But he could not in general pass that silver on to another merchant without having it taxed. Ultimately, a man found with untaxed silver in his possession was likely to have it confiscated.[1] This meant that anyone resolutely refusing to pay quinto or diezmo had to find a means of selling silver outside New Spain. Attempts, obviously often successful, were made to export silver through Veracruz. Endless memoranda were written by officials on this problem in the seventeenth century, of which one, the work of the senior oidor of the Audiencia of Mexico in 1663, is worth citing; partly because it is a clear statement, and partly because it

---

[1] See for this AT.Z, Reales Oficiales 2, Zacatecas 22 January 1604, 'Los apuntamientos que dieron los mineros sobre lo del ensayar ...', para. 4. Speaking of plata del rescate, a group of leading miners of Zacatecas noted '... this class of silver does not circulate nor does it pass from the merchant who receives it from the Indians or Negroes or other persons, without his first taking it to be taxed; first because it increases somewhat in value by being taxed, and secondly because it is not customary to transact with it; and however small the thing being bought, they [the sellers] will not hand it over if the silver is not taxed ...'.

was instrumental in the enacting of effective remedies.[1] The oidor, Calderón y Romero, noted that the export of untaxed silver had once been a minor affair, but was now very big business. Merchants sold to the Indies traders and to foreigners. And, not content with normal gains, they adulterated the silver with other metals. But it was not only merchants dealing in silver who engaged in the trade. Miners from the reales of New Spain had also discovered how profitable it was. Since there were no offices of the Treasury in the mining districts of New Spain proper besides that in Mexico City, and since tax could not be levied on silver except at a Treasury office, the normal procedure of these miners was to openly carry their silver out of their towns, saying that they were going to Mexico City to have it taxed. But once there, of course, they sold it clandestinely to bullion merchants from the fleets. At this point in his exposition, Calderón turned his attention to the northern mines of New Spain, New Galicia and New Biscay. There, he said, the Treasury could exercise much closer control over silver, because of the greater number of offices – the Reales Cajas of Guadalajara, Zacatecas, San Luis Potosí and Durango. In the jurisdiction of these Cajas, he observed, it was illegal to deal in silver that did not bear the *marca del quinto* (indicating registered, but untaxed, metal); moreover, a piece of silver could not legally be taken out of the district of a Caja unless it had actually been taxed.[2] Calderón affirmed that these regulations were enforced, and that as a result 'in these mining towns where there are Cajas and the marca del quinto, all silver and gold are marked, and there are no illegal exports of any considerable quantity'. This was possibly an excessively sanguine claim. Nevertheless, it was as a result of similar arguments that two new Cajas were created soon afterwards in the major mines of New Spain: at Guanajuato in 1665 and at Pachuca in 1667. The results appear to have been as hoped for. In Guanajuato, from 1665 to 1671, the income from silver taxes in fact exceeded a forecast based on the amount of mercury distributed; and the same happened at Pachuca from 1667 to 1671.[3] This was taken as evidence that the local presence of a Caja did restrict tax evasion. In the absence of any good reason for doubting that belief, it can be reaffirmed that at Zacatecas defrauding of the Treasury took place, but in the form of passing rescate silver as plata del diezmo. The Crown

[1] AGI Mexico 611, México 2 July 1663, Licenciado Don Francisco Calderón y Romero to viceroy, 'Sobre el extravío de la plata y oro sin quintar y que se ponga el remedio que su majestad tiene mandado' (n.f.).

[2] A slightly different formulation of the same law, namely, that silver should be taxed at the Real Caja nearest to its place of extraction, is given in *Recopilación* 1680, VIII x 9 and 11.

[3] AGI Mexico 39, R. 2, [final date] México 28 March 1671, untitled document signed by Gerónimo Pardo de Lago, on mercury distribution.

lost revenue, but the vast majority of silver produced passed through the processes of taxation, and was accounted. The accounts therefore reflect production with fair accuracy. One further minor aid to accuracy should also be pointed out. The Zacatecas accounts record not only the quantity of tax gathered, but also the number of marks of silver on which it was levied. Only in occasional years before 1700, and then generally in the eighteenth century, is it necessary to derive production from tax income.

The resolutely sceptical might at this point object that although most silver was presented for taxation at one rate or the other in Zacatecas, there still nevertheless remained the possibility of distortion of the record by malpractices of the Treasury officials. There exist, indeed, several reports accusing them of conducting their own business with royal monies. Considering the question, once again, from the point of view of the validity of the accounts as a record of silver production, two possibilities come to mind. If the officials took funds from the Caja after they had been entered in the account books, then the accounts themselves are not invalidated. If, on the other hand, they embezzled funds after they had been received, but before they had been entered in the accounts, then the accounts obviously understated true income. The great advantage of the second practice would have been that, if money embezzled never figured on the account, it could not be traced. The example may be imagined of a Treasury official supplying goods on credit to a miner. In due course, the miner would arrive at the Caja with a quantity of silver for taxation. A proportion of the silver would be taken as tax. And the official would pocket part or all of the tax as payment of the debt owed to him by the miner. In this way, only the Crown would lose; the official would be reimbursed and the miner would pay no more than the diezmo. The embezzled tax, never having been acounted, would never be missed. In practice, however, this fraud would have been difficult to carry out, unless there had been extensive collusion among various officials. Three separate accounts were kept of silver entering the Real Caja. The first was drawn up by the assayer at the casa de afinación; the second by a notary also at the casa de afinación; and the third by the Treasury officials at the Caja itself. In these accounts were recorded the amount, in marks, of silver presented by the miner; the amount, in marks, of the tax; and the amount, in pesos, of the tax. Taxation at the Real Caja was, in law, levied by the three Treasury officials acting together. As each account was completed, the miner witnessed and signed it. The account from one stage of the process was carried to the next, for collation.[1] Thus any fraud in accounting, if it were not to be noticeable, would have had to be

---

[1] These were statutory regulations. See articles 57 and 58 of *Ordenanzas del nuevo cuaderno*, 1584.

The Production of Silver

connived at by the assayer, the notary, the miner and three Treasury officials. Such harmony was far from impossible, but achieving it must have been something of a hindrance to peculation. Nor did these taxation procedures remain a mere legal fiction. Separate accounts from the casa de afinación and the Treasury in Zacatecas are often found; detailed day-books were remitted to the Tribunal de Cuentas and to Spain, together with summaries of the accounts. The accounting system of the Empire was not entirely lax. Embezzlement did occur; but if the Real Caja de Zacatecas is typical it did not absorb more than a small part of the royal income. In 1583 the Factor at Zacatecas was said to have taken 20,000 ducats from the Treasury.[1] On the face of it, this was a large sum, equivalent to some 3,400 marks of silver. But if the Factor had embezzled this amount over the previous five years, it would have represented only about 4 per cent of the Crown's income from silver taxes at Zacatecas in that time; and a correspondingly smaller proportion of the total income of the Caja.

It is a common criticism of Spanish American colonial accounts that they are so riddled with fraud as to be worthless as sources of information. The criticism cannot be decisively refuted. But it is clear, for the reasons given above, that there were restraining influences on fraud in silver at Zacatecas. The accounts may therefore be used with a degree of confidence. Graph 1 is probably a reasonably true picture of silver production in the district. It would be hard to defend its minor variations; but over the major fluctuations there can be little dispute.

There is, indeed, much evidence supporting the principal movements of the graph from many sources; and principally, of course, from the correspondence of officials and citizens of Zacatecas. To take an unequivocal example, observations of residents on the decline of mining in the second quarter of the seventeenth century may be quoted. Nicolás de Gueycoichea, depositario general of the city, wrote in 1652 that before the time of the derecho de Unión de Armas (which was first levied in Zacatecas in 1632) the town was 'in its greatest prosperity ("en sus mayores crecimientos"), since the principal vein of San Benito was being worked, from which was extracted much rich ore of very high quality, and silver was abundant ...[2]. But the words of the corregidor, spoken at a

---

[1] AGI Guadalajara 230, Z, 2, ff. 64v.-5, Madrid 19 April 1583, Crown to Viceroy Coruña. Reports had been received that the Factor of the Real Caja of Zacatecas had a fortune of 100,000 ducats, and supplied goods to miners, using Treasury funds, with the connivance of the Contador. He had taken, allegedly, 20,000 ducats from the Caja.

[2] AA.Z, 7, No. 24, Zacatecas 4 June 1652, Nicolás de Gueycoichea, depositario y procurador general, in introduction to an interrogatorio prepared by him on the excessive rate of alcabala levied in Zacatecas.

The Production of Silver

cabildo meeting held on 8 June 1652, only four days after Gueycoichea wrote, show what a change had overtaken Zacatecas in the intervening thirty years. Corregidor Fadríquez Dávila told the council that, in the six months he had been in Zacatecas, he had seen 'the miserable state the townspeople are in, for mining, being the principal strength (*nervio*) of the city and the thing on which commerce depends, is finished, having neither substance nor wealth; many merchants have departed, and their shops are closed ... so that there are scarcely ten vecinos of the city who are merchants; the houses and entire quarters are in ruins ...'.[1] This overwhelming decline of Zacatecas' fortunes between 1630 and 1650 is indeed the most marked and interesting feature of the town's history in the two centuries being discussed here, and, luckily for the historian, is reasonably well documented. It must be a central object of attention in this chapter, after a preliminary examination of mining production in earlier years.

One general comment on the discussion of silver production that follows will perhaps be apposite at this point. Variations in production should ideally be considered in close relation to costs and benefits in the mining industry. But unfortunately very little concrete information is available on costs. Miners did occasionally produce account sheets of their operations over a short period, but these were invariably drawn up with the aim of demonstrating to authorities that mining was unprofitable unless the price of mercury were reduced, or free slave-labour provided by the Crown, or some other relief furnished. Documents of this sort are clearly useless as sources of reliable information. Nor, unfortunately, is it possible to calculate the costs of amalgamation as against those of smelting. Even the price of labour is unknowable, since the cash wage was supplemented by pepenas, and, in many cases, board and lodging, which were costs directly borne by the miner. Costs of upkeep of plant, raw materials (apart from mercury and salt), and replacement of draught animals are similarly an unknown quantity. Yet, despite the impossibility of knowing specific costs with precision, in arguments advanced in explaining variations in production, the question of costs in general will always run near the surface, sometimes to emerge fully. Mining would obviously not have survived for long unless someone were making a profit from it.

During the period of the sixteenth century for which silver production is known, that is, from 1559 onwards, there were no remarkable gross variations in output. There are scattered reports on the state of the mines, but no serial information of value. Especially to be regretted is the lack of records of mercury arriving in Zacatecas before 1600. In their absence,

[1] AN.Z, LC 5, f. 36, cabildo of 8 June 1652.

little light can be thrown on production. The slight rise from 1565 to 1575 perhaps results from the continuing effect of the general introduction of the amalgam process, and from the discovery of new mines in the district (Fresnillo, 1566; Mazapil, 1568; Charcas, probably 1574). The subsequent fall in production in the second half of the 1570s and the early 1580s could be attributed to a shortage of labour after the epidemic of 1576 and 1577, and to the increasing gravity of the Chichimec war. These reasons were adduced in 1583 in a petition sent to the viceroy on behalf of the miners of New Galicia. Flooding of mines and a decline in yields of ore were also partly held responsible for difficulties in mining in the early 1580s.[1] Then in later years of the century, it appears likely that mercury became scarcer, or at least more difficult to obtain on easy terms, which could account for the nearly static silver production of the decade 1585 to 1595, and the definite decline in output from 1595 to 1600. After Enríquez took control of mercury distribution in 1572, and as imports from Peru fell, private dealings in quicksilver decreased in volume; and the credit offered to miners by the Treasury officials was less generous than that given by merchants. When selling mercury, said one oidor of Guadalajara, Licenciado Pinedo, in 1581, the merchant 'hazards himself at any risk'. But the Crown's officials, he went on, although selling at a lower price, demanded quick payment.[2]

If lack of mercury can be adduced only tentatively as the cause of stagnated production in the last fifteen years of the sixteenth century, it appears certain that mercury was the single largest determinant of variations in output in the seventeenth. The correlation between imports of mercury to the Zacatecas region and silver produced there from 1610, when mercury records effectively start, is so clear as to be beyond challenge. The correlation continues beyond 1650, but is less exact. (See Tables 4 and 9a, and Graphs 1 and 2.) To illustrate this point, comparisons can be made of mercury imported and silver produced in specified, shorter periods. The years 1610 to 1630 saw the largest arrivals of mercury in Zacatecas during the whole of the seventeenth century: a total of about 31,000 quintales. At the normal mercury-to-silver consumption ratio (*correspondencia*) of one quintal for a hundred marks, this mercury should have been good for 3,100,000 marks. In fact, production of plata del diezmo from 1610 to 1630 was 3,726,395 marks; which means to say that, if all production were by amalgamation, 120 marks would have been refined with each quintal of mercury. This figure is high, but by no means beyond possibility. The generally accepted correspondencia of one

---

[1] AGI Guadalajara 30, México 17 May 1583, petition of Alonso de Oñate to Viceroy Coruña.
[2] AGI Guadalajara 6, Guadalajara 8 March 1581, Licenciado Pinedo to Crown.

The Production of Silver

quintal per hundred marks was only a rule of thumb, mainly of use in forecasting, on the basis of past silver output, how much mercury a mining town or hacienda would need in some future period; or how much mercury should be issued to a miner by consumido. It was recognised that at some times and places ores were likely to be better than average, and consumption of mercury correspondingly lower. Observations of this sort had indeed been made of Zacatecas just before the turn of the century. In 1595 Viceroy Velasco had written to the king saying that, in a recent order for distribution of mercury by consumido, he had decreed that at Zacatecas a quintal of mercury should be issued to a miner for every 140 marks he brought for taxation.[1] Zacatecas' ores were evidently very good at the time, although Velasco later reduced the rate to the standard correspondencia. But about 1620, it was reported that yields in New Galicia were higher than ever; only shortage of mercury prevented greater silver production.[2] It can be said with confidence, therefore, that in the period 1610 to 1630, high silver production was the result of using the large quantities of mercury distributed for refining ores of good quality. Doubtless there was some production by smelting as well, about which a little must now be said.

There was firstly smelted rescate silver: metal produced from bought ores in small furnaces by people who were not miners. Rescate silver was in law taxable at a full quinto, and appears as plata del quinto in Table 4. The total registered quantity of this silver from 1610 to 1630 was 498,632 marks. This was a large sum, but only a seventh of the amount produced by amalgamation. Its existence therefore does not invalidate the argument that most silver in this period was refined by amalgamation, and that the very high observed output is the result of plentiful mercury. It is probable, of course, that some rescate silver was presented for taxation as plata del diezmo. Any such false presentation would, clearly, make it appear that less rescate silver was being produced than that stated in the account, and correspondingly more plata del diezmo. It seems especially likely that such a transfer occurred in the quinquennium 1625 to 1630, when, ostensibly, only 44,321 marks of rescate silver were presented and taxed, in comparison with 185,719 marks in the previous five years. The sudden decline is very suspicious. But even a fraud of this size would not have grossly distorted the registered production of plata del diezmo.

[1] AGI Mexico 23, R. 1, México 4 April 1595, Velasco II to Crown.
[2] AGI Guadalajara 8, R. 10, anonymous visitor to Zacatecas to viceroy (n.d., but certainly 1620), 'The miners of [New] Galicia are very hard pressed by not being able to continue refining in their haciendas, on account of the shortage of mercury; and the mines have richer ores than ever ...'.

The Production of Silver

The output of plata del diezmo might, however, be subject to another qualification, though not a distortion, that would undermine the argument for high production by amalgamation. 3,726,395 marks of plata del diezmo were registered from 1610 to 1630. The assumption has been, in calculating that this silver was refined with mercury at a correspondencia of 120 marks per quintal, that plata del diezmo, being in theory from miners' haciendas, was amalgamated silver. But smelted silver produced by the professional miner was taxed at a tenth, just as was amalgamated silver. Might not, then, the plata del diezmo be in large part the produce of smelting, and the supposed connection between mercury supplies and silver output consequently quite spurious? Fortunately, occasional data are available to meet this objection. In the first place, references to smelting works in Zacatecas itself are rare. Among the many descriptions of haciendas de minas in the city preserved in local archives, few were found of an *hacienda de fundición*; and those few referred to haciendas of the second half of the century. Smelting may, of course, have been practised as a subsidiary process in amalgamation haciendas, to which a furnace could have been added at slight marginal cost. In the other towns of the district there was at times a high proportion of smelting. From April 1606 to April 1608 in Sombrerete, for example, of 5,746½ marks produced, 1,758 were smelted and 3,988½ amalgamated.[1] Ramos, between May 1618 and May 1619, yielded a total of 35,352 marks, of which 19,542 were amalgamated and 2,283 smelted. How the other 13,527 marks were refined is not specified.[2] Again, in rather later times at Fresnillo, from January 1645 to April 1646, 3,223 marks were amalgamated and 6,631 smelted.[3] Many other examples could be given, showing a constant production of smelted silver in the smaller towns. But although constant, this production is insignificant in comparison with the total output of the district, which therefore appears to have consisted very largely of amalgamated silver. The figures just quoted incidentally reveal to what an extent Zacatecas dominated the lesser towns of the district in silver refining. Another Fresnillo account, from 1602, shows that in eight months of that year, 35,623 marks were registered there by the receptor.[4] Average yearly production in the whole Zacatecas district from 1600 to 1630 was about 186,500 marks; by rough calculations it can

[1] AT.Z, Reales Oficiales 2 (n.f.), record of *plata señalada* in Sombrerete, 1606–8.
[2] AT.Z, Reales Oficiales 3, plata señalada in Ramos, May 1618 to May 1619, by the *juez de azogues*, Miguel Zorrilla.
[3] AT.Z, Reales Oficiales 13, silver marked by the *administrador de reales azogues*, Captain Domingo de Santerbaez, from 8 January 1645 to 1 April 1646.
[4] AT.Z, Reales Oficiales 2, 'Plata señalada en el Fresnillo por Pedro de Torres, receptor, desde 3 de mayo hasta fin de diciembre 1602'.

be estimated that Zacatecas itself was contributing between two-thirds and three-quarters of this total.

In the decade 1630 to 1640 there was evidently a considerable reduction in the amount of mercury reaching the city. But, unfortunately, it is at this point that accounts become incomplete. No record remains of mercury from April 1633 to April 1635, although it is known that 4,997 quintales entered the almacén between February 1631 and December 1632. There is a full series of accounts for the second half of the decade, indicating the arrival of 4,200 quintales from May 1635 to December 1639. There were, apparently, long periods in which no mercury came at all; for example, from May 1635 to April 1637. In February 1637 the cabildo used the great shortage of quicksilver as an excuse for limiting the size of a gift (*servicio*) sought by the Crown to 1,500 pesos.[1] Considering the greatly decreased mercury supply, silver production in the decade is remarkably high. Again it is obvious that rescate silver was being masqueraded as plata del diezmo, thus inflating apparent output of the latter. Quantities of quinto silver presented after 1631 become almost negligible: far too negligible. But even quite a large fraud of this type could not explain how, from 1630 to 1635, some 1,070,000 marks were produced with the 4,997 quintales delivered in 1631 and 1632. A yield of over 200 marks per quintal is impossible, so clearly a considerable amount of mercury entered Zacatecas between 1632 and 1635. There is no good reason, on the other hand, to doubt the completeness of the mercury record from 1635 to 1640. Since silver output reached some 709,000 marks in these years, the apparent correspondencia is very high indeed, reaching nearly 170 marks per quintal. This is indeed a perplexing figure. It can perhaps be explained in part by supposing that quicksilver was more efficiently used when in short supply. Scarcity of mercury would put miners who refined ores of lesser quality out of business. Such a miner always made a lower profit, other things being equal, than one who had access to high-yield ores. He was therefore less able to pay off his mercury debt to the Treasury. In times when mercury was scarce, therefore, it would be given preferentially to the man with rich ores, and the yield of silver per quintal would be expected to rise. This, though, cannot be a full explanation for a correspondencia as high as 170 marks. Allowing that the accounts are accurate, possible contributory causes are that a considerable quantity of mercury from the first quinquennium remained to be used in the second; or that, as mercury became scarce, production by smelting increased.

In the following decade, the concurrence between mercury received and silver produced is much closer to the normal ratio. 1,224,832 marks

[1] AA.Z, LC 3, ff. 338v.–9, cabildo of 9 February 1637.

of plata del diezmo came from 10,933 quintales, at an average, therefore, of about 111 marks a quintal. In the first half of the decade, the ratio, as indicated by the account, was 93 marks a quintal; in the second, 135. This disparity suggests, of course, that mercury was carried over from the first quinquennium into the second.

The 1640s are the last years in which the relationship between silver output and mercury received lies within the limits of the generally accepted correspondencia. After 1650, the number of marks produced far exceeds possible output from the mercury arriving in Zacatecas; although it is indisputable that the trends of the graphs showing silver production and mercury arrivals continue to be the same. It is only the magnitude of variations that now becomes disproportional. To take a single, fairly extreme, example: from 1665 to 1670 production was 719,141 marks (discounting rescate silver), and the total quantity of mercury arriving, 2,054½ quintales; the indicated correspondencia thus reaches some 350 marks a quintal. If so much silver was produced by amalgamation, a fundamental improvement in technique had occurred. There is no evidence for such an advance.

The explanation lies in greatly increased output of smelted silver in Sombrerete. The first sign of what was to prove a major boom comes in May 1646, with an undertaking made by one Captain Graviel Suárez to the Treasury officials that he would return to Sombrerete from Zacatecas (where he had been living) to assume his position of *administrador de azogues.* He had previously held the post for some time, but had been without work because the mines and the town were all but abandoned. Six months previously, however, miners had cleared and drained old workings, and had located rich ores suitable for smelting. This discovery was the subject of a letter from the Fiscal of the Audiencia of New Galicia to the king in August 1646. Old mines had been re-explored, and revealed ores yielding 7 to 12 marks of silver per quintal. Flooding prevented the immediate working of the mines.[1] If this report is accurate, the yields were such as had not been seen in the Zacatecas district for almost a century. If it is recalled that the normal silver content of a quintal of ore at Zacatecas was 1½ ounces, then the significance of ores at Sombrerete giving 56 to 96 ounces will need no emphasis. Enthusiastic accounts of Sombrerete's prosperity begin to appear from the Audiencia of New Galicia in the early 1650s.[2] The upward turn of the district's total pro-

[1] AN.Z., MH 1646, f. 9v., Zacatecas 5 May 1646, obligación of Captain Graviel Suárez; and AGI Guadalajara 10, Guadalajara 18 August 1646, Fiscal to Crown.

[2] See, for example, AGI Guadalajara 10, Guadalajara 8 March 1653, president of the Audiencia to Crown. The veta principal of Sombrerete, long since flooded, but drained in 1646 and worked since then, was the richest vein in New Galicia, he said.

duction from 1650 to 1655 was probably the result of recovery at Sombrerete. And even the subsequent fall of the graph showing total output, in the period 1655 to 1665, does not preclude continued prosperity at Sombrerete, but rather reflects the deepening depression of Zacatecas itself. An indication of the lasting wealth of Sombrerete is given in a report by the Audiencia to the Queen Regent in July 1673, saying that the ancient prosperity of the mines there had been restored – a reference to Sombrerete's sixteenth-century fortunes; and that in 1671, 101,629 marks had been presented for stamping.[1] If annual production remained at this high level for the whole quinquennium 1671 to 1675, then Sombrerete was yielding nearly half the silver refined in the whole district during that period (1,164,823 marks). This same report reaffirmed that all this silver was smelted.

The quinquennium 1670 to 1675 was the first in which a separate record was kept of smelted and amalgamated silver – an innovation which itself was recognition, although belated, of the importance of smelting. The accounts are summarised in Table 6 and the totals shown in Graph 3. Of a total output of some 1,159,000 marks, 700,000 were smelted. If the Audiencia's report of July 1673 was correct, Sombrerete could have produced over 500,000 of these marks. The remaining 459,000 were amalgamated, presumably with the 3,632½ quintales arriving from September 1670 to June 1674. Indicated correspondencia was therefore about 126 marks a quintal: above the norm, but well within the bounds of possibility. The point to be stressed is that in the first half of the decade almost two-thirds of total output was smelted, and nearly half the total came from Sombrerete. This state of affairs continued until the end of the decade. Smelted silver still comprised well over half the total. Ouput of amalgamated metal rose slightly, following a small increase in the mercury supply.

In 1681 the importance of Sombrerete was given acknowledgement by the creation there of a separate Real Caja. At this point, of course, miners from Sombrerete and its surrounding towns ceased to pay taxes in Zacatecas, with the result that the amount of smelted silver shown in the Zacatecas accounts fell abruptly. (See Graph 3.) This decrease is further support for the contention that most smelting took place in Sombrerete. On the other hand, the quantity of amalgamated silver presented in Zacatecas fell only slightly. The decade 1680 to 1690 was the last prosperous one for Sombrerete. Already, in fact, by the time of the establishment of the Caja, signs of decline were visible. In a report of December 1679, miners of the town complained that the mines from which they extracted their smelting ores (principally, one called El Pabellón)

[1] AGI Guadalajara 12, Guadalajara 12 July 1673, Audiencia to Queen Regent.

were deep and flooded. Since the best smelting ores were at depth, they had decided to turn to amalgamation processing, for which they could obtain ores nearer the surface. Six amalgamation haciendas were already built. They needed quicker access to mercury supplies, and thought that the local presence of a Real Caja would facilitate this.[1] Exhaustion of rich ores apparently continued to afflict Sombrerete. Its decline from 1690 onwards is reflected in the fall of total regional production from 1690 to 1705. (See Graph 1.) After 1705, the graph begins to move upwards again, as the Zacatecas mines entered a new boom. It may be supposed that this was the result of a greatly increased supply of mercury; but research on mercury supplies was not extended beyond 1700.

How had the mines of Zacatecas fared while Sombrerete was enjoying its years of splendour? If all their output had been refined with mercury, production would have followed the course of the mercury graph downwards, sinking to a mere 150,000 or so marks in the quinquennium 1660 to 1665. But possibly the decline was not as grave as that. In the first place, rather more mercury arrived in Zacatecas from the late 1650s onwards than is recorded in Graph 2. Direct remittances from Mexico City to miners, not passing through the Real Caja in Zacatecas, may have added as much as a fifth to the total imports recorded in the Treasury accounts. (See note 3 of Table 9a.) There is also evidence of useful restoration work being done in the mines themselves around the mid-century. In 1652, the president of the Audiencia wrote to the king saying that important drainage operations were under way in nineteen mines on the Veta Grande, as well as at Sombrerete. It was further reported in March 1653 that the works at Zacatecas had been successful. The vein, after being flooded for sixteen years with 50 varas of water (about 150 feet), had now been drained to a flood level of 6 varas.[2] After that, there is no word about the state of the mines until 1675. According to the Treasury officials in that year, ores of very good quality were being extracted.[3] And in 1681 the president of New Galicia informed the king that mining was prospering (*boyante*) at Zacatecas.[4] There is other unequivocal evidence that wealth was returning by this time. After 1681, Zacatecas' contribution to total regional output can be seen. From 1681

---

[1] AGI Mexico 52, R. 3, Sombrerete 15 December 1679, 'Informe de los mineros de Sombrerete'. This is an enclosure with México 6 July 1681, Paredes to Crown, 'No. 5', which refers to the reasons for establishing a Real Caja in Sombrerete.

[2] AGI Guadalajara 30, Guadalajara 19 March 1652, president and Audiencia to Crown; and AGI Guadalajara 10, Guadalajara 8 March 1653, president to Crown.

[3] AT.Z/VO, Zacatecas 20 November 1675, Treasury officials to Archbishop Payo Enríquez. They described the mines as being 'en buen corriente de ley de metales'.

[4] AGI Guadalajara 15, Guadalajara 1 July 1681, president of Audiencia to Crown.

The Production of Silver

to 1685, some 600,000 marks were presented for taxation at the city's Treasury. Excepting a slight increase in the period 1690 to 1695, production remained at about that level until 1700; after which, it climbed quickly. A central feature of this revival of Zacatecas is that a large part of the silver being produced was smelted: rather under a half in the twenty years for which there are records, 1685 to 1705. So it is clear that at some time in the mid-century good smelting ores were found in Zacatecas and possibly some of the smaller towns. Apparently, miners were forced into smelting by shortage of mercury. It is noticeable that in the last twenty years of the century, production of smelted silver at Zacatecas rises and then is steady, while that of amalgamated silver gradually falls. (See Graph 3.) There appears to have been a strong undercurrent of smelting in the second half of the seventeenth century, which swelled in volume when mercury became scarce.

In summing up silver production in the Zacatecas district during the seventeenth century, therefore, it can be said that the period witnessed two booms: one from 1615 to 1635 and the other from 1670 to 1690. These peaks of output were followed by depressions of which the first and most serious ran from 1640 to 1665, and the second from about 1690 to 1705. The first boom was largely the fruit of mines in the close neighbourhood of Zacatecas, and can be attributed to the availability of large supplies of mercury. The second derived mainly from the mines of Sombrerete, where rich smelting ores began to be found about 1645. The decisive upswing of the second boom came after 1670, when silver from Zacatecas was added in increasing quantities to the rising output of Sombrerete. Whereas Zacatecas had previously devoted itself to refining by amalgamation, in the mid-century it began to employ smelting as well, while continuing amalgamation as far as supplies of mercury allowed.

After this unavoidably tedious account of the basic pattern of Zacatecan mining in the seventeenth century, a look at the state of mining at particular times may be illuminating. Reports of visitors provide occasional useful cross-sectional views of the industry, though of varying perceptiveness. Two visitas, one made in 1625 and the other in 1644, enable Zacatecas to be seen firstly at a time of prosperity, and then at a point well on the road to decay.

Francisco de Villarreal, accountant of the Tribunal de Cuentas in Mexico City, was sent to Zacatecas in 1625 by Viceroy Cerralvo, with a long list of tasks.[1] He was to audit the accounts of the Treasury, visit the

---

[1] The various parts of Villarreal's visita are in AGI Guadalajara 33. His reports date from January to June 1626.

mines, and investigate the activities of Treasury officials, notaries, assayers, alcaldes mayores, receptores de azogues, and miners – among others. He arrived in Zacatecas on 4 August 1625. His reports are not as informative as might be wished; they do not reflect at all clearly the current prosperity of mining. Indeed, one extraordinary order given to Villarreal bade him account for the *decadence* of the mines. It can only be supposed that the miners, as ever predicting disaster, had managed to persuade the newly-arrived viceroy that Zacatecas' unprecedented wealth was on the verge of disappearing: a prediction not to be realised for another ten years. Villarreal allowed himself to be instilled with a similar feeling, for he argued, perhaps accurately enough, for the issue of more mercury on deposit, by saying 'mining has much of agriculture, since if it is not continuously fostered, it needs to be replanted'. He conducted his visit with energy, visiting ninety-five haciendas de minas in the Zacatecas district (embracing parts of New Galicia, New Biscay, and the real of Sierra de Pinos, which geographically lay in New Spain). Forty-two of these haciendas were in Zacatecas, or within a radius of ten leagues of the city. Since Villarreal noted that in 1603 the same district had contained only forty-five haciendas, it is difficult to see how any idea of overall decline could have entered his mind. The ores currently being worked were of moderate to low yield, so that the correspondencia was the normal 100 marks to a quintal of mercury. But many new mines had been discovered, and it appeared that San Martín, Fresnillo and Ramos were enjoying rich ores. Of the ninety-five hacienda owners in the district, only four (unfortunately not named) were truly rich. In Zacatecas itself, much of the visitor's time was devoted to attempting to persuade miners to collaborate in draining important mines of the Veta Grande. The essential working was Palmillas, which, he said, had been responsible for Zacatecas' recent wealth, but which had flooded in 1624. Other major mines on the Veta Grande, now all flooded, were La Albarrada Grande, Albarradón, Las Isletas, El Gajuelo de Tolosa, Los Gajuelos Grandes, Las Demasías and Santa Clara. But all efforts to make the owners of these mines join forces in draining them proved useless, 'because it is difficult to reconcile so many people who, with differing reasons, wish to emphasise their small [economic] capacity ...'. In September 1625, Villarreal, after much negotiation, succeeded in having pumps installed in Palmillas, which were to be operated by forty-three Negro slaves contributed by all interested miners. But when the time came for pumping to commence, only Agustín de Zavala and Juan de Oñate sent their quotas of slaves. No efforts or threats were sufficient to induce the other miners to participate in the project.

The Production of Silver

Clearly the problems of flooding were not so grave as Villarreal made out, which is perhaps why the mine-owners proved so recalcitrant. If production was falling slightly in the two years preceding his visit, and continued downwards in 1626 and 1627, it rose to levels near the previous maximum in the early 1630s. But by the time of the second visita to be quoted here, 1644, annual production was barely a half of what it had been in the best years of the 1620s. This visita, undertaken by the senior oidor of the Audiencia of Mexico, Don Francisco de Rojas y Oñate, was the outcome of a royal order to Salvatierra of 12 October 1642, instructing him to arrange collection of the mercury and salt debt in Zacatecas and other mining towns.[1] Rojas wrote with profound gloom of Zacatecas' woes, a gloom which must have settled on him as soon as he arrived, for he was prostrated immediately with 'a grave disorder of the stomach, occasioned by the change of water, that of this city being all so bad that it cannot be drunk'. It is to be suspected that his illness upset his judgement so as to make him especially receptive of the miners' grievances – grievances which they were quick to state. A petition was rapidly prepared and presented to him by two mining deputies. It declared that there had been a great scarcity of mercury in the previous seven years. There had also been shortages of labour, especially of Negro slaves. Nearly all the slaves previously employed in Zacatecas had died, and far fewer were being brought from Africa. In earlier years there had been so many that the lack of Indian labour had not been felt; but it was being felt now. The petition continued with the observation that the richest mines were flooded. Recent times, furthermore, had brought higher prices of food, and of steel, iron, candles and other necessary goods. There had been years of drought, causing the death of mules and other animals. Refining works therefore lacked power, so that even the wealthiest miner could operate only one stamp-mill. The final consequence of this depressing series of difficulties was that aviadores were reluctant to advance credit to miners, who were obliged to devote their meagre output of silver to the purchase of maize and meat to feed 'the few servants who have remained alive ... the exercise of mining being, on account of this and other hardships, so difficult that the service of his majesty alone obliges us to continue with it'.

To this grievous report, Rojas added his own gloss. Sixty haciendas

---

[1] For Rojas' visit, see AGI Mexico 76, R. 1, '1644. Visita de la Caja Real de Zacatecas, que hizo el Licenciado Don Francisco de Rojas y Oñate, oidor más antiguo de México, y cuenta que da de ello [sic], con varios testimonios'. This consists of two documents: a copy of a letter from Rojas to the Crown, dated México 14 September 1644; and a copy of the relación of the visit, of which the final date is México 15 February 1644.

existed in Zacatecas, but only eight were running; and those, at a loss.
'And it is to be noticed that all the houses of these miners, not excepting
a single one, have the look of a hospital, [being] without any ornament,
jewel or silver, nor anything worth a peso, and not having food for the
morrow ...'. No buyers could be found for haciendas standing idle. And
matters were if anything worse in the smaller towns, in Ramos, Fresnillo,
Sombrerete, Charcas and Sierra de Pinos, 'for in some of them there has
not remained any trace of haciendas or miners, and where some sign does
remain, there are only one, two or three miners, but so destitute of credit,
fortune and even the manner (*forma*) of miners that it is impossible to
extract a real from them ...'. In making this last observation, Rojas was
alluding to his central task of collecting the mining debt of the district.
He estimated that the miners of the lesser towns owed 300,000 pesos, and
that this sum was totally irrecoverable. Miners in Zacatecas owed only
200,000 pesos, some of which could be collected, although great care
would be necessary in order to avoid destroying the fragile mining
industry that remained in the town. The Treasury officials were therefore
instructed to collect the debt by quinceno (which meant, of course, that
only those miners still producing silver would be paying off their debts).
Fully convinced of Zacatecas' plight by the entreaties of the miners and
his own observations (having spent fifty-one days in the city), Rojas
ordered the distribution of 400 quintales of mercury from the almacén.
By doing this he undoubtedly relieved the industry of some pressing
difficulties. But equally he thwarted his own prime purpose, which was
to reduce the mercury debt. Like many predecessors in a similar position,
he argued that to have mercury lying idle in store benefited no-one. So
he proclaimed the sale of this mercury for spot cash. And like many
predecessors, he was met with the argument from the miners that they
were too poor to pay cash. So he yielded, as others had done, to the extent
of distributing mercury on short credit. It should be paid for out of silver
produced, and the miners' stocks of quicksilver constantly replenished.
This, of course, was precisely the depósito and consumido scheme that
had given rise to all debts owed by miners for mercury.

The mining community of Zacatecas clearly set out to give a worse
impression of their situation to the visitor than was really the case. After
all, Rojas had come to collect money from them. Nevertheless, he went
away quite persuaded by their arguments, the force of which becomes
more apparent when it is added that he was not the first visitor to be
sent to Zacatecas by Salvatierra. The viceroy, soon after his arrival in
New Spain in 1642, had dispatched Don Pedro de Oroz, alcalde de
crimen of the Audiencia of Mexico, with the same mission of debt

collection in Zacatecas. Oroz had been able to do no more than Rojas finally did: leave the local Treasury officials to gather what they could by quinceno. Salvatierra had therefore ordered Rojas' visita as a more stringent measure. But all Rojas achieved, according to an informed correspondent in 1645, was 'to disillusion the viceroy and the junta general [de hacienda, and show them] that most of those debts were irrecoverable, on account of the death and destitution of the debtors, and the abandonment and decay of the haciendas de minas ...'.[1]

The petition presented by Zacatecan miners to Rojas makes it quite clear that lack of mercury was not the sole restriction on the production of silver, although it certainly headed their list. The other troubles of which they complained are worthy of some consideration. First, there was a series of fortuitous disasters: drought, bad harvests, high food prices, death of labourers, slaves and animals. The sequence of events is too common in history to demand elucidation. These misfortunes were of a sort to afflict a large area, not merely the Zacatecas mining district. This is certainly true of weather, agriculture and food prices. But the question of labour is more interesting. Was Zacatecas basically suffering from the demographic collapse of the aboriginal peoples of New Spain, which had begun almost immediately after the Conquest? Or were there quite local and quite specific reasons why a labour shortage should have occurred in the late 1630s? The great decline of Indian population appears indisputably to have taken place in the sixteenth century, though the lowest point was probably not reached until 1650.[2] If the Indian labour force available in Zacatecas varied, therefore, in some direct and proportional way with the total aboriginal population, it would seem strange that there was sufficient labour to work mines and haciendas during the boom of 1615 to 1635, but not sufficient in the 1640s. It will be objected, perhaps, that the miners stated in their petition to Rojas in 1644 that previously the large numbers of Negro slaves had disguised the lack of Indian labour. But it is nevertheless undeniable that many Indians had come to work in Zacatecas during the boom years. It is only necessary to recall the observations of the vicar of the Franciscan monastery in 1622, already referred to in the discussion of Zacatecas' labouring population in chapter 6. He declared that the floating Indian population of the city was

[1] AGI Mexico 76, R. 1, México 25 February 1645, Fiscal Don Pedro de Melián to Crown, para. 12, 'Estado de las minas de Zacatecas y sus deudas'.
[2] S. F. Cook and W. W. Borah, *The Indian Population of Central Mexico, 1531–1610*, Ibero-Americana: 44, University of California Press, Berkeley and Los Angeles, 1960, *passim*; W. W. Borah, *New Spain's Century of Depression*, Ibero-Americana: 35, University of California Press, Berkeley and Los Angeles, 1951, p. 43.

very large: good pepenas could cause the numbers living in the northern part of the town to swell from 900 to 2,000. In 1625, Francisco de Villarreal found 730 Indians working in Zacatecas and Pánuco; but these were employees of the haciendas de minas alone, not Indians who engaged in actual mining. The total number could have been some 1,700, as is suggested in chapter 6. The most obvious inference to be drawn from these observations is that there were enough Indians available to man the Zacatecas mining industry, so long as the rewards were attractive enough. The validity of this argument could only be judged, admittedly, from a comparison of wages in Zacatecas and in other occupations open to Indians elsewhere. And since neither wage is known, a conclusive proof cannot be offered. Or perhaps Indians came to Zacatecas in search of work, not having been employed for a wage before at all, but merely living in their pueblos from subsistence agriculture. In this case, lack of Indian labour in Zacatecas would not imply true competition for labour between different industries and places, but merely the preference of the worker for an undisturbed, if poor, life to salaried labour. Such speculation must remain idle until much more is known about the numbers of Indians employed in advanced economic activities – especially mining and hacienda agriculture – in seventeenth-century New Spain; and, in particular, about wages in that century. To return to Zacatecas: it seems more likely that the availability of Indian labour there depended on the prosperity of mining, than the prosperity of mining on the availability of labour.

There were, to be sure, specific reasons for scarcity of labour at Zacatecas in the late 1630s. Documents from those years support the miners' claims of 1644 that disease had wrought disaster among the labour force. Because of much illness the year before, the corregidor recommended the cabildo in 1637 to reappoint a city doctor, whose post had been allowed to lapse. Zacatecas' relatively cold climate probably caused it to be spared the endemic diseases of the lower regions of Mexico, but it could not be immune from illness, especially in times of food shortage. A still more local cause, in time and space, of scarcity of labour was the major silver strike made in 1630 at Parral, far to the north of Zacatecas. Tello, writing perhaps twenty years after the event, observed that Parral had attracted from Zacatecas not only labour, but mine-owners themselves.[1] Viceroy Cadereita, convinced by the miners of the reality of labour scarcity in Zacatecas, agreed in 1636 to their proposal for special imports of Negro slaves directed to the mines of the city. The miners suggested that an asiento for 500 slaves a year should be instituted. The scheme was sub-

[1] Tello, *Crónica miscelánea*, pp. 779–80.

mitted to the Consejo de Indias, which deliberated on it for two years without reaching a decision.[1]

The migration of labour to Parral, and complaints in the 1640s from Zacatecan miners about 'poaching' of their Indians by mine-owners in other towns, undeniably suggest that the labour market was a sellers' market, and that there was therefore an insufficient number of Indians willing to engage voluntarily in mine work at the wage rates some miners wished, or were able, to pay. These observations lead naturally to questions about the elasticity of Indian labour supply, and thence to still more elusive considerations of the economic preferences of Indians, if indeed these can be generalised for Indians living in different parts of New Spain at this time. At what wage rate, and to which Indians, did, for example, salaried mine work become preferable to subsistence agriculture? For lack of evidence, these matters cannot be explored here. What is clear is that at no time was there an absolute lack of labour for mining in New Spain. There are no complaints of shortage of workers, for instance, during the second boom of the Zacatecas district in the later part of the century. The total number of Indians in New Spain can have been very little greater in the period of this boom, 1670 to 1690, than it was at the postulated nadir of aboriginal population, 1650.

Why, then, did Zacatecas fail to attract sufficient labour in the late 1630s and the 1640s? A simple explanation would throw the blame directly on to lack of mercury. Without mercury the miner could not produce silver with which to pay his workers. If there were long periods during which no mercury arrived, as for example between 1635 and 1637, interruption of work would leave Indians unoccupied and the miners without income. In such a situation, free labour would clearly drift away. To attribute all Zacatecas' woes to shortage of mercury, however, and to enquire no further, is too simple an explanation. Why was there not more mercury? To answer this question, it will be necessary to examine the Crown's attitude to silver mining, and then what will prove to be a related matter, the profitability of the industry.

The silver miners of America were for many years, in the eyes of the Crown, a community to be cosseted. It was, in principle, to everyone's benefit that nothing should be done to hinder the production of silver. For this reason, miners were exempted by law from imprisonment for debt; nor were any of their tools, slaves or parts of their plant to be

---

[1] See AGI Mexico 31, Cuaderno 1, f. 29v., México 2 May 1636, Cadereita to Crown, 'Hacienda y azogues', para. 2; AGI Mexico 33, Cuaderno 2, f. 24, México 22 July 1637, Cadereita to Crown, 'Hacienda Real', para. 23; AGI Mexico 34, Cuaderno, f. 82v., México 12 July 1638, Cadereita to Crown, 'Hacienda Real', para. 2.

distrained for debt. Only when they owed money to the Crown were these exemptions waived.[1] In the last quarter of the sixteenth century, of course, miners very quickly contracted debts to the Crown for mercury and salt. The local Treasury officials and other lesser administrators in mining towns responsible for collecting these debts applied the law vigorously, seizing the haciendas of miners who failed to pay. Their zeal was not born just of a desire to serve the Crown, but rather of self-interest; for they were likely to have to balance out of their own pockets any account on which payment was due, but not made. Local officials apart, however, the attitude of the higher administration of New Spain towards miners, for much of the later part of the sixteenth century and the early part of the seventeenth, was generous. In 1580, Viceroy Velasco and the Treasury officials of New Spain drew up an *auto* recommending that miners, and the alcaldes mayores who issued mercury to them, should not be pressed for debts: 'the will of his majesty is that miners shall be favoured'. This auto was secret, and designed for the guidance of Treasury officials alone. '... The said alcaldes mayores and miners shall hear nothing of it, so that it shall not be the cause of greater delay in the payment of what they owe – rather, they [the alcaldes] shall be given to understand that they should constrain the miners to pay, and that they should imprison them and their guarantors, as at present some alcaldes mayores do ...'.[2] This was deviousness rare in Spanish colonial government, indeed. The attitude to miners established by this order was generally preserved by succeeding viceroys, and manifested itself in, for example, the liberal distribution, on deposit, of stocks of mercury found in the almacén of Mexico City. The last, and possibly the largest, general issue of quicksilver was that ordered by Guadalcázar in 1619, which included the release from the store in Zacatecas of 1,000 quintales.[3] The inevitable effect of the issue was to swell the already large mercury debt. Guadalcázar tried to remedy the situation by sending a visitor to Zacatecas in 1620, to collect as much as possible of what miners of the city and district owed. The total at this time amounted to over 356,000 pesos. The visitor was dispatched with a secret order reminiscent of Velasco's secret auto of 1580. If it seemed likely, the order said, that collecting the debt would cause future restriction of the haciendas' output, then the visitor should prudently consider means of long-term recovery of the debt, with payments being made by instalment. No-one should be given

---

[1] *Recopilación* 1680, IV xx 1.

[2] AGI Mexico 258, México 22 March 1580, 'Auto que dieron los oficiales reales sobre el buen recaudo del azogue que se entrega a los mineros'.

[3] AT.Z, Reales Oficiales 5, México 3 July 1619, 'Mandamiento para los jueces oficiales reales de Zacatecas, asienten los depósitos de azogues ...'.

The Production of Silver

reason to suspect, though, that collection would not be stringently pursued.[1] Five years later, the next visitor to Zacatecas, Francisco de Villarreal, claimed to have found proof that liberality to miners in the matter of mercury paid. In 1603, he wrote, there had been forty-five haciendas de minas in the district with depósitos; the debt owed by these haciendas had come to 401,252 pesos. But in 1625 there were ninety-five haciendas with depósitos, and the debt was only 273,000 pesos. These facts, he thought, showed that depósitos stimulated mining without causing debts to grow.[2] He perhaps failed to take into account that the quality of ores in Zacatecas had probably been good from the beginning of the century until the early 1620s. It was lower, though, by the time of his visita, and he apparently thought it had always been so. Nor did he mention that in 1603 the use of magistral was unknown. Its general introduction as a reagent in amalgamation soon after that date may have caused the number of haciendas de minas in New Galicia to multiply for reasons quite separate from the distribution of mercury on deposit.

The policy of liberality to miners, which Villarreal's opinions echoed, was not to last much longer. In chapter 7 the sequence of events leading to a fundamental change in official attitude towards mining has been recounted. Chinchón's fears for the safety of Indian workers at Huancavelica led in 1630 to the diversion of much mercury from New Spain to Peru. For the remainder of that decade Peru continued to receive the lion's share of mercury exports from Spain, probably because it had long been a larger producer of silver than New Spain, and was thought to have more need of mercury. New Spain was consequently deprived of mercury – in which deprivation Zacatecas shared. Mercury also, at long last, came to be regarded as a commodity to be sold, if not at a profit, at least not at a loss. This led in 1634 to strict orders from Madrid bidding colonial authorities to sell mercury henceforth for spot cash alone, and to collect the existing debt immediately. The penurious Spanish Treasury of the 1630s could not afford the luxury of being a creditor. It had too many creditors of its own.

The new stringency in debt collection was certainly felt in Zacatecas by the early 1640s. Its practical effect was the two visitas of Oroz and Rojas y Oñate in 1643 and 1644. Although these visitors were anything but sanguine about the possibility of fully recovering what was owed to the

---

[1] AGI Mexico 74, R. 2, México 25 August 1620, Guadalcázar's 'Instrucción particular y secreta para Don Juan de Cervantes Casaus ... corregidor de la ciudad de Zacatecas ... para visitar la Real Caja y tomar cuentas a los oficiales reales de ella ..'. Also Cervantes' subsequent 'Relación por mayor de las deudas ...', Zacatecas 26 November 1620.

[2] AGI Guadalajara 33, Zacatecas 28 January 1626, 'Puntos esenciales a que se redujo la visita de minas que hizo el Contador Francisco de Villarreal ... Depósitos de azogues'.

Crown, their efforts to do so piled disaster on disaster for the miners. A partial list of haciendas confiscated, drawn up in January 1644 (that is, after Oroz' but before Rojas' visit) shows that a minimum number of thirteen had been distrained for debts. The normal practice was to offer confiscated haciendas for sale or rent, but there were no bidders for eight of the thirteen. Only three, according to the list, were definitely still running, under lease or new ownership. Of the original owners, some were imprisoned and some had simply left Zacatecas.[1] In May 1644, Rojas reported that of sixty haciendas in Zacatecas, only eight were still running. A typical case of confiscation was that suffered by Bartolomé Hernández, who is mentioned in the list cf January 1644 as owing 5,067 pesos to the Treasury, for which debt he had been imprisoned. His hacienda de minas lay a quarter of a league from Zacatecas – whether above or below is not stated – and evidently on a stream, for it was unusual in having a stone-built dam to provide water for the incorporadero. It was leased for three years, beginning from 1 January 1644, to Felipe Flores and Andrés de Niebla, who were to pay rent of 650 pesos a year. Half of this sum was to be paid directly into the Treasury against Hernández' debts.[2] The hacienda was small and dilapidated. Of its two molinos, only one was running, and that with very worn iron-ware in the stamps. The other molino lacked many of its components, and its gearing was unserviceable for lack of teeth on the driving wheel and pinions. There were two houses for Indian workers, but their roofs were without shingles. The inventory mentions nine donkeys for carrying ore, but no mules to power the machinery. The permanent labour force was minute: one mulatto slave and two Indians, one to drive animals and the other a combined mill-operator (*molinero*) and tenatero. Hernández also owned some mines, or shares in mines, which were included in the lease. The tenants evidently found the hacienda uneconomic, even at the very low rent they paid (650 pesos were only 80 marks of silver). After sixteen months of the lease had elapsed they had paid no rent, and indeed had contracted a debt of their own to the Treasury for 867 pesos. So again the hacienda was distrained, and the lease ended. The later story of the hacienda is not known.

The dangers of collecting debts ruthlessly, and without regard to the circumstances of each miner, are illustrated by a letter of the Zacatecas Treasury officials to the Tribunal de Cuentas in 1648. It is at first sight strange to see the Treasury officials defending a miner here against the

---

[1] AT.Z, Reales Oficiales 12, Zacatecas 21 January 1644, an untitled summary of confiscations of mining haciendas, drawn up by Mateo de Herrera on the orders of the Treasury officials.

[2] AA.Z, 6, No. 51, Zacatecas 24 December 1643, 'Escritura de arrendamiento que otorgó Bartolomé Hernández, vecino de esta ciudad ... de su hacienda de minas ...'.

Crown's claims, when in earlier years they had been so energetic in pursuing miners for debts. But they were doubtless right in this case. They related that visitor Oroz in 1643 had arranged the lease of an hacienda, previously belonging to one Antonio de Figueroa, to Bartolomé Bravo and Diego de Leura. Leura had since died. The debt on the hacienda in 1643 had amounted to 20,000 pesos, 17,500 of which Bravo had paid off in the first five years of the lease. Perhaps the officials had been criticised for failing to collect Bravo's debt sooner; for they explained that they were proceeding with all caution in recovering the outstanding balance. If they took action against Bravo, his creditors would instantly desert him. Bravo was engaged in substantial improvements in a mine called San Juan, and was also draining another mine called la Cata de Escobedo. Over the five previous years he had paid more than 50,000 pesos in tax on silver produced. His continuing prosperity was therefore in the interest of the Treasury.[1] In later years, Bravo's wealth, in mines and lands, increased greatly.

Few miners, however, were as fortunate or as enterprising as Bartolomé Bravo. Those who were not continued to suffer the depredations of the Treasury. Pedro de Oroz visited Zacatecas for a second time in 1654, seizing and leasing mills. Another visitor, Don Francisco Lorenzo de San Millán, came ten years later with the same mission. He had a list prepared of haciendas confiscated over the previous few years.[2] Since March 1657, nine had been seized. All had subsequently been leased, for rents only slightly greater than nominal, varying from 150 to 1,300 pesos a year. (For the sake of comparison, it may be noted that a large hacienda at Pánuco, with four molinos, was sold in 1607 for 50,000 pesos.) Several tenants, however, were unable to produce even enough silver to pay their rents, largely because of scarcity of mercury.

By the 1660s it must have been clear to even the most hard-headed of visitors that little more could be extracted from the Zacatecas district. Various, probably incomplete, accounts show that some twenty-five miners in Zacatecas itself owed, on 30 April 1659, 248,670 pesos. In the three following years, the Treasury officials managed to recover only 27,246 pesos, leaving an outstanding debt to the Crown in 1662 of 221,424 pesos.[3] A similar survey later in the 1660s revealed that some thirty-seven miners of the Zacatecas district, excluding those of the city,

---

[1] AT.Z, Reales Oficiales 11, Zacatecas 16 August 1648, Treasury officials to Tribunal de Cuentas in Mexico City.

[2] AT.Z, Reales Oficiales 19, Zacatecas 1664 (n.e.d.), untitled summary of confiscations by Felipe de Espinosa.
AT.Z, Reales Oficiales 23, various loose sheets forming part of accounts of the mining debt, 1659 to 1662.

owed 189,149 pesos on 31 December 1663, and 165,840 pesos on 28 February 1668. In the intervening four years the Treasury had gathered in only 23,309 pesos.[1] It is doubtful whether the outstanding debts of the 1660s were ever recovered. By this time many of those who had originally contracted the debts had died, or had moved away. The period 1640 to 1660 witnessed the disappearance of many long-established mining families of the city, after first their incomes had been reduced by lack of mercury, and then their fortunes (or what remained of them) borne away by successive visitors. After about 1660, though, few new debts for mercury were contracted by miners. This resulted from a fundamental change in the financing of mining, which will be described below.

First, however, it is necessary to ask how mining debts ever arose. The institutional processes by which they were first incurred and then grew, are, of course, quite clear. Credit systems such as consumido and depósito plainly made it easy for miners to contract an initial debt, and then live with it. The Crown's credit systems, developed in the 1570s, were, in the circumstances of those years, a necessary imitation of existing credit devices operated by merchants. The miner, after discovering new deposits, clearly might need credit while extracting and refining his first ores. These early debts were allowed to persist. But was it necessary that they should persist? Why did miners not pay them off once they began to produce silver in quantity?

Some attempt can be made to answer these questions in the case of Zacatecas. The first explanation that comes to mind is, naturally, the heedlessness which is held to be a traditional feature of the miner's character everywhere, and at every period of history. There was certainly lavish spending on luxury goods in Zacatecas, despite Rojas' account of the austerity of miners' houses in 1644. The wills of miners and their widows are frequently replete with Eastern silks and Persian carpets. In the early decades of the seventeenth century, money was also poured into ecclesiastical building. Nor did miners neglect to make provision for their souls through censos and capellanías, which seemed slight burdens when they were first imposed on a man's estate, but in harder times sapped capital relentlessly. Free spending, therefore, disposed of profits, leaving little with which to pay for mercury. If another depósito was in the offing, there was little cause for worry. To attribute all the financial troubles of miners to free spending, however, would be to cast a rather

---

[1] AT.Z, Reales Oficiales 21, 'Relación jurada y firmada que nos los jueces oficiales de la Real Hacienda de esta ciudad de Nuestra Señora de los Zacatecas damos ... de las cantidades cobradas de debido cobrar de deudas de los mineros de los reales de minas del distrito de esta caja ...', (n.e.d.) 1668.

The Production of Silver

exaggerated slur on their intelligence. An equally good reason for their failure to acquire and preserve capital was the normal pattern of inheritance of goods in a miner's family. Very few miners indeed made any attempt to entail their estates so as to prevent them from being split up after death. The normal pattern of inheritance was, therefore, the equal division of an estate among the widow and children. Since families were not necessarily agreed about how the inheritance should be used, capital was often dissipated between one generation and the next.

Even this, though, cannot really explain how miners came to be unable to pay the Crown for the mercury and salt that it supplied to them. It does not explain, for instance, how Francisco de Villarreal could say in 1626, after fifteen years in which the Zacatecas district had yielded unprecedented amounts of silver, that of ninety-five mine and hacienda owners, only four were truly rich. Admittedly, his criteria of wealth are unknown, and he may have been exaggerating the difficulties of miners in order to create a case for the increased distribution of mercury that he considered necessary. But the statement remains astonishing. It suggests, in fact, that there was little profit to be made from mining, even when it was apparently at its richest. Indeed, it would not be unreasonable to go further, and suggest that at times, even though large quantities of silver were produced, mining was basically unprofitable. It is at this point, of course, that lack of knowledge of the costs of mining becomes a true hindrance to explanation. In particular, it would be desirable to know at what yield, other things being equal, ores became profitable. There is evidence, though admittedly not overwhelming, that ores in Zacatecas before 1620 were of high quality. Possibly the Veta Grande, and in particular the mine Palmillas, may have continued to yield rich ores into the early 1620s. But Villarreal noted in 1626 that ores were of low to moderate quality. He also reported that the ninety-five haciendas of the district owed the Crown 273,000 pesos for mercury and salt.[1] In 1638, the total debt of the district, according to the Treasurer of the Real Caja of Zacatecas, stood at 671,679 pesos.[2] Over twelve years, therefore, in which silver production tended to decline, at first slowly and then precipitously, the Crown appears to have granted credit of nearly 400,000 pesos to the miners of the Zacatecas district, in the form of issues of mercury and salt. There is no reason why this sum should not be regarded as a subsidy made by the Crown to mining. With the aid of this subsidy, a great deal of silver was produced. But whether it was produced economically is

[1] AGI Guadalajara 33, Zacatecas 28 January 1626, Villarreal's 'Puntos esenciales ...'.
[2] AGI Guadalajara 33, Madrid 10 September 1676, relación de méritos sent by Captain Francisco Gómez Rendón, former treasurer in Zacatecas, to Crown.

another question. And if Zacatecas was not producing economically, what of other silver mines in New Spain? Possibly the Crown had some dim inkling that supplying mercury to American silver mines was not bringing adequate returns, when the order went out for instant collection of mercury and salt debts in 1634. Even an imprecise analysis of the costs and benefits of mercury supply would have been far beyond the accounting of the time, since not only direct levies on silver output would have had to be included, but also all the other tax incomes which silver in the long run created. Nevertheless, a general dissatisfaction with the mining industry's endless demands for mercury may have reflected an economic truth: that silver mining in America was no longer profitable.

To make such a statement is perhaps to extrapolate too widely from the case of Zacatecas. To support it, evidence would be required showing that other major silver mines in America suffered a decline in ore-yields, or some other affliction causing increased costs, at the same time as Zacatecas. Certain specific failings of the Crown's system of mercury distribution can, however, be observed in Zacatecas, and were probably general in America. One basic disadvantage of the system was that credit was in general given without discrimination. Mercury was normally distributed to all miners with little regard to the quality of their ores and to the state of their haciendas. This was particularly true in times when mercury was plentiful; when it was scarce, rather more selectivity may have been used. The quantity of mercury a miner would require in a certain period was sometimes assessed, but the use he might make of it was left to chance. This practice no doubt enabled many miners refining bad ores to stay in business for a time, but was of doubtful utility to the Treasury in the long run. The same lack of discrimination persisted when the time came for stringent debt collection, with equally deleterious results. It was naturally the view of the central Treasury authorities in Mexico City that the whole mining community of the Zacatecas district was responsible for the mercury debt, and that all its members should be pursued with equal rigour for what they owed. It was then the task of the local Treasury officials to point out that some miners, although at present indebted, had the capacity to earn profits for themselves and provide taxes for the Crown, and should therefore not be too closely pressed for debts; while others had no chance of operating economically, and should therefore be forced to pay their debts as far as possible.

Without information on costs which there is no means of obtaining, it is impossible to say exactly when Zacatecas' mines became uneconomic. A reasonable estimate would be the mid-1620s. Ultimately the health of mining depended on the yield of ores; and Villarreal considered these to be at best moderate in 1626. The subsequent high silver production until 1635 was therefore achieved at the increasing expense of the Crown, as well as of those miners who may still have had cash in hand. It is no wonder, if these speculations are not too far from the truth, that in the late 1630s miners in Zacatecas were unable to pay Indian labourers the wages necessary to retain them in Zacatecas instead of drifting to Parral, or to attract them from their towns. The Crown's avid collection of debts in the 1640s and 1650s aggravated the difficulties caused by poor ores in Zacatecas. Gómez Rendón, Treasurer of the Real Caja, claimed to have collected by 1654 all but 70,000 of the 671,679 pesos owed by miners in 1638.[1] Admittedly some further small distributions of mercury were made in the intervening sixteen years (for example, the 400 quintales issued by Rojas in 1644). Notwithstanding, the withdrawal of over 600,000 pesos of liquid capital from the mining industry was hardly calculated to encourage miners to carry out the clearing and drainage of mines, and the prospecting, that were necessary if new sources of rich ore were to be uncovered, and restoration of mining thereby achieved.

It was, indeed, high-grade smelting ores at Sombrerete that revived the region's output. Zacatecas began to contribute to this revival in the 1670s; in considerable part, apparently, by imitating Sombrerete and refining smelting ores. Smelting did not necessarily demand heavy investment, since plant was of quite cheap construction. In the four final decades of the century, it is true that most transactions in refining works recorded in notarial books refer to amalgamation haciendas. Nevertheless, there are occasional sales and leases of smelting works.[2] Even simpler and cheaper than building a totally new plant for smelting would have been the adaptation of amalgamation haciendas to the new task. The existing stamp mills could have continued in use. In the inventory of an amalgamation hacienda in 1663, there is a reference to a complete smelting works contained within the larger premises, with furnaces for smelting and refining (that is, probably, cupellation), and machinery-driven bellows.[3] If conversions, or semi-conversions, of this type took place frequently, the puzzle of how Zacatecas produced so much smelted silver without having many smelting works would be solved. A further question then

---

[1] AGI Guadalajara 33, Madrid 10 September 1676, relación de méritos of Captain Francisco Gómez Rendón.

[2] See, for example, AN.Z, IG 1686, ff. 145v.–6v., Zacatecas 4 May 1686, a power of attorney granted by Cristóbal del Castillo to Don Francisco Martínez del Castillo, enabling him to raise a censo of 1,500 pesos on a small smelting hacienda, newly built on the loma de la Carnicería. The hacienda had ore-crushing machinery and one furnace.

[3] AA.Z, 8, No. 54, Zacatecas 9 February 1663, inventory of an hacienda belonging to Juan de Gastelu, drawn up on his death.

immediately arises. How did miners obtain ores suitable for smelting? The smelting process was by nature less able to handle large amounts of low-grade ore than amalgamation; therefore, at some time in the mid-century, ores of great richness must have been located. Where these ores came from is admittedly a mystery. Perhaps Bartolomé Bravo discovered them through his works of renovation on the Veta Grande; perhaps imitators of his advanced methods of linking and extending underground workings had success equal to his. But how could miners have undertaken these clearly expensive projects for renovating old mines? What financial resources remained to them, when they had apparently been deprived of all capital by the Treasury? The answer lies in private financing, which grew to previously unknown proportions in Zacatecas in the second half of the seventeenth century.

By the time the Crown began to issue depósitos of mercury in the 1580s, merchants had long been selling goods to miners on credit. The business of avío, or supply, was seen as the inevitable accompaniment of mining. The aviador not only profited from supplying miners with goods; he also took advantage of the miner's usual indebtedness to insinuate himself into the process of silver production. He became a *rescatador*. The word had two meanings, related but distinct. The rescatador was first a man who bought silver cheaply in an unfinished state with a view to refining it himself. He might buy pepenas from mine labourers and smelt them in a parada de fuelles; or he could simply make use of his power over miners indebted to him to oblige them to sell him crude amalgam. He then merely distilled off the mercury and dispatched his miner to declare the refined silver at the Treasury as plata del diezmo. He thus obtained the double advantage of buying silver cheaply and avoiding payment of the full quinto due on rescate silver. A natural development from this type of transaction was the purchase of fully refined silver at discount. The second class of rescatadores consisted of men who engaged in this business. It was realised very soon that both classes were to a large extent undesirable; the purchaser of unfinished silver defrauded the Crown of part of its silver tax, and the purchaser of finished silver charged what were regarded as usurious rates of interest to the miner.[1]

The purchase of finished silver appears to have started when a need

---

[1] See AGI Guadalajara 5, clause 40 of Mendiola's ordinances of Zacatecas 6 March 1568, in 'Averiguaciones ... Contreras y Guevara ... 1570', f. 132v. Mendiola here prohibits merchants from owning furnaces. Their practice was to sell goods to Indians and Negro mine-workers and demand payment in pepenas or even in stolen ores. For the rescate of finished silver, see AGI Guadalajara 30, Zacatecas 2 April 1587, Baltasar de Bañuelos to Crown.

The Production of Silver

arose in Zacatecas for silver coin. Coin – usually referred to simply as *reales* – was always scarce in New Spain because much of that struck in the colony's only mint, in Mexico City, was remitted to Spain as tax or in private transactions. Its place in general circulation was partly taken by unminted silver, but since such silver was of limited negotiability, there was a constant demand for coin. It was, moreover, the custom in Zacatecas to pay mine-workers in coin. And unless the miner was willing to carry his silver to the capital for minting, he had to buy coin from a *rescatador de reales*. The discount rate at the end of the sixteenth century was one real per peso: that is, to buy eight coined reales the miner paid nine reales in taxed silver.[1] Purchase of coin at this rate of discount soon became transformed into a system of cash loans at interest. The rescatador offered coin for repayment in silver at one real per peso, or one peso per mark (the same ratio), in a certain time. The normal period in the late sixteenth century was forty or fifty days.[2] Then the same rate of interest came to be used in the payment of debts on goods.[3] The merchant gained rather more than is immediately apparent, for he obtained payment in silver of above standard fineness. Up to the early years of the seventeenth century, a mark of taxed silver was officially valued at 65 reales (8 pesos, 1 real); this value appears to have been attributed to all silver produced by miners, regardless of variations in purity. But silver produced by amalgamation was of near perfect fineness, and a mark of it was worth 67 or 68 reales in coin. So for every 65 reales he sold or distributed in credit, the rescatador, with his interest and with the gain in fineness, received 75 or 76 coined reales in return. From this profit he had to deduct the cost of taking his silver to Mexico City, and mint charges. Freight costs are difficult to

---

[1] Citizens of Zacatecas, and inhabitants of New Galicia in general, continually suggested to viceroys and the Crown that a mint should be set up in the north, preferably in Zacatecas. Demands became especially vociferous after 1603, when Viceroy Monterrey tried (with little success) to ban the circulation of unminted silver, because it afforded possibilities for defrauding the Treasury. But no mint was founded in Zacatecas until 1813. The authorities believed that the volume of silver that would be coined would not be enough to cover costs, and that there was too much danger of fraud in an isolated mint. There are references to the question, too frequent to enumerate, in AGI Guadalajara 5, 7, 8, 30, 51, and in AGI Mexico 19.

[2] See AGI Guadalajara 30, Zacatecas 2 April 1587, Baltasar de Bañuelos to Crown. Bañuelos painted a sad picture of miners subjected to the greed of the rescatadores. Every fifty days, the miners had to raise a new loan to cover the previous one and its interest. The principal of each succeeding loan thus grew, and the miner became ever more deeply indebted, until in the end he suffered bankruptcy.

[3] See AGI Mexico 258, Nueva España 10 October 1603, 'Sobre el beneficio de los mineros' (a report by one Alonso de Peralta Sidonia, a vecino of Mexico City), f. 2v. 'The merchant gives clothes or money for forty or sixty days, to be paid for in silver, with rescate; for on each mark he takes six reales, and in many places, eight; and this is an established business.'

determine. Mintage amounted to three reales a mark.[1] The profit of the rescatador or *aviador* was probably not great, although the interest seemed extortionate to his customers.

But, at however great a cost, the miner became dependent on his aviador. It is difficult to trace the development of the avío system; arrangements must often have been informal, and conditions would naturally have varied according to the conditions of each loan, the ability of the miner to pay and the capital of the aviador. No contracts for avío were found in the notarial archives of Zacatecas. Nevertheless, it is clear that as the Crown withdrew its credit on mercury and began to collect its debts, from the mid-1630s onwards, miners came to rely increasingly on private funds. Documents contain increasingly frequent references to the necessity and fragility of the private avío system. The Treasury officials of Zacatecas, when advocating leniency in collecting debts from Bartolomé Bravo in 1648, pointed out that the first consequence of bringing pressure to bear on him would be that his aviadores would abandon him. The same officials, in a letter to the Tribunal de Cuentas three years later, gave even more revealing evidence of the extent to which private credit had penetrated and dominated the industry. Explaining why they had failed to collect certain debts, they said that the aviador had first claim on a miner's earnings. When the miner came to the Treasury to have a quantity of silver taxed, the aviador accompanied him. A tenth of the silver was taken for the Crown in the normal way; the aviador next stated how much the miner owed him, and took it; and lastly, debts owing to the Crown for mercury were paid out of the silver that remained. If this sequence of payments were not preserved, the officials said, miners would not be able to find aviadores. And that, they implied, would be the end of mining.[2]

The source of the aviadores' capital must also remain largely a matter for speculation. In the days of prosperous commerce in Zacatecas, trading profits doubtless provided resources for avío. It is also possible that the earnings of merchants from their much-criticised illegal smelting furnaces were a useful source of capital for loans. So aviadores of the city had a means of raising money on the spot. But all avío did not originate in Zacatecas. There is evidence of movement of capital from Mexico City into mining in the north. This movement doubtless took place from the very earliest days of mining, but it seems to have increased towards the

---

[1] See *Recopilación* 1680, IV xxiii 8. Seigniorage was 1 real. Mint officials were paid from a levy (*braceaje*) of 2 reales per mark.

[2] AT.Z, Reales Oficiales 11, Zacatecas 18 April 1651, Treasury officials to Tribunal de Cuentas.

The Production of Silver

middle of the seventeenth century. The corregidor of Zacatecas noted in 1652 that not only had many merchants left the city, but those who remained were financially dependent on the capital ('with funds from correspondents in Mexico City').[1] Depression of regional commerce had obviously left the way open for the merchants of the capital to establish themselves in the provinces, in effect buying out local traders who could no longer survive on their small businesses. The years of the mid-century are also marked by the appearance of the *mercader de plata*, who was a rescatador on the grand scale. He bought unminted silver in vast quantities, and acted as the ultimate source of credit for agents living in mining towns. Men calling themselves mercaderes de plata appear in Zacatecas in the 1650s. Captain Joseph de Villarreal was one. His installation, in 1654, as alguacil mayor, a member of the cabildo, was a sign of his importance in the town. His transactions in credit with miners were so large that, at the time of his death in 1680, he was owed debts of 139,000 pesos. But his capital was not his own. He dealt with two pairs of mercaderes de plata living in Mexico City: Captains Joseph de Retes and Dámaso de Zaldívar, and Captains Juan de Urrutia Retes and Luis Sáenz de Tagle.[2] From February 1659 to January 1669, Villarreal had received 609,805 pesos in coin from Joseph de Retes, and returned 601,755 pesos 6 reales in silver.[3] It was with the same Retes family that Don Andrés de Estrada, corregidor of Zacatecas from 1678 to 1684, traded in silver. This commerce was one of the charges brought against him in his residencia. Crown officials were, of course, strictly forbidden to engage in trade within their jurisdictions; and it is indeed difficult to imagine any trade more likely to prejudice justice and fair administration than rescate and avío. It was said in June 1684 that since the corregidor had been in Zacatecas, he had received 2,500,000 pesos in coin from his aviadores in Mexico City; he provided avío for a large number of the most prominent miners of the city – among them, Don Juan Bravo.[4]

From these local agents of the mercaderes de plata most miners obtained avío. Direct dealings with Mexico City were not common, although there are records of some loans made without intermediaries. It was no doubt more convenient for borrowers, and safer for creditors, that loans should be made on the spot, where direct supervision of payment was

[1] AN.Z, LC 5, f. 36, Zacatecas, cabildo of 8 June 1652.
[2] AN.Z, JL 1676–80, ff. 246–50v., Zacatecas 7 April 1680, will of Captain Joseph de Villarreal.
[3] AGI Mexico 267, 'Autos contra Joseph de Villarreal ... 1671', ff. 443–50lv., 'relación jurada' of Captain Joseph de Retes, mercader de plata.
[4] AGI Escribanía 389, 'Residencia del General Don Andrés de Estrada ... año de 1684 ...', f. 80–80v., testimony of Pedro Botello, Zacatecas 17 June 1684.

possible. The system of granting credit developed in such a way as to give the greatest possible security to the creditor. The aviador preferred distributing small amounts of cash to the miner at frequent intervals to handing over large sums every few months. Villarreal, in 1664, said that every week he gave his customers the credit they needed, obtaining from them a receipt. Miners deposited their silver with him as they produced it; and when enough had accumulated to form a barra (an ingot of 130 to 135 marks), they took it to the Treasury for taxation. Having paid the tenth, the miner settled his account with the mercader de plata or aviador in taxed silver. Villarreal said he charged interest at 6 reales a mark. By this time it was generally recognised, both in official and private dealings, that the value of silver varied with its fineness. A mark of amalgamated silver was now valued at 70 reales in coin. So it is clear that the interest rate had fallen from the beginning of the century, when it stood at 8 reales on a mark valued at 65 reales. Having bought a mark from the miner for 64 reales, Villarreal then sold it at 67 to the mercaderes de plata of Mexico City for whom he acted.[1] Thus the rescate of 6 reales was divided equally between him and the central creditors. The decrease in the rate of rescate can perhaps be attributed to the enormously increased scale of the system in the mid-seventeenth century in comparison with credit dealings at the start of the century.[2]

As credit from private sources became more freely available in the second half of the seventeenth century, debts to the Crown were more quickly paid. Up to about 1650 the Treasury had frequently had to persist ten years or more in collecting payment for a particular consignment of mercury; and always a final part of the debt remained unpaid. But after then the value of a consignment was normally recovered within months.[3] Obviously the miner now drew on private credit to buy his mercury. The mercury debt was thus transferred from official to private accounts, as is shown by the miners' observation in November 1677 that they were indebted to the extent of over a million pesos with aviadores. Not all of this sum represented purchases of mercury, of course.

---

[1] AGI Mexico 267, 'Autos contra Joseph de Villarreal ... 1671', ff. 163–4v., Zacatecas 13 January 1664, 'Declaración en la cárcel del Alguacil Mayor Joseph de Villarreal'.

[2] Rescate rates were not always 6 reales per mark in the second half of the century. On loans of lump sums of cash, they varied, presumably according to the reliability of the debtor, between 4 and 6 reales; and on such loans time limits for repayment were stated. Four months was a common period, although longer credit could be negotiated. See various loans in AN.Z, FE 1656, FE 1659, FE 1664, FE 1671, JL 1672, JL 1673, FE 1676, JL 1676–80, IG 1685, *passim*.

[3] See, for example, AT.Z, Reales Oficiales 26, various *relaciones juradas*, given by the Treasury officials of Zacatecas, of twenty-two consignments arriving from 2 September 1667 to 16 December 1679.

The Production of Silver

It also comprised loans of cash, and credit on general mining goods.[1] Despite the size of this debt, and the impression of inefficiency in mining that it inevitably suggests, there is every probability that credit was given more selectively by aviadores and mercaderes de plata than it had been by the Treasury. The aviador was no doubt careful to investigate the promise of the mines and hacienda of a prospective client. So credit, and hence the mercury brought with that credit, went to those who could make the best use of it. There is evidence for this in the relatively high correspondencia of the 1660s, 1670s and 1680s. From 8 November 1664 to 31 December 1686, 14,983 quintales of mercury were sold to miners of Zacatecas and Pánuco, who produced with them 1,731,231 marks of silver: at an average, therefore, of $115\frac{1}{2}$ marks a quintal.[2]

Up to this point, production of silver in the Zacatecas district has been discussed purely in relation to local and short-term causes and effects. But as a silver producer, Zacatecas was, of course, closely linked with other economies besides that of New Spain; particularly direct was the link with the European economy, through the Atlantic trade. It should therefore be said that the seventeenth-century history of Zacatecas – the history of a period with wide variations in silver output – was enacted against the background of a European economy in which the value of silver, in terms of gold, was fast falling. The decline was swiftest during the first half of the century, in the early part of which one unit of gold, for the first time, became equivalent to more than twelve of silver. The decline of the value of silver, in gold terms, was particularly rapid from 1620 to 1640. In the second half of the century the ratio of the two metals widened far more slowly, remaining between one to fourteen and one to fifteen.[3] Zacatecas, with its heavy production of silver in the first thirty-five years of the seventeenth century, doubtless made its contribution to the widening of the bimetallic ratio before 1650, and thus decreased the value of its own product against gold. The coincidence of the most rapid divergence of the two metals with the peak years of Zacatecas' output is also interesting to note, although the coincidence can hardly be more than fortuitous. Variations in the bimetallic ratio had many causes, of

---

[1] AGI Mexico 612, México 16 February 1678, 'Sobre la nueva forma de la distribución y repartimiento de los azogues', foliated 1–64; in this, ff. 9v.–13, 'poder' of the miners of Zacatecas, Zacatecas 24 November 1677, signed by Felipe de Espinosa.

[2] AT.Z, Reales Oficiales 30, Zacatecas 22 June 1687, 'Relación jurada y firmada que yo el Capitán Don Luis de Bolívar y Mena ... doy ... de la marca de plata que se ha hecho en esta Real Caja ... desde 8 de noviembre del año pasado de 1664 hasta 31 de diciembre del de 1686 ...'.

[3] *The Cambridge Economic History of Europe*, vol. 4, eds. E. E. Rich and C. H. Wilson, C.U.P., 1967, ch. 7: F. P. Braudel and F. Spooner, 'Prices in Europe from 1450 to 1750', pp. 384–5, and figs. 5 and 11.

which a boom in Zacatecas must have been a rather minor one. If, though, Zacatecas' boom proves to be typical of American silver mines, and particularly of those of Peru, in the years 1610 to 1640, then the connection between increased silver output and divergence of the ratio will appear rather closer.

The decline of Zacatecan mining after 1635, can, of course, be linked with this decrease in the value of silver in terms of gold; and the slow recovery of the late seventeenth century, with the steadying of the divergence between gold and silver. But in a situation where gold was not a standard, as it was not in much of seventeenth-century Europe, variations in bimetallic ratios did not necessarily coincide with variations in the value of silver in terms of goods – that is, the everyday purchasing power of silver. The miner would plainly, in general, be more concerned with how much food his silver would buy than with how much gold. Remaining for the moment on the eastern side of the Atlantic, it is thus worth noting that the average European price of wheat, expressed not in money of account but in weight of silver, reached a maximum, for the period under study, in the early 1630s. There had been a previous peak, only slightly lower, in the early 1590s.[1] That is to say, the price of silver, expressed in terms of wheat, reached a minimum at the end of the sixteenth, and a slightly lower minimun in the 1630s. Now, if it is legitimate to adduce imports of American bullion into Europe as a cause of price increases in the second half of the sixteenth century (an argument which seems well-established, though frequently contested), it is equally legitimate to adduce the corresponding decline in the value of silver in terms of goods as a cause of depression in American silver mining. Even if there is no connection between bullion imports and European price rises, then the mere decline of the value of silver in terms of goods, for whatever reason, would tend to mean decreasing profits to miners. It may seem strange to put forward European price rises as a cause of the decline of silver mining. But this is merely to invert the relationship that is normally claimed to have existed between bullion and prices. The economic connections between the New World and the Old did not move only in an easterly direction. They were circular; and the view of these connections that presents itself to the historian varies, depending on whether he breaks into the circle on the American or European side. There is an observable coincidence between variations in Zacatecas' output and variations of silver values in Europe, just as there is between

---

[1] Braudel and Spooner, 'Prices in Europe', figs 11 and 19. The authors consider the wheat-price series to be the dominant price series for Europe in the period they discuss. It both led and reflected the prices of other commodities.

changes in silver output and changes in the bimetallic ratio. In broad terms, the value of silver in Europe in terms of wheat decreases until the early 1630s. Production at Zacatecas is high until the mid-1630s. High silver output is thus ostensibly related to price increases of wheat. There comes a point at which silver is under-valued in relation to wheat. Silver production becomes uneconomic; output falls, making silver relatively scarcer, and wheat cheaper, in silver. After the 1630s, the value of silver in wheat increases quite steadily until the end of the century. Production of silver in Zacatecas falls until the 1660s, and then begins to rise. No short-term correspondence between silver output and European silver values could be hoped for. Only long-term trends might be expected to coincide. It is possible, therefore, that the recovery of Zacatecan mining in the last third of the seventeenth century is related to the continuing increase in the value of silver in Europe.

To make these connections, of course, is to beg many questions. It is to assume, in the first place, that the degree of interdependence between the European and American economies remained the same, over time. As a hypothetical example, let it be supposed that variations in the European prices of a certain good (say, wheat), during the years 1600 to 1610, produced parallel variations in the prices of the same good in New Spain during the same period. Would there be any increase or reduction in this hypothetical correlation of wheat prices in Europe and New Spain over the following fifty years? It seems very likely that there would be a reduced correlation, if only because New Spain, by 1660, was growing far more of her own wheat. It is plain, in short, that America became progressively more self-sufficient economically in the seventeenth century. One consequence of this would be that the importance to her of the value in Europe of her exports (including silver) would decrease. These are problems in need of much investigation, and no attempt to solve them can be made here. Much light would be thrown on the subject if comprehensive information were available on prices in New Spain, and other Spanish colonies, in the seventeenth century.

The silver miner himself had no direct connection with the foreign markets for his product. Privately exported silver, between the hacienda de minas and its destination, whether Seville or Manila, passed through many hands: those of the aviador, the mercader de plata, and the merchant engaging in the trans-oceanic trade. Between them, these middlemen might have absorbed any extra profit deriving from the increased value of silver on foreign markets, leaving no benefit for the miner; or conceivably they may have tolerated decreased profits when external silver values fell. The miner, in any case, had ultimately to take for his silver the price offered by the aviador. His notion of the value of silver (and therefore, of whether he was making profits or losses) thus sprung from very local circumstances, and not from any knowledge of what silver might be worth in Seville or Antwerp. Local prices of goods, in silver, were obviously of more importance to the profitability of his hacienda than European prices. And, as has been several times lamented here, prices in New Spain in the seventeenth century are all but unknown. From the sparse figures for bread and wheat prices in Zacatecas shown in Table 2, no clear or major long-term fluctuations in the price of this grain can be deduced. It is perhaps possible to discern a fall in the price of bread after 1640. But these prices, being fixed by the cabildo, do not necessarily correspond to the normal run of costs of grain. Nor is any information available about the price of maize, the staple cereal of the Indians living in Zacatecas. Hardly anything more conclusive, further-more, can be said of the prices of meat, as listed in Table 3. A decrease in prices of beef and hides, but not of mutton, is apparent from 1640 onwards. Meat sold outside the asiento, however, might have fetched prices rather different from those proposed by the asentista when bidding for the contract. It is quite probable, naturally, that many prices did fall in Zacatecas after 1640, merely because of the depressed state of mining. If prices followed silver output downwards, the fall would have improved the profitability of only the few miners who managed to maintain their individual production; to the remainder, suffering falling revenues, a decrease in prices would have been at best an alleviation of their ills. Any lag of prices behind output during the recovery of mining in later times would, obviously, have benefited miners. But price data are so incomplete that it cannot be said whether such a lag occurred.

The influence of long-term variations in the value of silver (as expressed in commodity prices) on the production of that metal in New Spain was obviously of major importance. But, in the case of European silver values, distance makes correlations uncertain; and in the case of silver values in New Spain, lack of data on prices is the obstacle to useful conclusions. There is, however, one clear change in the valuation of silver, in terms of money of account, in effect a price change, which occurred in the seventeenth century and which worked in the miners' favour. The standard value of a mark of taxed silver was held to be 65 reales. This valuation presupposed that the silver was of the fineness normally achieved by smelting; and all silver was taken to be of this quality. Amalgamated silver, however, was purer. During the first half of the seventeenth century, it appears that aviadores and rescatadores came to pay producers of amalgamated silver rates closer to the intrinsic value of the metal – usually calculated at 70 reales. Although it is impossible to trace this change in the valuing of silver, it certainly appears to have taken place by the middle of the century. How much of the increased valuation was generally absorbed in higher discount rates for avío, it is impossible to say. It will be recalled that, at the beginning of the century, discount amounted to 8 reales on a mark valued at 65 reales; and that Joseph de Villarreal, in 1664, charged 6 reales on a mark valued at 70 reales. It would therefore appear that miners received 57 reales for a mark produced around 1600 and 64 reales in 1664. The value of silver in terms of money of account thus appears to have risen by some 12 per cent in the first sixty years of the century.

This figure is, of course, calculated on the basis of only two quotations of discount rates. Much more information than has come to light would be needed to substantiate it. And to evaluate it as an influence on mining prosperity would again demand information on prices in New Spain which does not exist. Like all evidence of long-term economic changes affecting the history of silver mining in New Spain, its existence may merely be noted, and judgement reserved until new data are uncovered. There is no reason, on the other hand, to reserve judgement on the local and particular causes of mining prosperity and depression in Zacatecas, as they have been described in this chapter. These may now finally be resumed.

Production in the sixteenth century did not exhibit any wide fluctuations. Where variations exist, they may be attributed to new discoveries of ore (in the 1560s and 1570s), lack of labour (after the great epidemic of the late 1570s), and the Chichimec war (in the 1580s). The rise in production from the beginning of the new century to the mid-1620s was the consequence of liberal distribution of mercury by the Crown. Ores at this period were probably of high quality, and mining profitable. But by 1625, yields were beginning to fall. Mining appears to have become fundamentally unprofitable, although production remained high until 1635 because large quantities of mercury continued to arrive. Even these large quantities, however, were not as great as they might have been. For in the 1630s a far higher proportion of European mercury than ever before was directed to Peru. Lack of mercury was severely felt in Zacatecas in the second quinquennium of the 1630s. Moreover, by this time, collection of debts owed to the Crown for mercury and salt was beginning in earnest. For lack of mercury, miners could not produce silver; and the silver they had was gradually taken from them by Treasury officials and visitors. Indian labour, no longer finding adequate rewards in Zacatecas, abandoned the mines. The loss of labour was accentuated by disease and movement of Indians to Parral. Thus silver production in Zacatecas, which fell catastrophically from 1635 to 1640, continued to decline in the 1640s. No hope of recovery seemed possible. Recovery occurred, nevertheless, in the form of silver smelting at Sombrerete, hitherto a minor producer in comparison with Zacatecas. While Zacatecas' output apparently continued to decline, parallel with the fall in mercury supply, in the 1650s and 1660s, Sombrerete smelted silver in ever-increasing quantities. In these years, growing amounts of private capital, compensating for the Crown's withdrawal of credit, appear to have been invested in mining. This capital had its ultimate origins in Mexico City, and probably in a small number of merchant families, whose source of wealth is not yet known. Perhaps their capital derived in the long run from the Atlantic trade, by this time long since declined, or from trans-Pacific trade. These new financiers of mining made it possible for the renovation of existing mines to be undertaken, as is illustrated by the activities of Bartolomé Bravo in Zacatecas. Renovation led to the rediscovery of rich ores. These gave rise to the swift resurgence of mining production in the Zacatecas district from 1665 onwards. Sombrerete contributed most to this resurgence, but Zacatecas itself recovered, partly by imitating Sombrerete and turning to smelting. Mercury supplies to Zacatecas also rose considerably after 1670. One reason for this could have been that the extensive availability of private credit now enabled miners to pay for mercury with spot cash. If they were able to do this over all New Spain, the Crown would have been encouraged to increase the supply to the colony in general. Imports of mercury from Peru arriving in Zacatecas from 1670 onwards are evidence for this supposition. Mercury was also probably used more efficiently than hitherto, because of the selectivity of private creditors in granting loans to miners. Production in the district rose to a long plateau from 1675 to 1690, which was higher than the previous peak of 1620 to 1625. After 1690 it declined, but less sharply than it had after 1635, and largely on account of the exhaustion of Sombrerete's rich ores. By 1720, Sombrerete was producing only a small fraction of what it had yielded thirty years before. Zacatecas, on the other hand, had achieved yet new heights of output.

CHAPTER 9

CONCLUSION: PLUS ULTRA

The history of Mexico in the second half of the sixteenth century and in the seventeenth as a whole is a vast and so far largely unpainted canvas. Any limited study, such as this one, while answering some questions, can hardly fail to raise others and to leave connections unmade or only badly made.

This study throws light on an episode in the northward expansion of New Spain. The power of wealth as a force in extending Spanish settlement into hostile regions is scarcely shown better anywhere than in the creation of the towns of the Zacatecas district. It appears, also, that this expansion into the lands of rich minerals was a prime cause of the development of the agricultural regions of the Bajío and Michoacán. Settlement and farming activities trailed in the wake of the silver rush. The city of Zacatecas was a great magnet in the north for much of the later part of the sixteenth century and the early years of the seventeenth, drawing roads, supplies and men to itself from central Mexico. And as, for many years, the effective northern terminal point of the Camino Real de la Tierra Adentro, Zacatecas was not only a destination in itself, but also a centre of distribution and trade for a wide area of the northern plateau, embracing New Biscay and New León, and ultimately, New Mexico. Up to the time of the Parral strike, in the early 1630s, this northern area was empty and unproductive of all but cattle. Zacatecas stood in it as a bridgehead, an outpost in the wilderness – gateway to all the kingdoms of the north, as the citizens said.

Zacatecas maintained its dominant position in the north because of the wealth of its mines; the wealth which, so the townspeople claimed, made it the second city of New Spain. There is no doubt about its predominance as a mining centre. From Graph 2 and Table 9b it is clear that, at various times in the seventeenth century, the district received between 25 per cent and 65 per cent of all the mercury arriving in New Spain. Mercury was distributed by the authorities of Mexico City among the various mining towns of the colony according to their estimated need, and Zacatecas always received by far the largest proportion of the available mercury. In 1609 it was thought that the total demand in New Spain was for 4,170 quintales a year, of which Zacatecas needed 1,000. Its nearest rivals were Tasco and Sultepec, which claimed 600 and 500 quintales respectively; the Real Caja de Durango, from which all New Biscay was supplied, received only 350 quintales.[1] In 1648, the viceroy estimated that the mines required 6,000 quintales, of which 2,000 should go to Zacatecas. Its nearest competitors now were Guadalajara (for the mines of western New Galicia) and Durango (for the mines of New Biscay), each of which should be assigned 700 quintales. After them came Tasco, Pachuca and Guanajuato, needing 655, 600 and 435 quintales respectively.[2] So if it may be assumed – and there is no good reason to do otherwise at the moment – that other mines in general produced smelted and amalgamated silver in the same proportions as the Zacatecas district, then that district was by far the single most important mining area of New Spain. And – it may be repeated for the last time – the great majority of amalgamated silver produced in the district came from the mines of the Serranía de Zacatecas itself. In 1598, the mines and haciendas de minas of the city were employing nearly a third of all the free labourers (*naborías*) working in the mines of New Spain.[3]

So much is clear. But it is less clear how the history of Zacatecas is to be interpreted in the light of existing knowledge (scant though it is) of seventeenth-century Mexico. It is a sad comment on the colonial historiography of Spanish America that Borah's suggestive essay *New Spain's Century of Depression*, published almost twenty years ago now, has prompted little new research into the history of New Spain after the initial conquest, and before the far-reaching changes of the mid-eighteenth century.[4] There are obvious points of contact between the findings laid out in this study of Zacatecas and the scheme of seventeenth century Mexican history suggested by Borah. There is, indeed, a depression in the

---

[1] BM Add. MS. 13,992, f. 513, 'Tanteo del azogue que las minas de esta Nueva España han menester en cada un año para su beneficio y cómo se reparten los 3,177 quintales [que] vinieron en la flota [del] General Juan Gutiérrez de Garibay', anon., n.d. Gutiérrez commanded the fleet of 1609 to New Spain.

[2] Matilla Tascón, *Historia ... de Almadén*, p. 233, note 250, quoting AGI Indiferente General 1777, unidentified expediente of 28 August 1648.

[3] The mines of the Audiencia of New Spain and of Zacatecas together held this labour force: 1,022 Negro slaves, 4,606 naborías and 1,619 repartimiento Indians. Zacatecas had no repartimiento Indians at all, but 130 slaves and 1,014 naborías. See 'Relación del estado que tienen las minas de esta Nueva España ...', an enclosure with AGI Mexico 24, R. 1, No. 7a, México 24 April 1598, Monterrey to Crown.

[4] There are obvious exceptions to this generalisation. Borah himself, with his colleagues at Berkeley, has pursued demographic and price history. Chevalier's *La formation* is a work of major importance on the period; but although published after Borah's essay, it was written before it. Gibson's *The Aztecs* is another central work, touching on many themes stated by Borah; though its geographical limits are narrow. The answer to many of the questions raised by Borah will doubtless come from M. Jean-Pierre Berthe, in his promised major study of Mexican economic and social history from 1550 to 1700. It is hoped that this work, the fruit of many years' research, will reach published form in the near future.

seventeenth century. Shortage of labour, which Borah proposed as the root of the depression, does appear in Zacatecas. But there is also a deal of contradiction between the development of Zacatecas and Borah's model. Most strikingly, whereas his 'century of depression' begins with the great matlazahuatl epidemic of 1576 to 1579, Zacatecas' decline starts with the collapse of silver production after 1635. But is it permissible to compare Zacatecas' particular decline in silver production with the general decline of the colonial economy, as outlined by Borah? To answer this question, some clarification of what he meant by 'depression' is required.

Starting from the incontestable fact of the sixteenth-century demographic disaster afflicting the aboriginal population of New Spain, Borah postulates a decrease, proportionate to the loss of working population, in agricultural production.[1] This decrease in available food supply threatened the well-being of colonial cities, whose largely white populations were dependent on Indian labour for their sustenance. The price of food rose in the late sixteenth century. There is, Borah claims, further evidence for shortage at this time in the series of regulations controlling prices, regrating and distribution that were issued in Mexico City.[2] There is no doubt about the promulgation and enforcement of such regulations, nor about price increases. But it may be questioned whether they constitute evidence of a long-term shortage of food, or whether they were the outcome merely of short-term scarcity resulting from a brief run of bad harvests. Borah then goes on to suggest that the decline of aboriginal population seriously hampered mining. He quotes as an example the case of Pachuca, where the number of Indians available to miners under repartimiento dwindled almost to nothing by the mid-seventeenth century.[3] To adduce this reduction as evidence of a decline at Pachuca is far from conclusive, however; for, as Borah himself points out later in the essay, repartimiento labour in mines was largely replaced, certainly by the middle years of the century, by free and debt-bonded labour. Indeed, the development of new and more efficient labour systems is the burden of the second part of Borah's essay. And it is at this point that his conclusions become somewhat puzzling. For it seems that things were not so bad, after all. The response of the colonists to a threatened labour shortage, following the disappearance of 80 per cent to 90 per cent of the native population, was remarkably quick. Negro slave labour was available in some quantity to help out. And when

[1] Borah, *Century of Depression*, p. 5.
[2] Borah, *Century of Depression*, pp. 24–5.
[3] Borah, *Century of Depression*, p. 26.

repartimiento of Indians failed to produce sufficient men to work land and mines, Spanish employers secured permanent sources of labour through the free wage system and through debt peonage. As early as 1590, labour obtained under these systems was being more efficiently employed than ever before on *latifundia* – the great estates that largely replaced Indian tributes as the source of food for Spanish cities.[1] This progression in the efficiency of use of Indian labour leads Borah to the conclusion that even at the minimum level of population, reached about 1650 and at a figure of some 1,500,000, there were enough Indians to provide 'essential services'; indeed, there were more than enough, if they could have been persuaded to devote much of their time to supporting the white population. The white-populated cities did not starve, although, Borah states, they certainly suffered occasional near-famines.[2] Mining, however, did suffer from a lack of Indians. Production increased up to 1600, but then underwent a slow decline until 1631, and a precipitous one thereafter to 1660. Although, Borah says, not enough is known of the possible causes of the changing prosperity of mining, 'shortage of labor was probably a major factor in the decline following 1600 ...'.[3]

The general impression carried away by the reader after a careful examination of *New Spain's Century of Depression* is that the depression was not so severe as appeared to be promised in the opening pages. The growing white and near-white population managed to continue feeding itself, and Indians under debt-peonage were better off than when exposed to the demands of repartimiento. In what, then, did the depression postulated by Borah consist? Primarily, it appears to have been a quite expected decline in total agricultural production (and possibly locally-produced textiles) following the decline of the aboriginal population. But the correlation between falling Indian population and falling production was not high. Mining output, for instance, continued to rise long after the worst of the Indian depopulation had ceased. And even if what might circumspectly be called gross national product did decline, according to Borah's own statements there is reason to think that production per head remained steady or even rose.

The view of New Spain's seventeenth-century economy that emerges from the final pages of Borah's essay is therefore far from totally black. The comparison of this view with Zacatecas' history in the same period raises interesting and suggestive questions. One inescapable fact is that Zacatecas, founded in the late 1540s, and therefore rather before the final

---

[1] Borah, *Century of Depression*, pp. 34–7.
[2] Borah, *Century of Depression*, p. 43.
[3] Borah, *Century of Depression*, pp. 43–4.

downward plunge of Indian population that culminated in the epidemic of 1576 to 1579, maintained prosperity throughout the second half of the sixteenth century, and rose to even greater wealth in the early decades of the seventeenth. At times it certainly suffered from labour shortages. But these shortages, as is argued in chapters 6 and 8 in discussions of labour supply, appear to have been more the consequence of impoverishment of the mines than the cause of it. Shortage of labour did not prevent the Zacatecas boom of 1615 to 1635 from taking place, nor that of Parral in the 1630s, nor that of Sombrerete from 1670 to 1690. How far it inhibited these booms is, of course, impossible to say. But if the general conclusions of this study are correct, then labour supply was not the major determinant of mining output. If there was a single major determinant, it was the supply of mercury; though mercury, as should be clear by now, was not the beginning nor the end of the story. Its supply must always be considered in the light of credit, and hence in the light of the fundamental profitability of mining, since credit was not forthcoming unless it yielded returns.

It is, of course, possible to attribute Zacatecas's general freedom from labour shortage to the efficiency of the system of free, salaried labour. The system, because it made for permanency of a labour force, also made for the development of greater skills. It allowed, in theory, a larger proportion of the Indian population to be continuously employed in Spanish-controlled activities than did repartimiento. Such arguments would support the second part of Borah's thesis. But to speak of labour systems without reference to the economic occupations they served is to beg the question. Here, the rise of Zacatecas can be seen as symptomatic of a far deeper change in the economy of New Spain than a mere improvement of efficiency in the employment of Indians. The economy of the colony, it could be argued, for much of the sixteenth century, was little different from the subsistence economy of pre-Spanish times. But the economy of New Spain in the seventeenth century, in many respects, was plainly of a capitalist nature. In the sixteenth century, the white community lived on the surplus produced by a vast number of Indians working in a very primitive economic system. In the seventeenth, Spaniards lived on the product, broadly and ultimately, of their own enterprise and of an economy that was in its general outline of contemporary European design. This transformation of the economic structure of New Spain was forced upon the colonists, to be sure, by the removal of the great majority of the Indian population. But once the transformation had taken place (manifesting itself in such institutions as textile *obrajes*, agricultural and stock-raising estates, a plant-equipped mining industry, debt peonage and free wage labour), the prosperity of the colony was no longer limited to the surplus produced by the aboriginal population, but varied in response to a far wider range of economic circumstances. Shortage of labour thus became only one of a number of limitations on output in a given industry or activity. It is in a sense misleading to speak of an economic 'depression' of New Spain in the seventeenth century, in comparison with prosperity in the sixteenth. The two centuries are not economically comparable; or rather, the first half of the sixteenth century is not comparable with the seventeenth, for the change towards an economy in which capitalist institutions played a large part clearly began in the second half of the sixteenth.

Since the time of writing of *New Spain's Century of Depression* it has, of course, become clear that New Spain's economic decline took place rather later than that essay suggested. Chaunu's work on trans-Atlantic trade plainly shows that New Spain did not fail as a market for European goods until the third decade of the seventeenth century. It is difficult to reconcile this high demand for European goods, continuing into the early 1620s, with any postulated depression of New Spain resulting from a decline in Indian population in the sixteenth. Indeed, Chaunu himself finds the reconciliation very difficult. From 1596 to 1620, the years of maximum activity in the trans-Atlantic trade in the whole period he studies, New Spain was the driving force of the Carrera de Indias. It was the destination of almost exactly half the tonnage leaving Spain for the New World; and trade fluctuations with New Spain led to general fluctuations in trade with America. But the 1620s brought a rapid deterioration of New Spain's position. In the quinquennium 1616 to 1620, it received 51·2 per cent of the tonnage from Spain; from 1621 to 1625, 43·19 per cent; and in the succeeding quinquennia, 28·58 per cent and 29·82 per cent. In the same period, outward bound tonnage to Tierra Firme (that is, in the main, destined for Peru) increased from 36·04 per cent (1616 to 1620), to 37·73, 53·35 and 51·23 per cent (1631 to 1635).[1] The proportional increase of trade to Tierra Firme took place, however, within a general decline of trans-Atlantic commerce, starting in the 1620s and continuing beyond the closing date of Chaunu's study, 1650. This decline was the dominant seventeenth-century trend in trans-Atlantic trade, as growth had been characteristic of the sixteenth century. Chaunu states categorically on several occasions that it was the failure of New Spain as a market which ended the sustained high level of trade from 1590 to 1620, and which was responsible for the downward trend in

[1] Pierre and Huguette Chaunu, *Séville et l'Atlantique*, Paris 1955–9; 8 vols., here vol. 8, 2(*bis*), pp. 1534–5.

the long term.[1] The failure of New Spain as a market, he regards as a consequence of the general economic failure of the colony. And this failure he interprets according to Borah's scheme in *New Spain's Century of Depression*: that is, primarily as a consequence of demographic decline. But why, it may be asked, should this economic failure become particularly apparent in the 1620s? The maximum rate of decrease of Indian population had long since passed. Chaunu is forced to postulate a sudden crisis in the early part of the decade. A critical threshold of Indian population, a little below 2,000,000, was reached. The economy of New Spain was suddenly restrained. The first activities to suffer were those which fed long-distance trade.[2]

Chaunu readily concedes that his explanation of the decline of New Spain is hypothetical, and is formulated in the absence of specific information. It is open to many objections. The most obvious one, inherent in the argument itself, is vagueness. It is plain that the figure of 2,000,000 taken by Chaunu to be the 'critical' level of Indian population is selected quite arbitrarily. The economy of New Spain appears to falter in the early 1620s; Indian population had fallen by that time to about 2,000,000; therefore 2,000,000 was the level of Indian population below which the economy of New Spain could not survive. Such is the reasoning. But why should the critical level not have been 5,000,000 or 500,000? Simply not enough is known about how many Indians were employed, and in which occupations, to make any induction from population levels to economic activity possible.

The second objection derives from considerations of New Spain as a market for European goods. It is clear, despite all the European and Spanish price movements, Spanish and international political influences, wars, crises of ship-building, and multifarious psychological pressures among merchants which Chaunu has so brilliantly interwoven in explaining the vagaries of trade with Spanish America, that trans-Atlantic commerce ultimately depended on the state of the markets in America. In these markets, basically New Spain and Peru, there had to be demand for European goods and (the necessary condition of demand) means of paying for imports. Chaunu largely infers market conditions in America from the behaviour of the trade, and this is a quite reasonable procedure. If selling proved difficult in America, then the market obviously lacked demand. There was strong evidence by the early years of the seventeenth century that demand in New Spain for many European exports was declining. The merchants of Seville suffered a grave set-back in 1609 by

---

[1] Chaunu, *Séville*, vol. 8, 2(*bis*), p. 1557.
[2] Chaunu, *Séville*, vol. 8, 2(*bis*), pp. 1559–60.

being unable to sell exports at Veracruz. A similar market crisis in New Spain appears to have occurred in 1619.[1] Chaunu notes these symptoms of a grave decline in demand, and adduces them as a major cause of the collapse of trans-Atlantic trade in the 1620s. He appears, however, to attribute decline in demand in that decade not so much to a glutting of New Spain's market for European goods (or, more accurately, to the substitution of home-produced goods for imports), as to a fall in economic activity in the colony, and hence a loss of exportable produce to pay for goods from Spain. Hence he is inclined to follow and adapt the arguments of *New Spain's Century of Depression*, suggesting that the colony became a bad market because it fell victim to economic depression; and it fell victim to economic depression because the Indian population passed a critical minimum level.

Full elucidation of the questions surrounding the behaviour of the market in New Spain in the 1620s, and its effect on the Carrera de Indias, would require more information than is currently available on many topics. It is an incontrovertible fact that the merchants of Seville were able to sell far fewer goods in New Spain than they had in the previous two decades. But is it permissible to infer a general economic depression there from a falling-off of the market? Information presented by Chaunu himself gives good reason for doubting this argument. The single largest export of New Spain, balancing (and, according to Chaunu, driving) trade with Spain, was silver. It is true that the colony, by the early seventeenth century, was less exclusively a silver exporter than she had been in the sixteenth century, and than Peru continued to be. In 1609, for instance, her exports to Europe consisted (by value) of 65 per cent silver and 35 per cent other goods: cochineal, hides, indigo, wool, dyes, dye-woods and medicinal plants.[2] It may be supposed that the proportional value of exports other than bullion continued to rise after this date. Nevertheless, silver was the largest single component of New Spain's trading balance with Europe. Now, there is no reason to think that silver production in New Spain fell during the 1620s. Production at Zacatecas was higher in the first half of the decade than ever before, and continued high until the middle of the 1630s. Zacatecas was producing a large fraction of Mexican silver at this time, perhaps a third (if it is assumed that mercury distribution to different mining districts reflects output in them); so that it alone would have had considerable influence on total production, even if other mines were failing. But such failure is unlikely to have

---

[1] Chaunu, *Séville*, vol. 8, 2(*bis*), pp. 1499–1500.
[2] J. Lynch, *Spain under the Habsburgs. Volume Two. Spain and America 1598–1700*, Oxford 1969, p. 185.

occurred, since, other things being equal, silver production varied in the short-term with the supply of mercury. And Chaunu shows that imports of mercury to New Spain were higher in the three quinquennia of the period 1615 to 1630 than in any earlier period.[1] It seems likely, therefore, that unless there had previously existed very large-scale smelting, which ceased in the 1620s, the total output of silver in that decade in New Spain was higher than ever before.

If Chaunu is right in thinking that it was the capacity of the colonies to produce exportable goods that basically impelled the Atlantic trade, then this conjunction of high silver output with falling imports in New Spain is indeed difficult to explain. The difficulty is resolved, however, by supposing that, at this time, the market in New Spain was conditioned not so much by the availability of goods exportable to Spain as by pure demand for European commodities. This shift of emphasis puts New Spain in a dominant position in the trade; the colony's needs were now determining the varieties of goods that merchants could hope to sell there. From being an external provider of easily-tapped wealth for Europe, New Spain now became the discriminating customer. This argument, of course, is explicitly stated by Chaunu when he notes the difficulties encountered by Spanish merchants in selling goods at Veracruz in 1609 and 1619. But primacy in his discussion of the decline of trade still goes to the economic collapse of New Spain.

A full demonstration that trade to New Spain declined in the 1620s owing to a fall in the colony's demand for European goods would obviously require an examination of types of exports in previous years, and of the possibilities of local production of substitutes. It is, unfortunately, the precise nature of the exports which is the least known aspect of them. Chaunu suggests that the majority in the difficult year of 1619, as previously, were 'pondéreux alimentaires', of which wine formed a large part. If this is so, is it possible that agriculture in New Spain had become able by this time to produce enough foodstuffs to eliminate the need of imports from Spain? Again, the question of labour supply is raised. If agricultural production depended, ultimately, on the level of Indian population, then it is difficult to see how such production could have been insufficient to feed the colony without help from Spain before 1620, and yet large enough after that date to obviate, or greatly decrease, the need for food imports. After all, the Indian population was still falling. If, on the other hand, the critique made of *New Spain's Century*

---

[1] Chaunu, *Séville*, vol. 8, 2(*bis*), pp. 1974–5, 'Appendice III'. The present writer is not in agreement with Chaunu about the exact size of these imports; but they were certainly higher than any previous ones. See Table 10a.

of Depression earlier in this chapter is correct, then it is quite possible that hacienda agriculture and stock raising, and plantation cultivation, had improved in efficiency and output to a degree that did make New Spain self-sufficient in food. Agriculture may well have freed itself from dependence on very large reserves of labour, just as mining had. More efficient production of other commodities, such as textiles and leather goods, may have made New Spain progressively more independent of Europe for a wide range of supplies.

Much of this argument is conjectural. Yet it seems more plausible than Chaunu's arbitrary 'critical' level of population, and at least suggests reasons for New Spain's failure as a market at a time when her major export, silver, was probably being produced in very large quantities – perhaps larger than ever before. The argument also suggests that the economy of New Spain, far from suffering any decline in the early seventeenth century, became more healthy; at least, to the extent of making the colony self-sufficient in foodstuffs. This economic strength can only have been reinforced by the growth of silver production, consequent upon increasing supplies of mercury; for silver mining was clearly the dynamic sector of the economy. The question of what became of this increased supply of silver must obviously be asked. How much was remitted to Spain, how much to other destinations in the Empire, and how much retained in New Spain?

E. J. Hamilton shows imports of precious metals to Spain from the American colonies in this period. He gives total amounts of registered Crown and private imports, and the proportions of the total coming from New Spain and Peru.[1] From his Charts and Tables it may be calculated that in the period 1580 to 1620, New Spain supplied a fairly constant 36 per cent of bullion imports – in absolute figures about 10,625,000 pesos ensayados per quinquennium. Peru supplied the remainder: some 21,000,000 pesos, on average, per quinquennium. From 1616 to 1620, at 36 per cent of the total, the import from New Spain was some 10,836,000 pesos ensayados; and from 1621 to 1625 almost the same amount (10,800,000 pesos), although New Spain's proportional contribution to the total import from America rose to nearly 40 per cent. From 1626 to 1630, both as an absolute sum and a percentage, her contribution was much diminished: about 5,250,000 pesos and 21 per cent. In the following quinquennium, 1631 to 1635, New Spain's percentage was still low (about 22 per cent), and since total imports from America were falling, her contribution as an absolute sum was down, at roughly 3,740,000 pesos.

---

[1] Earl J. Hamilton, *American Treasure and the Price Revolution in Spain, 1501–1650*, Cambridge, Mass. 1934; Table 1 and Charts 1 and 3 (pp. 34, 35, 43).

Conclusion: Plus Ultra

Thenceforth until the end of Hamilton's statistics, 1660, New Spain yielded on average about 30 per cent of bullion imports to Spain from America – bullion imports which were falling precipitously (from 17,110,854 pesos, 1631 to 1635, to only 3,361,116 pesos, 1656 to 1660). In each of the two quinquennia of the period 1616 to 1625, therefore, New Spain provided some 10,800,000 pesos ensayados of bullion (very largely silver) in Seville. Registered imports from the colony fell in the following quinquennium to only 5,250,000 pesos, at Seville. But in 1628 the fleet from New Spain was lost to the Dutch at Matanzas, off Cuba, with perhaps 6,000,000 pesos aboard.[1] If this bullion had arrived at Seville, imports from New Spain would actually have been higher than in the previous two quinquennia. The true slump of bullion exports from New Spain therefore came after 1630, when, in the quinquennium 1631 to 1635, only 3,740,000 pesos were registered at Seville. The figure continued to fall thereafter.

Imports of silver from New Spain registered at Seville were, of course, equal to registered exports from the colony to Spain, barring losses during the voyage, such as the catastrophe of 1628. Counting the Matanzas loss as an export from New Spain, therefore, it is clear that remittances of bullion thence to Spain tended to increase, as absolute quantities, from 1615 to 1630. This increase is additional evidence for the prosperity of mining in the 1620s. What bearing does it have on the discussion of New Spain's market and economy in the preceding pages?

It is at first sight contradictory that the volume of New Spain's imports from Spain was decreasing while her exports of bullion to Seville were rising. Was not silver the major commodity balancing trans-Atlantic trade? There could be several explanations for this discrepancy. First there is the possibility that the trade had not declined in value as much as it had declined in volume. Secondly, it is possible that with abundant silver at her disposal, New Spain was reverting to an older pattern of trade, and paying for her imports mainly with precious metals and less with other goods (cochineal, etc.). Thirdly, there is the possibility that the increase of bullion exports reflected an increase in Crown remittances, and not in private ones. Indeed, the first effect of a rise of mining output would be to increase the tax yield of the diezmo; and as silver spread through the economy, other tax yields would also rise. It is unfortunately impossible to derive from Hamilton's figures separate quantities for Crown and private bullion imports to Spain from each American viceroyalty, although he gives totals in each category for America taken as a whole. There is evidence from documents, however, that remittances of Crown

[1] Lynch, *Spain and America*, p. 174.

Conclusion: Plus Ultra

silver from New Spain to Spain were very high in the 1620s, and indeed in the early 1630s. Gelves reported in 1623 that he had managed to increase the sum sent to Spain (from an unspecified previous amount). The returning fleet of 1623 carried 1,862,580 pesos de oro común (including 100,000 in defence expenditure for Havana).[1] In 1631 Cerralvo claimed that he had gathered the largest remittance since the conquest of New Spain: 1,316,562 pesos de oro común had left the Treasury of Mexico City for the fleet, to which sum the income of the Real Caja at Veracruz remained to be added.[2] Cadereita stated in 1636 that he had dispatched a fleet with some 2,000,000 pesos aboard for the Crown; but this may have been the accumulated income of two years.[3] It may well be, in view of these large remittances, that the high, indeed increasing, levels of bullion exports to Spain from New Spain in the 1620s were to an important degree the outcome of large Crown remittances, while private remittances perhaps declined. After 1630 there was a sharp and unequivocal fall in all bullion imports from New Spain, but again, probably, with Crown silver declining less rapidly than private silver.

The slight growth of total bullion remittances to Spain in the 1620s falls far short of accounting for all the increase in silver output which large supplies of mercury in that decade probably stimulated. Increased Crown income was certainly absorbed in the costs of Imperial defence, borne by the Treasury of Mexico City. New Spain financed the defence of most of the Caribbean, and of the Philippines. The enormous burden of these costs is well illustrated by a document of 1623 prepared by Treasury officials of Mexico City. It quotes remittances to Spain and the Philippines from New Spain in the four years 1618 to 1621. 1,653,253 pesos de oro común had been dispatched for military expenditure in the Philippines; and rather less, 1,500,595 pesos, to Spain. Furthermore, only 1,141,552 pesos of the remittance to Spain were in cash; the remainder consisted of cochineal belonging to the Treasury. A further, but unspecified, sum of money had been disbursed for defence expenditure in Havana, Santo Domingo, Puerto Rico and Florida.[4] Defence costs in the Philippines were probably unusually large in these years, perhaps on account of anticipated Dutch interloping there. But, as historians are coming

[1] AGI Mexico 30, R. 1, México 7 June 1623, Gelves to Crown, 'Sobre materias de hacienda', para. 1.
[2] AGI Mexico 30, R. 4, México 9 September 1631, Cerralvo to Crown, 'materias de hacienda', para. 2.
[3] AGI Mexico 31, R. 3, México 17 April 1636, Cadereita to Crown, 'gobierno', para. 11.
[4] AGI Mexico 30, R. 1, México 8 May 1623, 'Relación de los envíos que se hicieron a Castilla por cuenta de la Real Hacienda ... los cuatro años pasados ... gobernando el Señor Virrey Marqués de Guadalcázar ...'. Signed by Gaspar Valle de Acuña and Don Juan de Cervantes Casaus.

increasingly to recognise, it was as much defence expenditure in America as failure of mining that caused decreasing returns of Crown bullion from the colonies to Spain in the seventeenth century.[1] As foreign pressure on all parts of Spanish America (and the Philippines) grew, the colonies proved equal for many years to financing their own defence. But the inevitable concomitant of self-defence was less free wealth for remittance to Spain.

The rising cost of defence goes far towards explaining why Crown remittances to Spain from Mexico were not higher in the 1620s. But if the Crown's share in the postulated mining boom of the decade was thus absorbed, what became of the private share? As Chaunu demonstrates, it appears to have been progressively less dedicated to trade with Europe. Chaunu himself suggests a partial answer. He believes that the growing white (*criollo*) population of New Spain, and particularly of Mexico City itself, became in the seventeenth century a society dedicated to conspicuous consumption (in his own word, 'superconsommatrice').[2] More bullion was being retained for internal circulation; perhaps more was merely being fashioned into ornaments. Largesse may have been the characteristic of the early decades of the seventeenth century. In Zacatecas, it will be recalled, the period 1610 to 1620 was the time of ecclesiastical building; when, for instance, a rich miner donated 100,000 pesos to the Society of Jesus for a new college and church. It is difficult to reconcile these considerations with the notion of economic malaise in New Spain, with the concept of the 'century of depression'. Lynch is obliged to admit this same difficulty. While in general adopting the view that depletion of Indian population led to insuperable problems in agriculture, mining and manufacture, he nevertheless states that Treasury income in New Spain reached a peak in 1623, to decline 'but not substantially' after 1625. 'A hypothesis of depression', he says, is not easily reconciled with this evidence for 'sustained economic activity'.[3] It is indeed not at all easily done. Fortunately, the difficulty is removed if it is conceded that New Spain in all probability experienced economic growth until the 1620s.

The general development of the colony's economy after the 1620s remains unclear. The two major yardsticks by which attempts have normally been made to measure it – Crown remittances to Spain and the progression of external trade – are unreliable for the reasons given in previous pages. Remittances to Spain fell because of the increasing cost

[1] Lynch, *Spain and America*, pp. 199–200.
[2] Chaunu, *Séville*, vol. 8, 1, p. 751.
[3] Lynch, *Spain and America*, pp. 203, 212.

of Imperial defence, and trade probably declined, in large part, because New Spain no longer needed imports from Europe. Essential serial information on the progress of internal economic life in the seventeenth century is not yet available. But even Borah is obliged to concede that in the mid-century, the cities contrived to obtain, in most years, food sufficient for their needs. Did they also obtain sufficient cloth, shoes and craft-goods in general? Did the volume of internal exchange vary, and if so, in accordance with what? These are questions still to be resolved.

In certain respects, Zacatecas may prove to be a model for New Spain in this period. Its use of free labour and capital have already been pointed out as probably being typical of developments in important productive processes in New Spain in the late sixteenth and early seventeenth centuries. It is even possible that since Zacatecas was the colony's major silver producer, its prosperity was a major contributory cause of general prosperity, and its decline an influence for general decline. There is a further general sense in which Zacatecas' history is characteristic of that of New Spain in the seventeenth century. The subject of this concluding chapter has largely been New Spain in the first four decades of that century. These were years of profound changes in Zacatecas and in New Spain; as, indeed, in Spain and Europe. Zacatecas saw the rise and fall of its first major boom; New Spain ceased to be the prime mover of the trans-Atlantic trade, and seemingly became a self-sustaining colony in all important senses. Zacatecas prospered, and then suffered, on account of variations in the supply of mercury and of administrative decisions to exercise stringency with miners where leniency had previously been the rule. Its depression was therefore the direct result of the imposition of external controls – controls applied, in all probability, without realisation of their ultimate effects. Madrid decided to send mercury to Peru rather than to New Spain; Madrid decided to collect the mining debt in 1634. Zacatecas did not recover until new sources of finance for mining were tapped. These sources were the mercaderes de plata, natives of New Spain, and the possessors of capital held in Mexico City. Their reward for participation in mining was a part of the silver formerly paid to the Crown. By establishing claims over miners through credit concessions, they inserted themselves into the process of silver production and deprived the Crown of part of its tax income. They, or their aviador agents, produced silver taxable at a fifth, and either neglected to tax it altogether or obliged miners to tax it at a tenth. The miner, however, became independent of the Crown's credit. Native capital of New Spain, by the mid-seventeenth century, supported the mining industry. And mining, if the Zacatecas district is typical, recovered with the aid of this local capital. Exploration and working of veins was renewed. Mercury supplies increased again as the Crown found that miners were able to pay spot cash.

A similar growth in self-sufficiency was characteristic of all New Spain in the early part of the seventeenth century. This self-sufficiency was basically economic, though it may easily be surmised that economic independence was conducive to the development of a distinctive criollo society among white and near-white inhabitants of the colony. The increasing apartness of New Spain from Europe was not the result, as in the case of Zacatecas, of the imposition from without of restraints on prosperity and the subsequent overcoming of those restraints. It was, paradoxically, the result of fashioning in the New World a diversified and, in contemporary terms, capitalist economy of European type; and of using this economy to exploit the rich assets of Middle America for Middle America's advantage. New Spain, by the 1620s, was able to dispense with Europe as a purveyor of goods and of capital. She ceased to be (as Chaunu characterises all America) an external fountain-head ever pumping wealth across the Atlantic for the sustenance of the European economy, and increasingly conserved her wealth for her own use. New Spain, and Spanish America after her in general, became the financier of her own defence, the supplier of her own needs, and the home of her own distinctive society.

No claims of originality are made for these observations, which are inherent in Chaunu's work, and clearly expressed by Lynch. The ultimate conclusion that Lynch draws from them has not been stated here, however, and should perhaps be remarked upon. He writes of a 'fundamental shift of balance within the Hispanic world', and a movement of that world's 'centre of gravity' across the Atlantic, as a result of the patent economic growth of Spanish America in the seventeenth century.[1] Spain, he says, became the lesser partner in the Empire. These comments seem to imply that the Spanish colonies assumed political power which had previously been Spain's; for it is difficult to see how the Empire's 'centre of gravity' could move (though the expression is imprecise) without carrying political power with it. But little political authority, at least in relation to Europe and the outside world, attached to Spanish America until almost two centuries after New Spain first manifested her economic independence. The seventeenth-century drift of the American colonies away from the metropolis in economic matters certainly weakened Spain as a political power in Europe, but it did not threaten her position as the centre of the Empire nor as a free political agent in Europe and the world.

Lynch, *Spain and America*, pp. 12–13.

Conclusion: Plus Ultra

Zacatecan silver from the district's second boom of the late seventeenth century probably entered the Treasury's chests in Seville in far smaller quantities than had silver from the first boom of that century. The Crown's former income now remained in large part to enrich the citizens of Mexico City. But the mercaderes de plata of the capital, men far more rich and powerful than Chevalier's *latifundistas* of northern New Spain, did not instruct the king in Spanish policy.

Table 1

TABLE I *Amounts of wheat and maize entering the Alhóndiga in Zacatecas*[1]

Period	Source Area[2]	Maize[3]	Wheat[3]
14 November 1634–	Bajío	366	4,304
31 December 1635	Intermediate	1,297	30
(February, March and	Michoacán	10	16
April, 1635, are missing)	Canyons	716	68
	Zacatecas	275	282
	North	none	184
	Not specified	387	364
	Total	3,051	5,248
January–December 1652	Bajío	none	4,005
	Intermediate	674	357
	Michoacán	none	444
	Canyons	1,621	69
	Zacatecas	1,094	102
	North	none	403
	Puebla	53	none
	Not specified	237	360
	Total	3,679	5,740
January–December 1675	Bajío	261	2,481
	Intermediate	824	130
	Michoacán	none	13
	Canyons	265	none
	Zacatecas	66	none
	North	none	none
	Puebla	44	100
	Not specified	1,134	950
	Total	2,594	3,674

Units: cargas.

[1] The libros de manifestaciones used in preparing this Table are from AA.Z' 5, No. 48; AA.Z, 7, No. 25; and AA.Z, 9, No. 23. There are books for other years, but they do not contain enough detail on sources of grain for useful conclusions to be drawn.

[2] *Source areas.* In the libros de manifestaciones a note is generally found of the town of origin of each consignment. In this Table the towns have been grouped into six areas. Where no note was found, and where it has not been possible to locate the town, entries are made under the heading 'not specified'. Towns thus entered were usually small producers; only in 1672 are the amounts so entered large.

Sources have been grouped thus:

1. *Bajío:* Apaseo, Celaya, Chamaquero, Guatzindeo, Irapuato, León, Querétaro, Salamanca, Salvatierra, San Miguel, Silao.
2. *Intermediate zone (between the Bajío and Zacatecas):* Aguascalientes, Lagos, San Luis Potosí (the latter in 1652 only).
3. *Michoacán:* La Barca, Irurapúndaro, Jaconaondo, Tlazazalca, Zamora.
4. *Canyons:* Atotonilco, Colotlán, Huajúcar, Juchipila, Mecatabasco, Tayagua, Teocaltiche, Tlacotlán, Tlaltenango.

237

Table 1

5. *Zacatecas:* Fresnillo, Jerez, Trujillo (hacienda), Zacatecas.
6. *North:* Durango (1652 only), Nombre de Dios, Nuevo León, Parras, Poanas valley, Ramos, Saltillo, Súchil valley.
7. *Puebla:* mentioned in 1652 and 1675, and is listed apart.

[3] Wheat was brought to Zacatecas as milled flour. Maize arrived as grain. The making of *tortillas*, the principal form in which maize is eaten, demands the softening of the grain with lime before grinding. When the flour is prepared, it must be used quickly. Hence it was neither necessary nor practicable to import milled maize. Maize used as fodder obviously did not need milling.

Table 2

Date	Pesos per carga	oz. of bread for 1 real	oz. of bran for 1 real
1561	18½–23	—	—
May 1598	—	22	—
June 1598	—	26	48
1602	11½	—	—
January 1605	—	26	—
1608	11½	—	—
November 1608	9¼	24	48
February 1609	—	26	52
July 1609	—	24	48
February 1612	—	21	42
September 1612	—	24	48
February 1637	—	24	48
July 1639	—	28	56
September 1640	10–10½	30	60
June 1644	12–13½	26	52
June 1670	—	28	56
July 1693	17–18	—	—
April 1695	30–36	—	—

Prices of bran (*acemitas*) are generally half those of bread.

Sources. AA.Z, LC 2, LC 3, *passim*, LC 9, ff. 138–9; AA.Z, 6, Nos. 43, 47, 57; AA.Z, 7, Nos. 8, 38; AA.Z, 8, No. 5; AA.Z, 11, No. 14; 1561 price from Ahumada, 'Información', p. 251; 1602 price from Mota y Escobar, *Descripción geográfica*, p. 73; 1608 prices from 'Relación ... de Zacatecas', *DII* vol. 9, p. 187.

Table 3

Table 3

TABLE 3 *Some prices of beef, mutton, hides and tallow, 1612 to 1691. All prices are expressed in reales; the prometido is in pesos*[1]

Year	Novillo (lb. per real)	Single carnero	Carnero (lb. per real)	Hide (novillo)	Hide (carnero)	Arroba of tallow	Prometido
1612–13	10	14	2½	11	1	28	500
1614–15	11	16	10	8	1	28	700
1616	9	16	2	12	2	28	400
1618	9	—	2	12	2	28	500
1619	8	—	2	12	2	—	500
1624–5	7	16	2	14	2	28–30†	700
1627–8	7	16	2	15	2	30	600
1640–1	15	12–13*	2½	8	—	20	1,000
1643–5	14	20–22*	1½	8	2	28	800
1645–8	14	16–20*	2	6	2	28	1,000
1648–50	12	16–20*	2	8	1	28	1,100
1652	11	16–20*	2	10	2	24	800
1691	10	11–13*	2½	8	2	20	600

* The lower price refers to carcase; the higher to animals on the hoof.
† The lower price for miners only.

[1] *Sources.* Prices shown here are taken from the periodic auctions of the meat-supply contract in Zacatecas. The auctions are to be found in legajos of the Ayuntamiento Archive of Zacatecas (AA.Z), as follows: 1612–13, 3, No. 8; 1614–15, 3, No. 24; 1616, 3, No. 25; 1618, 3, No. 32; 1619, 3, No. 36; 1624–5, 4, No. 27; 1627–8, 4, No. 81; 1640–1, 5, No. 85; 1643–5, 6, No. 37; 1645–8, 6, No. 64; 1648, 6, No. 92; 1650–2, 7, No. 14; 1691, 11, No. 19.

Table 4

TABLE 4 Silver presented for taxation at the Real Caja de Zacatecas in the sixteenth and seventeenth centuries (value in marks)[1]

Period[2]	Plata del diezmo	Plata del quinto	Total
1 January 1559–31 December 1559	62,398	22,297	84,695
1560	78,112	24,894	103,006
1561	68,189	39,351	107,540
1562	79,572	38,671	118,243
1563	100,980	30,894	131,874
1564	99,540	27,171	126,711
1565	104,276	23,110	127,386
1566	113,301	16,174	129,475
1567	127,595	11,761	139,356
1568	123,058	18,126	141,184
1569	124,266	13,701	137,967
1570	130,519	15,595	146,114
1571	111,564	33,794	145,358
1572	105,942	42,577	148,519
1573	116,510	49,400	165,910
1574	110,645	50,217	160,862
1575	116,762	54,242	171,004
1576	113,599	51,567	165,166
1577	84,991	32,377	117,368
1578	96,309	38,291	134,600
1579	91,914	36,608	128,522
1580	Account missing		
1581	85,500	33,995	119,495
1582	91,615	29,748	121,363
1583	93,069	24,215	117,284
1584[3]	88,000	28,000	116,000
1585	104,354	29,989	134,343
1586	Account missing		
2 April 1587–21 March 1588	85,386	24,171	109,557
April–December 1588	Account missing		
1589	99,887	28,514	128,401
1590	112,256	27,530	139,786
1591	103,542	31,532	135,074
1592	104,005	28,666	132,671
1593	82,137	24,158	106,295
1594	88,469	21,571	110,040
1595	90,447	20,512	110,959
(1 January 1596–28 March 1596	23,487	5,954	29,441)
1 April 1596–31 March 1597[3]	69,000	16,000	85,000
10 April 1597–23 February 1598	74,311	18,289	92,600
2 April 1598–31 March 1599	87,490	18,648	106,138
2 April 1599–31 March 1600[3]	92,000	16,000	108,000
1 April 1600–29 March 1601	96,822	20,269	117,091
2 April 1601–28 March 1602	96,388	18,672	115,060
1 April 1602–29 March 1603	113,741	18,920	132,661
3 April 1603–31 March 1604	119,363	21,572	140,935

z.—9   241

Table 4

Period[2]	Plata del diezmo	Plata del quinto	Total
1 April 1604–31 March 1605	109,325	19,503	128,828
April 1605–March 1606	Account missing		
1 April 1606–31 March 1607	124,463	22,291	146,754
1 April 1607–30 March 1608	126,706	23,087	149,793
10 April 1608–31 March 1609	127,580	27,286	154,866
1 April 1609–31 March 1610	110,154	26,470	136,624
1 April 1610–30 March 1611	138,285	25,579	163,864
1 April 1611–31 March 1612	151,248	27,573	178,821
1 April 1612–31 March 1613	159,955	25,973	185,928
(1 April 1613–13 December 1613	130,048	23,882	153,930)
1 April 1614–31 March 1615	170,107	26,936	197,043
1 April 1615–31 March 1616	206,227	31,569	237,796
1 April 1616–31 March 1617	175,432	27,541	202,973
1 April 1617–31 March 1618	178,213	20,648	198,861
1 April 1618–31 March 1619	196,936	28,376	225,312
1 April 1619–30 March 1620	223,905	30,525	254,430
1 May 1620–30 April 1621	160,601	20,255	180,856
1 May 1621–30 April 1622	182,678	52,206	234,884
1 May 1622–30 April 1623	214,286	53,952	268,238
1 May 1623–30 April 1624	218,813	37,903	256,716
1 May 1624–30 April 1625	211,504	21,403	232,907
1 May 1625–6 May 1626	217,914	14,765	232,679
7 May 1626–30 April 1627	185,967	9,489	195,456
1 May 1627–30 April 1628	188,463	6,342	194,805
1 May 1628–30 April 1629	233,375	3,995	237,370
1 May 1629–30 April 1630	192,438	9,730	202,168
1 May 1630–30 April 1631	?	?	224,889
1 May 1631–30 April 1632	234,930	10,157	245,087
1 May 1632–30 April 1633	205,652	4,614	210,266
1 May 1633–30 April 1634	216,377	3,309	219,686
1 May 1634–30 April 1635	205,207	3,008	208,215
1 May 1635–30 April 1636	?	?	172,358
1 May 1636–30 April 1637	149,230	1,492	150,722
30 May 1637–30 April 1638	135,556	2,305	137,861
1 May 1638–16 April 1639	136,935	6,630	143,565
18 April 1639–13 April 1640	117,695	7,683	125,378
17 April 1640–30 April 1641	113,178	7,308	120,486
(1 May 1641–6 March 1642	113,735	6,085	119,820)
8 March 1642–30 April 1643	129,545	14,691	144,236
1 May 1643–30 April 1644	121,365	3,960	125,325
1 May 1644–30 April 1645	110,879	2,673	113,552
1 May 1645–30 April 1646	110,719	2,617	113,336
(5 April 1646–4 January 1647	106,725	7,027	113,752)
(4 January 1647–30 April 1648	153,475	1,959	155,434)
(2 May 1648–3 January 1649	77,583	317	77,900)
(4 January 1649–13 June 1650	187,628	1,834	189,462)
(14 June 1650–1 February 1651	84,985	751	85,736)
(1 February 1651–30 April 1652	159,697	3,469	163,166)
1 May 1652–22 April 1653	125,146	2,207	127,353

Table 4

Period[2]	Plata del diezmo	Plata del quinto	Total
1 May 1653–30 April 1654	160,280	2,904	163,184
1 May 1654–30 June 1655	151,090	2,503	153,593
1 July 1655–30 June 1656	129,188	1,346	130,534
(8 July 1656–5 May 1657	87,697	482	88,179)
5 May 1657–30 April 1658	121,307	1,317	122,624
1 May 1658–30 April 1659	116,360	974	117,334
2 May 1659–30 April 1660	118,271	778	119,049
1 May 1660–30 April 1661	112,680	850	113,530
1 May 1661–30 April 1662	102,858	1,601	104,459
1 May 1662–30 April 1663	92,886	3,928	96,814
May 1663–April 1664	Account missing		
(1 May 1664–28 February 1665	73,638	4,725	78,363)
(28 February 1665–19 August 1666	154,008	3,218	157,226)
(19 August 1666–30 June 1667	104,339	1,554	105,893)
(1 July 1667–30 April 1668	115,492	806	116,298)
1 May 1668–18 May 1669	168,340	1,478	169,818
22 May 1669–30 June 1670	176,962	677	177,639
1 July 1670–17 July 1671	206,601	—	206,601

After this date, plata del diezmo is recorded under two headings: that produced by amalgamation (plata de azogue) and that produced by smelting (plata de fundición).

Period	Plata de azogue	Plata de fundición	Plata del quinto	Total
(17 July 1671–24 October 1671	20,020	42,324	—	62,344)
(24 October 1671–30 June 1673	139,077	236,024	2,463	377,564)
1 July 1673–4 June 1674	72,105	135,571	329	208,005
(4 June 1674–22 October 1675	145,666	161,408	3,235	310,309)
22 October 1675–30 November 1676	110,980	118,196	507	229,683
(1 December 1676–11 May 1678	136,428	266,040	1,069	403,537)
(12 May 1678–31 July 1679	127,726	197,520	555	325,801)
1 August 1679–30 June 1680	111,651	165,578	2,174	279,403
1 July 1680–30 June 1681	138,036	211,492	2,382	351,910
1 July 1681–30 June 1682[4]	124,922	96,006	2,064	222,992
1 July 1682–1 January 1684	Account missing			
(1 January 1684–24 September 1684	73,736	26,166	1,106	101,008)
(30 September 1684–31 December 1685[3]	107,000	30,832	1,566	139,398)
(1 January 1686–29 March 1687	127,789	37,343	2,047	167,179)
5 April 1687–12 March 1688	104,003	40,706	685	145,394
16 March 1688–1 May 1689	76,412	66,961	475	143,848
2 May 1689–19 April 1690	93,214	49,264	160	142,638
(20 April 1690–24 February 1692	108,560	114,026	918	223,504)
25 February 1692–30 April 1693	83,509	98,725	1,173	183,407
(1 May 1693–21 April 1696	238,567	182,655	521	421,743)
(22 April 1696–12 November 1697	103,997	79,587	—	183,584)
(15 November 1697–4 January 1699	18,562	84,927	—	103,489)

243

Table 4

Period	Plata de azogue	Plata de fundición	Plata del quinto	Total
5 January 1699–31 December 1699	48,294	90,338	351	138,983
1 January 1700–31 December 1700[2]	79,000	63,000	160	142,160
1 January 1701–31 December 1701	68,336	51,432	—	119,768
1702[2]	67,000	63,000	—	130,000
1703	Account missing			
1704[2]	74,000	62,000	500	136,500
1705[2]	88,000	91,000	450	179,450
1706[2]	62,000	77,000	—	139,000
1707[2]	71,000	64,000	—	135,000
1708[2]	85,000	71,000	—	156,000
1709[2,5]	183,000		1,000	184,000
1710[2,5]	196,000		—	196,000
1711[2,5]	229,000		—	229,000
1712[2]	104,000	70,000	—	174,000
1713[2,5]	185,000		—	185,000
1714[2,5]	157,000		—	157,000
1715	Account missing			
1716[2,5]	242,000		—	242,000
1717[2,5]	236,000		—	236,000
1718[2]	145,000	112,000	—	257,000
1719[2]	147,000	127,000	—	274,000
1720[2,5]	275,000		—	275,000

[1] *Sources.* Figures presented in this Table were taken from accounts of the Real Caja de Zacatecas (with the exception of those given for 1575–7) in the following legajos of AGI Contaduría: 841 (1558–74), 858 (duplicates of Zacatecas accounts in 'Real Caja de Guadalajara, Cuentas de Real Hacienda 1575–7, con duplicados'), 842A (1578–81, 1593–1605), 842B (1582–92), 850 (1606–13), 845B (1614–22), 845A (1623–38), 846A (1638–47), 846B (1647–55), 847A (1656–68), 847B (1668–74), 848A (1674–80), 848B (1680–97), 849 (1697–1720). Also used was AGI Guadalajara 413, 'Audiencia de Guadalajara. Duplicados de sujetos particulares del distrito de aquella audiencia: años de 1653–1693', which contains duplicates of the accounts of the Treasury at Zacatecas for the periods 1 July 1681–30 June 1682, 1 January 1684–24 September 1684, and 30 September 1684–31 December 1685. In most of these accounts the total yearly quantity of silver presented for taxation is given in marks. In a few years, only the tax yield of the quintos and diezmos is given, in pesos de oro común. From this yield the amount presented, in marks, may be calculated. See below, note 3.

[2] *Period.* Most of the figures presented here are taken from Libros comunes de cuenta, or summary accounts, drawn up yearly by the Treasury officials of Zacatecas. Thus most figures refer to silver presented for taxation over a period of twelve months. Until 1595, accounts were taken for the calendar year, January to December. Thereafter the financial year was generally counted from April to March, or later, from May to April. (Variations may readily be seen in the Table.) Since accounts were immediately closed when one of the Treasury officials died or was removed from office, and sometimes when a visitor arrived, interruptions of the normal accounting year were common. In the second half of the seventeenth century, periods of accounts were especially irregular and it is not always possible to give yearly totals. Where an account period is so much longer or shorter than twelve months that figures for that period are not comparable with those coming before or after them, the whole entry has been placed in brackets.

244

Table 4

³ *Derived totals.* As noted in 1 above, for some years, because of deficiency or loss of accounts, it was possible to record only the tax collected on silver presented at the Real Caja de Zacatecas, quoted in pesos de oro común. (Contaduría 849, containing accounts from 1697 onwards, gives brief summaries, in which only yields of diezmos and quintos in pesos are quoted.) Amounts, in marks, of silver presented for taxation may easily be derived from the tax yield. Until 1712, the only taxes levied on silver at Zacatecas were the quinto, diezmo and the *uno por ciento*. Each mark of silver was therefore taxed with a deduction of $1/5 + 1\%$ or $1/10 + 1\%$:

i.e. 20·8% or 10·9% (208/1000) or (109/1000).

Up to the end of the sixteenth century a mark of silver was valued, for the purposes of taxation, at 65 reales or tomines (i.e. 8 pesos de oro común, 1 real). Therefore, to convert the tax yields in pesos to amounts of silver presented in marks, the yield must be multiplied, for diezmos, by a factor of $(8 \times 1000)/(65 \times 109) = 1·129$; and for quintos, by a factor of $(8 \times 1000)/65 \times 208) = 0·592$. By 1700, a mark of pure silver was valued at 70 reales (8 pesos 6 reales) and on some silver a mintage tax (*señoreaje*) of 1 real per mark was charged. Thus the factor for conversion of tax yields in pesos to marks of silver presented must be changed for use with figures from the early years of the eighteenth century. By the method of calculation illustrated above, the following factors were determined: for diezmo + 1%, 1·048; for diezmo + 1% + señoreaje, 0·929; for quinto + 1%, 0·549. Figures arrived at by using these factors cannot be exact. They have been reduced to the nearest thousand, except in the case of quintos, which are so small that they have been reduced to the nearest fifty, or even ten, in one case (1700). In the period 1684–5 only the figures for plata de azogue have been derived.

⁴ From November 1681 silver produced in the district of Sombrerete was presented for taxation at the Real Caja established in Sombrerete in that month. Silver taxed there is recorded separately in Table 7.

⁵ In these years, plata de azogue and plata de fundición are not separated. An aggregate total is given.

Table 5

TABLE 5 *Five-yearly totals of all silver presented for taxation at the Real Caja de Zacatecas from 1560 to 1720*

Period[1]	Marks
1 January 1560–31 December 1564	587,374
1 January 1565–31 December 1569	675,368
1 January 1570–31 December 1574	766,763
1 January 1575–31 December 1579	716,620
1 January 1580–31 December 1584	582,415[2]
1 January 1585–31 December 1589	617,169[2]
1 January 1590–31 December 1594	623,866
1 January 1595–31 March 1600	532,138
1 April 1600–31 March 1605	634,575
1 April 1605–31 March 1610	735,046[2]
1 April 1610–31 March 1615	879,586
1 April 1615–31 March 1620	1,119,372
1 May 1620–30 April 1625	1,173,601
1 May 1625–30 April 1630	1,052,478
1 May 1630–30 April 1635	1,108,143
1 May 1635–13 April 1640	729,889
17 April 1640–30 April 1645	623,419
1 May 1645–13 June 1650	609,884
14 June 1650–30 June 1655	693,033
1 July 1655–30 April 1660	577,720
1 May 1660–28 February 1665	490,083[2]
28 February 1665–30 June 1670	726,874
1 July 1670–22 October 1675	1,164,823
22 October 1675–30 June 1680	1,238,424
1 January 1681–31 December 1685	600,000[3]
1 January 1686–19 April 1690	599,059
20 April 1690–April 1695	688,073[4]
April 1695–31 December 1699	566,637[4]
1 January 1700–31 December 1704	660,535[2]
1 January 1705–31 December 1709	793,450
1 January 1710–31 December 1714	941,000
1715 – account missing	—
1 January 1716–31 December 1720	1,284,000

[1] Wherever possible, the amount of silver taxed during a full 60-month period is shown. But because of irregularities in accounts, periods sometimes exceed, or fall short of, that number of months. There is an error of 8 months in the period 1686–90, which, as it appears in the Table, contains 52 months. Elsewhere the largest error is of 4 months (in 1665–70 and 1695–9).

[2] In these periods, a year or more is missing in the accounts. Quinquennial totals have been obtained by scaling the average amount of silver presented during the remaining years of the quinquennium. The following accounts are missing: January to December 1580, January to December 1586, January to March 1587, April to December 1588, April 1605 to March 1606, May 1663 to April 1664, and January to December 1703 and 1715.

[3] It is difficult to arrive at an accurate quinquennial total for silver presented at the Zacatecas Caja from 1681 to 1685, since accounts are missing from 1 July 1682 to 1 January 1684.

Table 5

Moreover, the first account of the quinquennium, running from 1 July 1681 to 30 June 1682, shows a figure containing some silver from Sombrerete, and is therefore of little use in calculating how much silver was taxed at Zacatecas itself. A round figure of 600,000 marks for the quinquennium has been arrived at by calculating the monthly average from 1 January 1684 to 31 December 1685, and assuming that the same average held good for the previous three years. The quinquennial total is therefore $(240,405 \times 60)/24$ marks $(= ca.\ 600,000)$.

4 The 421,743 marks given in the account for 1 May 1693 to 21 April 1696 were divided into three equal parts. Two parts were attributed to the quinquennium 1690 to 1695; one part to 1695 to 1699.

Table 6

TABLE 6 *Quantities of amalgamated and smelted silver presented for taxation at the Real Caja de Zacatecas from 1670 to 1705, in five-yearly totals (value in marks)*[1]

Period	Plata de azogue	Plata de fundición
1 July 1670–22 October 1675	459,000[2]	700,000[2]
23 October 1675–30 June 1680	486,784	747,334
1 July 1680–31 December 1685	455,000[3]	145,000[3]
1 January 1686–19 April 1690	401,419	194,274
20 April 1690–April 1695	351,113[4]	334,521[4]
April 1695–31 December 1699	250,375[5]	315,737[5]
1 January 1700–31 December 1705	376,336[6]	330,432[6]

[1] Figures are derived from Table 4. Sources are indicated in notes to that Table.

[2] It will be seen in Table 4 that separate accounting of smelted and amalgamated silver does not begin until July 1671. To provide a full quinquennium's figures here, therefore, silver production from July 1670 to July 1671 has been scaled in proportion to the smelted/amalgamated ratio from 1671 to 1675, and the results added to the appropriate totals. Figures for this quinquennium are therefore approximations.

[3] These figures are arrived at by scaling the total amount of silver believed to have been presented at Zacatecas in the period 1 January 1680 to 31 December 1685 in accordance with the ratio of plata de azogue to plata de fundición observable in the accounts of 1 January 1684 to 31 December 1685. See note 3 of Table 5.
A difficulty in arriving at totals for these years is that there is only one account for the period 1 May 1693 to 21 April 1696. To produce reasonable totals for the quinquennium 1690 to 1695, the plata de azogue and plata de fundición figures for the three years May 1693 to April 1696 were divided into thirds. Two thirds were included in the totals for 1690 to 1695 and one third in those for 1695 to 1699.

[5] See note 4 above.

[6] The period for which these figures are given appears to be six years, not five. But nothing is included for 1603, since the account for that year is missing. The figures relate therefore to a period of only sixty months.

Table 7

TABLE 7 *Silver presented for taxation at the Real Caja de Sombrerete from 6 May 1683 to 31 December 1720 (value in marks)*[1]

Period	Plata de azogue	Plata de fuego	Plata del quinto	Total
6 May 1683–1 December 1683[2]	13,000	67,000	500	80,500
2 December 1683–21 July 1684	21,000	54,000	—	75,000
August 1684–February 1688	Account missing			
18 March 1688–6 May 1689	30,771	131,380	198	162,349
6 May 1689–31 August 1690	32,774	138,157	353	171,248
1 September 1690–26 January 1692	20,909	156,772	1,298	178,979
February 1692–May 1694	Account missing			
5 June 1694–5 February 1695	18,212	34,533	100	52,845
6 February 1695–30 April 1696	22,371	70,691	—	93,062
1 May 1696–20 May 1697	12,000	46,000	—	58,000
21 May 1697–5 November 1699	11,000	76,000	—	87,000
6 November 1699–18 May 1701	13,000	51,000	—	64,000
19 May 1701–26 February 1703	16,000	37,000	100	53,100
27 February 1703–21 August 1705	20,000	50,000	—	70,000
13 August 1705–31 December 1706	20,000	11,000	—	31,000
1 January 1707–31 December 1707	13,000	38,000	—	51,000
1 January 1708–31 December 1708	8,000	20,000	—	28,000
1 January 1709–31 December 1709	7,000	19,000	—	26,000
1 February 1710–31 March 1711	7,000	22,000	—	29,000
1 April 1711–27 January 1712	2,000	11,000	—	13,000
28 January 1712–27 January 1713	5,000	26,000	—	31,000
28 January 1713–27 January 1714	4,000	12,000	—	16,000
28 January 1714–31 December 1714	6,000	14,000	—	20,000
1 January 1715–31 December 1715	7,000	8,000	—	15,000
1716	10,000	10,000	—	20,000
1717	6,000	12,000	200	18,200
1718	4,000	17,000	—	21,000
1719	4,000	13,000	—	17,000
1720	2,000	9,000	—	11,000

[1] *Sources.* AGI Contaduría 932 (Sombrerete accounts for 6 May 1683–21 July 1684 and 1 May 1696–31 December 1720). AGI Contaduría 931 (Sombrerete accounts for 18 March 1688–30 April 1696).

[2] Figures for all years except the period 18 March 1688–30 April 1696 are derived from tax yields by the method described in note 3 of Table 4. They are given to the nearest 1,000 marks.

Table 8

TABLE 8 *Five-yearly totals of all silver presented for taxation at the Real Caja de Sombrerete from 1681 to 1720*

Period[1]	Marks
1681–5[2]	640,920
1686–90[2]	640,920
30 April 1692–28 April 1697[3]	361,195
6 November 1699–21 August 1705[4]	187,000
13 August 1705–31 December 1709	136,000
1 February 1710–31 December 1714	109,000
1 January 1715–31 December 1719	91,200
(1 January 1720–31 December 1720	11,559)

[1] Because the account periods of the Sombrerete Caja from 1683 to 1699 are irregular, and because accounts for those years are not continuous, it is impossible to derive useful quinquennial totals from the figures presented in Table 7 for the last years of the seventeenth century. Quinquennial totals for 1681–99 are therefore taken from other sources, described below in notes 2 and 3.

[2] These figures are taken from H. L. Heldt, *Historical Sketch of the Sombrerete Mines* (Sombrerete, Zac., 1911), p. 5, where it is stated that from 1681 to 1690 inclusive 1,281,839 marks of silver were presented for assay and taxing at Sombrerete. This figure has simply been halved to give quinquennial totals for 1681–5 and 1686–90. The resulting figures of 640,920 marks for each quinquennium cannot, of course, be exact representations of amounts of silver taxed. But there is evidence that production during the whole decade 1681–90 was steady. It will be seen from the yearly totals given in Table 7 that average monthly production from 6 May 1683 to 21 July 1684 was 10,746 marks; and from 18 March 1688 to 31 August 1690, 11,505 marks. This is some evidence that production in the two quinquennia 1681–5 and 1686–90 was roughly equal. Heldt does not give sources for his production figures, but they appear quite accurate. For example, his total (p. 6) for the decade 1701–10, of 292,295 marks, corresponds closely to the total indicated by Table 7 for the same years – 288,000 marks.

[3] This figure is from AGI Contaduría 931 – 'Sombrerete. Con relación de oficiales reales desde 1692 hasta 1696': an expediente relating quantities of silver received from various mining towns in the district of Sombrerete from 20 April 1692 to 29 April 1697.

[4] From November 1699, quinquennial totals are derived from yearly totals given in Table 7.

Table 9a

TABLE 9a *Amounts of mercury arriving and being distributed in Zacatecas in the seventeenth century*[1]

Period[2]	quintales	libras
September 1608–March 1610	1,352	50
April 1610–March 1615	6,027	70
April 1615–April 1620	9,009	2
November 1620–December 1624	5,949	—
January 1625–December 1629	10,299	43
February 1631–December 1632	4,997	43
May 1635–December 1639	4,200	—
January 1640–November 1644	6,298	59
February 1645–November 1649	4,695	—
November 1650–December 1654	3,600	—
July 1655–August 1659[3]	2,000	—
July 1660–October 1664	1,631	$7\frac{1}{2}$
December 1665–August 1669	2,054	49
September 1670–June 1674	3,632	66
March 1675–December 1679	4,060	17
June 1680–November 1684	5,354	70
December 1685–January 1689	2,986	73
January 1690–March 1694	3,444	56
October 1695–December 1698	1,596	75

[1] *Sources*. Amounts of mercury actually distributed to miners at Zacatecas from September 1608 to April 1620 are given in the *sumarios de cargos y datas de azogues* to be found in AGI Contaduría 843A and 843B. After 1620 the sumarios do not show distribution. All figures in this Table for the years after 1620 refer to arrivals of mercury in Zacatecas. Up to 1632 and for 1637–8, figures for incoming consignments of mercury are taken from accounts of payments made to carters who carried mercury from Mexico City to Zacatecas. These accounts, included in the sumarios, tell not only how much the carter was paid, but also how much quicksilver he transported. There are no sumarios for 1633–5; but those for the period 1620 to 1656 in general are in AGI Contaduría 843A, 844, 846A and 846B. Sumarios become progressively less detailed after 1620, so information on mercury arrivals given here for the years after 1640 is taken from documents in AT.Z. See the *libros manuales* of the *ramo de consumido y quinceno* in Azogues 1 (1642–54), Azogues 2 (1655–60), Azogues 3 (1662–79), Azogues 4 (1681–9) and Azogues 5 (1697–1704). See also AT.Z, Reales Oficiales 14, 18, 22, 23, 24, 26, 27, 29, 30 and 31 for scattered summaries of accounts of mercury payments and taxes.

[2] Mercury did not arrive in Zacatecas at regular intervals. Because of this, it is not possible to give yearly totals of incoming consignments; and to record each consignment separately would not be illuminating. So, for ease of comparison-making between different periods, five-yearly totals are given. For some years, loss of accounts or scarcity of information has prevented the compiling of a full quinquennial total. In any given period of five years, the first date indicates the first consignment arriving in that quinquennium, and the second date, the last.

[3] There is reason to think that the figures given here for the years after 1660 understate the amounts of mercury reaching Zacatecas. This is because in 1658, for the first time, issues of mercury were made to individual miners in Zacatecas directly from Mexico City. These issues were not handled by the Treasury officials of Zacatecas, and so they do not

Table 9a

appear in the accounts from which this Table is compiled. It is difficult to say how much these remittances to individuals added to total arrivals. Sources are very few. But one period for which full information is available is January 1658 to September 1663. In this time, the grand total of all mercury arriving in Zacatecas was 2,399½ quintales; of which 519½, or about 22 per cent, were sent directly to individuals. Again, in 1687, of 726 quintales sent to Zacatecas and Sombrerete, 126, or some 17 per cent, were consigned to individual miners directly. Thus it seems (although on slight evidence, for it is not clear how often these individual issues were made) that the amounts of mercury actually reaching Zacatecas in the last forty years of the century may well have been about a fifth greater than the figures in the Table indicate. Sources for this supposition are: AGI Mexico 611, an untitled expediente of mercury accounts and related documents referring to receipts of mercury in New Spain from 1650 to 1669, foliated 2–426, here f. 277v., 'Distribución de azogues en los reales almacenes de esta ciudad de México de la Nueva España, desde el año de 1651 hasta fin del de 663'; and a 'Certificación con individualidad de la forma en que se han repartido así los azogues que había en los almacenes el día en que Vuestra Excelencia tomó posesión como los dos mil y cien quintales que trajeron los navíos del cargo del Almirante Real Don Francisco Navarro' – which is an enclosure in Monclova to Crown, 'No. 20', México 10 August 1687, in AGI Mexico 612.

Table 9b

TABLE 9b *Total distribution of mercury in New Spain, and mercury assigned to Zacatecas, in certain years*

Year	New Spain	Zacatecas		
1609(?)[1]	4,170*			1,000*
1630[2]	3,262			2,000
1632[2]	3,415			2,000
1636[3]	5,398*			2,000*
1651–64[4]	25,565			7,019
1675[5]	2,448			800
1686–7[6]	2,139	Zacatecas	526	} 726
		Sombrerete	200	
1695[7]	4,329	Zacatecas	945	} 1,110
		Sombrerete	165	

Units: quintales. Figures are to the nearest quintal.

* Figures thus marked refer to estimated demand for mercury. Other figures are for quantities of mercury actually distributed.

[1] BM Add. MS. 13,992, f. 513, 'Tanteo del azogue que las minas de esta Nueva España han menester en cada un año para su beneficio y cómo se reparten ...'; (n.d., but almost certainly 1609).

[2] AGI Mexico 35 R. 1, 'Del gobierno en la Nueva España. 1639. Para la carta del Virrey, No. 19. "Testimonio de los autos sobre el repartimiento de los azogues que el año de 637 vinieron a cargo del Capitán D. Baltasar de Torres y el Marqués de Cardenosa" '. (Final date) Madrid 5 September 1639, ff. 25, 26–26v.

[3] AGI Mexico 31, Cuaderno 1, ff. 189–90v, 'Relación de los azogues que son precisos cada año para los consumidos y depósitos ordinarios de todos los puestos y reales de minas de esta Nueva España y cajas de ella'; anon., n.d., but certainly 1636.

[4] AGI Mexico 611, Untitled expediente of mercury accounts and related documents referring to receipts of mercury in New Spain from 1650 to 1669; foliated 2–426. Here, ff. 189v–239, 'Data y distribución de dicho azogue'.

[5] AGI Mexico 612, México 13 November 1675, Archbishop Payo to Queen Regent, 'No. 5'.

[6] AGI Mexico 612, México 10 August 1687, Monclova to king, 'No. 20'; containing 'Certificación con individualidad de la forma en que se han repartido así los azogues que había en los almacenes el día en que Vuestra Excelencia tomó posesión como los dos mil y cien quintales que trajeron los navíos del cargo del Almirante Real D. Francisco Navarro ...', Treasury officials to viceroy, México 11 July 1687. Before 1681, mercury destined for Sombrerete was sent to Zacatecas. But in that year Sombrerete received its own caja real. To maintain comparability with previous figures, the sum of consignments to Zacatecas and Sombrerete must obviously be given here.

[7] AGI Mexico 64 R. 1, 'México, y Abril 17 de 1696 años. Decreto y certificación del Contador de azogues y tributos de los que en el aviso y flota se recibieron y como fueron repartidos; y haber en los reales almacenes cinco quintales solamente'; signed by D. Fernando Deza y Ulloa; final date, México 23 April 1696.

253

Table 10a

TABLE 10a Five-yearly totals of all mercury exported from Spain to the New World, 1565 to 1700, according to destination[1]

Period	New Spain	Peru	Honduras	New Granada	Santa Marta	Santo Domingo
1565–9[2]	4,804	[3]	—	—	—	—
1570–4	9,352	—	—	—	—	—
1575–9	13,336	—	199	—	—	—
1580–4	8,274	—	501	—	—	—
1585–9	12,537	—	466	499	—	—
1590–4	14,445	—	222	150	—	180
1595–9	12,027	—	—	60	—	100
1600–4	15,340	—	—	78	—	—
1605–9	15,062	3,031	—	—	—	—
1610–14	16,665	1,000	—	—	—	—
1615–19	24,032	—	280	300	—	—
1620–4	21,646[4]	10,502	399	1,100	200	—
1625–9	19,108[4]	9,006	401	1,100	—	—
1630–4	17,785[4]	13,051	99	1,121	—	—
1635–9	5,124[4, 5]	18,276	?	?	?	?
1640–4	18,624	16,740	?	?	?	?
1645–9	8,969	?	?	?	?	?
1650–4	12,362[4]	4,358	?	?	?	?
1655–9	10,808[4]	?	?	?	?	?
1660–4	7,390[4]	—	—	760	—	—
1665–9	9,043[4]	—	150	300	—	—
1670–4	12,328	—	—	606	—	—
1675–9	11,100	—	—	300	—	—
1680–4	8,724	—	—	500	—	—
1685–9	9,603	—	—	—	—	—
1690–4	6,792	—	—	300	—	—
1695–9	10,150	—	—	200	—	—
(1700	2,494	—	—	—	—	—

Units: quintales. Figures are to the nearest quintal.

[1] Sources. 1565–93, to all destinations – AGI Contaduría 331, 'Cuentas del Factor Don Francisco Duarte respectivas a azogue; desde 1562 a 1593, con documentos por duplicado. 1º, cargos y datas de estas cuentas en 2 ramos'. (Ramo 1 to 1579, ramo 2 from 1580 to 1593); 1594–1634, to all destinations, except New Spain 1624–34, – AGI Contratación 4324, 'Contratación de Sevilla. Libros de Cargo y Data de Azogues recibidos y entregados por los Factores. En 4 números'. (No. 1, 1580–1610; No. 2, 1607–21; No. 3, 1623–34); 1624–34, to New Spain – AGI Mexico 31, 'Audiencia de México. Cartas y Expedientes del Virrey, vistos en el Consejo, años de 1632 a 1636', (the final item in this), 'Cuaderno de cartas que el Marqués de Cadereita, Virrey de la Nueva España, escribió a su Magestad, el año de 1636' (foliated 1–254, here ff. 187–8v.); 1636, to New Spain – AGI Mexico 31, Cuaderno, f. 131, Mexico City 15 June 1636, Cadereita to king, 'Gobierno'; 1638, to New Spain – AGI Mexico 34, Cuaderno, f. 81, Mexico City 12 July 1638, Cadereita to king, 'Hacienda Real'; 1640, to New Spain – Chaunu, Séville, vol. V, p. 360, quoting AGI Contratación 5118, Veracruz 15 July 1641, Treasury officials to Casa de la Contratación; 1642–8, to New Spain – AGI Indiferente General 1777, 'Relación de los azogues que se han enviado a la Nueva España desde el año de 1642 hasta este de 648 que son 23,182 quintales y los

Table 10a

que escribió el Marqués de Cadereita son necesarios al año que son de 8,000 a diez mil al año'. (n.d., anon.); 1635–44, to Peru – AGI Contaduría 404, 'Relaciones de los gastos de Galeones y Flotas con varios oficios y ordenes desde 1610 a 1704', No. 3, 'Cuentas de los azogues entrados en las Atarazanas de Sevilla, y de los remitidos a las Indias; con varias ordenes y otros papeles sobre este asunto. 1623 a 1660'; 1650–67, to New Spain – AGI Contaduría 1002, 'Asientos y Cuentas de Azogues: desde 1571 a 657' (sic), R. 4, 'Relación con cargo y data de los azogues remitidos a Nueva España de que se hicieron cargo los oficiales Reales de México, cuyo producto remitieron en la flota del General Adrián Pulido'; 1651–8, to Peru – AGI Contaduría 404, No. 3 (see full title, above); 1661–1700, to all destinations – AGI Contratación 4324, No. 4 (see full title, above).

Figures for yearly remittances of mercury to America are given by Chaunu, in *Séville*, vol. VII, 2(*bis*), pp. 1958–71. Any discrepancies between his figures and the quinquennial totals given here may be attributed to occasional use of different sources and differences in interpreting the accounts. It is necessary, though, to point out one printing error in Chaunu's table. On page 1962, all figures under 'Îles' should be moved one column to the left, to fall under 'Honduras'. It is quite clear from Chaunu's quoted source, AGI Contratación 4324, that in these years (1615–25) no mercury was sent to the Caribbean islands. But it was sent to Honduras.

² Official exports of mercury to America (almost certainly to New Spain, since amalgamation was first introduced there) began several years before 1565. But available figures are not sufficiently reliable for a useful quinquennial total to be compiled. AGI Contaduría 403, No. 1, R. 7, 'Azogues. Tanteo del gasto y aprovechamiento que se pudo sacar dellos desde abril de 1559 hasta fin de diciembre 1571', shows that 3,312 quintales were available for despatch from Seville to New Spain in the years 1559 to 1566.

³ Blank spaces in this table indicate that, as far as is known, no mercury was sent in the period referred to. Question marks indicate that no documentary source was found for the destination and period referred to, and therefore that the possibility of exports cannot be excluded.

⁴ For the years 1626–36 and 1650–67, accounts were used which showed quantities of mercury received in New Spain, and not (as elsewhere in this table) amounts despatched from Spain. This was done in order to achieve the closest possible approximation to the amounts of mercury actually available in New Spain for mining purposes. The use of such accounts has the double disadvantage of reducing comparability with other figures for exports to New Spain, and reducing comparability with exports to other destinations, notably Peru. But since mining in New Spain, or in part of it, is the subject of this study, it was felt that these disadvantages were worth incurring. Amounts actually *exported* to New Spain in the period 1620–34 were: 1620–4, 21,747 quintales; 1625–9, 23,884 quintales; 1630–4, 12,999 quintales. (AGI Contratación 4324, Nos. 2 and 3). For 1635–9, see note 5 below. There is no full account of exports from Spain to New Spain in the 1650s. A 'Relación de las partidas de azogue que desde el año dcli parece se han remitido a la provincia de Nueva España en esta manera ...' (Seville 13 July 1662, Casa de la Contratación to king) in AGI Indiferente General 1780, shows, however, that exports in the quinquennium 1655–9 were 10,811 quintales. The amount received in New Spain was 10,808 quintales. This 'Relación' and AGI Contratación 4324 No. 4 show that exports from 1660–4 totalled 8,848 quintales, and from 1665–9, 9,072 quintales. The discrepancy between the 7,390 quintales received in New Spain in the years 1660–4 (see the table) and the 8,848 quintales dispatched, was caused by the capture of two boats carrying mercury to New Spain in 1663, one by the Moors off North Africa, and the other by the English off Jamaica. (AGI Indiferente General 1780, Mexico City 11 February 1664, Conde de Baños to D. Francisco Ramos del Manzano.)

⁵ This is a minimum figure. Sources consulted yielded figures only for 1635, 1636 and 1638. Chaunu, however, in *Séville*, vol. V, pp. 308, 314, quotes manuscripts suggesting that mercury was exported in 1637, though in unknown quantities. It seems clear that none went to New Spain in 1639. (Chaunu, *Séville*, vol. V, pp. 342, 346 note 7.)

Table 10b

TABLE 10b Five-yearly totals of mercury produced at Almadén and Huancavelica; and mercury provided under asiento from Idria; 1571 to 1700[1]

Period	Almadén	Huancavelica
1571–4	3,800 (1573–4)	7,871
1575–9	11,400	19,154
1580–4	10,600	43,240
1585–9	12,800	31,247
1590–4	13,331	40,413
1595–9	13,394	28,706
1600–4	15,207	20,105
1605–9	17,332	14,440
1610–14	18,622	30,677
1615–19	24,531	30,919
1620–4	23,462	29,424
1625–9	22,868	13,446
1630–4	22,209	21,640
1635–9	14,750	27,433
1640–4	11,481	26,593
1645–9	(1,749 – 1645 only)	25,924
1650–4	—	32,723
1655–9	—	34,046
1660–4	—	25,656
1665–9	—	20,229
1670–4	—	28,865
1675–9	—	25,072
1680–4	—	25,664
1685–9	—	17,450
1690–1700	—	57,534

Period	Idria
1620–ca. 1625	16,000[2]
1626–8	over 3,000[3]
1632–6	6,000[4]
1636–40	16,000[5]
1641–5	16,000[6]

Units: quintales. Figures are to the nearest quintal.

[1] Sources. For Almadén, Matilla Tascón, Historia de ... Almadén, pp. 107, 111, 121, 122, 137, 171, 182 (seven asientos with the Fuggers, from 1573 to 1645). No series of production figures is known for the years after 1645. For Huancavelica, Lohmann Villena, Las minas de Huancavelica, 452–5. For Idria, see notes 2–6.

[2] First asiento with Federico Oberolz. AGI Indiferente General 1777, Madrid 24 April 1621, Consulta of Consejos de Indias and de Hacienda.

[3] Second asiento with Federico Oberolz. 3,000 quintales were delivered in 1626, but Oberolz' later bankruptcy interrupted delivery of the remaining 6,000 due under the contract. It is not known how much was eventually supplied. AGI Indiferente General 1777, Madrid 24 April 1630, Consulta of Consejo de Indias.

Table 10b

[4] First asiento with Antonio Balbi. AGI Indiferente General 1777, Madrid 22 June 1636, Consulta of Consejo de Indias.

[5] Second asiento with Antonio Balbi. AGI Indiferente General 1777, Madrid 8 May 1640, membrete of Secretario Juan de Otálora Guevara (Consejo de Hacienda) to the Conde de Castrillo.

[6] Third and last asiento with Antonio Balbi. AGI Indiferente General 1777, Madrid 18 February 1644, membrete of Secretario Juan de Otálora Guevara to D. Gabriel de Ocaña y Alarcón.

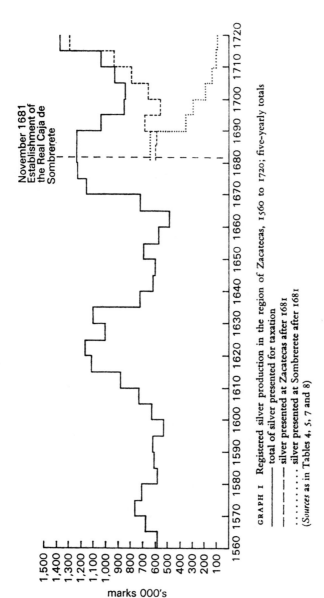

GRAPH I Registered silver production in the region of Zacatecas, 1560 to 1720; five-yearly totals

——— total of silver presented for taxation
– – – – silver presented at Zacatecas after 1681
· · · · · · · · silver presented at Sombrerete after 1681
(*Sources* as in Tables 4, 5, 7 and 8)

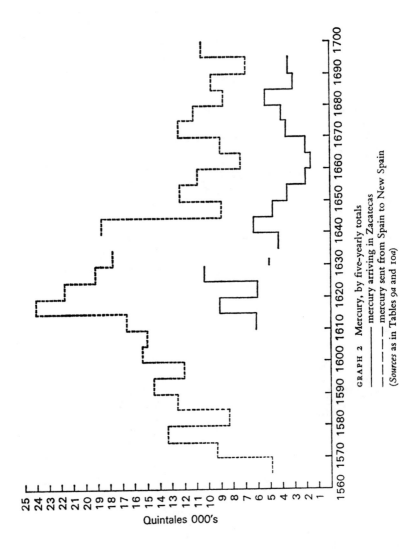

GRAPH 2 Mercury, by five-yearly totals
– – – – – mercury arriving in Zacatecas
———— mercury sent from Spain to New Spain
(*Sources* as in Tables 9*a* and 10*a*)

260

GRAPH 3 Registered silver production in the region of Zacatecas. Smelted and amalgamated silver presented at Zacatecas, 1670 to 1705; five-yearly totals
——— amalgamated silver
– – – smelted silver
(*Sources* as in Table 6)

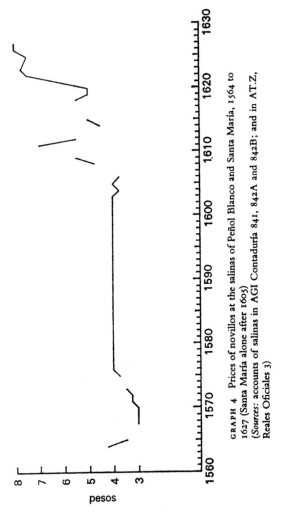

GRAPH 4 Prices of novillos at the salinas of Peñol Blanco and Santa María, 1564 to 1627 (Santa María alone after 1605)
(*Sources:* accounts of salinas in AGI Contaduría 841, 842A and 842B; and in AT.Z, Reales Oficiales 3)

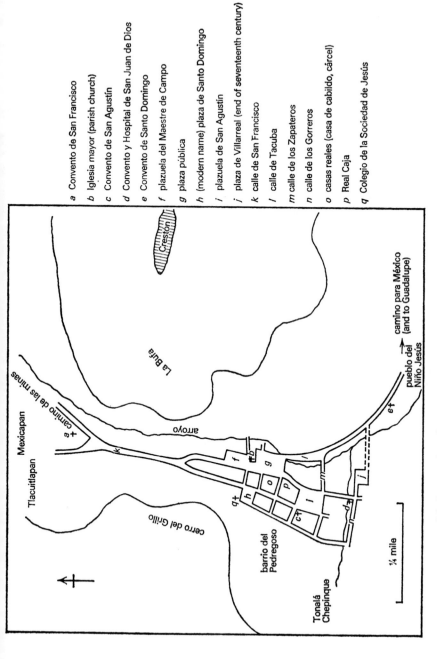

a Convento de San Francisco
b Iglesia mayor (parish church)
c Convento de San Agustín
d Convento y Hospital de San Juan de Dios
e Convento de Santo Domingo
f plazuela del Maestre de Campo
g plaza pública
h (modern name) plaza de Santo Domingo
i plazuela de San Agustín
j plaza de Villarreal (end of seventeenth century)
k calle de San Francisco
l calle de Tacuba
m calle de los Zapateros
n calle de los Gorreros
o casas reales (casa de cabildo, cárcel)
p Real Caja
q Colegio de la Sociedad de Jesús

PLAN I A basic street plan of Zacatecas in the **seventeenth** century

263

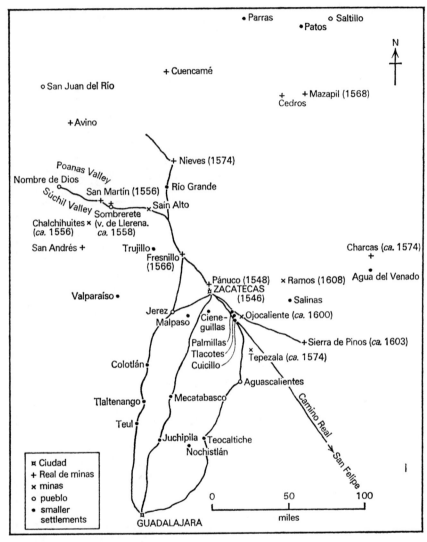

PLAN 2 Towns and roads in the region of Zacatecas and Guadalajara, with dates of discoveries of mines

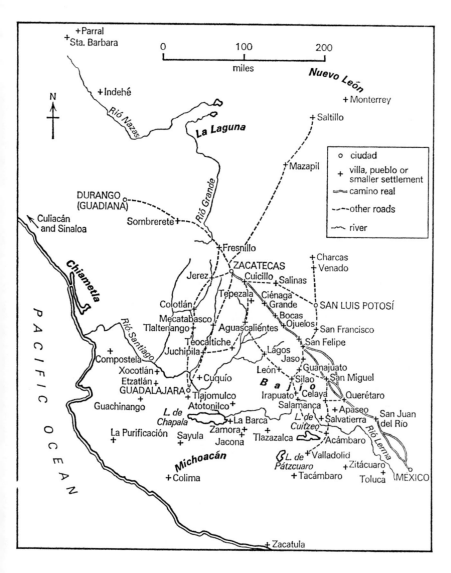

PLAN 3 Towns and roads in New Galicia, and parts of New Spain, New Biscay and New León

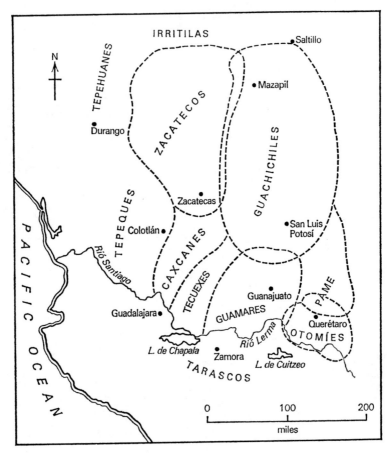

PLAN 4 The northern nations

APPENDIX I

A good description of a tina appears in AN.Z, FE 1678 (n.f.), in a lease contract dated Zacatecas, 22 June 1678. Matías Tenorio, a miner of Zacatecas, leased his hacienda de minas to Cristóbal Carrasco. The inventory of the works includes a description of the washing shed. 'El lavadero contiene ocho tijeras enlatadas, todo cubierto de tajamanil, a medio servir, gualdra, rueda, dos lanternillas, eje con sus guijos y cinchos, y toda la dentazón nueva y bien tratada, peón con cincho y guijo espeque con sus cuartas y horquetas, una tina grande, bien tratada, con tres cinchos y guijo, corriente y moliente, todo bueno, una tinilla chica de apurar con sus cinchos y otra de limpiar plata pequeña.' Although the exact meaning of some technical terms is not clear, a reasonable translation is as follows: 'The washing shed contains eight trusses, with rafters, the whole being roofed with wooden shingles, in moderate condition; the principal upper cross-beam (of the machinery), the main driving wheel, two pinions, the shaft with journals and iron binding-straps, all the gear teeth being new and in good condition; a smaller shaft with strap and journal, a paddle with four cross-pieces and spikes, a large vat, in good condition, with three iron straps and an iron bearing, all in good running order; a smaller purifying vat, with iron straps and another small vat for washing small pieces of silver.' The phrase 'espeque con sus cuartas y horquetas' presents some difficulty, and is here taken to mean the paddle assembly rotating in the vat, called in other inventories simply 'el molinete'. It was probably a central spindle (espeque) with four arms attached to it at right-angles (cuartas), each of which bore upward-pointing prongs (horquetas). It appears that, in this lavadero, there was only one large powered vat. The two smaller tubs may have been hand-operated. The 'tinilla chica de apurar' was probably used for further washing of the pella after it had been drawn off from the main vat. The 'plata pequeña' washed in the other small vat may have been metal sweepings or perhaps small pieces of native silver.

APPENDIX II

Records of the population of Zacatecas are scarce and scattered. The numbers shown here were obviously roughly counted, and the writers did not always count the same category of inhabitants, which makes comparison between successive figures difficult. Almost all records refer to Spaniards alone, and most limit themselves to the number of vecinos. This number should be multiplied by a factor of four to five to give an approximation to the total Spanish population.

Year	
1549	Over 300 Spaniards engaged in mining.[1]
1554	300 vecinos and over 1,000 'otros tratantes'.[2]
1572	300 vecinos (miners and merchants) in the *vicaría* of Zacatecas, and 1,500 Indians normally resident; also a number of transient natives and merchants.[3]
1584	1,300 Spaniards 'de confesión' and many Indians.[4]
1585	Over 400 vecinos, 'toda gente noble y rica'.[5]
Late sixteenth century	500 Spaniards and 500 slaves.[6]
1602 to 1605	About 300 vecinos. 100–200 'sobresalientes españoles ... que entran y salen a negocios unos y otros a traer mercerías'. 60–70 children of Spanish vecinos. 10–12 Portuguese and Italians. About 800 Negro and mulatto slaves, of both sexes. About 1,500 Indians in cuadrillas, but these come and go so freely that no set figure can be given.[7]
1608	Over 1,500 Spaniards – men, women and children. These include 100 Spanish mineros. They are described as 'casi todos criollos, hijos de españoles venidos de Castilla'. About 3,000 Indians and Negroes (including mestizos and mulattos) – men, women and children.[8]
1621	300 vecinos. Many others 'yentes y vinientes'. Innumerable Indians and Negroes.[9]
1640	500 Spanish vecinos.[10]

[1] AGI Guadalajara 31, 22 October 1549, Juan de Ojeda to Emperor.
[2] AGI Guadalajara 51, Tlajimaroa 10 September 1554, oidor Lebrón de Quiñones to Príncipe.
[3] AGI Guadalajara 55, Guadalajara 23 December 1572, bishop elect of New Galicia to Crown.
[4] CDHG vol. 3 (No. 3), pp. 232–4, Nueva Galicia 16 July 1584, Bishop Alzola to Crown.
[5] AGI Guadalajara 236, AA, 1, Barcelona 20 May 1585, real cédula to president and oidores of New Galicia and to viceroy, quoting report of vecinos of Zacatecas in their petition for the title of 'city'.
[6] Antonio de Herrera, *Historia general de los hechos de los castellanos en las islas y tierra firme de el Mar Océano* (edition of Madrid, 1934–, vol. 1, 74).
[7] Mota y Escobar, *Descripción*, 65–6.
[8] DII, vol. 9, 182, 'Relación de Zacatecas ... 1608'.
[9] Arregui, *Descripción*, p. 125.
[10] Borah, *Century of Depression*, p. 12, Table 5; quoting Juan Díez de la Calle, *Memorial y noticias sacras y reales del imperio de las Indias Occidentales*, Madrid 1646, f. 93.

GLOSSARY

Some common mining, and related, terms

Alhóndiga. A grain exchange.

Aviador. A supplier of goods to miners. He might supply goods on credit, if necessary; or extend credit in cash.

Avío. Mining supplies: goods or cash credit.

Barretero. A mine labourer employed in cutting ores with a *barra*, or crowbar.

Beneficio de patio. The open-air amalgamation process.

Caballería. An area of land 1,104 × 552 varas; equal to about 106 acres.

Carga. As a dry measure of grain, 5·32 bushels (5·15 U.S. bushels).

Casa de afinación. An assay office (an institution of the royal Treasury).

Colorados. Silver ore with a high content of iron oxide.

Consumido. The device by which a miner's stock of mercury was maintained. On registering silver with the Treasury, he was issued with the amount of mercury it was calculated he had consumed in producing that silver.

Correspondencia. The ratio of silver produced to mercury consumed, in the amalgamation process of silver refining. The normally accepted ratio was 100 marks of silver to one quintal of mercury; but, depending on the quality of silver ores, the ratio could vary from 80 to over 120 marks to a quintal.

Crestón. The exposed part of a vein, on the surface.

Cuadrilla. A miner's labour force, generally living in his hacienda de minas, and working his plant and his mines.

Depósito. A miner's stock of mercury, which in the first instance was issued to him by the Treasury on credit, and which he was intended to preserve at a constant level, through consumido (q.v.).

Diezmo. A tenth: the tax levied by the royal Treasury on silver produced by recognised miners.

Grano. A twelfth of a tomín or real (q.v.).

Hacienda de minas. A silver refining plant: more correctly and fully termed 'hacienda de sacar plata por el beneficio de azogue' (or 'de fundición', if a smelting plant).

Incorporadero. The yard of an hacienda de minas in which amalgamation took place: the Zacatecan term for the more usual 'patio', as in 'beneficio de patio'.

Glossary

Lavadero. The part of an hacienda de minas in which the crude mixture of amalgam and waste earth and rock material was washed.

Magistral. Probably a mixture of copper pyrites and iron pyrites; an essential reagent in the amalgamation process, discovered in the first decade of the seventeenth century.

Malacate. A whim.

Marca del diezmo. A mark placed on a bar of silver showing that it was 'plata del diezmo' (q.v.).

Mark. 8 ounces of silver.

Mayorazgo. An entailed estate, usually descending by primogeniture; though conditions attaching to mayorazgos were variable.

Metal. The usual term for ore (*not* refined metal).

Mercader de plata. A large-scale dealer in silver. Generally based in Mexico City, he bought finished silver for coin, operating through agents – aviadores and rescatadores – in mining towns. The source of much mining capital in the seventeenth century.

Molino. A stamp mill (in an hacienda de minas).

Negros. Silver ore with high lead sulphide content.

Noria. Generally, a chain of buckets for raising water; though more properly a water-wheel with the same function.

Parada de fuelles. A small furnace for smelting silver ores, usually operated by men who were not recognised miners.

Pella. The washed amalgam of mercury and silver.

Pepenas. An indeterminate quantity of ore which labourers were permitted to extract from mines for their own use and profit.

Peso de oro común. The common accounting unit of the Treasury in New Spain. It consisted of 8 reales or tomines, each valued at 34 maravedís. The peso was therefore of 272 maravedís.

Plata del diezmo. Silver produced by a recognised miner, generally with ores from his own mines, and in his own hacienda de minas; and therefore assessable at a tax rate of one tenth ('diezmo').

Plata del rescate. In general, silver produced from bought or stolen ores, and refined by men who were not recognised miners. It was taxable at a full fifth ('quinto').

Plata dezmada. Silver that had been taxed at one tenth.

Plata quintada. Any silver that had been taxed (see 'quintar').

Pósito. A grain store, in a municipality.

Quinceno. A fifteenth: the fraction of a miner's current silver production normally taken by the Treasury in payment for mercury and salt issued to him on credit.

Quintal. 100 pounds (about 46 kilograms).

Glossary

Quintar. The common term for 'to tax', with reference to silver. Its meaning was not restricted to taxing at the rate of a fifth. The expression 'quintar del diezmo' is frequently found.

Quinto. A fifth: the tax levied by the royal Treasury on silver not produced by recognised miners.

Real. One eighth of a peso, synonymous with 'tomín'.

Real Caja. Any local branch office of the royal Treasury.

Real de minas. A small town specialised in mining.

Rescate. With reference to silver, purchase: purchase either of finished silver, or of ores.

Rescatador. A man who bought unfinished silver, in order to refine it himself; or one who bought finished silver from a miner, for coin, at a discount.

Sitio de ganado mayor. An area of land 5,000 varas square; about 4,338 acres.

Sitio de ganado menor. An area of land 3,333 varas square; about 1,928 acres.

Socavón. In a mine, an adit for drainage or ventilation; or simply for access to workings.

Tahona. A device for grinding ores very finely, by means of heavy stones slung under a rotating arm.

Tenatero. A mine labourer carrying ores from the face to the surface in a 'tenate' (hide bag).

Tequío. The amount of ore to be extracted in a given time by a mine labourer contracted to a miner; by extension, the contract itself.

Tina. A washing vat for separating amalgam from crushed rock and earth.

Tomín. One eighth of a peso; synonymous with 'real'.

Vara. 0·838 metre: 32·99 inches.

ON PRIMARY SOURCES

Two large and well-known archives were investigated. One, the Archivo General de Indias in Seville, yielded very large quantities of valuable material. The other, the Archivo General de la Nación in Mexico City (with its companion, the Archivo Histórico de Hacienda), yielded hardly anything of use. The AGN's riches are largely of the eighteenth century, and furthermore, the archive appears to have smaller holdings for the northern provinces of New Spain than for lands in the jurisdiction of the Audiencia de México proper. No comment is needed here about these important archives. Many readers will be familiar with the range of their contents, and those who are not might refer to Lino Gómez Canedo's *Los archivos de la historia de América. Período colonial español* (2 vols., México 1961) for a general guide and references to more detailed catalogues. The type and variety of documents consulted in the AGI and the AGN will be clear by this stage from footnotes to the text. A list of legajos and volumes seen is given below.

Other well-known manuscript collections consulted were those preserved in the British Museum, the Biblioteca Nacional in Mexico City, and the Bancroft Library of the University of California at Berkeley. Parts of the microfilm collection held by the Museo Nacional de Antropología in Mexico City were also used. These sources yielded occasional items of great interest, but no continuous runs of information.

The remaining archives that were investigated are those of Zacatecas itself. Since little information is available about local Mexican archives, a few words about Zacatecas' collections will not be out of place, and may give some indication of what the diligent researcher can expect to find in similar provincial towns elsewhere in Mexico. In Zacatecas itself, two archives proved to be valuable sources for the topics and period being studied. The first was the archive of the town council, the cabildo, and has been referred to here, in accordance with normal Spanish terminology, as the Archivo del Ayuntamiento. It is housed in the Presidencia Municipal. (Shortly after research was completed in 1967, the Presidencia was moved, on peremptory order of the state governor, to another building. The archive, which had previously been arranged in fair order in a room of its own, was last seen in a heap on the floor of a room in the new Presidencia. It is to be hoped that by this time it has been put back in order.) This collection contains the following major items: the books of transactions of the town council (libros de cabildo) from

1587 to the end of the seventeenth century; a small number of vellum-bound books of royal and viceroyal orders received in Zacatecas in the sixteenth and seventeenth centuries; a few legajos of papers relating to land titles in the sixteenth, seventeenth and eighteenth centuries; and a series of legajos of miscellaneous papers relating to local government – for example, inspections of shops, orders issued by corregidores and the cabildo, lists of inhabitants drawn up for various purposes, and property transactions. These legajos were a most valuable source. Fortunately they have been sorted into chronological order by caretakers of the archive, one legajo to a decade, beginning with a few papers from the final years of the sixteenth century. (The Ayuntamiento collection continues, of course, into the eighteenth and nineteenth centuries, in ever-increasing abundance.) The second archive in Zacatecas to yield important information was the Archivo de Notarías. This is kept as part of the modern judicial archive of the state, the Archivo del Supremo Tribunal de Justicia del Estado de Zacatecas. Although the books of protocols forming the notarial archive scarcely fill a cupboard, it took many weeks' work to peruse even those relevant to this study. The bulk of the material dates from about 1645 onwards. Notaries generally produced a book for each year. The typical contents of notarial books will be well known: wills, dowries, powers of attorney (*poderes*), certain sales and contracts, I.O.U.'s – in short, any transaction or declaration made by a private citizen and requiring official formulation. The notaries of Zacatecas often also acted as scribes for the Treasury officials of the city, usually when it was necessary to draw up a declaration of debts owed by individuals to the Treasury. When the debtor was a miner, he usually owed for salt and mercury. There are many volumes mainly consisting of debt acknowledgements in the notarial archive.

There are several other archives in Zacatecas. If there had been any chance of seeing it, the Cathedral archive would doubtless have proved informative. But a mere transient Protestant could hardly hope to penetrate to the treasures hidden in the depths of the sacristy, however persistent his efforts and however willing the help of Catholic, historically-minded friends. This was a disappointment, for the archive is known to contain sixteenth and seventeenth-century manuscripts, in the form of the *libros de gobierno* of the parish church of that period and records of the religious fraternities (*cofradías*) of the city. Some of these items were filmed in 1948 and may be read on film in the Museo Nacional de Antropología in Mexico City. Parish registers for the period under examination seem to have disappeared altogether, apart from one mutilated register of births, confirmations and marriages for the years

On primary sources

1616 to 1620 which survives in the Biblioteca Pública del Estado. The small archive of the present parish church, Santo Domingo, was searched, but no registers of any age came to light. Similarly the archives of Zacatecas' monasteries have been dispersed or destroyed. The Palacio de Gobierno, seat of the state administration, has a very large collection of manuscripts; but the earliest items there are from the last quarter of the eighteenth century.

One major Zacatecan archive, for better or for worse (probably for better, as far as its safety is concerned) is no longer in the city. This is the archive of the colonial Real Caja, which until quite recently formed part of the archive of the modern Treasury department in Zacatecas. In 1952, it seems, it was bought by the University of Michigan, and is now housed in the William L. Clements Library of that University, in Ann Arbor, Michigan. Much fundamental material was taken from it for this book. Since it has no official title, it has been referred to here, perhaps clumsily, as the Archivo de la Tesorería de Zacatecas. The papers were sorted and put into rough chronological order by Professor Philip Powell in 1954. He placed them in box files, which he arranged by decades. The largest section of the collection, Powell entitled 'Treasury Correspondence and Records'. It begins in 1561 and ends in the nineteenth century. Since it contains papers and accounts of the Treasury officials of Zacatecas, it has been given the title in references here of 'Reales Oficiales'. Specific references in this section are difficult to make, since although Powell sorted the papers into decades, he did not order them within the decades. And as there are frequently several boxes-full for a ten-year span, manuscripts for a single year may be found in any one of six or seven files. Nor were the files numbered. For expediency's sake, therefore, numbers were simply pencilled on the spines of the box files in the order in which they were taken from the shelf and consulted. The numbers correspond to the chronological sequence of the manuscripts as nearly as present arrangements allow. But this archive deserves proper sorting and cataloguing. 'Reales Oficiales' contains a wealth of detailed material on the working of the Real Caja in Zacatecas. Of exceptional interest were the records of silver production in the smaller towns of the district (records unavailable elsewhere), and of quantities of mercury distributed throughout the region. Day-books of various accounts gave full lists of miners and vecinos for some years. The collection also contains various books of viceregal and royal orders directed to the Real Caja; long accounts of mercury received and sold in the seventeenth century; and some information on Indian affairs in the district of the Caja.

On primary sources

A list of manuscripts inspected during the preparation of this book follows. For the sake of brevity, only the numbers of legajos, volumes, files, etc., are given. To quote their titles would be prohibitively long.

Archivo General de Indias, Seville
Contaduría 669; 675; 677–80, 682, 684, 685, 686, 690, 691, 693, 694, 695A, 695B, 696–8, 702, 705 (accounts of the Real Caja de México, 1581–1603); 841–50 (accounts of the Real Caja de Zacatecas, 1544–1720); 856–60, 863 (accounts of the Real Caja de Guadalajara, 1559–1610).

Escribanía de Cámara 380A, 380B, 389.

Audiencia de Guadalajara 1–4; 5–27 (correspondence of the president and oidores of the Audiencia, 1534–1700); 30; 31; 33–5; 41; 45; 46; 51; 55; 56; 64; 65; 114; 230–2; 236; 303; 413; 423.

Indiferente General 77; 450; 755; 1767; 1777; 1778; 1780; 1792.

Audiencia de México 1; 19–66 (correspondence of the viceroys, 1536–1699); 72–90 (correspondence of the Audiencia, 1597–1700); 91; 92; 258; 267; 285; 320; 611; 612; 1064; 1846.

Patronato 75, 78A, 80, 238.

Archivo General de la Nación, Mexico City
Mercedes 3. Real Hacienda 1. Inquisición 5; 10; 16; 17; 19. Tierras 699; 700.

Archivo Histórico de Hacienda, Mexico City
Tesorerías 1505–9.

Biblioteca Nacional, Mexico City (Archive)
MS. 9 (72.32) OJE.

Archivo de la Provincia del Santo Evangelio de México (partly conserved in the Biblioteca Nacional), Caja 58.

Museo Nacional de Antropología, Mexico City (Microfilm collection)
Zacatecas microfilm, spools 2 and 7.

Archivo del Ayuntamiento, Zacatecas
Libros de cabildo 2; 3; 6–8 (books 1 and 4 are missing; book 5 is kept in the Archivo de Notarías; books 2 to 8 cover the years 1587–1697).

On primary sources

AA.Z, Cédulas 2 (cédulas to the cabildo, 1636–44). AA.Z, Cédulas 4 (marked on the spine, 'Núm. 4–1655. Cédulas del cabildo 1629 a 1655-4').

AA.Z, folder (a cardboard folder entitled 'Siglo XVI – Reales Cédulas').

AA.Z, 2–11 (loosely-tied bundles of documents, without covering or titles; each bundle contains documents for one decade, 1600–1700).

AA.Z, Propiedades 1–3.

Archivo de Notarías, Zacatecas
(The majority of this collection consists of books of protocols, now without covers and titles. They are identified here and in footnotes by the initial of the notary and the year. The names of notaries are given in the list of abbreviations at the beginning of the book. The letters RH placed after the year of a volume indicate that it contains Treasury – Real Hacienda – records, drawn up by a notary while acting as scribe to the Treasury officials.) The following books were examined:

BN 1682–3 (one volume); DV 1687; FE 1651, 1653A (January to June), 1653B (May to August), 1656, 1659, 1664, 1668(RH), 1671, 1673, 1674, 1675, 1676, 1678, 1679, 1680(RH), 1684; IG 1685, 1686, 1690; JL 1672, 1673, 1674, 1675, 1676–80 (one volume), 1681, 1682, 1682A (January to March), 1683; JM 1683, 1684, 1684–5(RH), 1684–5, 1688–9(RH); LF 1695; MH 1645, 1646; MR 1650; PC 1614.

This archive also contains a small number of lawsuits, of which the following were examined: AN.Z, Protocolos 1 (the only sixteenth-century volume in the archive, containing proceedings in a mining case starting in 1549. It is in a paper folder bearing the dates 1589, 1592, 1593, Siglo XVI. The first folio of the MS. is marked 'Núm. 47'); AN.Z, 1664 (marked 'Núm. 1', and recording proceedings taken in relation to the hacienda called Monte Grande de Escobedo); AN.Z, 1645–52 (marked 'Tostado: Real Hacienda Núm. 25'); AN.Z, 1661 (marked 'Autos de Doña Isabel de Castilla').

Archivo de la Tesorería de Zacatecas, William L. Clements Library, Ann Arbor, Michigan
AT.Z/VO (one box of viceregal orders, 1601 to 1711); AT.Z, Azog. 1574–84 (register of disbursements of mercury in Zacatecas, 1574 to 1584); AT.Z, Quintos 1 (the first box of accounts from the *ramo de quintos y diezmos* in this archive. The series continues, but later documents were not consulted. This box contains accounts for the years 1575 to 1580);

On primary sources

AT.Z, Reales Oficiales 1–31 (boxes from the section called by Powell 'Treasury Records and Correspondence', covering the period 1561 to 1699); AT.Z, Azogues 1–5 (accounts of the *ramo de consumido y quinceno* of the Zacatecas Treasury, covering the period 1643 to 1704).

Bancroft Library, Berkeley, California
M–M 1714 (containing correspondence of Viceroy Enríquez in 1572).

British Museum
Additional MS. 13,992.

SELECT BIBLIOGRAPHY

Works cited in the text and in footnotes

AGRICOLA, Georgius. *De Re Metallica.* Translated from the first Latin Edition of 1556, with Bibliographical Introduction, Annotations and Appendices upon the Development of Mining Methods, Metallurgical Processes, Geology, Mineralogy and Mining Law from the earliest times to the late sixteenth century, by Herbert Clark Hoover and Lou Henry Hoover, London 1912.

AHUMADA SÁMANO, Pedro de. *1562. Relación de los Zacatecos y Guachichiles*, México 1952.

'Información acerca de la rebelión de los indios zacatecos y guachichiles, a pedimento de . . .', México 20 March 1562. *Colección de documentos inéditos para la historia de Ibero-América*, ed. Santiago Montoto, vol. 1 Madrid 1927, pp. 237–368.

AITON, A. S. *Antonio de Mendoza, first viceroy of New Spain*, Duke University Press, Durham, North Carolina 1927.

ALONSO BARBA, Alvaro. *Arte de los metales*, Madrid 1640, ed. used, Madrid 1729; and the English translation by R. E. Douglas and E. P. Mathewson, New York 1923.

AMADOR, Elías. *Bosquejo histórico de Zacatecas*, vol. 1, Zacatecas 1892.

ARCILA FARÍAS, E. *Comercio entre Venezuela y México en los siglos XVII y XVIII*, México 1950.

ARLEGUI, el Padre José. *Crónica de la Provincia de N.S.P. S. Francisco de Zacatecas*, México 1737, ed. used, México 1851.

ARREGUI, Domingo Lázaro de. *Descripción de la Nueva Galicia*, (Edición y estudio por François Chevalier. Prólogo de John Van Horne), Seville 1946.

BÁNCORA CAÑERO, Carmen. 'Las remesas de metales preciosos desde el Callao a España en la primera mitad del siglo XVII', *Revista de Indias*, año XIX, 1959, No. 75, pp. 35–88.

BANCROFT, H. H. *History of the Pacific States of North America*, vol. 5, *Mexico, vol. II, 1521–1600*, San Francisco 1883.

BARBA, A. A. See Alonso Barba, Alvaro.

BARGALLÓ, Modesto. *La minería y la metalurgia en la América española durante la época colonial*, México 1955.

BASALENQUE, Fray Diego, *Historia de la Provincia de San Nicolás de Tolentino de Michoacán*, ed. used, México 1963.

Select bibliography

BAYLE, Constantino, S. J. *Los cabildos sueclares en la América española*, Madrid 1952.

BATAILLON, Claude. *Les régions géographiques au Mexique*, Paris 1968.

BELEÑA, Eusebio B. *Recopilación sumaria de todos los autos acordados de la Real Audiencia y Sala de Crimen de esta Nueva España, y provisiones de su superior gobierno*, 2 vols., México 1787.

BIRINGUCCIO, Vannoccio. *The Pirotechnia of Vannoccio Biringuccio*, English translation from the Italian, by C. S. Smith and Martha T. Gnudi, New York 1942.

BORAH, W. W. *New Spain's Century of Depression*, Ibero-Americana: 35, University of California Press, Berkeley and Los Angeles 1951.

'Un gobierno provincial de frontera en San Luis Potosí, 1612–1620', *Historia Mexicana*, vol. 13, No. 4, pp. 532–50.

and COOK, S. F. *Price Trends of some Basic Commodities in Central Mexico, 1531–1570*, Ibero-Americana: 40, University of California Press, Berkeley and Los Angeles 1958.

BOYD-BOWMAN, P. 'La emigración peninsular a América: 1520–1539', *Historia Mexicana*, vol. 13, No. 2, pp. 165–92.

BRAUDEL, F. and SPOONER, F. 'Prices in Europe from 1450 to 1750'. (Ch. 7 of *The Cambridge Economic History of Europe, vol. IV. The Economy of Expanding Europe in the Sixteenth and Seventeenth Centuries*, ed. E. E. Rich and C. H. Wilson, London 1967).

BURKART, Joseph. 'Description du filon et des mines de Veta-Grande, près de la ville de Zacatecas, dans l'état du même nom, au Mexique', *Annales des Mines*, troisième série, vol. 8, 1835, pp. 55–87.

BUSTAMANTE, I. M. *Descripción de la Serranía de Zacatecas, formada por ... 1828 y 1829*, Zacatecas 1889.

CARANDE, Ramón. *Carlos V y sus banqueros*, 3 vols., Madrid 1943–68.

CARO BAROJA, J. *Los vascos, etnología*, San Sebastián 1949.

CARRERA STAMPA, Manuel. 'The Evolution of Weights and Measures in New Spain', *HAHR*, vol. 29, 1949, pp. 2–24.

CASTAÑEDA, Carlos E. 'The Corregidor in Spanish Colonial Administration', *HAHR*, vol. 9, 1929, pp. 446–70.

CHAUNU, Huguette and Pierre. *Séville et l'Atlantique*, 8 vols., Paris 1955–9.

CHEVALIER, François. *La formation des grands domaines au Mexique. Terre et société aux XVIe–XVIIe siècles*, Paris 1952.

Colección de documentos inéditos relativos al descubrimiento, conquista y organización de las antiguas posesiones españolas de América y Oceanía, sacados de los archivos del Reino y muy especialmente del de Indias, 42 vols., Madrid 1864–84.

Select bibliography

COOK, S. F. and BORAH, W. W. *The Indian Population of Central Mexico, 1531–1610*, Ibero-Americana: 44, University of California Press, Berkeley and Los Angeles 1960.

DÁVILA GARIBI, J. I. P. *La sociedad de Zacatecas en los albores del régimen colonial, actuación de los principales fundadores y primeros funcionarios públicos de la ciudad*, México 1939.

DEL HOYO, Eugenio. 'Don Martín de Zavala y la minería en el Nuevo Reino de León', *Humanitas. Anuario del Centro de estudios humanísticos*, (Universidad de Nuevo León), No. 4, 1963, pp. 411–26.

DOMÍNGUEZ ORTIZ, A. *Política y hacienda de Felipe IV*, Madrid 1960.

DUNNE, P. M., S. J. *Pioneer Jesuits in Northern Mexico*, University of California Press, Berkeley and Los Angeles 1944.

DUSENBERRY, W. H. 'The Regulation of Meat Supply in Sixteenth-Century Mexico City', *HAHR*, vol. 28, 1948, pp. 38–52.

ENCINAS, Diego de. *Cedulario indiano, recopilado por . . .*, 4 vols. (facsimile edition), Madrid 1945–6.

FLORES, Théodore. *Etude minière du district de Zacatecas*, México 1906.

FLORESCANO, Enrique. 'El abasto y la legislación de granos en el siglo XVI', *Historia Mexicana*, vol. 14, No. 4, pp. 567–630.

FONSECA, Fabián de and URRUTIA, Carlos de. *Historia general de real hacienda, escrita por orden del Virrey Conde de Revillagigedo*, 6 vols., México 1845.

FOSTER, George M. *Culture and Conquest. America's Spanish Heritage*, Chicago 1960.

GAMBOA, Francisco Xavier de. *Comentarios a las Ordenanzas de Minas, dedicados al católico rey, nuestro señor, Don Carlos III*, Madrid 1761.

GARCÍA, Trinidad. *Los mineros mexicanos*, México 1895.

GASCA, el Presbítero José del Refugio. *Timbres y laureles zacatecanos, o cantos a Zacatecas, con notas crítico-históricas, escritos por . . .*, Zacatecas 1901.

GIBSON, Charles. *The Aztecs under Spanish Rule. A History of the Indians of the Valley of Mexico, 1519–1810*, Stanford and London 1964.
Tlaxcala in the Sixteenth Century, Yale University Press, New Haven 1952.

GÓMEZ CANEDO, Lino. *Los archivos de la historia de América. Período colonial español*, 2 vols., México 1961.

GÓNGORA, Mario. *El estado en el derecho indiano. Epoca de fundación, 1492–1570*, Santiago de Chile 1951.

GUTHRIE, Chester L. 'Colonial Economy. Trade, Industry and Labor in Seventeenth Century Mexico City', *Revista de Historia de América*, No. 7, December 1939, pp. 103–34.

Select bibliography

HALLECK, H. W. (editor and translator). *A Collection of Mining Laws of Spain and Mexico*, San Francisco 1859.

HAMILTON, Earl J. *American Treasure and the Price Revolution in Spain, 1501–1650*, Harvard University Press, Cambridge, Mass. 1934.

HAMMOND, G. P. and Agapito Rey. *Don Juan de Oñate, Colonizer of New Mexico, 1595–1628*, 2 vols., University of New Mexico Press, Alburquerque 1953.

HARING, C. H. *The Spanish Empire in America*, New York 1947.

HELDT, H. L. *Historical Sketch of the Sombrerete Mines*, Sombrerete, Zac. 1911.

HERRERA, Antonio de. *Historia general de los hechos de los castellanos en las islas y tierra firme del Mar Océano*, 17 vols., Madrid 1934–56.

HUMBOLDT, Alexander von. *Ensayo político sobre el reino de la Nueva España*, ed. used, México 1966.

JAMES, Preston. *Latin America*, New York 1950.

JARA, Alvaro. *Tres ensayos sobre economía minera hispanoamericana*, Santiago de Chile 1966.

JIMÉNEZ, MORENO, W. *Estudios de historia colonial*, México 1958.

KURI BREÑA, Daniel. *Zacatecas civilizadora del Norte. Pequeña biografía de una rara ciudad*, México 1944.

LAS CASAS, Gonzalo de, 'Guerra de los chichimecas (1571–1585)', in Hermann Trimborn, *Fuentes de la historia cultural de la América precolombina*, Madrid 1936, pp. 152–85.

LAUR, P. 'De la métallurgie de l'argent au Mexique', *Annales des Mines*, sixième série, vol. 20, 1871, pp. 38–317.

LEE, R. L. 'Grain Legislation in Colonial Mexico, 1575–1585', *HAHR*, vol. 27, 1947, pp. 647–60.

LOHMANN VILLENA, Guillermo. *Las minas de Huancavelica en los siglos XVI y XVII*, Seville 1949.

LÓPEZ PORTILLO Y WEBER, José. *La conquista de la Nueva Galicia*, México 1933.

LÓPEZ DE VELASCO, Juan. *Geografía y descripción universal de las Indias, recopilada por el cosmógrafo-cronista . . . desde el año de 1571 al de 1574*, ed. of Madrid 1894.

LYNCH, J. *Spain under the Habsburgs. Volume Two. Spain and America 1598–1700*, Oxford 1969.

LYON, G. F. *Journal of a Residence and Tour in the Republic of Mexico, in the year 1826, with some account of the mines of that country*, 2 vols., London 1828.

MATILLA TASCÓN, A. *Historia de las minas de Almadén. Vol. I (Desde la época romana hasta el año 1645)*, Madrid 1958.

Select bibliography

MECHAM, J. Lloyd. *Francisco de Ibarra and Nueva Vizcaya*, Duke University Press, Durham, North Carolina 1927.
'The *Real de Minas* as a Political Institution', *HAHR*, vol. 7, 1927, pp. 45–83.
Memoria en que el gobierno del Estado Libre de los Zacatecas da cuenta de los Ramos de su Administración al Congreso del Mismo Estado, Zacatecas 1831.
MENDIZÁBAL, Miguel Othón de. 'Carácter de la conquista y colonización de Zacatecas', in *Obras completas*, vol. 5, México 1946, pp. 75–82.
'Compendio histórico de Zacatecas', in *Obras completas*, vol. 5, México 1946.
MIRANDA, José. *Las ideas y las instituciones políticas mexicanas. Primera parte, 1521–1820*, México 1952.
MOORE, John Preston. *The Cabildo in Peru under the Hapsburgs*, Duke University Press, Durham, North Carolina 1954.
MOTA Y ESCOBAR, Alonso de la. *Descripción geográfica de los reinos de Nueva Galicia, Nueva Vizcaya y Nuevo León*, ed. of Guadalajara 1966.
MOTA PADILLA, Matías de la. *Historia de la conquista de la Provincia de la Nueva Galicia, escrita por ... en 1742*, eds. of México 1870 and Guadalajara 1920.
Ordenanzas para descubrimientos, nuevas poblaciones y pacificaciones, San Lorenzo 3 July 1573, in *HAHR*, vol. 4, 1921, pp. 745–9.
OROZCO Y JIMÉNEZ, Francisco. *Colección de documentos históricos inéditos o muy raros referentes al Arzobispado de Guadalajara (publicados en forma de revista trimestral ilustrada por el Ilmo. y Rvmo. Sr. Dr. y Mtro. Don ...)*, 6 vols., Guadalajara 1922–7.
PEÑA, Moisés T. de la (ed.). *Zacatecas económico*, México 1948.
PARRY, J. H. *The Audiencia of New Galicia in the Sixteenth Century. A Study in Spanish Colonial Government*, C.U.P. 1948.
The Sale of Public Office in the Spanish Indies under the Hapsburgs, Ibero-Americana: 37, University of California Press, Berkeley and Los Angeles 1953.
PASO Y TRONCOSO, Francisco del. *Papeles de Nueva España (2a. serie)*, 9 vols., México 1905–48.
PIERSON, W. W. 'Some Reflections on the Cabildo as an Institution', *HAHR*, vol. 5, 1922, pp. 573–96.
PIKE, Fredrick B. 'Aspects of Cabildo Economic Regulations in Spanish America under the Hapsburgs', *Inter-American Economic Affairs*, vol. 13, 1959–60, pp. 67–86.
'The Cabildo and Colonial Loyalty to Hapsburg Rulers', *Journal of Inter-American Studies*, vol. 2, 1960, pp. 405–20.

Select bibliography

'The Municipality and the System of Checks and Balances in Spanish American Colonial Administration', *The Americas*, vol. 15, 1958, pp. 139–58.

POWELL, P. W. 'Presidios and Towns on the Silver Frontier of New Spain, 1550–1580', *HAHR*, vol. 24, 1944, pp. 179–200.

Soldiers, Indians and Silver. The Northward Advance of New Spain, 1550–1600, University of California Press, Berkeley and Los Angeles 1952.

'Spanish Warfare against the Chichimecas in the 1570's', *HAHR*, vol. 24, 1944, pp. 580–604.

'The Chichimecas: Scourge of the Silver Frontier in Sixteenth-Century Mexico', *HAHR*, vol. 25, 1945, pp. 315–38.

'The Forty-Niners of Sixteenth-Century Mexico', *Pacific Historical Review*, vol. 19, 1950, pp. 235–49.

REAL DÍAZ, J. J. *Las ferias de Jalapa*, Seville 1959.

Recopilación de leyes de los reinos de las Indias, mandadas imprimir y publicar por la majestad católica del rey Don Carlos II, nuestro señor; va dividida en cuatro tomos, con el índice general, y al principio de cada tomo el especial de los títulos que contiene, Madrid 1680, ed. used, Madrid 1841.

'Relación de Nuestra Señora de los Zacatecas, sacada de la información que, por mandado del Consejo, en ella se hizo el año de 1608', *DII*, vol. 9, pp. 179–91.

RIBERA BERNÁRDEZ, J. *Compendio de las cosas más notables contenidas en los libros del cabildo de esta ciudad de Nuestra Señora de los Zacatecas, desde el año de su descubrimiento 1546 hasta 1730*, Zacatecas 1732, ed. used, México 194–, Biblioteca de la Academia mexicana de la historia, vol. 2.

Descripción breve de la muy noble y leal ciudad de Zacatecas, México 1732, ed. used, that published in *Testimonios de Zacatecas*, selección de Gabriel Salinas de la Torre, México 1946.

SARFATTI, Magali. *Spanish Bureaucratic Patrimonialism in America*, Institute of International Studies, Berkeley, California 1966.

SIMPSON, L. B. *Exploitation of Land in Central Mexico in the Sixteenth Century*, Ibero-Americana: 36, University of California Press, Berkeley and Los Angeles 1952.

Studies in the Administration of the Indians in New Spain. III. The Repartimiento System of Forced Native Labor in New Spain and Guatemala, Ibero-Americana: 13, University of California Press, Berkeley and Los Angeles 1938.

SMITH, R. S. 'Sales Taxes in New Spain, 1575–1770', *HAHR*, vol. 28, 1948, pp. 2–37.

Select bibliography

STANISLAWSKI, D. 'Early Spanish Town Planning in the New World', *Geographical Review*, vol. 37, 1947, pp. 94–105.

TELLO, Fray Antonio. *Crónica miscelánea y conquista espiritual y temporal de la Santa Provincia de Jalisco en el Nuevo Reino de la Galicia y Nueva Vizcaya y descubrimiento del Nuevo México*, ed. of Guadalajara 1891.

VIDAL, Salvador. *Estudio histórico de la ciudad de Zacatecas*, Zacatecas 1955.

VILLASEÑOR BORDES, Rubén. *La Inquisición en la Nueva Galicia (siglo XVI)*. *Recopilación, introducción y notas por el Dr*..., Guadalajara 1959.

WEST, Robert C. 'Surface Configuration and Associated Geology of Middle America', *Handbook of Middle American Indians*, vol. I, Austin, Texas 1964, pp. 33–83.

The Mining Community of Northern New Spain: the Parral Mining District, Ibero-Americana: 30, University of California Press, Berkeley and Los Angeles 1949.

ZAVALA, Silvio. 'La amalgama en la minería de Nueva España', *Historia Mexicana*, vol. II, No. 3, pp. 416–21.

INDEX

Index

Index

Index

interest (on private credit to mining), 211, 214, 219
iron, 76, 149
Izmiquilpan, 147

Jerez de la Frontera, 34, 36, 59, 111, 117, 118
Jesuits, 39; land-owners, 120; in Zacatecas, 46-7
Juchipila, 7, 21, 110n 1, 111, 118
jurisdiction: (territorial) of cabildo of Zacatecas, 110-11; conflicts of, 86-9

labour: free wage, 124-5, 222n 2, 224, 225; number of Indians employed in silver mining, 127-8, 222n 2; origins of Indians, 128; 'poaching', 125-6; shortage, 128-9, 199-201, 219, 223-5; systems in silver mining, 121-9
la Fuente, Licenciado Gaspar de, 69
Lagos, 60, 61, 62, 66, 111
Laguna, la, 2
lama, 141
lead, 22, 23-4, 147
leather, 75
lentils, 74
León (town), 20, 34, 66
León, Miguel de, 120
Lezcano, Doña Francisca de, 119
libros de cabildo, 81-2
libros de manifestaciones, 60
livestock: in New Galicia, 68, 72; in New Spain, 72-3; in Zacatecas district, 2, 41, 68-73
Lorenzo de San Millán, Don Francisco, 205

machinery (in silver mining), 132-8 passim, 141, 142-3, 267
magistral, 143-4, 147, 203
maize, 59-63 passim, 65, 238n 3
malacate, 132, 134, 135
Mantuan war, 161
marca del diezmo, 182, 183
marca del quinto, 184
Marcha, la; see Martínez de la Marcha, Hernán
Martínez, el Bachiller, 85-6
Martínez de la Marcha, Hernán: Ordinances, 16, 75, 123-5; visitor to Zacatecas, 15-16
Matanzas (Spanish treasure fleet captured off), 231
matlazahuatl, 127, 223
Mazapil, 27, 35, 61, 111, 114; silver deposits, 30
mazos, 137

meat: asientos, 69-71, 101, 218; dried, 74; prices in Zacatecas, 71-3, 218; supply to Zacatecas, 68-73
Medina, Bartolomé de, 138
Mendiola, Don Francisco Gómez de, 85, 86, 124, 146
Mendoza, Viceroy Don Antonio de, 5, 19, 20, 21, 58
mercaderes de plata, 91-2, 213-15, 234
merchants: in cabildo of Zacatecas, 99; evading tax on silver, 182, 183-4; itinerant, 77-8; in partnerships, 78; trading in mercury, 173; in Zacatecas, 77-8
mercury, 22, 130, 201; debts, 87, 165, 174, 176, 177, 197, 198, 199, 202-8, 214-15; determining silver production, 188-92, 194-5, 219; distilled from pella, 141; distribution in Zacatecas, 178-80, 188, 191-2, 198, 202, 220; exported to New Spain, 162-4, 170-2, 229, 255n 4; exported to Peru, 162-4; fraud in, 174-5; land freight, 171, 172; prices, 154, 157, 161, 171-3; private trading in, 173; production, 154-70 passim; sea freight, 170, 172; shortage (general), 104, 163-4 (in New Spain), 164 (in Zacatecas), 188, 197, 214-15; sources, 151-70 passim
Mexicapan, 56
mezquite, 2, 146
Michoacán: fish producer, 74; grain producer, 58, 64, 221; home of Indians moving to Zacatecas, 128; mercury in, 151; sugar producer, 74
migration of Indians, 36-7
miners, mines, mining: see silver miners, etc.
mint, 211n 1
missions: Augustinian, 19; Franciscan, 19, 24, 39; Jesuit, 39
mita (at Huancavelica), 152-63 passim
Mixton war, 5
molinos, 136-8; in various mines of New Spain in 1597, 139
Monroy, Juan de, 107
Monte Grande, 110n 1, 111
Monterrey, 39
Montesclaros, Viceroy Marqués de, 152, 155, 156
morteros, 137
mulatto slaves, 122, 123-4
mules, 134, 137, 141, 142; breeding, 117; in trains, 21

naborías, 124, 222n 2

Index

Index

Index

Index

CPSIA information can be obtained at www.ICGtesting.com
Printed in the USA
BVOW07s0607260814

364253BV00001B/26/A